D1522599

Praise for *Health Advocacy, Inc.*

"This riveting history of the breast-cancer movement chronicles, analyzes, and evaluates the relationship between patient-advocacy organizations and the pharmaceutical industry. The author's autoethnographic observations shine brilliantly, and the issues she raises should incite debate about the need for medical reform and new health policy."

– **SERGIO SISMONDO**, professor of philosophy, Queen's University and co-editor of *The Pharmaceutical Studies Reader*

"This is a powerful insider account, coupled with excellent scholarship, of Big Pharma's doings in relation to the breast cancer movement. After reading this book, the only thing I wanted was more – more information on how this work applies to other countries and to other health advocacy movements. This is a vitally important book."

– **EVELYNE DE LEEUW**, director of the Centre for Health Equity Training Research and Evaluation (CHETRE) at the University of New South Wales, Australia

"Sharon Batt, herself a breast cancer survivor, weaves the personal with the political to tell the story of how most of the breast cancer movement ended up in the arms of the pharmaceutical industry. Abandoned by the federal government as it increasingly adopted a set of neoliberal values, the patient breast cancer groups turned to the drug companies for funding, and in doing so lost their way."

– **JOEL LEXCHIN**, MD, Professor Emeritus, Faculty of Health, York University and author of *Doctors in Denial: Why Big Pharma and the Canadian Medical Profession Are Too Close for Comfort*

"I recommend this book to anyone who wants to understand the government policy changes and the manipulations, conflicts of interest, and very human dynamics that undermined the integrity of the breast cancer patient/survivor movement and skewed patient advocacy towards pharmaceutical industry interests. Sharon Batt's meticulous research lays bare the troubling dynamics of drug industry funding and explores better ways to protect women's health."

– **ANN SILVERSIDES**, award-winning health policy journalist and author of *AIDS Activist: Michael Lynch and the Politics of Community*

"Sharon Batt has given us a riveting account of how health advocacy in Canada became colonized by the pharmaceutical industry. As a leader in the breast cancer and women's health movement, she provides a compassionate and scholarly overview of the moral and ethical dilemmas many health activists faced when Big Pharma came knocking at the door. *Health Advocacy, Inc.* describes the public policies that were behind these heart-wrenching debates on the front lines and provides a roadmap back to independence."

— **COLLEEN FULLER,** cofounder and president, PharmaWatch Canada

"A searing indictment of industry subversion of 'patient' groups. Batt chronicles the rise of industry fronts and industry-influenced patient groups that arose in parallel with (and as a result of) the rise of neoliberalism. She demonstrates how the same tools employed by industry to influence doctors are used to influence key patient groups in ways that patients may not recognize. Required reading for all lay groups tempted by industry money."

— **JEANNE LENZER,** associate editor, *British Medical Journal,* and author of
The Danger within Us: America's Untested, Unregulated Medical Device Industry and One Man's Battle to Survive It (forthcoming)

"As a public intellectual whose work spans the worlds of journalism, the women's movement, breast cancer advocacy, and the social studies of medicine, Sharon Batt provides a nuanced analysis of the vexing problem of political advocacy and industry funding. This book has important implications not only for health policy and patient advocacy but also for the broader political conversation about neoliberalism, democracy, social movements, and social fairness."

— **DAVID J. HESS,** professor of sociology, Vanderbilt University, and author of
Undone Science: Social Movements, Mobilized Publics, and Industrial Transitions

Health Advocacy, Inc.

Health Advocacy, Inc.

How Pharmaceutical Funding
Changed the Breast Cancer Movement

SHARON BATT

UBCPress · Vancouver · Toronto

26 25 24 23 22 21 20 19 18 17   5 4 3 2 1

Printed in Canada on FSC-certified ancient-forest-free paper
(100% post-consumer recycled) that is processed chlorine- and acid-free.

Library and Archives Canada Cataloguing in Publication

Batt, Sharon, author
Health Advocacy Inc. : how pharmaceutical funding changed the
breast cancer movement / Sharon Batt.

Includes bibliographical references and index.
Issued in print and electronic formats.
ISBN 978-0-7748-3384-4 (hardcover). – ISBN 978-0-7748-3386-8 (PDF). –
ISBN 978-0-7748-3387-5 (EPUB). – ISBN 978-0-7748-3388-2 (Kindle)

1. Patient advocacy – Canada. 2. Breast – Cancer – Research – Canada – Finance.
3. Pharmaceutical industry – Canada. 4. Medical policy – Canada. I. Title.

R727.45.B38 2017   362.10971   C2017-902017-X
                                                              C2017-902018-8

Canadä

UBC Press gratefully acknowledges the financial support for our publishing program of the Government of Canada (through the Canada Book Fund), the Canada Council for the Arts, and the British Columbia Arts Council.

This book has been published with the help of a grant from the Canadian Federation for the Humanities and Social Sciences, through the Awards to Scholarly Publications Program, using funds provided by the Social Sciences and Humanities Research Council of Canada.

Printed and bound in Canada by Friesens
Set in Zurich, Univers, and Minion by Artegraphica Design Co. Ltd.
Copy editor: Judy Phillips
Proofreader: Kristy Lynn Hankewitz
Indexer: Judy Dunlop
Cover designer: Martyn Schmoll

UBC Press
The University of British Columbia
2029 West Mall
Vancouver, BC V6T 1Z2
www.ubcpress.ca

Contents

Acknowledgments

This book has had a long evolution and owes a debt to more people than I can mention here. First and foremost, I thank the participants in my research, who generously shared recollections of their experiences. Several have died, and I regret that I will never know what they would have thought of this account. The willingness of each participant to engage with the issue supported my belief that the events recounted here matter to the community, past and present. I hope my rendition of our collective journey merits the trust they put in me and opens a path for further exploration.

My research is based in part on documents, experiences, and memories from the 1990s, when some of the research participants and I were active in Canada's breast cancer community. I owe the opportunity to conduct a formal study to my years as a fellow in the CIHR Training Program in Ethics of Health Research and Policy, jointly sponsored by the Department of Bioethics at Dalhousie University and the W. Maurice Young Centre for Applied Ethics at UBC. Through this program I became part of an extraordinary community of professors and research fellows grappling with contemporary ethical issues in medicine. Among those whose work inspired and informed my own were Janice Graham, Susan Sherwin, Françoise Baylis, Nuala Kenny, and Janet Atkinson-Grosjean. Other professors at Dalhousie whose contributions enriched this research were Paul Pross, Ingrid Sketris, and Wendy McKeen (now at York University). I also learned from members of Dr. Graham's lab for science studies research in medical anthropology, the Technoscience and Regulation Research

Unit. Throughout my initiation to the field of science studies, the work of David Hess of Vanderbilt University was a guiding light.

I had financial support for my research from numerous sources at Dalhousie University: from the CIHR Training Program in Ethics of Health Research and Policy, from Dr. Janice Graham's CIHR grant, titled "Risks and Regulation of Novel and Therapeutic Products," and from a Nora Stephen Oncology Summer Studentship.

From a personal standpoint, I could not have completed this long haul of a late-in-life project without the support of my family, including my beloved late sister Sylvia and mother, both of whom died of cancer too soon to see me complete my research. Ted Schrecker and William Stewart made valuable comments on draft manuscripts. I owe a huge debt to my many friends in the women's health community, particularly to the members of Women and Health Protection, for their moral and intellectual support. Each of them has thought deeply about the questions at the heart of this research; their insights are a strong influence throughout the text.

Finally, I thank Darcy Cullen at UBC Press for her patience and unflagging support over the several years of the manuscript's transformation from proposal to final text. I am grateful to two anonymous reviewers who provided thoughtful critiques of the manuscript, pushing me to rethink weak sections while maintaining the overall vision. In the last stages of editing and production, a team of creative minds at UBC Press materialized, including Ann Macklem, Nadine Pedersen, and Judy Phillips; their collaborative spirit and attention to detail never failed to impress me. Finally, defamation lawyer Roger McConchie's careful review spotted numerous weak claims and helped me raise them to legal standard.

Preface

This book has a personal side, as a coming-to-terms with an unfinished chapter of my past. When I was diagnosed with breast cancer in 1988, I already had spent two decades as a politically engaged journalist and editor, working mainly for feminist and consumer protection magazines. Following my diagnosis, I turned my research and writing to breast cancer and the politics of the disease, which at the time was scarcely explored. AIDS activists were blazing the way to a new form of disease activism, and I was struck by the contrasting invisibility and silence of breast cancer patients. That those of us living with a disease should contribute to shaping relevant health policies seemed obvious from a social justice perspective; that our lived experience was a necessary complement to the knowledge researchers and health practitioners had of the disease seemed equally clear. I cofounded Canada's first breast cancer patient advocacy group and wrote a book, *Patient No More: The Politics of Breast Cancer*, published in 1994 by Gynergy Books. As I wrote in the introduction to that book, the central task I saw for patients as activists was "to develop and advance a coherent perspective of our own. Our voice must be a counterweight to the medical point of view that dominates discussions of the disease" (p. xiii).

Throughout the 1990s, I divided my time between writing about breast cancer and activism in the breast cancer movement, working not only in Canada but also in the United States, Australia, and Europe, including the United Kingdom. During this decade of intense engagement, the breast cancer movement grew and changed. I welcomed the growth, but one change profoundly disturbed me: breast cancer groups had become increasingly dependent on the pharmaceutical industry for funding. In journalism, the pitfalls of financial conflicts of interest are well understood. Consumer protection magazines like the one I worked on for six years take no advertising, so that they can credibly assess products on the market. The feminist magazine community I was part of in the 1970s understood the power of advertising that relentlessly reinforces feminine stereotypes. Curiously to me, many of the breast cancer activists I knew seemed comfortable accepting money from the pharmaceutical industry, despite the widespread dissatisfaction with the array of toxic cancer drugs of dubious benefit. Health policy makers took these alliances in stride as well, and even encouraged them. A movement that had begun as a force for much-needed change began to seem to me like part of the problem.

I withdrew from grassroots community work in the breast cancer movement in 1999. Two successive university appointments of two years each gave me the space to reflect on the hurly-burly years of activism, when time to read had been in short supply. I discovered the wealth of scholarly writing about social movements, where health activist movements were still regarded as a new, and largely unexplored, phenomenon. Dalhousie University, where I was teaching, had just launched a program to train scholars in the ethical issues that pervade health policy and health research. I became a fellow in the program to study the movement in which I had recently been an active participant, in particular, the community's engagement with big pharma.

My goal in this book is to provide an understanding of the relationships Canadian breast cancer groups developed with the pharmaceutical industry, and how these alliances evolved. Although I don't claim that my findings tell the whole story or that I include all relevant points of view, I have tried to provide a rigorous interpretation of a rich array of material, inclusive of multiple, competing perspectives. Far from having the last word, I hope to open debate on a topic too long in the shadows.

Health Advocacy, Inc.

Introduction

THE SECRET WAR AMONG PATIENT GROUPS

There's always been a huge war between people within the community, between those who accept pharma funding – as if it were black and white, you know, the "pharma-takers" – and the sanctimonious ones on the other side who feel they've never been tarnished by that conflict.

        – BETH KAPUSTA, CANCER ACTIVIST AND FORMER CANCER PATIENT

Few who know the patient advocacy community in Canada would deny that two hostile camps are a long-standing reality. This was not always the case, though the beginnings of the "huge war" Beth refers to are now lost in time. One aim of this book is to reconstitute the process of division as it played out in one segment of the community that speaks for patients: that of grassroots breast cancer groups in Canada. This story is worth telling in its own right. However, the narrative has wider resonance – beyond the breast cancer movement, beyond Canada, and even beyond patient activism. In Canada and the United Kingdom, scholars and health activists have documented splits in various patient communities over pharma funding – funding from the pharmaceutical industry. Activists in the breast cancer movement in the United States and Germany have described similar ruptures. In each case, one patient group decided not to accept funds from the pharmaceutical industry and broke with the larger community, in which the practice had become prevalent. Among patient organizations representing different diseases in Ireland, in France, and in the United

States, researchers have documented varying practices in relation to the pharmaceutical industry. These accounts hint at painful internal struggles but do not depict the process of contestation that took place over time. This book does.[1]

One may ask, why go there? Struggles within social movements are sometimes seen as tedious exercises in ideological hairsplitting, or the result of petty personality conflicts. When the individuals involved are sick – sometimes terminally – the divisions may seem all the more bewildering. When I was active in the breast cancer movement in the 1990s, exasperated onlookers would sometimes say, "Why can't everybody just get along? You should all be fighting together, against breast cancer!" One assumption underlying this book is that the "pharma fights" within patients' movements matter a great deal and that they have not been given their due. Divisions within movements signify a struggle among members to define a reality that is central to their world; deconstructing the struggle reveals how social groups create and defend competing knowledge systems. In the case of patient organizations, the struggle is over what meanings we assign to drugs and drug companies, and to the health and regulatory systems that control access to therapeutic technologies.

Understanding these struggles in patient groups matters, because in many democracies, including Canada, patients are now important policy actors. In the 1980s, both in Canada and in the United States, HIV/AIDS activism expanded the boundaries of health activism to include political action by patients. AIDS activists argued that patients have an "embodied knowledge," derived from their first-hand experience of their illness as it affects their everyday lives.[2] Health policy makers and drug regulators began to take the patients' perspective more seriously, acknowledging patients as interested parties in research and policy decisions. Patient advocacy groups have proliferated, and their views are solicited, even mandated, at many levels of health governance. The rise of patient groups is thus politically important and would seem to count as a democratic gain, giving voice to previously silent, powerless constituencies of patients. But if groups within the patient community deem their differences significant enough to warrant waging internecine wars, anyone concerned about health policy should ask, what is at stake here? A related question is whether partnerships between pharmaceutical companies and patient organizations have contributed to a more democratic, participatory system of science governance.

Within the physician community, a similar tension over pharma funding has been examined for decades. Should physicians accept industry-funded trips to exotic places to attend educational talks? Should they accept big pharma's free meals? Is it okay to use pens bearing company logos? What about free samples from drug sales reps, to give to indigent patients? Physicians disagree on the answers, sometimes bitterly so. Although the debates about conflicts of interest in medicine are not yet resolved, they clearly matter. If corporate largesse encourages physicians to prescribe drugs when they are not appropriate, or to perform unnecessary medical procedures, the potential for harm is obvious. Quite apart from whether pharma funding influences the practice of medicine, the profession depends on the trust of patients, whose vulnerability magnifies the physician's power; on these grounds, physician and ethicist Howard Brody has argued, the potential of influence alone is reason enough for physicians to refuse industry funds or gifts. The debates within the patient community over pharma funding have had less exposure, but the parallels are striking.[3]

Also striking in their similarity are debates about corporate funding within other segments of the nonprofit, voluntary, or NGO (nongovernmental organization) sector. Since the early 1990s, alliances between activist groups and multinational corporations have proliferated. The World Wildlife Fund now accepts funding from Coca-Cola; the International Youth Foundation receives funds from Microsoft and Nike, among others; Oxfam has agreements with Starbucks and Unilever. This transformation has caused turmoil within NGO communities. Long-time Greenpeace leader Patrick Moore left that organization in 1986 and openly criticized it, "not for being corporatized, but for not working closely enough with corporations." On the other hand, when the Sierra Club accepted millions in donations from the gigantic gas driller and pro-fracking corporation Chesapeake Energy, outraged environmental activist, biologist, and author Sandra Steingraber said it was as if "anti-Fascist partisans had discovered that Churchill was actually in cahoots with the Axis forces."[4]

These concomitant conflicts suggest common underlying causes, and the broad strokes of my analysis at the national and international levels

coincide with that of others who have explored the sociopolitical transformations of the past three decades. In wealthy democracies, including
Canada, neoliberal governance regimes have reshaped state policies and
profoundly altered the funding practices that characterized civil society
organizations in the welfare state era preceding it. These macro-level
changes in funding practices have in turn changed the understanding of
concepts like advocacy and the social good. This transition has done much
to shape the group or meso-level politics within the patients' movement,
including competing advocacy agendas regarding pharmaceutical policies: What do patients need, anyway? And what policies will best address
these needs? Groups negotiate these questions and goals within a broader
political framework that has shifted over the past three decades, and that
continues to evolve.

I look at the macro-level forces through the lens of breast cancer patient
advocacy groups in Canada as they formed, gained recognition, grew,
and diversified over time. At the heart of the narrative is an examination
of how groups grappled with an ethical question: Can they accept pharma
funding and still advocate for drug treatment policies that serve the best
interests of patients? We'll look at how members of the community with
different perspectives developed competing ethical arguments, how one
argument achieved precedence over another, and how the outcome shapes
understandings about drugs. Also explored are what power relationships
are at play as two factions struggle to each have its perspective seen as true,
and how shifts in national and transnational policies influenced debates
within the groups.

What Are PHANGOs and Why Do They Matter?

My research draws on extensive research within Canada's breast cancer
community for two decades beginning in 1988 and documents the process
by which pharma funding became the norm within the patient advocacy
community. Tying the existence of these alliances to the politics of neoliberalism and its culture of partnership, I coined the word "PHANGO,"
meaning pharma-funded NGO, and referencing a vocabulary that characterizes NGOs according to their relationships with sponsoring partners
– for example, BONGOs, DONGOs, GONGOs, QUANGOs, and BINGOs.[5]
Anthropologist William Fisher maintains that this proliferation of NGO

acronyms can be counterproductive, since their creation and use is inconsistent and "often derives from a narrow objective on the part of the analyst." Although this criticism could be made of the term "PHANGO," I believe that terms designating a collaborative arrangement between a class of NGOs and a financial sponsor have value.[6]

First, I wanted to avoid the term "astroturf group," which references the fake-grass product and is used pejoratively to refer to groups with covert industry funding that present themselves as grassroots organizations while lobbying to promote corporate interests. Although the term is sometimes applied to any patient group that accepts pharma funding, I agree with Steven Epstein that the suggestion of a front group is best reserved for "one end of a continuum," that is, pharma-funded groups created by pharmaceutical companies to promote their products or gain support for regulatory approval.[7] My research in Canada's breast cancer community depicts a more complicated reality. In some groups, members actively debate the issue of pharma funding, with the weight of opinion shifting back and forth over time. In others, ambivalence is a constant: pharma funding is deemed acceptable under some circumstances but not others, and offers are continually negotiated. A few groups were rumoured in the community to be pharmaceutical-industry creations, but the organizations' leaders told a different story, and I was not able to determine the truth. Taking this variability into account, I intend the term "PHANGO" to be descriptive rather than pejorative, denoting the full range of groups that have one or more pharma partners but which may vary widely in their terms of engagement.[8]

This use is in keeping with Fisher's admonition that "what is at issue is not ... whether a specific association is or isn't an NGO, a QUANGO, a CONGO ... but what happens in specific places and at specific times."[9] He argues in favour of ethnographic studies that highlight the rich diversity of NGOs, depicting them as arenas that internalize battles from the larger society. In coining the term "PHANGO," with its allusion to the tango, I mean to capture this spirit of continual improvisation and struggle to adapt to local conditions, as well as the process of ongoing collaboration with a partner, which may be tinged with antagonism.

As well, by using the terms "patients' movement" and "breast cancer movement," I mean to exclude the large, established disease charities, such as (in Canada) the Canadian Cancer Society and the Canadian Breast Cancer Foundation. Both are primarily fundraising organizations that distribute funds to researchers and, in the case of the Cancer Society, provide professionally led and volunteer services. Although their structures may include patients as staff or volunteers, they are not self-help or advocacy organizations run largely by patients (the two charities merged in late 2016).

The alliances between patient organizations and corporations that are my focus here are specifically those with pharmaceutical companies – not, for example, the cause marketing alliances that many patient groups have formed with corporations. Cause marketing is a type of marketing in which a company links one of its consumer products to a popular charitable cause.[10] To gain market share and burnish its image, the company gives the organization in question a portion of the proceeds from sales, in exchange for attaching the organization's name or logo to the product. Cause marketing has linked breast cancer charities to spring water, yogourt, jeans, makeup, kitchenware, cars, and even guns. If there's a common thread in this list, it's that the products have no obvious relationship to the disease. A company that engages in cause marketing flaunts the alliance because it wants to forge a connection, in the public's mind, between its product and the cause. Drugs, by contrast, have everything to do with disease. Pharmaceutical company alliances with patient organizations therefore raise questions, some of them legal, about marketing. Pharmaceutical companies may prefer to fly under the radar when supporting patient groups because, unlike ordinary consumer products, drugs are highly regulated. Their marketing and use is controlled because they can harm health as well as improve it. Patient-group advocacy with pharmaceutical company sponsors thus have the potential to distort policies that have been put in place to protect the public health. This concern is at the heart of my investigation.

Patient Advocacy Groups, Science Research, and Health Policy

The interdisciplinary field of science and technology studies (STS), in which my research is situated, is the study of how social actors affect the creation and interpretation of scientific knowledge. Recognizing that science is a human endeavour means science is never neutral but is affected by scientists' values, politics, and agendas. STS research goes beneath the mask of neutrality that science sometimes wears to show the socially constructed aspects of science and science policy. A critical STS inquiry assumes that scientific discovery should contribute to the public good, and analyzes science policy, governance, and funding with the aim of advancing equality and other social justice goals.[11]

STS researchers study patient groups and health movements because the groups bring lay expertise to bear to politically shape the scientific agenda, and because the organizations have an inherent interest in the science and technologies that are applied to predicting, diagnosing, and treating disease, says Steven Epstein, whose ethnography of the AIDS movement in the United States is the bellwether STS analysis of a patients' movement. Interest in social movements and activist groups is relatively recent in STS literature. Early incarnations of STS focused on scientists and their laboratories. Critical STS provides a powerful lens for examining social justice issues in health movement and patient groups, yet researchers in the field have been slow to problematize the pharma funding of these groups, or the broader issue of commercialization in science.[12] Although many researchers have acknowledged the issue of corporate ties in health-related and patient organizations, their interest in challenges to dominant cultural authorities has led some to selectively study the more radical health organizations. The result is a tendency to conceptualize the groups as social movement organizations when in fact many – such as those with corporate ties – may be "contributing to the intensification of biomedicine's authority and further widening its jurisdiction."[13] Health activism, then, can bring about change that is progressive or regressive.[14]

Perhaps more intriguing, a patients' movement can do both at once. The AIDS movement in the United States is, arguably, an example of the latter. In his 1996 *Impure Science: AIDS, Activism and the Politics of Knowledge*, Steven Epstein documents how AIDS activist groups changed the practice of medical science by demanding changes in the clinical trials process used to test the safety and efficacy of HIV/AIDS medications. With a cry of "Drugs into bodies," they contested the ethics of placebo-controlled trials that required desperately ill patients participating in trials of new medications to risk being randomly assigned to the "no drug" arm of a trial. There is little doubt that pressure from the patient community accelerated the pace of research and dramatically slowed the pace of deaths, particularly in wealthy countries.[15]

The groups also altered American drug policy by challenging the American drug regulator, the Food and Drug Administration (FDA), to approve new drugs for HIV/AIDS more quickly, shifting the agency's priority from safety to access. Here, the cost-benefit balance of patient activism is more ambiguous. The macro-level political economy environment in which American AIDS activist groups functioned remains in the background in Epstein's treatment; however, the rise of AIDS activism in the 1980s coincided with the rise of neoliberal politics. Activists were aware that some of their demands for regulatory change meshed comfortably with the goals of the conservative administration of Ronald Reagan, as the following passage makes clear:[16]

> The FDA was killing the drug companies and preventing useful products from getting to market, the [conservative] argument ran; the best solution would be to repeal the Kefauver-Harris amendment, which had granted the FDA the authority to assess the safety and efficacy of drugs. "Especially considering who was the president, we had concern" about adding fuel to the deregulatory movement, recalled David Barr of ACT UP/New York: "But it wasn't enough concern that it would stop us from doing what we were doing." Soon, an unlikely alliance had developed – usually tacit, but sometimes explicit – between AIDS treatment activists and conservatives, leaving consumer protection groups and treatment liberals on the other side.[17]

In highlighting the impact of AIDS activist groups on research and regulatory policy, Epstein's study illustrates how actors with noncredentialled expertise can leverage their power to affect the practice of medical science and the regulation of medical technologies. This knowledge is not simply a less sophisticated grasp of the knowledge experts possess, but an epistemology that merits study in its own right. Medical anthropologists use the term "embodied knowledge" to characterize a type of experiential, lay knowledge based on the ways in which people experience their bodies and make sense of a bodily state (well-being, health, illness) in their everyday lives. The term shifts the idea of understanding of a disease state away from expert knowledge to what is learned first-hand from the day-to-day experience of living with an illness. Embodied knowledge incorporates cultural variables: one's history, language, politics, and local (including scientific) knowledge. It may differ from, or align with, expert knowledge. STS theorizing addresses this embodied quality in its attention to the "intermingling of humans and non-humans;"[18] in the case of a drug, the nonhuman entity literally acts on and becomes one with the patient's body.[19]

HIV/AIDS activism enlarged the critique of both the pharmaceutical industry and the drug regulatory agencies while adding a new dimension to health activism: collective pressure on researchers to target their research to particular diseases, and on drug regulators to provide access to novel treatments still in the pipeline. The first wave of the AIDS activist movement, which began in the United States in the early 1980s, combined demands for drugs with a strong critique of the pharmaceutical industry. More recently, analysts within the movement have voiced cautions about the potential of pharma funding to soften AIDS activism's critical edge.[20] Steven Epstein distinguishes between co-optation, in which "the radical potential of an activist critique is blunted or contained," and incorporation, when the insights of patient advocacy transform biomedical practice.[21] Co-optation is problematic, whereas incorporation is a sign of a movement's success, but the two processes may be hard to distinguish, as they can appear similar or may both be happening at the same time. As an ambiguous example of what might appear to be co-optation, Epstein cites the moderation of AIDS activists' political goals and methods over time, a change that he attributes in part to changes in the research trajectory and in part to activists' advances in their understanding of AIDS. In this case, he says, "blunt and accusatory terms such as 'cooptation' appear unhelpful." As if to illustrate the caution that activists' policy stances reflect a complicated trajectory of learning by multiple parties, in June 2015, two cofounders of the AIDS Treatment Action Group joined with former FDA commissioner David Kessler to oppose a new US bill, the 21st Century Cures Act, on the grounds that it could "substantially lower the standards for approval of many medical products, potentially placing patients at unnecessary risk of injury or death." Rapid access to new treatments was good for patients, the trio argued, only if it was restricted to serious or life-threatening diseases and paired with rigorous follow-up to ensure that the treatment actually improves patients' lives.[22]

The Dual Nature of Drugs

Epstein's analysis points to the need to study movements over time and also implicitly raises the issue of gender politics. The early AIDS movement grew out of the largely male gay activist movement and bore the imprint of gay activism at the time, including confrontational tactics and relatively young, educated, white, middle-class, urban leaders. The women's health movement, which dates to the 1960s, also had young, educated, white, middle-class leaders but a less confrontational political style and a different historical relationship to medical treatments. Women's embodied knowledge included their central role in human reproduction, as well as their experiences as family caregivers in times of both sickness and health. Abby Wilkerson provides an especially thoughtful analysis of the contrasting attitudes toward drug regulation between feminist and gay male activists, based on the different ways the medical profession stigmatized each community. Whereas healthy women have often been prescribed drugs to make their bodies conform more to a male ideal, physicians and other health professionals were reluctant to treat patients with AIDS.[23]

Feminist scholars have documented a long history of women's groups advocating for health and medical choices that are more holistic and inclusive than those based on a heterosexual, male-centred, biomedical model. The women's health activists who were part of the post-1960s feminist movement began to analyze structural reasons for women's exploitation, including violence against women, the medicalization of their bodies, the denigration of their caregiving roles, and the control pharmaceutical companies exercised over women's bodies and emotional states. This control spawned an antagonism toward the pharmaceutical industry, but the anger was not based – as it was in the early AIDS movement – on a belief that their plight merited more attention from the medical establishment. Rather, women were outraged by pharmaceutical company ads that reinforced demeaning stereotypes of women and by the harm they suffered from the misuse and overuse of drugs to treat normal conditions (like pregnancy), or states that had social roots (like depression). In short, "Drugs into bodies" was far from being the cry of the women's health movement; where drugs were concerned, women's health activists wanted effective health protection laws, and they looked to government agencies, like the FDA and (in Canada) the Health Protection Branch of the federal Department of Health, to provide them.[24]

The contrasting view of drugs in the early AIDS movement and the women's health movement is no anomalous fluke. Aside from the radically different ways in which medicine treated healthy women and gay men with AIDS – overtreating the former and shunning the latter – drugs, by their nature, evoke both desire and fear: they can cure and they can poison.

Pharmaceutical drugs and their antecedents, such as herbal remedies, have long been recognized as potentially useful, but also dangerous, interventions. *Pharmakon*, the Greek word for drug, has multiple other meanings, from remedy and poison to magic, spell, and charm. Jacques Derrida, in an extended reflection on the term and its contradictory meanings, argues against seeking a stable essence in the inherently ambivalent and oppositional. Scholars of feminism's third wave have cautioned against an oversimplified critique of pharmaceuticals in women's health, arguing that women respond to medicalization in ambivalent ways, negotiating rather than rejecting medical procedures and pragmatically accepting medical relief from pain, infertility, or premature death. Critical analyses of patient groups thus need to capture the tension of appeal versus risk and exploitation inherent in our relationship to technologies, including drugs. When it comes to medicalization, women have the agency to reflect on and choose among available discourses and practices and are able to adapt them to their own needs and values.[25]

In the AIDS movement, this tension and capacity for adaptive response was evident in the activists' response to azidothymidine (AZT), the first of the AIDS drugs that "did something" to the immune systems of AIDS patients in clinical trials but also caused severe adverse effects in some patients, including anemia, nausea, and headaches.[26] Although activists recognized the drug's limitations, they initially saw AZT as an early rung on a ladder that would eventually lead to a cure – hence the "drugs into bodies" strategy, adopted in the hope of keeping patients alive until a better drug came along. By the early 1990s, however, AZT was still the front-line therapy, despite being marginally effective and disliked by patients, and activists began to shift strategy gears: rather than access for the patients of today, they wanted answers – even if they themselves were not the beneficiaries; they wanted good science that would someday lead to an effective therapy or cure.[27]

The double-edged nature of drugs has an economic aspect also. Historically, apothecaries (the predecessors of today's pharmacists), as well as governments, have sometimes adopted the stance of protector of people's health, regulating the prices of drugs and the truth claims of those who sell them; in other periods, officials allowed vendors to exploit the seemingly magical quality of drugs as a source of easy profits. Today's neoliberal regimes define pharmaceuticals as commodities vital to the expansion of knowledge-based economies and, to this end, Canada and other states have revised regulatory controls on the pharmaceutical industry to facilitate international trade in these products. Some analysts of pharmaceutical policy believe neoliberal governments have gone too far in recalibrating the regulatory balance, allowing economic interests to trump its responsibility to protect the public health. I situate the PHANGO within the morally charged debates about these regulatory changes.[28]

The Neoliberal Connection

Definitions of neoliberalism abound, to the point where some scholars argue that the term has lost all analytic usefulness. I disagree, siding with those who believe the neoliberal paradigm shapes contemporary political and economic life and can't be ignored; furthermore, despite various understandings of the term, agreement exists on neoliberalism's central philosophical underpinnings: that markets are valued in themselves and all human action should be directed toward intensifying and expanding them. To ground my analysis, I adopt David Hess's definition of neoliberalism as "both public policies and economic thought that have guided a transition in many of the world's economies toward the liberalization of financial and other markets, the privatization of public enterprises, and the retrenchment of government commitments to social programs."[29] Canada's economy has undergone such a transition, and the realignments in public policy are central to my narrative in three domains: the health care system, the regulation of pharmaceuticals, and the role of civil society.

A few caveats are in order, however, to address the concerns of skeptics. First, the expansion of markets into nonmarket domains does not proceed in a single predictable pattern. Social geographers Kevin Ward and Kim England suggest thinking about state restructuring as a process, an evolution that unfolds unevenly and dynamically under different conditions. Ongoing struggles, including the resistance strategies of some actors (e.g., unions, public intellectuals, activists), contribute to making the path of neoliberalization unpredictable. Thus, an expansion in state funding of health care (which Canada experienced during the period under study) may be consistent with a neoliberal agenda. A critical question is who benefits from this spending? If, for example, rising public spending on health care benefits corporate interests (e.g., the pharmaceutical industry) and certain elite groups (e.g., affluent citizens, specialist physicians), without improving the overall health of Canadians, public spending is arguably serving the market while eroding the system's social justice goals.[30]

Recognizing the influence of neoliberalism on national and global economies and public policies, Kelly Moore and colleagues call for explorations that identify new patterns in the interrelationships among industry, science, and social movements. For these scholars, conflict is important. Of particular interest to an understanding of neoliberalism are conflicts arising from countervailing pressures, "from industry and the 'right hand' of the state on one side ... and from civil society and the 'left hand' of the state on the other side."[31] The French sociologist Pierre Bourdieu's metaphor of the state's right and left hands recognizes that governments have two broad types of obligations that are sometimes in conflict: to support economic interests, via such agencies as the Ministry of Finance and the banks, and to provide citizens with needed protections and services, the task of ministries like defence, health, and education that must spend money to achieve their goals.[32] For Bourdieu, neoliberalism was an "infernal machine," bent on the destruction of all the collective institutions capable of counteracting its effects; the institutions in jeopardy were primarily those of "the state, repository of all the universal ideas associated with the idea of the *public*." The only hope he saw for the construction of a new social order oriented to solidarities and social values was for individuals and groups with a tradition of civil and public service to resist the vision of accountants.[33]

If civil society groups exist to protect and provide services that advance the public good and are available to all, they will tend to be aligned with the state's "left hand," but under neoliberal governments, the numbers of such groups advocating for pharmaceutical policy in the public interest have been dwindling, political theorist Hans Löfgren concluded in 2004. Löfgren studied the changing influence of consumer and patient advocacy groups in pharmaceutical policy in Australia and globally. He found contrasting perspectives among groups over pharma funding and concluded that groups today play contradictory roles in the pharmaceutical policy domain. Depending on their mandates, some resemble the critical social movements of the 1960s and 1970s, which questioned established experts and powerful institutions, but many others may be fully incorporated into dominant power structures and exhibit characteristics of corporations, "with chief executive officers, large budgets and business plans."[34]

Löfgren notes the usefulness of analyses that compare neoliberal governance models with those that preceded them, in which bargaining relationships between capital, labour, the state, and sectorial interests were kept at arm's length. Neoliberal governance, by contrast, is premised on the notion of partnerships between actors who span a wider range, and relationships are no longer arm's length. The emergence of pharma-funded patient groups reflects this political evolution. Löfgren concludes that Australia, like other industrially developed countries, still accepts government regulation of pharmaceuticals as necessary to the market economy, but the government's role is no longer to ensure public health above all; rather, governments strive to retain social acceptability while coordinating and facilitating international market exchange. To achieve this, neoliberal governments manage pharmaceutical policy by orchestrating negotiations among large numbers of public and private "stakeholders," organized in complex networks of partnerships. (The term "stakeholder," used to denote anyone who is affected by a course of action, is itself neoliberal terminology, writes Joshua Sharfstein, a physician and former commissioner at the FDA. In a critique of the term's proliferation in the health policy world, Sharfstein notes that the term's more common use denotes someone with a financial stake in the success of an enterprise. In health policy, those referred to as stakeholders – such as pharmaceutical companies – often do have a financial stake in discussions, but the interests of these parties can be at odds with good health policy, which advances public health while containing costs. Referring to everyone around the table as a stakeholder shrouds the deliberations in a dense fog, Sharfstein argues, obscuring differences in goals that should be made visible.[35] Following Sharfstein, I do not identify patients or patient organizations as stakeholders, though I do quote texts and cite individuals who use the term this way.)

Patient and other health sector advocacy groups play a prominent role in certain negotiating networks because a neoliberal regime awards various societal sectors a claim to political participation based on their different stakes in the uncertainties of the globalized world – what sociologists Ulrich Beck and Anthony Giddens have termed the "risk society."[36] Patient groups are awarded participant status in the drug policy arena because of their obvious stake in the availability, effectiveness, and safety of pharmaceuticals. In this capacity, part of their role is to articulate the amount of risk they consider acceptable in drug treatments. Historically, says Löfgren, Australian health and patient advocacy groups were allied with the Health Department on such regulatory matters as equity, accessibility, rational drug policy, and appropriate prescribing. Over the decade prior to his study, he concludes, the pharmaceutical industry had purposefully weakened the alliances with the Health Department through dialogue, collaborative marketing, and sponsorships.

As Löfgren's analysis implies, neoliberal regimes alter the national frameworks in which advocacy groups function and, some have argued, redefine the meaning of advocacy. Canadian feminist scholars have documented the ways in which neoliberal discourses and funding policies in Canada changed the political environment to weaken conflictual group activism and privilege a depoliticized, consumerist, noncontentious individual engagement in the political system. Having stripped away their advocacy role, governments rebranded civil society groups as the "voluntary sector." Lawyers Judy Fudge and Brenda Cossman propose that neoliberal policies encouraging alliances between health charities and drug companies set back women's equity struggles in the area of health. Governments in the new order now rely on health charities to provide their members with services that once were the domain of the health care system, so are loath to discourage these alliances, they say. Fudge and Cossman note that health charities now have extensive websites that carry useful information on topics like self-care and family support, which alleviates pressures on the health care system. At the same time, the sites have disease-specific information, including drug information, which will probably increase pressure on the health budget by promoting new, expensive, and not necessarily better drugs. Although nonprofit organizations are becoming larger, richer, more powerful, and more "corporate," Fudge and Cossman argue that they are losing their autonomy via strings to corporations.[37]

Patient-driven organizations and websites are evidence of what some theorists have termed "biological citizenship" or "biosociality," a new type of identity politics in which individuals with the same disease form organizations and assert rights based on patient status. These claims can arise from health harms, as when the post-Chernobyl citizens of the Ukraine mobilized to claim compensation for adverse health effects they suffered from radiation exposure; or they can be based on the perceived benefits of new health technologies, such as genetic tests and treatments. Paul Rabinow, Nicholas Rose, and colleagues argue that the new genetic discoveries arising from the Human Genome Project have led to the creation of groups whose members are susceptible to the same disease; they are, in Michel Foucault's terminology, a new episteme: sites of new knowledges and powers, based on genomics. Rabinow calls this new type of identity, formed in response to genetic technologies, "biosociality."[38]

For Rabinow, AIDS activism provided a model in which patient organizations could keep scientists honest by reminding them that the point of medical research is to alleviate suffering. By engaging scientists in ongoing dialogue about their work, such groups could counter the self-interested, sometimes arrogant, culture of science, which in the past had led to inhumane experiments. The ascendance of neoliberal regimes had replaced ruling elites whose values were shaped by humanism with managers who valued neither science nor humanism, Rabinow reasoned, so checks on science were particularly needed. Building on Rabinow's analysis, Nicholas Rose and Carlos Novas conducted case studies of partnerships among patient groups, biotech companies, and biomedical researchers. They propose the concept of biocitizenship to theorize innovative citizenship projects where patients and their allies sometimes lead in setting ethical standards and pushing scientific boundaries.[39]

These same scholars and others agree that the diversity in patient-centred groups calls for empirical research and theorizing to lend greater nuance to concepts like biocitizenship. Medical anthropologist Margaret Lock, for example, studied the support group networks that developed after Alzheimer's disease was named as a heritable condition in the late 1970s. She found that discussions at the meetings, attended mainly by family members involved in care giving, paid little attention to whether genes are implicated in the condition and instead focused overwhelmingly on practical coping strategies for caregivers. And in a theoretical analysis, Alexandra Plows and Paula Boddington argue that the "bio" prefix in "biocitizenship" risks obscuring debates that require urgent attention, including those between groups that mobilize to contest corporate power in the health field and those that support a gene-focused research and policy agenda while using pharma funding to mobilize. In a similar vein, Thomas Lemke, in a 2015 assessment of biosociality and its limitations, observes, "Power relations have not been adequately addressed in the analysis of biosocial communities."[40] He critiques the bulk of the theorizing and research that has come out of the biosociality concept as one-sided, giving too much weight to biomedical knowledge as a force constituting the identities of individuals and their organizations. The converse is also true, he argues: the hopes and needs of patients, and the visions and interests of scientific experts, simultaneously shape the conduct, interpretation, and application of medical research.[41]

Recognizing the diversity among patient groups, many researchers have developed classificatory systems to organize the types of organizations and their salient features, a practice that itself has led to a confusing array of typologies. Based on a 2008 review of the literature on patient groups and health movements, Steven Epstein identifies six important questions that underlie the diversity of these groups, suggesting that researchers should recognize that their research question will inevitably "chop up the universe of cases in a distinctive way."[42] Among Epstein's six dimensions, my research highlights primarily the groups' degree of independence from corporations, state agencies, or professional associations. A secondary question from Epstein's list that differentiated the groups is their relationship to medicalization: some groups seek medical recognition for a condition, whereas others contest or resist medical interventions.[43]

Pharma Funding of Patient Groups

Since 2000, the phenomenon of patient groups with pharma funding has attracted the attention of health policy makers, becoming a theme in the scholarly literature on health policy literature and medical ethics.[44] Nonetheless, the move to industry funding and the reasons for it have not been analyzed in detail. Most research on the groups consists of surveys, which establish the PHANGO phenomenon as real and widespread, and studies of websites and other public documents, which point to the covert nature of the funding and argue that both the industry and groups have a public responsibility to open their relationships to public scrutiny. Localized case studies of pharma funding within patient groups, which are less common, have shown that in Ireland, Finland, France, and the United Kingdom, groups differ among themselves in the stance they adopt to accepting industry funds.[45]

At a 2006 pan-European workshop, health researchers from ten countries came together to discuss health consumer and patient organizations in Europe and identified funding by drug companies as a major issue.[46] In most countries, researchers reported, groups had moved from self-help to greater political awareness and lobbying, but their financial and human resources were often limited. Their impact on policy was only apparent if powerful interests supported the organizations: the medical profession, state agencies, or the pharmaceutical industry. Workshop delegates worried (but had not demonstrated) that dependence on pharmaceutical companies increased the likelihood that the organizations would support the industry's interests, but recognized that funding from professional organizations and government could also compromise independence. These researchers considered the internal workings of health consumer and patient organizations to be inadequately documented but expressed concerns that some were not democratic or representative – no small details, since the participation of lay participants in decision making is meant to promote greater democratization in science.

In Canada, two physicians writing in Canada's medical journal of record made the claim in 2010 that organized political activism by patient organizations contributes to the misallocation of health resources because of inequalities in representation among disease groups. Paul Hébert and Matthew Stanbrook wrote: "Although federal leaders elsewhere have galvanized their citizens to develop national evidence-based health care institutions ... Canada's parliamentarians issue occasional impassioned pleas on behalf of specific patient groups fortunate enough to make their concerns appear politically expedient."[47] Canadian medical anthropologist Janice Graham notes the potential for groups comprising patients or their family members to publicly portray their members as "caring humanitarians" pitted against "cold guardians of the public purse" as they demand that a new, untested therapy be added to a drug formulary. Graham continues: "So we are prescribing and funding drugs, despite the lack of strong, publicly sponsored best-evidence of efficacy, to satisfy family (and, one presumes, clinician and industry) demands."[48]

Social groups use discourses – words, arguments, claims, visuals, and other modes of communication – to construct their social worlds, or understandings of reality. Discourses about pharma funding of patient groups thus provide windows into the way these contrasting social worlds are constructed. In 2007, the *British Medical Journal (BMJ)* invited pro and con commentaries on the question of whether patient groups should accept money from drug companies. Alastair Kent, director of the Genetic Interest Group (now Genetic Alliance UK) in London, England, argued that they should, because money from the pharmaceutical and biotech industries allows groups, including his own, to provide better services and support for the individuals and families they represent. There is nothing inherently wrong with pharma funding, he said, provided that "the source is acknowledged and there are no hidden strings." Besides, he continued, public money and grants from charitable foundations cannot be assumed to be strings-free either, as "no person or group will be overly keen to support a campaigning organization if they think that their money will be used to 'buy a stick to beat them with.'"[49]

In contrast, Barbara Mintzes, an epidemiologist at the University of British Columbia, wrote that funding to patient groups from industries that sell products to treat their illnesses involves an inherent conflict that compromises the groups' ability to provide impartial information and to speak on behalf of people who are ill. Mintzes cites three dangers to patients: disguised product promotion funnelled through a seemingly impartial party, confusion between the interests of the group and the corporate sponsor, and inadequate representation for patients when those interests diverge.[50] Although she welcomed steps to make funding arrangements more transparent, Mintzes contends that the problems remain: groups are reluctant to discuss safety concerns about a drug if they have received money from the company that makes it; similarly, the groups are likely to side with a sponsoring company in policy disputes over such issues as which drugs to insure. The evidence points to even small donations compromising a group's impartiality, said Mintzes, and industry-funded groups eventually may lose public trust.

Research Methodology and Its Underlying Rationale

This detailed examination of a national patients' movement's involvement with the pharmaceutical industry over an extended period is the first I know of. I use interviews, direct observation, and detailed analysis of documents from multiple sources to provide a fine-grained description with three main threads, each of which changes colour and texture over time: the development of PHANGO culture as seen from inside a movement, the effects of macro-level changes on local organizations, and the socially constructed meanings of medications.

The historical tracking of groups has two main purposes. First, only an analysis over time can answer questions about whether and how funding from pharmaceutical companies co-opts patient groups, since co-optation implies a process in which the donor corporations increase their influence within the groups in conjunction with funding. Second, the political-economic culture within patient organizations is shaped in no small measure by constantly changing policy decisions made at the macro-political level; these interactions can only be captured in a study that tracks their evolution.[51]

To expand on the first point, a critical question is whether, under the influence of a corporate donor, the group endorses positions on pharmaceuticals and related policies that are counter to its members' interests. As Epstein points out, a group's position may appear to move closer to that of industry for reasons unrelated to co-optation.[52] A similar logic underlies debates about the significance of "professionalization" in activist movements. In a common trajectory, groups outgrow their volunteer roots and adopt a more professionalized model with paid staff, secure funding, and recognition by establishment actors like physicians, health researchers, and decision makers in government. A rise in professionalism is sometimes viewed as inimical to grassroots activism, but Robert Kleidman, a sociologist who studies social movements, contests this claim as overly simplistic. Categorizing a group as either grassroots or professional assumes that professionalization moves the group's perception of issues closer to that of professionals and renders the group less able to represent the interests and knowledge of people at the grassroots. But, Kleidman objects, simply observing that the structure of a grassroots group (or movement) has become professionalized is insufficient evidence to conclude that the group has abandoned its commitment to grassroots objectives. Paid staff, for example, can be used to train local activists in radical tactics, making the organization more challenging to the status quo, not less. Kleidman urges social theorists to develop models that consider not only resources and political opportunities but also the values and strategies of movement professionals.[53]

Orla O'Donovan, who conducted research on pharma funding of patient groups in Ireland, rejects a straightforward astroturf/authentic dualism, for reasons similar to Kleidman's. Pharmaceutical companies have successfully defined themselves as a philanthropic force and as rightful players in Irish health activism, but research has yet to demonstrate that these ties have eroded the mandates of these organizations from contesting the status quo to accepting dominant structures and discourses. She poses the possibility that health advocacy organizations can both disturb orthodox understandings of health, illness, and patienthood while reinforcing pharma-centric health discourses and the commodification of health activism.[54]

On the second rationale for studying the groups over time, I wanted to illuminate the ways in which changes in macro-level policies affect advocacy groups concerned about drug regulation. To this end, my research spans three decades in which Canada underwent a radical transition, from welfare state to a nation in which governance structures were realigned to reflect the trade-based assumptions of neoliberalism and neoconservatism. Patient-centred health advocacy began its ascent on the cusp of this political restructuring: the high-profile AIDS groups began organizing in the mid- to late 1980s, and breast cancer groups soon followed, in the early 1990s. Many other disease-specific organizations have modelled themselves on these examples. Researchers in other sectors have documented how policy shifts reverberated through well-established civil society movements, such as services for children and families and the environmental movement; I ask whether groups within patients' movements felt their effects as well, and if so, how.[55]

By shifting attention from the work of scientists to that of patients, who are among the main users of scientific discoveries, I highlight unequal relationships of knowledge and power. How do patient groups understand the health technologies (especially drugs) that are developed in their name? How do they weigh social justice in the distribution and application of these technologies? And how do alliances with pharmaceutical companies affect these knowledge/power/justice equations – if they do at all?[56]

I made breast cancer groups in Canada the focus of my research in part because they constitute an important social movement in themselves, and one that other patient communities look to as a model. The rapid emergence and growth of the breast cancer movement is arguably the most remarkable example of health activism in the 1990s; yet, despite many fine scholarly investigations of this phenomenon, the theme of pharma funding in that movement's evolution remains largely overlooked. Also critical to my research, the evolution of breast cancer groups spans several decades – a necessary requirement for studying change over time. The scope of my research includes a period of overlap between the breast cancer movement and the women's health movement that preceded it by two decades. The two health movements bleed into one another – though not always harmoniously – and some individuals engaged in the earlier movement became leaders in the later one.[57]

From my participation in the breast cancer movement in the 1990s, I knew that the issue of pharma funding had been debated within many of the groups, and that these discourses developed in tandem with the debates about various treatment regimens these same companies were bringing to market. To understand the interrelationships between groups and drug treatment debates, I tracked the "social lives" of breast cancer drug treatments over the same twenty-year period. The concept of drugs having social lives recognizes that a drug acquires social meanings as it passes through its life cycle – the trajectory from development to actual use to eventual obsolescence.[58] Our understanding of a drug derives only in part from its objective qualities; a range of actors with varied values and vested interests add profoundly subjective meanings.

Drug companies understand this process well. Alastair Matheson, who worked for over a decade in communications in the pharmaceutical industry, explains that, during a drug's development, companies construct narratives that integrate scientific and marketing goals to shape scientific and medical knowledge about the new product. As the drug approaches market, the company often creates "key messages" that "describe the background area of medicine, why the drug is needed, how it benefits the patient, why it is superior to its competitors, and why it is cost-effective."[59] Patient groups comprise a relatively new addition to the array of social actors positioned to engage in this process of negotiated meaning making, which they can accomplish in a more politically effective way than individual patients.

I organize my narrative of the breast cancer movement's relationship with the pharmaceutical industry into three periods, each of which is defined by the practices, discourses, and struggles within the groups. Describing the phases of advocacy in a patients' movement this way highlights turning points at which the power relations shift and transform the relationships among players. I then identify underlying conditions and events at that particular moment and place that could have upset the continuity of daily practice. The resulting history emphasizes conflicts within the movement over the ethical arguments for and against industry relationships, shows points of stabilization, and makes visible the rules governing accepted practices.[60]

To capture the internal workings of the movement, I conducted interviews with forty women who had been decision makers at different points in time, and examined documents from the health advocacy organizations to which they belonged. I also drew from my own experiences as a former breast cancer patient who spent almost a decade in the breast cancer movement in the 1990s. I analyzed government reports, scientific literatures, industry documents, and media stories to situate these accounts of health activism in the scientific and policy contexts to which they belonged.

In addition to my interviews with health activists, I interviewed two key informants from the pharmaceutical industry, two from government policy circles, and one prominent cancer research scientist. Given the polarization within the community on this topic and to encourage a frank discussion of their views, I offered participants the option of speaking under a pseudonym. Some chose to do so, and these names are referenced in the text and shown in the Appendix in quotation marks.

How the Book Is Organized

The book has two main sections. Part 1 provides the policy background that informs the empirical investigation of the breast cancer movement in Part 2. The latter describes the growth of the movement over two decades, with a focus on relationships with the pharmaceutical industry. I conclude by examining the relationship between the movement and the industry and assessing what it means for health policy affecting breast cancer patients.

Part 1, comprising Chapters 1 and 2, relates the book's backstory: the dramatic reorientation in political philosophy that characterized Canada's transition from a postwar welfare state to a neoliberal state. From the early 1980s and into the 1990s, the country gradually aligned its policies with those of the Reagan and Thatcher governments in the United States and the United Kingdom respectively. The breast cancer movement, which had its origins in the late 1980s, is thus almost entirely a creature of the neoliberal period. Keeping in mind the unevenness with which neoliberalization proceeds, however, some structures and policies from the welfare state era remained in place into the early 1990s, and helped shape the early movement, as did activist resistance to the neoliberal project.

Chapter 1 outlines the central features of Canada's health system as it evolved, from the 1950s through the 1980s. The chapter provides essential background to Canada's publicly funded health care system – its significance and limitations, and some of the controversies it provoked. The contested nature of policy making is clearly seen, with its cast of characters working to push decisions one way or another, in a process that is seldom completely visible to the public. The transition to neoliberalism also saw dramatic changes in Canadian policies governing advocacy groups. Chapter 2 examines the pro-advocacy regulatory regime that governments developed in Canada's welfare state era and the resulting environment that enabled progressive social movements to flourish.[61] The latter part of the chapter considers conditions that began to reshape the funding of nonprofits.

Part 2 tells the story of the breast cancer movement's beginnings and growth, with a focus on the gradual development of relationships between the grassroots groups and the pharmaceutical industry. Chapter 3 documents an initial grassroots period, in which small local groups of women diagnosed with breast cancer began to voice dissatisfaction with aspects of their experience as patients. The pharmaceutical industry had little role in these early groups, and drugs were a relatively minor topic of discussion, until a series of changes converged to bring the groups into sporadic contact with the industry, stimulating internal discussions about whether drug companies were an acceptable source of funding. Chapters 4 and 5 describe a period of contestation in which groups struggled internally with the ethics of pharma funding. Chapter 4 looks at external forces that challenged the feminist opposition to pharma funding. Chapter 5 provides case examples of internal tensions as debates within the groups redefined movement contours. By the third and last phase of my analysis (Chapters 6 and 7), most breast cancer groups had opted to accept pharma funding, normalizing the PHANGO construct. Chapter 6 describes a change in the sociopolitical landscape supportive of these developments and documents a process that systematized relationships between the industry and movement activists in response to critical attacks on the partnership model. In Chapter 7, examples of pharma-funded advocacy campaigns identify steps in these advocacy "dances" and illustrate their potential to affect pharmaceutical policies.

In the Conclusion, I reflect on what my findings say about how PHANGOs are constructed and maintained, and on the meaning of these partnerships for democratic debate, health policy, and patient groups as sites of knowledge that can advance patients' interests.

PART 1

Canada's Health Care System Transformed
Neoliberalism and the Erosion
of the Welfare State

1

Canada's Health Policy Landscape

The 1980s in Canada were a time of policy upheaval. Social programs that had been developed over the previous four decades under a welfare state model were recast or replaced with programs designed to align the country's economic system with the neoliberal and neoconservative regimes imposed by Margaret Thatcher in Great Britain and Ronald Reagan in the United States. The policies constructed in Canada's welfare state era arose from long-standing, hard-fought discursive struggles with powerful opponents. The fragility of these programs has become apparent in the years since the mid-1980s as the country coped with a rising debt and moved to the free-market model, which relies on markets to meet all needs. We look here at three such program areas: publicly funded hospital and medical insurance; laws and regulations to address pharmaceutical drug safety, efficacy, truth claims, and pricing; and community-based advocacy groups (the topic of the next chapter).

Government-Funded Health Insurance

Canada's system of universal, publicly funded hospital and medical insurance is a defining characteristic of the country's policy landscape. Medicare, or publicly funded health care, is a legacy of the period in Canada's political-economic development from the mid-1940s to the mid-1970s in which a series of universal social programs were put in place and actively maintained. Few Canadians would claim neutrality in the debates about the country's social programs, and today the term "welfare state" is often used pejoratively. I stand, however, with analysts who contend that the creation of national programs to provide basic security to the sick, families, the unemployed, and the aged marked a high point for social justice in Canada. State supports for advocacy by marginalized and underrepresented groups are less known and understood, but they complement social programs. Designed to broaden the participation in democratic nation building, they keep social programs attuned to community concerns and breathe meaning into the equality ideal in citizenship. Indeed, the programs discussed here evolved in no small part through the advocacy of state-funded civil society organizations.[1]

Prime Minister Louis St. Laurent's Liberal government introduced Canada's publicly funded health care program in 1957 using a provincial template: Saskatchewan's public hospital insurance plan of 1947. The latter was the legendary brainchild of Tommy Douglas, who, as premier of Saskatchewan, was the first democratic socialist to lead a government in Canada. The essence of the original federal plan was that all Canadians are entitled to the same hospital care, regardless of ability to pay. Because health care delivery is a provincial responsibility under the Canadian Constitution, the federal government could not impose the plan but promised to pay half of all hospital expenses in any province that signed onto it. All ten provincial governments did so, enticed not just by the money but also by the plan's undeniable success in Saskatchewan and the enormous public support this generated. That province, meanwhile, had taken the additional step of expanding its plan to include the cost of visits to a physician. In 1966, the federal government followed suit, passing the Medical Care Act. A Royal Commission report on health services bolstered the decision to expand coverage with evidence that a single-payer, publicly funded, universal health insurance plan provides medical outcomes that compare favourably with those under privately funded systems, saves substantial administrative costs, and equalizes treatment across the entire population.

Under the Medical Care Act, the country's provincial and territorial governments maintained regulatory control over the hospitals and health service providers in their jurisdiction. Each province and territory could thus adapt health spending to local needs within the four principles the federal government attached to its transfer of tax dollars: public administration, comprehensive coverage, universality, and portability. Notably, medications, unless administered in a hospital, don't fall under the terms of universal health care. The two levels of government split responsibilities in the regulation of pharmaceuticals. The federal government regulates the safety, efficacy, and promotion of drugs, and sets some limits on pricing. The provinces establish their own drug payment systems, which include drug coverage programs for seniors and welfare recipients and, importantly for the discussion of patient advocacy, a drug formulary, which lists the drugs each government has decided to cover under its provincial insurance plan. Because each province has its own drug formulary, a particular drug may be publicly funded in one province and not in another.[2]

Significantly, the Hall Report (named after former justice Emmett Hall, who headed the Royal Commission that wrote the report) argued that the country's health care needs would best be met if pharmaceuticals and other core services (home care, nurse care, ambulances, and eye and dental care) were brought under the single-payer umbrella. The government decided to proceed gradually, however, reasoning that other services could be added later. Fifty years on, the single-payer system has yet to expand to cover these additional services, leading advocates of the public-funding principle to fault that decision as a political misstep. A 2012 report from the Senate identified a national pharmaceuticals strategy as a priority for health care reform in Canada and, in 2016, under a newly elected Liberal government, the question of how to fund pharmaceuticals once again moved to the fore. In April 2016, the Standing Committee on Health of the House of Commons began studying proposals for the development of a national pharmacare plan.[3]

From its inception, the single-payer system has had detractors. Provinces divided along lines of size and wealth: larger, wealthier provinces feared losing control of how they spent their money, whereas smaller, poorer provinces welcomed the guarantee of revenue to provide basic, costly services to their populations. Nurses and other unionized segments of the affected workforce have supported the plan, which ensures a large number of good jobs, particularly for women. Many companies too have supported the plan, which relieves them of having to provide their employees with health insurance for core services. Among voters, publicly funded health care quickly developed broad support because the system worked: as patients, they received good care at less cost than under a private plan. This strong voter support has meant that all Canadian political parties, from left to right on the spectrum, have ultimately endorsed single-payer health care, despite its origins in a democratic socialist party and despite opposition from companies and lobby groups that promote private enterprise.

Private insurance companies were obvious opponents to the single-payer system because governments took over their role in insuring basic hospital and physician services; however, all provinces allow private insurance to cover areas not covered by their plans, and five allow additional private insurance for services that are covered. Thus, employee health insurance plans and privately purchased insurance can cover any drug, including those that are not administered in-hospital or that a provincial government has excluded from its formulary (private plans have their own formularies).

Physicians were divided. Some believed the single-payer system undermined their professional independence; others saw it as consistent with their professional obligation to treat on the basis of need and welcomed a plan that ensured they would be paid for their services regardless of a patient's financial means. Physician support for the single-payer system, expressed individually and through the physicians' political advocacy organization, the Canadian Medical Association, is thus unstable and subject to internal factions. Each province and territory also has a medical association; these twelve organizations comprise autonomous divisions of the Canadian Medical Association and attend to responsibilities specific to their jurisdictions – for example, negotiating fee schedules. As a result, regional variations in rural-urban distribution, wealth disparities, and the like present another potential source of division.

A significant addition to the 1966 Medical Care Act was introduced in 1984 to combat threats to the plan's universality. A federal inquiry, again headed by Emmett Hall, and a citizens group, the Canadian Health Coalition, had warned then minister of health and welfare, Monique Bégin, that physicians were charging extra fees and provinces were spending their federal health care transfer payments on other priorities. With additional support from unions, health advocacy groups, and nurses, the health minister convinced Prime Minister Pierre Trudeau and his Cabinet to bring in new legislation, known as the Canada Health Act, to combat the renegade physicians and provinces. In replacing the Medical Care Act and the Hospital Insurance and Diagnostic Services Act, the Canada Health

Act set a new framework for transferring federal funds to the provinces; it reaffirmed the four conditions for federal funding and added a fifth, accessibility, to strengthen the national program. To qualify for federal funding under the new act, the provinces and territories had to adhere to all five principles:

- *Public administration* asserts that the administration of a province's health plan must be nonprofit and responsible to the provincial or territorial government;
- *Comprehensiveness* requires all hospitals to provide and pay for a specified menu of basic services;
- *Universality* affirms a uniform right to all insured services for all insured persons in the province;
- *Portability* guarantees that coverage travels with the individual when he or she moves from one province to another, changes jobs, or changes physicians; and
- *Accessibility* asserts that essential services provided must be similar for everyone and without user fees, though providers must receive "reasonable" compensation.

Together, the principles promote the values of solidarity, equity, reduced administrative costs, and a collective vested interest in the quality of services. The Canada Health Act was meant to address regional inequalities and to force compliance with the public system but would be effective only if the federal government was willing to enforce it. In 1986, physicians in Ontario tested government will. They went on strike, and the federal government withheld transfer payments to the province until the strike – lasting a total of twenty-three days – ended. This government resolve has weakened since the mid-1980s and confidence in the system has eroded (more on this below).

There were two main competing discourses about health care during this transitional period. One camp favoured a reliance on markets; they framed the debt and deficit as crises largely precipitated by the cost of programs like health care and by individuals dependent on them. The second camp opposed the free-market approach to health care and favoured maintaining the publicly funded system. Its proponents cited research that traced the federal government's debt to tax cuts to corporations and rising interest charges. The ongoing cuts to the program, they said, increased regional disparities in the provision of health care, which undermined the ethic of equality.

Early Drug Regulation

Although pharmaceuticals were excluded from medicare unless administered in a hospital as part of hospital care, the federal government intervened in other ways to regulate pharmaceutical drugs, including price controls and a ban on advertising to consumers. Despite being a minor player in the global pharmaceutical scene, Canada has shown a capacity to destabilize the pharmaceutical industry's well-honed discourses, primarily through its proximity to the United States, where differences in pharmaceutical policy have at times been striking, for reasons that are in large part structural. From its emergence in the early twentieth century, the pharmaceutical industry has operated from and benefited the economies of a few wealthy countries – initially Switzerland, Germany, and the United States.[4] Despite a few early indigenous companies, Canada did not develop a strong homegrown industry, and the country's relatively small population makes it a minor market for foreign companies. The United States' central place in the global pharmaceutical industry, combined with its stronger commitment to a free-enterprise model of health care, make comparisons between the two systems inevitable and ongoing, bringing to the fore contrasts that have ancient antecedents.[5]

Contemporary discourses about big pharma embody a long-standing, inherent tension between the industry's ethical obligations to the consumer and the business of making profits and contributing to a community's economic growth. In England, the adulteration of drugs, such as botanicals, had always been considered a serious offence, but enforcement flagged in the seventeenth and eighteenth centuries, allowing trade in so-called patent medicines to flourish. These highly profitable, widely advertised potents with secret ingredients that were sometimes poisonous or addictive were also marketed in the United States and Canada, until social reform movements in all three countries successfully challenged the claims of dishonest merchants and pushed for science-based regulation of food and drugs to protect the public from health catastrophes.[6]

Beginning in 1860 in England and culminating in the United States' Pure Food and Drug Act, passed in 1906, legislation to prohibit the adulteration of food, drink, and drugs was put in place and strengthened in both countries, using scientific testing methods to protect the consumer against unsafe products and fraudulent claims. Canada passed similar laws: the Adulteration Act of 1884, modelled on the United Kingdom's act of the same name, set standards for strength, quality, and purity, and criminalized the sale of adulterated food and drugs. In 1920, Canada replaced the Adulteration Act with its own Food and Drugs Act, based on the 1906 US legislation.[7] The US act created the Food and Drug Administration, or FDA, the first regulatory agency in the United States. Significantly, the act recognized industry as an inherently more powerful player than the average citizen. Food and drug manufacturers in the United States opposed the regulations and applied pressure on legislators, who struck the requirements that companies disclose all ingredients and refrain from false and misleading therapeutic claims. The act also failed to authorize a ban on unsafe drugs. Despite its weaknesses, the US Pure Food and Drug Act set a new standard that influenced laws and regulatory structures in other countries, including Canada, where the 1920 act set quality standards for foods and alcoholic drinks, gave the government the power to inspect products, and prohibited misleading advertising.[8]

The Modern-Day Drug Industry

As this regulatory framework for food and drugs was being honed in the United States, Canada, the United Kingdom, and elsewhere, the modern-day chemically based pharmaceutical industry was in its infancy, evolving within parent companies that produced synthetic dyes, petrochemicals, agrichemicals, and other chemical products. Drug development soon became a thriving industry in its own right. To distinguish its drug products from the discredited patent medicine trade, the burgeoning industry highlighted the scientific basis for its discoveries and adopted the term "ethical drug manufacturers" – an early example of corporate branding. The industry as we know it took flight with the mass production of antibiotics or anti-infective drugs in the mid-1930s. It expanded rapidly during and after the Second World War, a period of new drug discovery. Intensive experimentation to discover cancer drugs began in the United

States in the period immediately after the war, initially in secret and then publicly.[9]

As early as 1921, Swiss companies pioneered a structural model of global market control that remains largely intact today. Hoffmann-La Roche, Ciba, and Sandoz each assembled large research teams based in Switzerland that specialized in drug development, and distributed promotional experts throughout foreign markets via branch operations. Germany and the United States had thriving industries by the early 1940s, each with a similar, centrally controlled global reach. Leading firms headquartered in Germany included Bayer and Boehringer Ingelheim; the United States was home to Eli Lilly, Upjohn, Pfizer, and Merck. Britain, France, and the Netherlands subsequently gained entry to the elite club, and Japan followed in the 1970s. Other industrialized countries, Canada among them, had a negative balance of trade in pharmaceuticals, depending almost completely on the dominant foreign companies for the research, development, and manufacture of their drugs.[10]

The United States introduced the Food, Drug, and Cosmetic Act of 1938 in response to a drug disaster that caused 107 reported deaths, mostly of children, exposing weaknesses in the Pure Food and Drug Act. In the 1930s, sulpha drugs were widely used in the United States and Europe as an effective antibiotic treatment for diseases such as pneumonia and meningitis. The Tennessee-based company Massengill produced a liquid-form, sulpha-based antibiotic, which used antifreeze as a solvent and raspberry extract for flavouring. The company conducted no clinical tests before marketing its product, Elixir of Sulfanilamide. The new act required that a company, before it could market a new drug, had to conduct safety tests and submit an application to the FDA, demonstrating that the drug was safe when used according to instructions on the label. Furthermore, the government no longer needed to prove fraudulent intent, and it gained the right to make factory inspections and seizures. The Food, Drug, and Cosmetic Act also introduced the concept of a prescription drug; certain drugs were deemed too risky to be used without a doctor's supervision and could be dispensed only when the patient's physician prescribed the drug as treatment. Canada followed the United States' lead, in part because manufacturers were thought to be using Canada as a testing ground for the American drug market. In 1954, a modernized Canadian Food and

Drugs Act came into force, putting many of the same safeguards in place as in the US legislation – including the requirement that safety data be submitted to the federal government prior to licensing.[11]

The thalidomide tragedy in 1961 showed the potential for system failures to have far-reaching global consequences and prompted further tightening of drug safety regulations. A German company, Chemie Grünenthal, marketed thalidomide as a sleeping pill and as a remedy for morning sickness during pregnancy. The company had tested the drug on animals but had not tested for birth defects; the drug caused severe abnormalities when taken in the first trimester of pregnancy. In countries that approved the drug, including Germany, Canada, the Netherlands, Australia, and Japan, some eight thousand babies were born with absent or badly deformed limbs. One estimate put the number of such babies born in Canada at 115, although estimates vary and not all children survived.[12]

In the United States, beginning in 1957, Senator Carey Estes Kefauver led a decade of hearings into all aspects of the pharmaceutical industry. The inquiry's central concern was the industry's monopolistic structure, but the thalidomide tragedy empowered the Senate subcommittee to require evidence of efficacy and safety as a prerequisite to drug approval, a law known as the Kefauver-Harris Amendments. In 1963, Canada followed suit with amendments to the Food and Drugs Act, making approval for marketing a drug conditional on "substantial evidence" from manufacturers that the drug was both safe and effective in recommended clinical use.[13] Although health is a provincial responsibility under Canada's constitution, the regulation of drugs is deemed necessary for "peace, order and good government" and so falls under federal jurisdiction.[14] The Canadian Food and Drugs Act provides the broad framework of Canadian health protection law for pharmaceuticals, with details specified in regulations. All Western countries now include laws that incorporate the principle that a drug's efficacy and lack of toxicity must be verified, and all have adopted the clinical trial as the means of establishing efficacy.[15]

Canada's 1954 act and its 1963 revisions set out a step-by-step drug approval review system in which the company produces evidence for the Therapeutic Products Directorate of Health Canada (formerly the Department of Health and Welfare) to review. More recently, a parallel office, the Biologics and Genetic Therapies Directorate, was added to review biologic drugs and genetic therapies, following the same steps. (Conventional drugs are chemically synthesized and have a known structure; biologics are isolated from natural sources and include substances like sugars, proteins, cells, and genes.) The Canadian and American review processes are sufficiently similar that Canadian reviewers will accept the same submission as that made to the FDA, though they do not necessarily render the same decision. The process begins with an initial *preclinical phase* comprising bench and animal studies to provide preliminary evidence of safety and therapeutic benefit for a particular disease. If these studies are successful, the sponsor proposes human (clinical) trials on volunteer study participants. Clinical trials follow a three-step plan: *Phase 1* tests for safety and appropriate dosages on a small number of healthy human volunteers, except – significantly – for cancer and AIDS drugs, which, because of their toxicity, are tested on patients with the disease; *Phase 2* tests for safety and efficacy on a small number of people who suffer from the specific conditions for which the drug is intended; and *Phase 3* – a full-fledged clinical trial – is carried out using a sufficient number of closely observed patients to obtain reliable results on the drug's safety, efficacy, and optimal dosages compared with a placebo arm or other treatments. If the data from Phase 3 are satisfactory, the company may present a New Drug Submission to the Health Products and Food Branch, where government regulatory reviewers examine the extensive statistical data, analysis, and pharmacological information yielded by the clinical research. Reviewers can ask for additional information, or reject an application if the data is insufficient. Regulatory approval means that the company can market the drug in Canada.[16]

A new round of efforts to "modernize" the act began in 1998. Critics of the prevailing pro-market discourse in health policy, including women's health advocates, argued that "modernization" was a code word for relaxing regulations that restricted the industry's marketing opportunities. Ultimately, in 2014, the efforts of one individual led to tightened restrictions. When Terence Young, a former member of Ontario's provincial government, lost his fifteen-year-old daughter Vanessa to cardiac arrhythmia after she took the prescription drug Prepulsid, he was determined to curtail aggressive marketing of prescription drugs and to improve drug safety. Drug regulators in both the United States and Canada had issued safety warnings about Prepulsid and heart irregularities, but neither Vanessa Young nor her parents were warned of the drug's deadly potential. In 2008, Young ran successfully for federal Parliament, where he was able to push from within for changes to Canada's drug safety laws. On November 6, 2014, the Conservative government passed the Protecting Canadians from Unsafe Drugs Act, also called Vanessa's Law. The bill requires hospitals and clinics to report serious drug effects and empowers the federal government to recall unsafe drugs without the company's permission (a power that had been lacking), to fine companies up to $5 million for false or misleading claims, and to jail for up to five years anyone who contravenes the act or its regulations.[17]

Because clinical trials are based on a limited number of patients over a relatively short period, favourable clinical trial results do not mean the drug is safe for all patients, or that long-term side effects won't overshadow its benefits. Once on the market, drugs need to be monitored for side effects that are relatively infrequent and for long-term harms, a process known as post-marketing surveillance. This has been one of the weakest links in the drug review chain. First, though, let's look at another area of system weakness: drug pricing.

Containing Drug Prices: Canada's Decade-Long Fight

Overlapping the regulatory efforts to improve drug safety, effectiveness, and information, in 1958 the Canadian government began a ten-year struggle with the pharmaceutical industry over prices. By the mid-1950s, the price of drugs had become a policy concern worldwide, and governments everywhere began to critically scrutinize the industry's business practices. In the United States, Senator Estes Kefauver, a firm believer in price competition, undertook a five-year inquiry into the pharmaceutical industry that detailed an ingenious use of patents, trademarks, brand names, and promotional techniques – all of which ran counter to Kefauver's liberal, free-enterprise political convictions. He introduced a Senate bill "to make vital prescription drugs available to the people at reasonable prices," taking aim at anticompetitive patent and marketing practices that contributed to unnaturally high prices and misled physicians about drug effectiveness and safety.[18]

Through its national pressure group, the Pharmaceutical Manufacturers' Association, the industry vowed to fight the American bill "to the death,"[19] and succeeded in gutting the changes it most strenuously opposed – the section of the bill that governed patents and licensing procedures. As a result, the hearings had a limited impact on American legislation affecting drug pricing. The investigation's fifteen volumes of testimony nevertheless gave governments elsewhere ample insight into the methods the industry used to keep the price of pharmaceuticals high, and emboldened no fewer than seventeen countries to undertake their own investigations.

In Canada, the result was a series of studies and reports that found drug prices in the country to be among the highest in the world and identified patent protection as a major cost driver.[20] Newly elected Liberal prime minister Pierre Trudeau used the reports – The Green Book, the Royal Commission on Health Services' report, and the *Report of the Special Committee of the House of Commons on Drug Costs and Prices* (also known as the Harley Report) – to argue for a system that would overrule patent protection of pharmaceuticals and allow Canadian generic companies to manufacture and import drugs that were still under patent, a provision known as "compulsory licensing." This mechanism, recognized in the Paris Convention of 1883 as a means for national governments to prevent abuses resulting from the exercise of exclusive patent rights, allows a third party to manufacture a patented drug on the condition that the company pays the patent holder a royalty. The company holding the patent is obliged by law to issue the licence (hence the "compulsory" designation). Senator Kefauver's bill proposed introducing a compulsory licensing system in the United States, which would have allowed pharmaceutical companies there three years of exclusive patent rights, followed by fourteen years in which a compulsory licence system would apply. The Pharmaceutical Manufacturers' Association strongly opposed and ultimately defeated this proposal.

Compulsory licensing was an existing feature of Canada's patent law in the 1960s and was intended to ensure competition so that drugs would be available at the lowest possible price. The provision was seldom used, however, because the country's market was too small to support the manufacture of drugs, particularly lower-priced ones, and Canadian companies were not permitted to import drugs from companies outside Canada. The new law allowed Canadian generic companies to import a patented drug, rather than having to make it themselves. They then paid the fee, usually 4 percent, to the patent holder. The change was designed to increase price competition for pharmaceuticals, support a Canadian generic drug industry, and make drugs more affordable to Canadians.[21]

When the Canadian government began intensive work on pharmaceutical drug prices in 1958, seven or eight large international companies holding US patents dominated the Canadian market, and they viewed Canada as simply an extension of their domestic territory. The Canadian branch companies of American firms all belonged to the Pharmaceutical Manufacturers Association of Canada (PMAC), a pressure group with fifty-nine members from international companies that together represented 85 percent of the total Canadian market. A second organization, the Association of Canadian Drug Manufacturers, made up of about fifteen Canadian-based generic manufacturers, had 10 percent of the market.[22] The two groups generally had diametrically opposing views; PMAC considered its members to be "innovators" and excluded members of the Association of Canadian Drug Manufacturers from its membership on the grounds that they were "copiers." A subsidiary company was not likely to develop, manufacture, and market a product in competition with its parent company or to use compulsory licensing to compete with another brand-name company. The result was that the Canadian drug trade operated according to US patent law, which gave patent holders a legal monopoly on the sale of their products for up to seventeen years. Canada's Patent Act provided the same protection, but in 1963, Canadian-owned firms held fewer than 5 percent of the patents on drugs sold in Canada and had only 1 percent of the world's exports of drugs. Canadian subsidiaries of US companies charged as much or more for their drugs in Canada as they did in the United States, so prices in Canada were high by world standards.[23]

The recommendations in the Green Book and the Harley Report were designed to alter the structural features underlying high Canadian drug prices. The reports also singled out the pharmaceutical industry's promotional practices as factors limiting competition and contributing to high prices. At least 25 percent of net sales was spent to promote brand names and to undermine confidence in generic alternatives by implying that they were inferior. The two reports deemed the promotional material to physicians to be "excessive and objectionable" and proposed that generic names be required to appear on labels and in advertisements in a type "at least as large as that used for the brand name."[24]

PMAC vehemently attacked the recommendation for a compulsory licensing system as well as the proposed labelling changes, but its aggressive lobbying was so transparently insensitive to Canadian interests that the efforts proved counterproductive. One misstep was PMAC's claiming to be guided by ethical principles of "public service" while at the same time arguing that drug prices in Canada were actually low, because Canadians had to work relatively few hours to pay for their drugs. In other words, the companies based their pricing on what they judged Canadians could afford, rather than on the manufacturing cost or intrinsic worth of their products. PMAC further alienated potential allies in government, in Parliament, and in the media by misrepresenting its members' profit margins and the cost of quality control. In another tactic, the industry tried to use the thalidomide scandal to shift the discourse from drug costs to drug safety. PMAC's main concern, said one industry insider, was not a loss of profits from the relatively small Canadian market but that the legislation might set a precedent attractive to legislators and consumers of other countries – the United States in particular. The fact that the American companies behind PMAC were preoccupied until 1963 with their own fight with Kefauver and the US Congress contributed to the lobby group's clumsy efforts.[25]

The industry had expected the government to lower prices by merely eliminating a tax and was caught off-guard when the bill was tabled. From the beginning, senior civil servants who were guiding the proceedings from behind the scenes had intended a comprehensive strategy that went far beyond lowering prices. They wanted to promote a generic industry in Canada and to defeat what they perceived as the industry's arrogance. Drawing from the recommendations of the Harley Committee, Bill C-102 took a multipronged "package" approach that centred on attacking the patent system. Pierre Trudeau's newly elected government passed the Act to Amend the Patent Act and the Food and Drugs Act into law in 1969. By 1984, a commission of inquiry into the pharmaceutical industry, headed by Harry Eastman, concluded that the new regime had supported the development of a robust Canadian generic drug industry and saved the public an estimated $212 million in lowered drug prices in 1983 alone. By 1986, drug prices in Canada were 20 percent below those in the United

States. The cheaper drugs had made possible provincial drug subsidy programs for seniors and welfare recipients, while the multinational companies lost only 3.1 percent of the Canadian market to generic companies. Their profit levels in Canada remained above those of most other industrialized countries, except for the United States. The commission's report strongly recommended keeping the system of compulsory licensing, with perhaps some modifications to appease the industry.[26]

Pharmaceutical companies and their Canadian and US lobbying organizations, PMAC, and the Pharmaceutical Manufacturers' Association, continued to strongly oppose the Canadian compulsory licensing law, litigating the licences granted almost routinely, but Canadian courts took the position that containing drug prices serves a social purpose. In 1987, a Canadian federal trial court concluded that economic and trade goals are secondary to the Food and Drugs Act's primary purpose: the regulation of public safety.[27]

The Drug Safety Review and Approval System: It Sparkles on Paper, but ...

The compulsory licensing system succeeded in containing prices of essential drugs and spawning a homegrown generic industry, yet the regulatory regime designed to ensure drug safety had a more equivocal record. The Health Protection Branch was established under the Food and Drugs Act of 1952–53 as the act's enforcement agency. The mandate to approve new drugs so they can enter the market is a drug agency's "most formidable" power, writes legal scholar Patricia Carter.[28] Unfortunately, despite the apparently rigorous regulatory regimes put in place after the thalidomide debacle, drug-related tragedies continued in the decades following the 1963 revisions, often the result of claims based on evidence that was flimsy or absent. Journalist Nicholas Regush, who studied many of these safety failures, concludes that Canada's drug safety review system compares well with other developed nations only because globally the bar for drug reviews is so low.[29]

How is this possible? Once a drug is approved for marketing, the company can begin promoting it, and drug promotion has become a highly developed dark art. In Canada, as in most industrialized countries, the regulatory regimens governing pharmaceuticals introduced in the mid-twentieth century allowed manufacturers to promote drugs only to physicians, the designated gatekeepers of prescription medications. The rationale is that a physician's training and knowledge of a particular patient's case would allow him or her to decide whether a drug was appropriate to that patient's condition and safe enough on balance to warrant prescribing. Except for in the United States and New Zealand, drug regulators banned advertising directly to consumers on the grounds that patients are vulnerable targets for misleading claims and that drugs can cause serious harm. Under the banner of physician education, however, companies in Canada and elsewhere can promote the use of a new drug to physicians by a variety of methods, such as ads in medical journals and sales representatives deployed to visit physicians in their offices (known as "detailing"). These practices involve a range of questionable tactics designed to maximize "scripts" (prescriptions), regardless of whether the drug in question is the most economical and appropriate, or whether it is an appropriate treatment at all. American physician Jerry Avorn, reflecting in 2011 on the drug safety record in the half-century since thalidomide and the Kefauver commission, concluded that the term "ethical drugs," referring to prescription medications, "seems oddly archaic in a time of scandals about deceptive marketing practices and heavily advertised, costly medications that turn out to have major unreported risks."[30]

Among the concerns critics have raised are the industry's ability to circumvent regulations, its use of regulatory loopholes to make misleading claims that distort physicians' and the public's understanding of drugs, the industry's tendency to target women in its marketing campaigns, and the overreliance on clinical trials to demonstrate efficacy. On the latter point, David Healy argues that the 1962 decision to allow drugs on the market simply on the basis of two positive clinical trials was a mistake because showing that people given a drug have a statistically greater response on some measure compared with those given a placebo tells us almost nothing about cause and effect, while filling the market with drugs that "work" but which have not been shown to save or improve lives.[31]

Diethylstilbestrol (DES) and the Dalkon Shield are two examples of pharmaceutical products that suffered regulatory system failures. The synthetic sex hormone DES was developed in London, England, in 1938.

Beginning in 1940, without adequate testing for either safety or effectiveness, DES was given to pregnant women to prevent miscarriage and for gynecological and menopause-related symptoms. Despite a double-blind trial in the 1950s that showed DES had no benefit for pregnant women, the drug continued to be prescribed to prevent miscarriages until 1971, when a published report showed that it was associated with a rare vaginal cancer in the daughters of women who had taken it while pregnant. The Dalkon Shield, a contraceptive device, was also aggressively marketed despite lack of evidence to back the manufacturer's claims. As a medical device, the Dalkon Shield comes under the same regulatory regime as drugs. The American pharmaceutical company A.H. Robins, which purchased the Dalkon Shield in 1970 from a smaller company, sold an estimated 4 to 5 million devices before taking the Dalkon Shield off the market in 1974. The company was besieged by lawsuits claiming that the device caused miscarriages and sterility, as well as infections that were sometimes fatal.[32]

Depo-Provera, an injectable contraceptive, is another drug for which promotional material overstated benefits and downplayed potential harms. It was promoted to physicians through drug advertising in medical journals or at expensive dinners paid for by the manufacturer. Psychotropic drugs, notably tranquilizers, were promoted primarily to women as medical solutions to socially based anxiety. In the 1960s and 1970s, drugs like Valium (diazepam) accounted for approximately 20 percent of all prescription drug use in England, Canada, and the United States, with advertising to physicians specifically profiling emotionally distressed middle-aged women as the drugs' main potential beneficiaries. Ruth Cooperstock, a medical sociologist with the Addiction Research Foundation in Toronto, argued that the widespread use of these drugs depended on the social construction of anxiety as a physical disease, when the actual cause was gendered role pressures. Political change, she contended, is a more appropriate way to address such stresses. Cooperstock's critique speaks to David Healy's argument that the mere fact that a drug "works" in a clinical trial (women under stress became calmer on antidepressants) does not mean they improve or save lives.[33]

That DES, Depo-Provera, the Dalkon Shield, and psychotropic drugs were all marketed exclusively or primarily to women is no coincidence;

from the beginning, the industry understood women to be its major market. Women's health activists mobilized to form advocacy organizations and countercampaigns focused on particular pharmaceutical products.[34] Significantly, however, drugs to treat cancer were not part of this early critical discourse.

Tremors in Neoliberal Policy

Health care costs began to rise, and in 1987 the federal government responded by reducing its transfer payments to the provinces while giving them some of its areas of taxation. Throughout the 1990s, successive federal governments continued to cut spending for health (and other social programs), citing the need to balance the budget; the reduction was particularly sharp in 1996, when the federal government contributed only 15 percent of the total spent by provinces.[35] By reducing its direct contribution to health spending, Ottawa surrendered its main tool to enforce the Canada Health Act. The provinces could spend federal transfer payments as they chose, so the funds did not always go to health care and problems were not addressed. The system deteriorated, and the debate about publicly funded health care once again moved to the fore. Confidence in the system declined and the public, among others, began to question the system's sustainability. Social solidarity eroded as the more affluent chafed at the limited menu of available interventions and the requirement to wait their turn. Provincial governments downsized their staff and looked to civil society groups to fill the gaps in care as cheaply as possible.[36]

Drug regulation also underwent dramatic changes in the key areas of review times, post-marketing surveillance, financing of reviews, and patent protection. In the 1970s, Canada's review times were ranked ahead of the international standard, with a complete review of an "important, new" drug taking sixteen months; in the United States in the same era, the average review time for priority drugs was twenty-three months. Throughout the 1970s, however, the workload of the Health Protection Branch increased by about 10 percent a year, with no increase in staff. Review times slowed; by 1982, the head of the Bureau of Human Prescription Drugs was feeling pressured by drug companies to speed up drug approvals. Between 1985 and 1987, four published government reports expressed concern about a drug review backlog.[37]

Drug review times are an area of fraught debate. Pharmaceutical companies are strong advocates of rapid reviews, since the sooner they can get a drug to market, the longer they have to make a profit before the patent protection runs out. The industry uses the pejorative term "drug lag" to imply that bureaucratic processes within regulatory agencies are delaying access to important therapeutic advances and restricting the profits necessary for a healthy pharmaceutical industry. Advocates for whom drug safety is a priority are skeptical of rapid reviews, arguing that they compromise the review's central purpose: ensuring safety and effectiveness. Philip J. Hilts, in a history of drug regulation in the United States, argues that concern over "drug lag" is cyclical and becomes a political issue in conservative times. He deems the term meaningless because judgments about a drug's safety and efficacy must be made case by case. Few drugs are truly innovative; estimates of the percentage of new drugs approved that have a therapeutic advantage over existing drugs vary from less than 1 percent to 15 percent, depending on the definition of "innovative" and the country and year in which the study is done. Most new drug submissions are "me too" drugs – virtual copies of "blockbuster" drugs that have been profitable for other companies. For drugs that actually are innovative, taking the time to support a submission with better data than was initially provided may mean the drug will ultimately benefit more patients and harm fewer. Advocates of case-by-case reviews point out that reviewers should, and do, give innovative drugs priority, so the review times of these drugs are much faster than average. A discourse that equates "rapid review" with "more patients will benefit" thus masks the market forces that are the main impetus for speedy reviews and overlooks the potential harm of a drug rushed to market.[38]

Post-marketing surveillance (PMS) is a system to collect incidents of uncommon but serious drug harms from real-life usage after the drug is approved, and is another aspect of drug evaluation that became a battleground within pharmaceutical policy in Canada in the 1980s. PMS is essential to supplement clinical trials; the latter are limited in duration and cannot establish a drug's clinical risks and benefits over the long term. Furthermore, because they typically involve only hundreds or a few thousand patients, clinical trials can't detect safety problems that are relatively rare. The system for detecting these iatrogenic (i.e., medically caused) problems relied on physicians and hospitals filling out and filing voluntary reports of adverse drug side effects when they occur, and has been ineffective, since only a small proportion of such events are ever reported.

After the thalidomide debacle, two senior bureaucrats in the federal Ministry of National Health and Welfare pressed for a structured post-marketing surveillance system to replace the existing passive process. One of them, Dr. Edward Napke, the head of the Canadian Adverse Drug Reaction Monitoring Program, wanted to set up a system to collect, collate, and evaluate information on pharmaceuticals in use in the population. He could then feed the data back to the medical community and the drug industry. Dr. Ian Henderson, a colleague who headed the Bureau of Human Prescription Drugs, launched a complementary initiative, proposing that drug companies be required to monitor their drugs as a condition of sale. The federal government's preoccupation in drug regulation in the 1980s, however, manifested itself in rapid drug approvals, not post-market surveillance. In 1982, Napke's total budget was only $21,000. In a valiant but sadly desperate effort to do his job, he devised a makeshift system of pigeonholes and coloured tabs to indicate particularly severe drug reactions – a cluster of tabs of the same colour in the same or adjacent pigeonholes indicated a potential problem.[39]

As far back as the late 1970s, Montreal journalist Nicholas Regush concluded that political priorities had undermined the core purpose of drug reviews:

> Tough economic conditions led to government cutbacks. Programs that reviewed the safety of drugs and medical devices did not broaden according to plan. Staff shortages caused discontentment among overworked scientists and friction between them and their managers. By the early 1980s, government safety reviewers were under increasing pressure from their managers and industry representatives to speed up pre-market evaluations.[40]

Regush became interested in product safety regulations while writing a series of articles about the polyurethane-covered silicone breast implant known as the Même. His research convinced him that the federal government was sacrificing safety for faster approvals. Marketed to breast cancer patients as a prosthesis and to healthy women for breast augmentation, the Même began to make headlines in both Canada and the United States in the late 1980s. Safety concerns about breast implants were not exclusive to the Même – all implants deteriorate over time, and those that are silicone-filled can leach silicone into the body – but the brand attracted attention because of an unusual foam covering that broke down, releasing a chemical that was a potential carcinogen. In addition, women implanted with the product frequently experienced infections that ate through the skin – a result of unsanitary manufacturing conditions, which were revealed after an investigation.[41]

In his coverage of the Même affair in the *Montreal Gazette*, and later in the American magazine *Mother Jones*, Regush was struck by the federal government's apparent wish to minimize the problems with the implant rather than to take action. He was not alone. Health Canada scientist Pierre Blais, who had researched the implants, was fired when he brought his concerns to the attention of his superiors; women implanted with the device began to organize when they couldn't get answers to their questions about chronic pain and infections; a respected Montreal plastic surgeon spoke out, as did a member of Parliament and a university research chemist. After a 1990 meeting with then deputy minister of health Margaret Catley-Carlson, Regush concluded that a "trust-industry philosophy" had gradually eroded the internal culture at the Health Protection Branch, which regulated drugs and medical devices: according to Regush, Catley-Carlson "detailed her vision of a new partnership between government and industry: industry really wanted to do good because it was in industry's best interest to do so. Think partnership, not conflict. Crusaders who would keep industry in check were obso[lete]."[42]

Regush concluded that after a Conservative government took power in 1984, the mandate to protect consumer safety had gradually given way to one in which government and industry collaborated to advance the shared goal of promoting business. Other researchers documented evidence of this partnership model in the 1990s. In 1994, the pharmaceutical industry began to provide funding to the Therapeutic Products Directorate (TPD), the arm of Health Canada responsible for conducting the drug reviews. Up to that point, the TPD had been financed through government appropriations; gradually, the industry portion increased over the next decade to about half the directorate's total budget. In a 1997 memo to his staff, the director general of the TPD identified pharmaceutical companies as "clients." For advocates of drug safety, implying that drug companies were to be served and pleased because they were paying for a substantial portion of the reviews conflicted with the TPD's core purpose of monitoring the companies' submissions to ensure that the industry's pursuit of profits did not put human health at risk. The move to user fees followed a similar transition at the FDA in the United States, where a law known as the Prescription Drug User Fee Act was enacted in 1992 and has been renewed every five years since then. As in Canada, the pharmaceutical industry welcomed the government-industry partnership and public interest health groups opposed it.[43]

In 1998, Health Canada began issuing conditional approvals for drugs whose clinical benefit had not yet been verified but that were judged to be of high quality and with a favourable risk/benefit ratio. The move again fuelled fears that the industry had captured the government regulatory process. The stated rationale for the new category, known as a notice of compliance with conditions, or NOC/c, was to fast-track drugs for life-threatening diseases like AIDS and cancer. In keeping with this goal, the first NOC/c was given in July 1998 to the AIDS antiretroviral drug Rescriptor (delavirdine mesylate); yet in 1999, the TPD awarded the NOC/c designation to Relenza, a new drug for "uncomplicated influenza." Health Canada declined to make public the conditions attached to the approval, so prescribing physicians and patients had no way of knowing what risks taking the drug might entail. In fact, the company's patient information leaflet did not even mention that approval was conditional. The FDA in the United States also approved Relenza, overriding the recommendations of its advisory committee, which considered the evidence of benefit too weak to justify approval. One of the FDA reviewers, Dr. Michael Elashoff, resigned over the decision. These events led to speculation that both government regulators had given in to pressure from the industry to market a drug of minor therapeutic importance despite insufficient evidence to assess it.[44]

The 1990s also saw the federal government soften its position of direct-to-consumer advertising (DTCA) of drugs. Canada's Food and Drugs Act prohibits the advertising of prescription drugs to the public, a health protection measure designed to prevent drug companies from stimulating inappropriate demand for products. All wealthy industrialized countries except the United States and New Zealand prohibit DTCA on this basis. In 1975, Canada introduced a regulation within the act to allow the posting of the name, price, and quantity of a drug, a move designed to encourage pharmacies to post price comparisons. In the late 1990s, however, a regulatory change in the United States led to an explosion of television and magazine ads for pharmaceutical drugs. The ready availability of US television programs and magazines in Canada meant that Canadians were exposed to a barrage of cross-border drug ads. Although a system for blocking the illegal ads could have been devised and implemented, the federal government did nothing to restrict cross-border pharmaceutical advertising. Furthermore, in 1996 and 2000, it issued policy statements that reinterpreted the sole exception to the ban, permitting the display of name, price, and quantity. Under this new regime, drug advertising was prohibited only if both the name of the drug and its use were given. This new policy permitted two types of "made in Canada" drug advertisements, known as "reminder" and "disease awareness" ads for prescription drugs, both of which clearly violated the spirit, if not the letter, of the Canadian law banning DTCA. Reminder ads state the name of a product but don't say what condition it is approved to treat, whereas disease awareness ads talk about a condition but don't name the drug that is approved to treat the condition. Instead, the consumer is urged to see their doctor to discuss a new treatment for the symptoms described in the ad. Health Canada further relaxed its regulation of drug ads by failing to act on violations.[45]

The Health Care System and Breast Cancer Treatment

From the introduction of single-payer health care in Canada to the mid-1980s, the system served breast cancer patients quite well. Cancer care was typically carried out in hospitals, with follow-up by physicians, and both services were fully covered by the single-payer system. The lack of a national pharmacare program, which has since become a concern of cancer patients, had little effect on breast cancer patients before 1990, for several reasons. First, although a research program had been set up in the United States in 1954 to systematically search for "wonder drugs" that would cure cancer, the search had yielded little success by the early 1980s. Notable exceptions

were chemotherapy treatments for Hodgkin's disease and certain leuk-
emias and lymphomas; these comprised less than 5 percent of cancers and
affected mainly children. Second, until the early 1980s, breast cancer was
widely considered a local disease, so treatments were aimed at local control
using surgery and radiation. Both were hospital procedures, and end-of-
life care was also provided mainly in hospitals. Diagnosis and follow-up
care were the responsibility of physicians, so they too fell under the umbrella of fully covered services. Thus, despite the gaps in the single-payer
system, most aspects of cancer care were likely to be fully covered no matter
where in Canada a cancer patient lived and which of the standard medical
treatment(s) they were receiving.[46]

From the mid-1970s to the mid-1980s, a fundamental shift in thinking
about breast cancer took place that redefined the disease as systemic rather
than local. A major consequence of this redefinition was that researchers
and cancer treatment specialists began to take chemotherapy more seriously as a potentially effective treatment for breast cancer. Beginning in
the late 1960s and throughout the 1970s and 1980s, clinical trial results
gradually accrued, providing evidence that two types of drug treatments,
as defined by their mechanism of action, had benefits for breast cancer
patients.[47]

The first type were cytotoxic drugs, drugs whose mechanism of action
is to kill cells as they divide. By 1990, ten or eleven of these were in common
use for breast cancer.[48] But the treatments were extremely toxic, and many
cancer specialists were hesitant to adopt them without evidence of substantial effectiveness; also because of their toxicity, these drugs were typically given by intravenous drip and carried out as a hospital procedure.[49]
The second type of treatment was hormonal and worked by inhibiting or
stabilizing cell growth.[50] Of six hormonal treatments in use for breast cancer
in 1990, all were taken orally on a daily basis. The most commonly used
anti-hormonal treatment by far was tamoxifen, which was taken two times
per day.[51] Hospitals were not required to pay for self-administered pills
under the Canada Health Act, and payment for this treatment varied depending on the patient's province or territory of residence, and whether
the patient had coverage through an employer-sponsored or individual
private drug plan.[52] Despite this potential for inequity in accessing breast
cancer drugs like tamoxifen, the treatments were available in generic form

in Canada at a relatively low cost. Although cost was still significant for some women, gaining access to oral drugs was not the source of intense controversy it was to become.

In the late 1980s, a set of interconnected circumstances brought drug treatments for breast cancer to the policy fore. First, pharmaceutical treatments for breast cancer began to be seen as potentially life extending, even curative, especially if administered in the early stages of the disease, even though risk/benefit evidence of the treatments was still limited. Second, as a result of this shift in perspective, chemotherapy treatment options began to diversify. One example was a hypertoxic, costly procedure known as "high-dose chemotherapy with autologous stem cell rescue," which was being used experimentally and – particularly in the United States – outside of clinical trials. The procedure attracted attention in Canada, and some women who could afford to do so travelled to the United States for treatment.[53] In addition, two new breast cancer treatments, Taxol (paclitaxel) and Herceptin (trastuzumab), were in the development pipeline.[54] Third, a policy change in Canada delayed the use of generic versions of new drugs, removing a mechanism for keeping drug prices in Canada low. And fourth, the costs of new cancer drugs began to rise dramatically worldwide. Thus, before 1990, the lack of a national drug coverage plan within Canada's health care system had a limited impact on breast cancer patients' access to standard treatment. When neoliberal governments began to re-align policies in the late 1980s and early 1990s, however, drug access became a topic of active debate.

2

Health Advocacy Organizations in Canada

One of the main reasons the Consumers' Association of Canada formed was to balance, or provide a countervailing force to, the influence of powerful industry interests in the marketplace and in bureaucratic decision-making [at a time when] few standards, regulations, or sources of information existed to protect the health and well-being of families.

— WENDY ARMSTRONG, CONSUMERS' ASSOCIATION
OF CANADA (ALBERTA)[1]

The Rise of Health Advocacy Groups

From colonial times to the present, Canadians have formed organizations to influence public policy. Whether they are called advocacy groups, pressure groups, interest groups, or civil society organizations, they are a third major political actor, along with government and the private sector. Pressure groups have long been viewed as a mixed blessing, observes Paul Pross, who documented their role in Canadian politics from Confederation to the 1980s. They can perform unique, useful functions, such as communicating changing political concerns – a vital contribution in a democratic state. However, influencing the Canadian policy system requires resources beyond the capacity of most public interest pressure groups, and the legitimacy of a group can be hard to judge. Thus, two questions underlying my research – how community-based groups can attain adequate resources and how outsiders can assess a group's claim that it represents a particular constituency – are not new. What has changed in the past three decades is the larger political framework in which the groups operate.[2]

From the mid-1960s to the mid-1980s, civil society groups became more numerous, active, and publicity-conscious than they had been previously. With the advent of neoliberalism, traditional boundaries between civil society, government, and the private sector began to blur. The massive paradigm shift in the structure of global capitalism fundamentally redefined the relationships of all major actors in the system to one another, including those of advocacy groups. Numerous analysts of Canadian politics have concluded that a succession of globalized neoliberal regimes have altered the very concept of citizenship in Canada. Conflict and contestation – forms of group protest that were accepted in the 1960s and 1970s as ways of redistributing political power – are delegitimized, whereas activities that engage the individual consumer, client, and citizen are privileged.[3]

Despite the radical societal transformations underway, in the late 1980s or early 1990s, breast cancer advocacy groups that emerged in Canada and the United States borrowed discourses, structures, and tools of community activism from the women's health advocacy of first- and second-wave feminism.[4]

First-Wave Feminist Health Discourses

Affluent political reformers spearheaded Canada's first wave of feminism, which dates from the late 1800s to 1930. Their main goals were suffrage and recognition in law as persons; nonetheless, they responded to women's collective suffering and to their desire for better health services and more knowledge. An increased professionalization of medicine in the nineteenth and early twentieth century had usurped women's traditional roles as experts in childbirth, sexuality, menopause, and care of the elderly. These early feminist reformers claimed political representation for women based on the knowledge of family concerns gained through their experience as wives and mothers, including the care of sick family members. They contested the belief that women's bodies made them intellectually inferior and implicitly demanded more control over their bodies and lives.[5]

Two examples are the Victorian Order of Nurses (VON) and the Women's Institute (WI), both founded in 1897 with health-related missions and both led by socially privileged women. The VON, a cross-Canada network of visiting home-care nurses, was created after members of the National Council of Women of Canada shared "horror stories" of house-bound young mothers or their children dying in isolated communities in Canada because they were unable to gain timely access to medical care. The council appealed for help to the wife of the then governor-general, Lady Ishbel Aberdeen, who took up the cause. By year's end, the VON had admitted twelve nurses.[6]

Adelaide Hoodless, who cofounded the WI, was born Addie Hunter, the twelfth child of an Ontario farming couple, and had little formal education beyond elementary school. She married the son of a prominent furniture maker in Hamilton, left the farm, and joined Ontario's social elite. Hoodless cofounded the organization after her infant son drank contaminated milk and died, a tragedy that may have motivated her activism. The WI set up libraries and organized talks to increase rural women's education and civic engagement, particularly on issues related to food and healthy eating. Regional and national networks linked local groups, and the WI expanded to become international.

Tensions of class and other political influences shaped the internal discourses of these organizations, which were neither homogeneous nor static. Although the WI began as a conservative body that eschewed conflict and confrontation and resisted radical change, over time it afforded a space for activist members. In the mid-1910s, for example, the suffrage issue fanned class tensions within the WI. The wealthier members preferred to bypass the question; Hoodless, despite her own prominence in community affairs at the local and national levels, opposed women's suffrage "on the grounds that women exercised their influence through their sons and husbands."[7] Others saw the WI as a site for political action. Linda Ambrose and Margaret Kechnie, two scholars of women's history who studied the WI from the perspective of both privileged women and members who worked the farms, comment, "Certainly if one looks at the WI from the perspective of the rank-and-file members, it becomes clear that by the 1920s enlarging the sphere of women is precisely what typified the activity of this so-called 'conservative' organization."[8] As their analysis illustrates, a given organization can embody both progressive and status quo elements, with the mix changing over time.

Second-Wave Feminism and the Women's Health Movement

Feminism's second wave dates from the 1960s and 1970s and spawned an organized movement in Canada that was specifically dedicated to women's health issues, particularly concerns related to women's reproductive rights. The movement introduced the important innovation of consciousness-raising groups, at which women met for focused discussion about the structural reasons for women's exploitation. These groups became sites of feminist health research that relied on a critical reading of scientific literature measured against lay experiential knowledge and community values. The latter includes the process of analyzing and trying to redress what has since been labelled "undone science" or "socially constructed ignorance" – questions that remain unanswered because the research community has failed to investigate them.[9]

Three unifying themes of the women's health movement were (1) women have the right to knowledge about their own bodies; (2) much of the information about women's bodies in the medical and societal canon has been based on myth, not fact; and (3) laywomen possess valuable knowledge about themselves. This discourse emboldened women to research and produce their own health publications, sometimes in opposition to official knowledge claims. For example, feminist critique was evident from the first edition of the revolutionary *Birth Control Handbook*, which the Birth Control Committee of McGill University's Students' Council published in 1968, when providing contraceptive information was still illegal in Canada. In 1978, Canadian health activists launched *Healthsharing*, a quarterly feminist health magazine, which continued for fifteen years. In Montreal, sociologist Janine O'Leary Cobb published the newsletter *A Friend Indeed*, which contested the dominant medical paradigm for menopause, including hormone manufacturers' claims about the benefits of hormonal drugs.[10]

The women's health movement sometimes used confrontational tactics to change laws and policies. In 1969, the Liberal government under Pierre Trudeau's leadership removed birth control from the Criminal Code and passed the first law designed to make abortions legal in Canada, but a Therapeutic Abortion Committee in the hospital had to agree that the woman's life was in danger. Vancouver feminists organized the Abortion

Caravan to protest the requirement that the committee, not the woman, had the ultimate say. Pro-choice activists travelled from Vancouver to Ottawa, gathering supporters for the decriminalization of abortion along the way. Their demonstration in the House of Commons shut down Parliament. This action spawned a national abortion rights organization to support Dr. Henry Morgentaler, who had been charged for performing abortions in his Montreal clinic. Subsequently, abortion rights groups formed provincially and, along with other clinics run by Morgentaler, fought to make safe, legal abortions a woman's right.[11]

By the 1980s, government funding supported a cross-Canada network of a hundred women's centres that provided a range of alternative approaches to care. They moved feminist analyses of the social roots of women's health problems to the community level. The control that pharmaceutical companies exercised over women was central to this critical discourse. Despite the regulations introduced after the thalidomide tragedy, harmful pharmaceutical products involving women continued to come to market, forming the basis of a feminist analysis of the pharmaceutical industry. Women who had been harmed by drugs and medical devices mobilized to form grassroots women's groups like DES Action Canada and Dalkon Shield Action Canada. Barbara Mintzes, who began working at the Vancouver Women's Health Collective shortly after she graduated from university, first learned of the effects of diethylstilbestrol (DES) at a conference on women and pharmaceuticals:

> I went to a presentation that Harriet Simand [the cofounder, in Montreal, of DES Action Canada] gave. This was very soon after she had recovered from the surgery and such [that] she'd had from the cancer caused by DES exposure. The first responses Harriet had [when] she contacted [sources like] Health Canada to try to find out if there were others who had been exposed prenatally to DES and had been harmed by it ... was that [DES] wasn't really a problem in Canada – that it was prescribed much more often in the US. Then she and her mother ended up going to the press. And they had a massive response! They had thousands of calls from women who thought that they might have been exposed during pregnancy.[12]

Mintzes, who later went on to become a researcher in drug policy, joined Harriet and her mother, Shirley Simand, in their campaign to determine the extent of DES exposure in Canada. Official denials of any problem galvanized them to educate women about the drug's effects and about steps they should take if they thought they might have been exposed to it:

> I brought back a pile of brochures and started trying to get women involved ... I tried to find out a bit about what had happened in [western Canada], and the answer I got was that, "Oh no, it wasn't a problem here, maybe it was a problem a bit in Montreal." So that was an awareness-raiser for me.
>
> [With] any press work that we ended up doing on it, we certainly got calls from women who had no idea – who knew they had taken something during pregnancy and didn't know what it was, or they knew they had taken DES but they weren't aware of some of the extra gynecological exams and other things that they needed. It was an eye-opener!

The experience of having scales fall from their eyes took many forms and was an integral part of the learning that shaped the activists in the women's health movement. Janine O'Leary Cobb became active in women's health in 1984 when she began comparing notes with friends and colleagues about their experiences during menopause. Intrigued by their stories of what they were going through, she started a newsletter based in Montreal to counter the medical community's characterization of menopause as a disease. *A Friend Indeed*, the first newsletter to provide a woman's perspective on the experience of menopause, was an international success. When O'Leary Cobb first started the newsletter, she attended a meeting in Epcot, Florida, of the World Congress on Menopause. She explains her shock at the delegates' behaviour in an interview:

> I thought I could go down there and find all sorts of experts on menopause, women who were my age (I was about fifty at the time), and instead what I found was all these gynecologists, and the GPs too, who would sign in in the morning and then go off to the Epcot Center, or to

Disneyland or whatever it is, for the day, and then come back in the evening.[13] They didn't listen to any of the conference. And it just struck me as being such a cheat! That was a terrible eye-opener for me.

Like the women who participated in DES Action, O'Leary Cobb became part of a community of women who asked challenging questions of established medicine, based in part on the pharmaceutical industry's close relationship to physicians. She expanded:

[I was skeptical] of the kinds of claims that they would make. They had *no* proof that hormones were going to make life just a paradise for menopausal women. Their advertising was unrealistic, [so] the expectations that women had as a result of the advertising were unrealistic ... But there were some – and there still are some – companies that comport themselves in a more or less honest way.

On the other hand, [the gynecologists] behaved so badly that the women who were on the edges of this, we started connecting immediately. We began meeting and forming a loose organization of women ... who just were appalled at what was going on, at what the men were saying. A gynecologist got up and said there was no point in writing a book about menopause, women weren't interested in books. They liked little leaflets and things they could read quickly ... "You have to love them up because they're going through such a hard time, the dears. We have to get them into the office and get them on hormones" – that sort of thing. And we were all rolling our eyes!

The women's health movement of the 1970s and 1980s thus made public unethical prescribing practices that targeted women. They mobilized to have drug regulation enforced, and pushed the research community to reexamine basic assumptions about women's biology and information needs. They were not alone in their critiques of the dominant biomedical model. Researchers in the Canadian health policy community provided both moral backing and evidence-based support. Like-minded Canadian health professionals included Ruth Cooperstock, who developed a feminist analysis of the social meanings of antidepressants; Joel Lexchin, a Toronto physician who published *The Real Pushers: A Critical Analysis of the Can-*

adian Drug Industry; and Jim Harding, a sociologist based in Saskatchewan who documented the high rates of mood modifiers among elderly women and exposed links between the prescribing of these drugs to women and their conditions of poverty.[14]

Their overlapping concerns gave rise to informal and formal collaborations between health professionals, feminists critical of the industry, and grassroots activists in international development and consumer protection. One such collaboration spawned the play *Side Effects*, based on women's stories about the harmful effects of pharmaceuticals. The Ottawa-based international development group Inter Pares conceived and developed the idea at a workshop, then collaborated with a theatre company and local women's groups to develop the production. The play toured nationally in 1985, drawing support from local women's health groups and creating regional networks. A book project, *Adverse Effects: Women and the Pharmaceutical Industry*, was the product of an international, intersectoral coalition that had a strong Canadian component. *Adverse Effects* developed three interrelated themes: that women in rich and poor countries have a shared interest in access to safe, effective, affordable drugs; that potential threats to these goals include the pharmaceutical industry, governments, and organizations bent on population control; and that networks of local, national, and international citizens groups provide an important means of responding to abuses on the part of industry, government, and NGO actors.[15]

The Canadian women's health movement had extensive international connections. DES Action Canada had counterparts in the United States and in European countries where pregnant women had been given DES. The International Organization of Consumers Unions, which published the book *Adverse Effects*, set up Health Action International (HAI) in 1981 as an international activist watchdog group that would monitor the pharmaceutical industry on behalf of consumers' interests. Barbara Mintzes began working with HAI through her connections with DES Action groups in other parts of the world. She explains HAI's origins:

> HAI ... modelled itself on the international network on breast milk issues, on baby formula ... basically a movement to confront the international situation of unethical marketing of breast milk substitutes ...

Groups that had been working in pharmaceuticals saw a lot of parallels with that [baby formula] situation in terms of unethical marketing practices – particularly concerns about multinational companies that were marketing medicines in developing countries. Both in terms of which products were for sale, but also the lack of warnings about harmful effects and the promotion for uses for which there wasn't enough scientific evidence of effectiveness. So, the HAI network formed, to begin with, to try to press for a similar kind of WHO [World Health Organization] code on the unethical marketing of pharmaceuticals. And then it has expanded to deal with a whole range of other issues. The second issue that was very much a priority was the lack of access to essential medicines in many countries, which is still a major problem.

The International Organization of Consumers Unions also had member organizations in Canada from the consumer movement, including the Consumers' Association of Canada (CAC), which formed in 1947 from a network of women's organizations working with the Wartime Prices and Trade Board. The CAC had a long history of providing input to the federal government on food safety and pricing, including farm family safety. In an interview, Wendy Armstrong, a nurse, former member of the CAC National Health Council, and past president of the CAC affiliate in Alberta, describes the links she saw between the CAC and the concerns of new women's groups working on health and pharmaceutical issues:

The CAC arose from a coalition of women's organizations dedicated to improving the standard of living of Canadian families in the postwar era. One of the main reasons it formed was to balance, or provide a counter-vailing force to, powerful industry interests in the marketplace and in bureaucratic decision making ... The CAC's long history of involvement with both industry players and regulators in issues related to food safety and pricing meant it recognized the pharmaceutical industry as part of a larger chemical industry. Historically, the chemical products of these companies affected not only consumers but workers – farm workers, for example – as well as the environment. Pesticides, fertilizers, new biotech applications, and pharmaceuticals – they all pose many of the same health and safety issues, and the same regulatory challenges.

At the heart of these demands for change was the claim that the existing health protection system was inadequate because it accepted uncritically the biomedical model of health while ignoring the social and political drivers of drug and medical device use. Government policy reports at the time supported the critique of medicalization, and many in government were happy to see groups like DES Action Canada speaking out. Groups like the CAC and DES Action Canada were funded with government money precisely because they could bring forward issues that reflected community concerns. From the early 1970s to the mid-1980s, the Canadian government positioned itself as a leader in developing policies that emphasized a broad range of social determinants beyond the biological that contribute to health, including gender, poverty, and physical environments.[16]

Significantly, provincial and national government agencies, especially those responsible for health and the status of women, gave financial support to advocacy organizations concerned about drug and device safety and the misrepresentation of the scientific knowledge about drugs. The effect was liberating, as Barbara Mintzes explains: "Because I was working at a local women's health centre, I could do some local awareness-raising on the issues. I think what made [this work] possible was having resources that at the time were publicly funded." This was about to change. She recalls the Vancouver Women's Health Collective where she worked in the 1980s being 100 percent funded by the provincial government, "and then we moved, in a day, to zero funding."

Health Activism in a Neoliberal Age
As Canada gradually adopted the trappings of a neoliberal state, the health care system, the drug regulatory system, and social justice advocacy organizations all felt the effects of economic policies designed to align the country's political structures with global trade goals.

The effect was to radically alter the fabric of democratic politics, including the social contract that had evolved over a century between the state and the organizations that represent sectors within civil society. Social policy researcher Josephine Rekart points out that both the right and the left had critiqued the welfare state and each advocated a larger role for the voluntary sector, but for different reasons.[17] The right opposed the pursuit of egalitarian policies as inconsistent with its core beliefs in freedom, individualism, and inequality; the left argued that inequalities persisted under the welfare state, and that the latter served capitalism by exercising social control rather than fostering needed structural changes. Modern proponents of market economies, such as the Fraser Institute in Canada, valorized reduced public expenditure and less taxation; as a conservative think tank, it anticipated less public spending on social services and more personal responsibility if social functions were returned to the family, the voluntary sector, and the market. For the left, greater engagement from the voluntary sector offered the potential for diffusing power, direct participation of citizens in decision making, and more decentralized services responsive to local needs. It did not envision any less public spending on social services, but expected better outcomes.

Political scientist Alexandra Dobrowolsky observes that pre-1980s interest groups and social movements had carved a role complementary to political parties, providing specific expertise and acting as a prod to policy change when political actors failed to incorporate the interests of their communities into the broader platforms of political parties. Neoliberal governments began to adopt a rhetoric demonizing groups formerly seen as advancing "progressive," "equality," or "social justice" causes; and they backed their words with policy changes that reduced the capacity of these organizations to raise operating funds. In an analysis of the federal government's changing attitudes to civil society advocacy groups, Dobrowolsky captures the mood of the late 1980s:

> The [Progressive] Conservatives followed market imperatives, applied business techniques to government and moved to downsize programmes, privatize operations and deregulate the economy. [Prime Minister] Mulroney distrusted both the bureaucracy and extra-parliamentary interventions from others than those in the business community ... In comparison to the early 1980s, the climate for "interest groups" had turned substantially colder by the end of the decade. Given the Conservative government's priorities, there was little time or use for, and less and less money allocated to, advocacy groups.[18]

Federal and provincial government cuts to community group funding began to send shockwaves through the women's health community;

meanwhile, some groups, desperate for operating funds, weighed offers from the pharmaceutical industry. Movement activists began to worry about the ability of groups to provide unbiased information about health issues, including those related to pharmaceuticals. Barbara Mintzes recalls the period:

> [We] ended up having to go without core funding and to depend on various short-term project funding and to depend on staffing through employment assistance programs. So really, things were problematic in terms of the quality of service that we were providing to the public. They were programs that were quite short-term, so you could not have long-term staff. You couldn't get people properly trained to the point [where] they were at higher levels in their understanding of the issues and being able to provide information to the public. And so there were certainly discussions internally in our organization of where to go for funding. And we had decided at that point not to go to the pharmaceutical industry, or to any other health product industry.

Mintzes remembers "alarm bells" going off as word circulated in the women's health community of infertility groups receiving funds from manufacturers of infertility products and menopause groups receiving money from companies making hormonal treatments. Indeed, for members of groups that existed in part to monitor pharmaceutical companies' ethics, the very idea of taking funding from the industry was unthinkable. Anne Rochon Ford explains:

> I was involved with DES Action going back to around 1983 when it first started, so a good ten years ... I knew these people and this organization really well ... And the language that that group spoke around big pharma was *so* consistent. You never wavered from the place of betrayal and that they were the source of the problem, right? And so people wouldn't have *dreamed* of taking pharma money! It was just like, we would have laughed if it – I don't ever recall it coming up. If someone did [suggest it], they would probably have just been, you know, so squeezed out by embarrassment.

Because many DES daughters had fertility problems caused by their mothers using the drug during pregnancy, they turned to infertility groups for help. Ford took particular note of the decision by the Infertility Awareness Association of Canada (IAAC) to accept funding from a pharmaceutical company for its newsletter. As a support group, IAAC subscribed to the self-help philosophy of providing members with as much accurate information as possible, so they could decide for themselves on the best course of action. But the group had no operating budget, and it began taking money from Serono, the manufacturer of one of the drugs associated with in vitro fertilization. Ford recalls getting the IAAC newsletter in the DES office and reading it regularly. "I had been noticing that there was a change in the tone, in the level of critical perspective," she says. "They were also starting to look a little more slick."

In the 1980s, in vitro fertilization and other new reproductive technologies were at the forefront of potentially lucrative medical innovations, raising ethical, legal, safety, and social concerns about so-called test-tube babies and the commercialization of reproduction. In 1989, the federal government, led by Brian Mulroney, established a Royal Commission on Reproductive Technologies, providing the opportunity for public input; the women's health community weighed in, with a range of perspectives. As part of a research paper she submitted to the commission, Ford undertook a content analysis of IAAC's newsletter from 1985 to 1991, taking note of IAAC's industry funding and the association's focus on access to the new technologies. Overall, she concluded, the publication provided women and couples experiencing infertility with tools for coping with their "pain and despair," but also responded with "signs of hope, usually in the form of medically assisted reproductive techniques."[19] An early issue of the newsletter, in 1985, included four pages of treatment descriptions taken from a pamphlet produced by Serono. In all, Ford concluded, the newsletter was more positive about the technologies than neutral or critical, and the association had lost its analytic edge.

Leaders of new groups run by and for patients with specific diseases were often unfamiliar with the pharmaceutical industry and sensitivities about corporate sponsorships. One such woman, Lorna Stevens, whose young son had been diagnosed with a rare genetic blood disorder called neutropenia, started the Neutropenia Support Association in 1989 to help families coping with the disease. The same team of specialists were treating four other families in Winnipeg, where Lorna and her family lived, and one of the physicians asked Lorna if she would take the lead in bringing them together for mutual support. At the beginning, Lorna recalls, the families were "neophytes in volunteerism"; they simply agreed on the tremendous need for information. Their first project was to establish an information library, but they also wanted to encourage research into the condition. They formed a registered charity so that they could raise funds and issue tax receipts to donors as part of an early period of gradual growth. Lorna explains:

> In 1989, we raised $700 selling calendars. In 1990, we had a fashion show and a baseball tournament ... And then we thought, "Oh, we need a newsletter," and "Oh, we need a toll-free number," and "Oh, we need a website." And it just keeps on going, right? [*Laughs.*] ...
>
> Early on, I approached some drug companies for money to publish a newsletter. We received $1,000 each from Amgen, Sandoz, and Schering, which covered three years of published newsletters. They were hands-off – the money was for the printing. Then, in 1993, we approached Amgen Canada for money to publish two booklets, in French and English. They gave us a grant of $10,000 and we acknowledged them on the back [of each booklet].[20]

When the booklets appeared, one of the physicians advising the group suggested that it should not accept any further pharma funding. "[He] picked up on the fact that, because we were using the drug company logos, we were perceived as being in the pocket of pharma," Lorna said. She didn't feel the group had done anything wrong in asking for or accepting funds from the companies, but did not want to be wrongly perceived. "We made an executive decision in '91 or '92 to raise all the money ourselves."

For twenty years, the group depended on volunteers and raised money with an annual golf tournament at which donors could sponsor a hole for $100, with pharmaceutical companies sometimes making contributions on this basis. The group receives calls from across Canada and has requests for information from around the world. In retrospect, Lorna wonders if the group *should* have gone for pharmaceutical company grants, which might have enabled it to hire a part-time fundraiser and provide more services. People can only volunteer for so long, she told me in 2016, and the pharma companies have always been extremely helpful and professional in dealings with the group. As their most dedicated volunteers retire, burn out, or cope with health demands of their own, she expects the group will someday have to fold.

Some of the industry overtures to patient organizations in the 1990s were the result of a formal initiative by a former Liberal Cabinet minister, Judith Erola, who lost her seat in the Progressive Conservative sweep of 1984. She became president of the Pharmaceutical Manufacturers Association of Canada (PMAC) in 1987, remaining in that position until 1998. In the government of Pierre Trudeau she was the minister of consumer and corporate affairs and also held the Cabinet portfolio for the status of women. She told me that when she went into the pharmaceutical industry, she believed the protection of intellectual property was essential but also that, if the industry was to flourish in Canada, it had "an obligation to participate in the whole issue of the Canadian health care system, and they had to be good corporate citizens." In both protecting the industry and pushing it to engage in social issues, she said, "I always said that I was a policeman on two fronts."[21]

Within PMAC, she created the Women's Advisory Committee, in part as a mechanism to institute broad reforms to support women within the industry with projects such as onsite daycare, but also to encourage pharmaceutical companies to promote women's health in Canadian society. These projects included an industry-funded university research chair in women's health and funding for women's health organizations in the community. Reflecting on her reasons for wanting the industry to fund grassroots women's health groups, she said:

> I encouraged those companies ... they had to spend 10 percent of their sales on research in Canada – well, I felt it wasn't enough to just spend the money on research. That's fine, but [they also needed] to understand what it [the money] could do to support various groups in the country that were desperately in need of support, and women's health was one of them.

The Complicating Precedent of AIDS Activism

The reconfigured relationship between government and civil society organizations was not the result of a one-way process. In Canada, as in the United States, HIV/AIDS activism within the gay community was redefining health activism to include radical political action by patients. Among cancer patients, demands for access to treatments outside the culture of allopathic medicine have a long history. AIDS treatment activism, by contrast, targeted the drugs developed by mainstream researchers and companies. This movement enlarged the critique of both the pharmaceutical industry and drug regulatory agencies, while adding a new dimension to health activism: collective pressure on researchers to target their research to particular diseases, to modify clinical trial design, and to exert pressure on drug regulators to provide access to new treatments still in the pipeline.[22]

The first wave of the AIDS activist movement, which began in the United States in the early 1980s, combined demands for drugs with a strong critique of drug regulators and the pharmaceutical industry. Dr. Michèle Brill-Edwards experienced this period of activism as a senior drug reviewer at the federal Department of Health (now Health Canada) and, as she told me, witnessed a similar dynamic in Canada:

> There was a crisis period where the minister was being burned in effigy for lack of access to AIDS drugs and lack of research in Canada. There were demonstrations on Parliament Hill. There were headlines regularly, weekly, criticizing the department for what it was not doing. And finally, there was a very embarrassing CBC-TV program that showed that we at Health Canada would block access to a drug that was made in Toronto but it was shipped off to – I think it was the Bahamas – and then imported back in so it could be legally accessed [*laughs*]. The insanity of that – I mean, the drug actually wasn't important. It was rather a fraudulent drug. But it did make the point that this is how crazy this regulatory process is, and here are these dying patients who see this craziness. And it's – you know, they're inflamed, and rightly so.

The day after the demonstration, at 8:30 a.m., Brill-Edwards was appointed as senior drug regulator responsible for HIV/AIDS drugs, giving her a unique vantage point from which to witness both the activism and the government's response to it:

> From my perspective ... the activist approach to AIDS was a dramatic change in the social fabric. And all of the patient advocacy groups that have come since really took their model from AIDS ... It changed the balance of power in the AIDS research game such that those paid in the public interest were reminded that if they failed to serve the public interest, they would, they could be damaged. And that was dramatic ... It produced dramatic change. After that, the AIDS activists had a much, much larger say in things. The result was a model where patients [with other diseases] had a much, much larger say.

Like the American AIDS movement, the Canadian movement in the 1980s featured attention-grabbing, symbolic public actions, critical of government and of drug companies. At the fifth international AIDS conference in Montreal in 1989, for example, activists took to the stage in advance of Prime Minister Brian Mulroney's opening remarks to chastise him for not speaking about HIV/AIDS in the previous five years when he had led the government. Ann Silversides wrote that the activists "shift[ed] the conference away from being solely an industry platform to ensuring the needs and concerns of people living with HIV/AIDS were acknowledged."[23]

In the early days of the AIDS movement in Canada, AIDS activists met with representatives of the women's movement to share political analyses and strategies. Areas of common ground included the constraints advocacy imposed by accepting government funding, strategies for confronting the state, and the ways in which the medical establishment and the pharmaceutical industry medicalized gender-related behaviours. One significant divergence between the two movements, however, was over the issue of access to drugs. With its focus on the health concerns of women in their reproductive years, the women's health movement emphasized the potential hazards of drugs and wanted strong safety standards; AIDS activists focused first and foremost on drugs as potential remedies.[24]

Numerous analysts of drug regulation have parsed the AIDS activists' demands for early access to new drugs and asked whether they helped corporations and neoliberal governments in their push to relax safety regulations and speed new pharmaceuticals to market.[25] Steven Epstein found that the movement's perspective on drug regulation changed over time, from the early attacks on the Food and Drug Administration (FDA) and demands for faster access to new drugs in the 1980s to a realization in the 1990s that good science was ultimately the route to effective treatments. In his history of the FDA, Philip J. Hilts concurs. In 1994, leaders in the political far right, including Newt Gingrich and the Competitive Enterprise Institute, launched an anti-FDA advertising campaign and tried unsuccessfully to enlist leaders in the AIDS movement. Accusing the drug regulator of discouraging innovation and blocking profitable products from coming to market, the campaigners wanted "to dismantle the FDA, to roll back the scientific standards of the 1962 law and turn over the 'review' of drugs to private companies hired by the drug manufacturers themselves."[26] Leaders in the AIDS movement explained to Hilts that, even at the height of their struggles with the FDA, in 1988, they were never against regulation; rather, they wanted the agency "to be flexible and intelligent about development and approval of drugs." Another explained, "We don't want ourselves or our friends to die from taking unsafe drugs, and we disagree with the radical deregulators of the right who would abolish all efficacy requirements."[27]

John Abraham and Courtney Davis, who analyze drug regulation from a base in the United Kingdom, observe that whatever effect AIDS activism may have had on the regulatory regime in the United States, drugs that are potentially life-saving comprise a tiny minority of those reviewed and should be viewed as a special case. And yet the shift at the FDA in the 1990s to accelerated reviews and other means of extending patent protection was far broader and included treatments that offer no significant therapeutic efficacy over existing therapies – which make up the vast majority of drugs that gain approval.[28]

At the same time that the early AIDS activists lobbied for access to new medications, they also challenged pharmaceutical industry practices they saw as unethical. Brill-Edwards recalls:

They were largely at odds with the industry. The [early] AIDS activists saw the industry as – I would not say enemies, but certainly as treacherous entities. You know, they saw the dilemmas. They unmasked the close rapport, the too-close rapport between the companies that wanted a product on the market and the experts and researchers who "collaborated" with them. And they unmasked the hollowness of much of medical research.

So on those two points it was the AIDS activists who did their home-work and tracked down the two hundred, three hundred, four hundred thousand dollar "honorariums" that were flowing from the companies involved in AIDS research to the expert staff at NIH [National Institutes for Health, in the United States], who were getting paid public salaries but who were taking this private money through the back door.

The HIV/AIDS movement developed tactics that had no counterpart in the Canadian women's health movement. Lori Waserman, a graduate student in Canadian Studies, analyzed that movement in the 1970s and 1980s and concluded that, although women's health activists felt rage at their treatment in the medical system, they had been socialized to be treated dismissively and so acted quietly, forming support groups and engaging in public education, rather than demanding better treatment "with the same kind of gusto" as the (largely male) activists in the early HIV/AIDS movement. Furthermore, the belief that one could demand access to new drugs and still critique the drug companies ran deeply in the AIDS activist culture.[29]

In some respects, then, the two movements were a study in contrasts: female versus male leaders; the healthy and the gravely ill; demands for tighter drug safety regulation versus demands that regulations be changed to speed access to new drugs. Both movements were highly critical of the pharmaceutical industry; women's health activists, however, protested quietly, distanced themselves from drug companies, and urged more attention to social determinants of health. Members of the early AIDS movement confronted the industry, demanding "drugs into bodies," a seat at the negotiating table, and changes to clinical trial design so that no clinical trial participant would go without drug treatment. In essence, they were looking at drugs from two different sides.

Drugs as Chameleons
Drugs have an inherent Janus-faced identity; they can both help and hurt

the patient. In an essay titled "Plato's Pharmacy," inspired by Plato's *Phaedrus*, Jacques Derrida explored the multiple meanings in antiquity of the concept of pharmakon (pharmacy). Translating "pharmakon" as "remedy" is always partial, Derrida argues; "pharmakon" also means poison, charm, magic, love potion, and paint. The essence of a drug is that it has no essential nature.[30]

The modern cancer pharmacy thus belongs to a long line of substances whose unstable identities make their cultural meanings highly susceptible to social filters. Because a drug's effects are often variable and unpredictable, a discourse can focus on or exaggerate one aspect and ignore or play down the other. Anthropologist Emily Martin shows how manufacturers of psychotropics use this malleability, hiring marketing firms to brand their drugs with "personalities" that capture the drug's contradictory characteristics in an appealing way. Based on feedback from focus groups of potential users, an advertising agency might promote a drug to be "[like] Hillary Clinton ... [she's] strong and tough and knows what she wants to do, and yet [is] sensitive to social issues." Such a drug would "work really well" but would also have "a feminine sort of feeling."[31] The concept of drugs as actors with multifaceted, socially constructed personalities is useful in understanding the way the contested meanings of drugs shape-shift over time and across speakers.

This plasticity of meaning is evident in cancer treatments. Cancer is one of the most dreaded diseases in contemporary life and, as a remedy, chemotherapy is sometimes depicted as an armed protector – "powerful drugs patrolling the body, destroying wayward cancer cells."[32] At the same time, the toxicity of chemo treatments is legendary, with effects on the patient that include nausea, vomiting, fatigue, and hair loss. Less often mentioned is that cancer drugs can inflict lasting damage and even kill the patient. Indeed, the drugs used to treat most cancers confer modest benefits; some argue, however, that the prevalence of the disease means that small improvements in treatment can translate into many lives extended or saved.[33] Among experts, whether and when a cancer drug treatment is appropriate can be highly controversial.

When chemotherapy gained stature as a potentially useful treatment for breast cancer in the 1970s, two classes of drug treatments gained credibility, each with its adherents and detractors. Both drug types were considered adjuvant or "helping" treatments, to be used in combination with local treatment (surgery and/or radiation). In 1976, a cancer research group in Milan put the combination cytotoxic chemotherapy regime known as CMF (cyclophosphamide, methotrexate, and 5-fluorouracil, also called 5-FU) on the map as an adjuvant treatment for premenopausal women with stage 1 or stage 2 breast cancer; that is, cancer that could not be detected in vital organs.[34] By 1995, research had shown that CMF, initially found to reduce the risk of recurrence in premenopausal women, also reduced the risk of death, and that benefits extended to older, post-menopausal women. A combination known as CAF, in which Adriamycin (doxorubicin) replaces methotrexate, showed similar efficacy.[35]

These findings generated several debates about the relative advantages of combination cytotoxic chemotherapy, measured against the risks of these treatments. One controversy was that, although the drugs improved survival rates for stage 2 cancer, only some women saw these benefits, and the drugs had significant toxicity; furthermore, they had not been tested on women diagnosed as stage 1, whose disease was presumably even more curable.[36] Medical historian Barron Lerner summarizes the dilemma of the latter:

> At least 80 percent of women treated with surgery for clinical stage 1 disease survived without a recurrence for ten to twenty years, indicating they were probably cured [i.e., without chemotherapy]. Of the remaining 20 percent who might benefit from chemotherapy, only a minority, perhaps one fifth, avoided death or a recurrence as a direct result of receiving chemotherapy. Thus the vast majority of women treated for adjuvant chemotherapy for stage 1 breast cancer would experience no actual benefit from this therapy, only the side effects, such as nausea, vomiting, fatigue and hair loss. These drugs also led to suppression of the bone marrow, making patients susceptible to infections, some of which could be life-threatening. Risk of future leukemias was another potential complication.[37]

Faced with the conundrum of uncertain benefits and high toxicity, regulators and oncologists, especially in the United States, leaned toward the potential benefits. Regulatory agencies approved cancer drugs for the market before their effectiveness had been demonstrated, using tacit strategies that relax the post-thalidomide criteria for drug approvals. Furthermore, regulators tended to show less concern for safety than they would with a drug to treat a disease like arthritis. In a 1992 book on the practical, legal, and ethical problems of introducing new cancer treatments, Christopher Williams writes, "This difference in emphasis means that toxic drugs can be used for potentially fatal diseases that would never gain a license for less serious indications." Physicians are free to prescribe a drug for indications beyond those for which they are approved, using their judgment to deal with the ambiguity. The result, Williams asserts, was the absence of adequate data and "willy-nilly" usage of the drugs in practice.[38]

The second pharmacological treatment for breast cancer introduced in the 1970s, the anti-estrogenic drug tamoxifen, generated a contrasting discourse about adverse effects. Although even proponents of cytotoxic chemotherapies acknowledged the drugs were tough on patients, breast cancer specialists described tamoxifen's risks as "usually minimal" compared with those of cytotoxic chemotherapy, "for the most part ... well tolerated," and even "non-toxic."[39] The most common side effects were hot flashes, nausea and vomiting for one or two months, vaginal spotting, and weight gain. But some patients experienced more severe effects, including depression, loss of appetite, headache, loss of vision, blood clots, and, in one study, endometrial cancer. In 1990, when the American breast surgeon Dr. Susan Love published her book on breast health and breast cancer aimed at a lay audience, she cautioned, "Tamoxifen should not be considered lightly."[40]

Unlike cytotoxic chemotherapy, which kills cells as they divide, tamoxifen inhibits cancer cell growth by blocking the routes by which estrogen (a breast tumour stimulant) enters the tumour. In 1977, the FDA approved the use of tamoxifen for postmenopausal women whose breast tumours depended on estrogen to grow (i.e., cancers classified as estrogen receptor-positive, or ER+), but the approval was based on what researchers and regulators call a "surrogate endpoint."[41] The putative post-thalidomide litmus test for drug efficacy is the clinical trial showing the drug significantly extends survival time and alleviates symptoms. With cancer drugs, except with childhood cancers, actual evidence of extended life (let alone cure) is unusual. The surrogate endpoint, that is, a biological response to the drug, such as tumour shrinkage or extended time-to-disease recurrence (two effects of cytotoxic chemo regimens), has become the standard for showing efficacy. This much weaker standard of evidence suggests the drug might, in time, be shown to extend life. Tamoxifen's demonstrated effect in the 1970s and 1980s was that the drug reduced the risk of cancer in the opposite breast, suggesting the possibility of extended survival time. Many oncology drugs have been approved based on the hope of a yet-to-be-demonstrated real benefit, even though the practice meant researchers were pursuing "the finding of correct answers to the wrong question."[42] To the unwary, however, the act of drug approval sends a signal that the drug meets the higher standard of efficacy. In the case of tamoxifen, the believers turned out to be right. Combined results of clinical trials published in 1988 – eleven years after its FDA approval – found that tamoxifen did meet the standard of extending survival time, by an average of two years after five years of follow-up, an improvement in survival of 5 to 6 percent. By 2004, the women had been followed for fifteen years and the improvement in survival was 6.8 percent for premenopausal women and 8.2 percent for postmenopausal women.[43]

Both these types of chemotherapy had moved into standard practice in Canada by 1990, despite uncertain benefits and risks for individual patients. Physicians were divided on when to give chemotherapy, or whether to give it at all. In his 1992 assessment of the problems of introducing new cancer drugs, Christopher Williams noted that powerful vested interests and the lack of scientific clarity could sideline patients' interests:

> The decision as to whether drugs [should] be used has been left to the discretion of the individual clinician, [to] market forces (including drug company promotion) and to a lesser extent clinical trials or "directives" ... from governmental bodies or research organizations ... However, these may also be used as a way of gaining a tacit acceptance of a new drug without demonstrating whether it is beneficial to the patients.[44]

A Curious Omission
Despite the Canadian women's health movement's focus on pharmaceuticals, the debate about drug treatments and other breast cancer issues were

virtually absent from movement discourse. Lori Waserman, studying the reasons for the omission in 1997, concludes that although breast cancer had the conditions for politicization, women's health activists of this period, despite their awareness of the disease, were preoccupied with reproductive health issues.[45] The enormous control that the law, medicine, and religious institutions wielded over reproductive rights contributed to this concentration; so did the personal centrality of these issues to many of the movement's young, healthy leaders, whose reproductive concerns structured their contact with the medical profession. Feminist struggles over medicine and reproduction seemed never-ending and they resurfaced in a new form with the advent of reproductive technologies. Indeed, second-wave women's health activists tended in general to neglect health problems that kill women – smoking and lung cancer being another example. For life-threatening conditions, Waserman says, "It is difficult not to turn to the medical profession," even when medical knowledge is wanting and treatments are controversial, so the treatment of diseases was thought to be "outside the realm of politics," until AIDS activists changed that perception.[46] Finally, Waserman noted that the emphasis on and idealization of women's breasts as cultural symbols of a woman's worth contributed to women feeling too ashamed or embarrassed to talk about breast cancer.[47] By the late 1980s, women's health centres began to lose funding, curtailing the ability of activists to take on new issues.[48]

A few individual women with breast cancer had framed the disease politically, however.[49] One of the most prominent was Rose Kushner, an American journalist who turned to activism after her diagnosis of breast cancer in 1974. Kushner's activism is sometimes cited as a precursor to the breast cancer movement of the 1990s.[50] As Barron Lerner recounts the story, the year after her diagnosis, Kushner not only wrote an investigative book, *Breast Cancer: A Personal History and Investigative Report*, she also set up a counselling centre for women out of her own home.[51] And although US-based, Kushner travelled widely and was known in Canada and beyond. She actively sought to compare cancer treatment practices in the United States with those abroad and in the process met cancer specialists the world over; in addition, through her book and counselling service, she established a reputation as a lay expert among women with breast cancer. Her stance toward medical practice, particularly the then routine use of mastectomy in the United States, was that of a well-educated, critical consumer. She confidently, writes Lerner, "discussed and evaluated the medical literature. Too many physicians, she argued, had the science all wrong."[52] In the 1980s, the decade before an organized breast cancer movement took shape, thousands of women turned to Kushner for "the truth" about breast cancer treatments. I was one such woman. After being diagnosed with stage 2 breast cancer in 1988, I discovered her book *Alternatives* in the local library and was immediately drawn in by her detailed, cross-cultural, critical account of breast cancer history, treatments, and politics. My oncologist had recommended that I enter a clinical trial designed to compare the efficacy and toxicity of three regimens of CAF, and the prospect of subjecting my body to such a toxic treatment terrified me.

Kushner was critical of a push from some medical oncologists, in the late 1970s, to extend the use of cytotoxic chemotherapy from patients with stage 3 and 4 diagnoses to women diagnosed with stage 2 cancers. She was not impressed, either, when Gianni Bonadonna's research team in Italy published its clinical trial data in 1976 to show that the combination chemotherapy regime CMF significantly reduced the risk of recurrence in these women. Risk of recurrence is just a surrogate endpoint, and Kushner argued (as did many oncologists) that the researchers' follow-up time of fourteen months was too short to conclude that the benefits of such a toxic treatment were worth the risks to women whose cancers might never prove lethal. Based on her investigation of medical practices in other Western countries, Kushner concluded that oncologists in the United States were particularly prone to adopting aggressive treatment modalities on the basis of preliminary evidence.

When her cancer recurred in 1981, Kushner decided to take the anti-estrogen pill tamoxifen, produced in the United States by Stuart Pharmaceuticals and marketed under the brand name Nolvadex. Like adjuvant chemotherapy using CMF, tamoxifen was still experimental, but Kushner agreed with its adherents in the medical community who promoted it as having fewer side effects than combination chemotherapy. She wrote scathingly of the "toxic" regimens that were being recommended for postmenopausal women and accused the physicians who encouraged them of being insensitive to their patients' quality of life.[53]

In a 2007 article, Barron Lerner disclosed a little-known fact: that Kushner had developed a financial arrangement with the pharmaceutical company that made Nolvadex. Assessing Kushner's perspective in the debate about tamoxifen's relative risks and benefits for postmenopausal women compared with CMF, he concludes that financial support from the makers of tamoxifen helped shape her advocacy:

> As her opposition to chemotherapy continued, her confidence in tamoxifen as an alternative treatment grew. At some point, she purchased stock in Imperial Chemical Industries (ICI), the British company that manufactured Nolvadex, and regularly mentioned the medication in her frequent articles and lectures on breast cancer. When her book, *Alternatives: New Developments in the War on Breast Cancer*, was published in 1984, a natural alliance was formed: ICI and its American affiliate, Stuart Pharmaceuticals, were eager to help publicize the book, which was not only an excellent treatise on the disease but also spoke very favorably about their product. Kushner received travel funding from the two companies, enabling her to appear at meetings and to sell her book. Stuart Pharmaceuticals also bought 10,000 copies of *Alternatives*, distributing them to physicians as gifts.[54]

That wasn't all: ICI donated money to Kushner's advisory centre and contracted her to write the text for a patient information leaflet about Nolvadex, in which she claimed the therapy had no side effects.[55] Kushner was fifty-nine when she died in 1990 of cancer-related causes.

Lerner's article floored me. The toxicities of cytotoxic chemotherapy drugs are a valid concern; so is the research community's tendency to prematurely hype every new finding as an important breakthrough. However, if I had known at the time that Kushner was in the pay of the drug's manufacturer, I believe I would have given less weight to her assessment of cytotoxic chemotherapies in relation to tamoxifen, which (contrary to Kushner's view at the time) has its own toxicities. Ironically, in seeking to avoid the bias toward toxic medical treatment that I assumed was characteristic of medical specialists, I put my trust in someone who had a vested commercial interest in the system.[56]

I have little doubt that her belief in tamoxifen's superiority over cytotoxic chemotherapy was genuine. I would also guess that, as her renown increased, the demands of her work outstripped her personal resources and made the funding from Stuart Pharmaceuticals seem a fair trade-off. History, I would suggest, has proven her wrong. Despite the new treatments drugs introduced in the past two decades, cytotoxic chemotherapies remain reliable workhorses in the breast cancer treatment arsenal, as does tamoxifen.

Lerner concludes that Kushner's interactions with the manufacturer of a drug that she was taking, and which she so enthusiastically endorsed, put her in a conflict of interest that provides a cautionary tale "about individuals who function simultaneously as patients and spokespeople."[57] He argues, however, that the mid-1980s were a period of transition in ethical standards within medicine from an earlier time, when "largesse from industry was tolerated, even lauded"; for this reason, he says, even though she apparently never publicly disclosed her relationship with ICI and Stuart Pharmaceuticals, we should not judge Kushner by "our modern ethical standard."

Lerner's assessment that the standard of the 1970s and 1980s was more tolerant of conflicts of interest than our standard today is perhaps peculiar to medicine, where ethical standards concerning commercial conflicts have lagged behind social institutions like the judiciary, government, and media. Since Kushner was first and foremost a journalist, working in a field whose codes of ethics have long recognized the need to avoid conflicts of interest while covering a story, I found her undisclosed alliance with the maker of Nolvadex jarring. And I question Lerner's assertion that this example discredits patients who act as spokespeople; rather, the issue raised is whether any spokesperson – patient, physician, researcher, or policy maker – can avoid having his or her judgment affected by industry support. For these reasons, Lerner's account of Kushner's financial arrangement with ICI and Stuart Pharmaceuticals stands as a fascinating harbinger of what was to come.[58]

PART 2

From Grassroots to Contestation to Partnership
The Breast Cancer Movement and Big Pharma

3

Beginnings of the Breast Cancer Movement

We all came together from our dissatisfaction with various aspects of the status quo.

– CAROLYN GIBSON BADGER, 2009

Movement at the Grassroots

Burlington, Ontario, 1989

Patricia (Pat) Kelly was in her late thirties and had two young daughters when she was diagnosed with breast cancer. She was desperate to discuss her breast cancer experience with others in the same situation when a mutual friend introduced her to Barb Sullivan, a nurse who had also had breast cancer. The two women placed an ad in the local paper, inviting other breast cancer patients to meet at the YWCA. Thirty-five women showed up to the first meeting. "And it was amazing," Pat recalls. "We just sat in a circle, and women started telling their stories."

The women decided to meet once a month. The local Canadian Cancer Society held monthly support group meetings at their offices in town, so a delegation of three approached the society to ask that younger women, in particular, be told about the meetings at the Y. Three men and two women who worked for or were members of the board of the Cancer Society met formally with them but expressed concern about whether they intended to discuss treatments. "Well, of course we will," one replied. "But you're not qualified to give treatment advice!" was the response. The three survivors countered that the point of exchanging experiences was not to advise one another but to share knowledge. They in turn questioned the expertise of the Cancer Society's group leaders after learning that they had not themselves had cancer, did not seem to grasp the value of peer support, and were running a support group that appeared to have no active members. The new group continued to meet and became the Burlington Breast Cancer Support Services. Within two years, it had its own donated meeting space in a shopping mall.[1]

Montreal, Quebec, 1989–91

I was a journalist working in Montreal as an editor on a consumer protection magazine published by the Quebec government when I was diagnosed with breast cancer. In 1989, while still undergoing chemotherapy treatment, I was struck by the contrast between the passivity and invisibility of cancer patients and the high profile of AIDS activists at an international conference in the city. I wrote an op-ed article for the local newspaper about the culture of optimism in the breast cancer world, which masked the punishing treatments and the failure of research to advance the understanding of the causes of the disease. I exhorted cancer patients to organize, as AIDS patients had done. Among the responses I received was a note from a breast cancer patient named Carolyn Gibson Badger, which ended with the comment that I sounded like an activist and an invitation: to call her if I ever decided to start a group.

Two years later, I began meeting every month with Carolyn and two other Montreal women with breast cancer, Margaret Waller and Kathy Glass, and in April 1991 we held our first public meeting to launch the group – a patient organization focused on advocacy rather than on support. Eighteen years later, Carolyn reflected, "I have a sense that we all came together from our dissatisfaction with various aspects of the status quo. In those early meetings, we were all alarmed by the rising breast cancer rates and were concerned that so much effort was directed to drug trials and so little to understanding the cause of the dramatic increase in rates. We quickly determined that prevention should be our primary focus."[2]

St. Catharines, Ontario, 1990–91

Paula McPherson, a young lawyer from St. Catharines, had just had her first child and was practising law in Toronto when she was diagnosed with breast cancer. Throughout her pregnancy, she had felt knowledgeable, in control, and confident about making decisions, thanks to the countless resources available to her. As a cancer patient, by contrast, she felt "cut adrift ... Every bit of information I had to work hard to get."[3] She set about researching the disease and was shocked to learn that over twelve thousand women and men were being diagnosed every year in Canada, and that five thousand Canadian women a year were dying of it. She was equally shocked to discover that the causes of breast cancer were unknown. The focus of research had to shift to cause and prevention, she concluded.[4]

In early 1991, she set up a nonprofit charitable organization to promote understanding of the connections between the environment and breast cancer, built on the public interest research group (PIRG) model developed in the early 1970s by American consumer activist Ralph Nader. She called the group the Breast Cancer Research and Education Fund, and its slogan was "Fight back! Stop it before it starts." To address a second concern, the neglect of the psychosocial stress of uncertainty after a cancer diagnosis, Paula founded a self-help group, similar to the one in Burlington, in which women could share experiences and resources about living with breast cancer in a positive, informal atmosphere. In just two and a half months, it had twenty-two members.[5]

Montreal and Vancouver, 1990–91

Marcella Tardif was forty-five in January 1990 when she was diagnosed with breast cancer. Over the next six months she had numerous biopsies and lumpectomies, until finally a doctor recommended she have a mastectomy. The idea of losing her breast terrified her; she wanted to look feminine. The doctor reassured her that a breast implant would allow her to have the mastectomy with no long-term change to her appearance. In June she had a single operation to remove her breast and insert an implant. Alarming secretions, swelling, and pain began almost immediately and continued for months. Her surgeon said the implant was not the source of her problems, but when she finally obtained a second opinion from a general surgeon, he advised her to have the implant removed immediately. She did so and the symptoms subsided.

Outraged by the plastic surgeon's denials, she told her story on a television talk show and the next day, she says, "the phones were ringing off the walls because women were phoning in to tell me, 'I had this happen to me!'"[6] She formed a breast implant support and advocacy network with Linda Wilson and Joy Langan, two women from British Columbia who had heard her story. They named their network Je sais/I know – when they had told one another their experiences, they found themselves nodding and saying, "I know, *Je sais.*" The group's founders were determined to call physicians to account and to pressure the government to stop the implantation of unsafe products in women's bodies.[7]

Parliamentary Hearings Provide a Platform

Between 1989 and 1991, small pockets of women in Canada began launching new meeting places, under their own control, where they could discuss their experiences of living with breast cancer, collectively formulate questions they felt were important, and take action to have these questions answered. Their activities were simple and familiar: they met at one another's homes or at community centres to exchange personal experiences; they researched the disease at their local library, bookstore, or medical school; they discussed what they had read; and they told their stories to the media. At the same time, their effect was startling: they were raising questions about the disease and the practices in place to deal with it that had not been articulated before. Their organizations became sites of knowledge construction – new ways of looking at breast cancer based on experiences and reflections of women who had the disease.[8] They could move their claims forward, however, only if others involved in the process of knowledge making recognized their groups as sources they would have to consult.

The opportunity to become involved in the knowledge-making process came in the fall of 1991, when a parliamentary subcommittee on the status of women began a study of breast cancer and breast implants.[9] The national hearings initiated a chain of events that put breast cancer on the federal government's policy agenda. For the groups, the hearings were the chance to put women's experiences on the public record. Representatives from each of the four groups mentioned above, and several others, appeared before the all-woman subcommittee of members of Parliament, chaired by Barbara Greene from the then-ruling Progressive Conservative Party of Canada. The subcommittee, too, sought to reinvigorate the breast cancer issue. According to member Dawn Black of the New Democratic Party, the subcommittee members each had friends who had been diagnosed and so felt deeply committed to the proceedings.[10]

The subcommittee called on a range of policy actors as witnesses but chose to give women from the nascent community groups a prominent role. The resulting synergy was such that the hearings can fairly be said to have co-constructed the Canadian breast cancer movement. The emerging movement in the United States was also a strong influence, providing the organizations in Canada with models and contacts. The pharmaceutical industry, by contrast, had little or no role in shaping these early groups.

Transcripts from the parliamentary hearings document the social world of breast cancer in Canada at the time and provide a rich record of the discourses on breast cancer issues. Forty-eight people from the breast cancer arena testified over a period of eight months. Of these, medical researchers comprised the largest category by far, with twenty-nine witnesses, clinical trialists, and treatment researchers dominating. Next in number to the researchers were eleven self-identified patients and/or representatives of grassroots patient organizations. Although speaking from various perspectives and organizations, the activists collectively emphasized the gulf between what patients needed and what researchers, physicians, and professionalized charitable organizations serving patients were providing.[11]

The established charities claimed to be serving the needs of cancer patients with information booklets, hospital visitations, and fundraising programs for patient services and research, but members of the emerging grassroots groups found these projects wanting. Indeed, they said that the established agencies sometimes withheld information in a way that circumscribed patients' knowledge of the disease and misrepresented the inadequacies and failures of treatments. In short, patients and their families wanted to be treated as resourceful collaborators in the shaping and using of knowledge, not as passive, dependent "patients" lacking expertise. Furthermore, having redefined the established actors as failed providers of the knowledge patients sought, they positioned their own organizations as the solution to these unmet needs. They wanted nothing less than to participate in the breast cancer policy community, the inner circle that affects government policy in this domain.[12]

Thematically, the activists who testified covered a wide range of concerns, including lack of information on which to make treatment decisions; inadequate emotional supports; harsh and often ineffective treatments; perceived paternalism on the part of physicians, researchers, and cancer charities; shock at learning that breast cancer rates were rising for reasons that were still largely unknown; and their difficulty gaining access to new and potentially life-saving treatments. This latter theme was neither more nor less central to the women's demands than the others; a decade later, however, it would be the leitmotif defining the movement.

The testimony of one patient presaged a plea still heard with regularity. Sylvia Morrison, from the Burlington Breast Cancer Support Services, was perhaps the first breast cancer patient within Canada's breast cancer movement to publicly advocate for systemic changes that would provide patients faster access to novel, expensive treatments. In riveting testimony, Morrison described the rapid advance of her cancer and her decision to go to the Memorial Sloan Kettering Cancer Center in New York for a second opinion, and then to Roswell Park Cancer Institute in Buffalo to have a treatment that was not approved for use in Canada.[13] Despite a vigilant practice of self-examination and frequent mammograms prompted by her family history of breast cancer, she had been diagnosed just eight months earlier with a tumour that had already metastasized. In view of her desperate situation, her oncologist in Hamilton recommended high-dose chemotherapy (HDC) with bone marrow transplant (more on this in Chapter 7).

Showing an impressive grasp of Canada's drug regulatory system, Morrison argued that patients like her should have easier access to experimental drugs. Some of the American treatment teams specializing in HDC had begun using two such drugs to boost the patients' production of white and red blood cells, thereby speeding the patient's recovery and shortening the hospital stay. Neupogen (filgrastim) is a synthetic protein that stimulates the production of a type of white blood cell. Epogen (epoetin alfa) is human erythropoietin produced by recombinant DNA technology and used as a therapeutic agent to increase red blood cell levels. When Morrison testified in 1991, Neupogen was considered experimental in Canada and was not licensed; Epogen was licensed and indicated for AIDS but was not approved for breast cancer treatment. Specialists at her local

Canadian centre told her that the treatment was not offered in Canada because it had not been proven to have better five-year survival rates than standard treatments. But such proof was a logical impossibility, she pointed out, because "the drug has not even been available for five years."[14] Yet, the statistics available "indicate[d] that it [was] very promising," she said. "Do we have to wait five years before we give our women the opportunity to take advantage of research and experimental procedures going on elsewhere?" The costs of her treatment in the United States and related expenses "bankrupted us," she stated, emphasizing that her family was financially "in better shape than the majority of Canadians." In their final report, members of the subcommittee wrote sympathetically that Morrison was luckier than most to have access to "cutting edge" treatment options.[15] Yet, a decade later, the treatment was relegated to the dark pages of cancer treatment mistakes, a hypertoxic failed experiment, perpetuated by desperation, greed, and fraud.[16]

The parliamentary hearings on breast cancer were heading into their sixth month when the subcommittee heard from the only two witnesses from the pharmaceutical industry who would appear before them. Gordon Postlewaite was the director of university and scientific affairs for the Pharmaceutical Manufacturers Association of Canada (PMAC), the multinational industry's lobbying organization in Canada, and Leonora Marks was PMAC's director of publications.[17] In spoken testimony in May 1992, the two echoed Morrison's lament that Canada lagged in its approval of new drug treatments.[18] A supplementary PMAC brief, "Response to the Review of the Canadian Drug Approval System," reinforced this theme, praising Canada's drug approval process for its "enviable standard of safety" but calling for a "renewed mission statement that would include a goal to make safe modern therapeutic advances available at the earliest possible time."[19]

The two industry representatives did not enjoy the same warm reception as the patients who testified at the hearings. In a series of pointed questions, committee member Dawn Black challenged Postlewaite and Marks about what the two referred to as "a consumer information campaign" – it was actually "an advertising campaign," asserted Black. Not so, Postlewaite and Marks countered; the campaign was a public service designed to inform consumers about the medications that their member companies produced. The messages provided information the public wanted, they argued, but that Canadian physicians and pharmacists had failed to provide.[20] Indeed, PMAC had sponsored consumer information seminars and appointed advisory panels with the specific goal of designing programs for consumers to fill the gaps in information available to the public about medications, particularly for seniors and women. Dawn Black broached another sensitive topic: users' complaints about drugs and devices. She proposed a consumer registry, because people had "nowhere to turn" when they encountered problems. Once again, Postlewaite and Marks recast the point: consumers wanted to be more involved in decision making, they said, and PMAC's outreach efforts responded to this demand.

This testimony supports the account that PMAC's then-president Judith Erola provided in an interview, in which she envisioned industry-sponsored consumer information sessions and advisory panels as a means to promote women's health and consumers' interests in the larger Canadian society.[21]

The Pharmaceutical Policy Environment

To understand PMAC's position, and the frosty attitude of some witnesses and committee members to the industry, it helps to consider the rapid changes underway in pharmaceutical policy at the time of the parliamentary hearings. Despite Canada's 1987 legislation to delay compulsory licensing by seven years as a condition of the Free Trade Agreement (FTA) with the United States, the American pharmaceutical industry remained concerned that compulsory licensing would set a precedent – indeed, the Canadian experiment had attracted attention in Europe.[22] Furthermore, by 1992, Canada had become one of the US industry's largest markets for pharmaceuticals, with imports of US$845 million.[23] Apart from direct pressure from industry, the US government was eager to increase protection for the exports of the growing American biotechnology industry.[24] Negotiations for the North American Free Trade Agreement (NAFTA) were under way, broadening the FTA to include Mexico. The Canadian government, still under the Mulroney Conservatives, anticipated that the terms of NAFTA would force it to abandon compulsory licensing and in 1993 acted in advance (NAFTA came into force January 1, 1994).

The government passed Bill C-91, bringing into law the Patent Act Amendment Act, which abolished compulsory licensing for pharmaceutical products altogether and extended patent protection of brand-name drugs to at least twenty years. The bill also retroactively voided all compulsory licences obtained after December 20, 1991. To further appease the industry, in 1993, Canada added a new regulation to the patent act. The Patented Medicines (Notice of Compliance or NOC) Regulations prohibited Health Canada from approving a generic drug until after the courts had ruled on any claim of alleged patent infringement. This latter regulation facilitated the brand-name companies' efforts to delay the introduction of generic drugs and hobbled the generic drug industry. A brand-name company had only to argue that its patent had been infringed and an injunction of up to two years was granted; the onus was on the generic company to prove that it had not violated patent law. In return for these concessions, the industry promised to invest at least $400 million or 10 percent of its Canadian sales in research and development by the end of 1996. So that the government could maintain some control over prices, Bill C-91 increased the power of the Patented Medicine Prices Review Board, giving it the authority to order reductions in prices deemed excessive (by comparison with prices in seven economically similar countries), to impose penalties to recoup excess revenues, and to take away the company's market exclusivity.[25]

The exchange between members of the parliamentary committee and the two representatives of PMAC captured some of the unease within the health policy community about the American-dominated pharmaceutical industry and its power. Concerns that "consumer education" could bleed into advertising, and the lack of recourse for patients who suffered side effects from drug treatments and medical devices (such as breast implants), arose from a consumer protection perspective, but researchers were wary too. Two previous witnesses, both physician researchers, had criticized the industry for spending too much money on advertising and too little on research. If Canada was trading its highly successful compulsory licensing system for a promise of research funding, where was the money? Judging from comments that dotted the hearings, the industry was a long way from being regarded in the medical research community as a good corporate citizen. Indeed, investments in research and development improved, but remained low compared with the industry's rates of spending internationally. By 2000, the industry was investing $945 million in Canada – an increase, but still the lowest rate of spending among the comparator countries the Patented Medicines Prices Review Board used to determine Canadian price controls.[26]

The Community Grows

In September 1992, the subcommittee summarized its findings in a report titled *Breast Cancer: Unanswered Questions*, which, as the subtitle suggests, highlighted the many troubling gaps in knowledge about breast cancer. The most striking feature of the subcommittee's recommendations is the attention given, at every turn, to including the "experience and expertise" of breast cancer activists and survivors,[27] and of support, advocacy, and consumer group members, in all manner of decision-making bodies, from breast cancer curriculum review committees to cancer research agencies. The subcommittee further proposed that the federal Department of Health assist with developing the necessary infrastructure of lay expertise for all of this consultation. This endorsement came with a caveat: the movement would not be "disruptive." This assurance appeared in a section of the subcommittee's report headed "Advocacy and Activism," which began, "There is often a tendency to equate activism and advocacy with large scale 'disruptive' behaviour. The subcommittee received an overwhelming message from the breast cancer survivors and activists who appeared before us that this is not their intention."[28]

Since none of the survivors who appeared before the committee either advocated or disavowed disruptive behaviour, this may have been the subcommittee's way of preemptively circumscribing the type of activism its members were prepared to endorse, and perhaps of countering in advance anticipated opposition; alternatively, the statement may simply reflect the demeanour of activist witnesses. The preamble goes on to specify:

> Their goal is to raise the profile of breast cancer as a major national health issue, to support appropriate research on breast cancer, to encourage an increase in research funding, particularly with respect to research into

the cause of breast cancer, to ensure that women and their families have access to up-to-date information on the disease, and to offer emotional support to women who are living and dying with the disease.[29]

The subcommittee's enthusiasm for a movement of patient organizations was thus framed within a vision, not of leadership or critique (as had distinguished the women's health movement), but of service-oriented support, and of advocacy that would eschew disruptive tactics while promoting the subcommittee's goal of moving breast cancer to the front of the research and policy agendas. In flagging the causes of breast cancer as a research priority, however, the subcommittee left wiggle room for advocacy challenges to the status quo. Although this modest proposal encountered some resistance from the then minister of national health and welfare, Benoît Bouchard, the subcommittee's vision prevailed in the end.[30]

During the hearings and beyond, the groups proliferated and expanded their activities to include a mix of peer support, education, and – from a variety of small-*p* political perspectives – advocacy. By February 1992, the group advocating for safe breast implants, Je sais/I know, had over eight hundred members across Canada, and Marcella Tardif had an office in east-end Montreal, where the phones rang constantly with calls from women whose doctors had dismissed their symptoms as unrelated to their implants. A Montreal group, Breast Cancer Action Montreal, was drawn to an emerging theory advanced by epidemiologist Devra Lee Davis. She challenged the claims that environmental toxins were a minor contribution to cancer, suggesting that more cancers than previously thought could be prevented by public health measures.[31]

Regionally, the province of Ontario proved a particularly fertile locus of growth for new organizations. At the time of the parliamentary hearings, Ontario lacked a breast cancer patient group dedicated to advocacy, and in late 1992, Pat Kelly, one of the activists who had testified before the subcommittee, cofounded the Toronto-based Alliance of Breast Cancer Survivors. The same year, following up on the recommendations in *Breast Cancer: Unanswered Questions*, Pat and Anne Rochon Ford, a long-time women's health activist, applied for funding from Health Canada's Ontario Region office to start a provincial network of breast cancer support groups.

They received a grant of $200,000 over two years to assist women who wanted to start self-help groups in their local communities; by the fall, the project was well underway, with fifteen local groups of various sizes.

I found no evidence that any of the breast cancer organizations formed before the 1991–92 parliamentary hearings had received funding from the industry. In their testimony to the subcommittee, in newspaper accounts of these start-up projects, and in interviews I conducted, members of the early groups cited shoestring budgets relying on volunteer labour, small membership fees, community goodwill, occasional modest legacy donations when members died, and small project grants from foundations or from their provincial or municipal governments. The earliest overture from the industry that I uncovered was in the spring of 1993. Breast Cancer Action Montreal and the Alliance of Breast Cancer Survivors, two groups that had begun with an explicit advocacy mandate, each staged public events in their respective cities to debate the pros and cons of the newly launched Breast Cancer Prevention Trial (BCPT). The BCPT was a large US-Canada clinical trial designed to determine whether tamoxifen, the breast cancer treatment drug, would be effective as a breast cancer preventive. Sue Groves, who was a member of the board of the Alliance of Breast Cancer Survivors, recalls, "[The panel on tamoxifen as a preventive] was one of the few big things we did ... I was approached by a pharma rep at that event. I remember her giving me a card and saying, 'We would like to help you.'" The overture would be one of many similar encounters for Sue, who remained active in breast cancer groups throughout the 1990s.

> And I slowly – at the beginning I was pretty innocent about this, not because I expected to take the money but because I couldn't really see why they'd be interested in us – It was more like, "Ooooh! That's interesting!" You know, that Pollyanna kind of thing. And then it dawning on me, "Oh, there's another agenda here."

Offers from the industry soon became both routine and a source of internal stress. Sue adds:

> There wasn't an event that we were at where I wasn't offered something like that kind of card ... where we would have a table in a community,

and these pharmaceutical cockroaches would come up and, you know, shove their cards in our face. And we talked about it [in the group], because there were some members who would say, "If we're struggling so badly, why *can't* we take this money?" And it really became an ethical thing.

As the breast cancer movement grew and more groups took on an advocacy role, the federal government tightened its policy regarding advocacy by civil society groups. Under Canada's welfare state regime, community-based groups had been eligible for government grants and could usually also gain registered charity status, a designation that Revenue Canada (now Canada Revenue Agency) awarded as long as the organization restricted its advocacy to small-*p* political stances and did not align itself with a particular political party. Groups could thus issue tax receipts to donors – a boon to their fundraising efforts. As far back as 1978, however, on the cusp of Canada's turn to neoliberalism, the federal government started to rein in the political activities of registered charities, even to the point of forbidding groups to write letters to the editor.

Breast Cancer Action Montreal had an early brush with the crackdown on civil society advocacy. The group began its fundraising in the tradition of movement organizations from the welfare state era. Its initial budget came from individual donations at the first meeting and from selling memberships at $20 each. By January 1993, the group's minutes recorded a budget for 1992 of $2,000, raised from memberships, donations, and small fundraising events, like a yard sale. The group applied for charitable tax status in the fall of 1992. In January 1993, Revenue Canada refused the group's application on the grounds that the group engaged in political advocacy. Why, members wondered, did the Canadian Cancer Society merit charitable status, whereas a group of patients who felt the society was not adequately addressing patients' interests and needs did not? With the help of a sympathetic lawyer working pro bono, the group appealed the decision, emphasizing its educational aims. In February 1993, Revenue Canada approved the application for charitable tax status. The group's annual revenues gradually increased: to $5,500 in 1994 and to $25,000 in 1996. The incident was prescient, however, of the ill-defined boundary between nonprofit educational work and political advocacy, and the ease with which this ambiguity can be leveraged to selectively sideline groups by starving them of resources if they seem to be threatening the status quo.

The relationship between federal government decision makers and the grassroots movement revived in early 1993. Plans moved ahead for a national consensus conference, to be called the National Forum on Breast Cancer, with Health and Welfare Canada (i.e., the federal Department of Health, now rebranded as Health Canada) providing the core funding and the organizational leadership of two public health physicians. As well, two national research agencies and two major cancer charities contributed both financial sponsorship and planning personnel. Notably, the pharmaceutical industry played no part in the planning process, nor did it contribute funding to support the meeting. Pat Kelly and I had both testified at the parliamentary hearings and were invited to jointly chair one of four planning subcommittees, the Support, Advocacy and Networking (SAN) Subcommittee.[32] The role of the subcommittee was to ensure that women with breast cancer from across the country were included throughout the planning process and participated in the forum itself with their families and other supporters. This goal was largely accomplished. An article in the *Globe and Mail*, for example, hailed the conference as a watershed event, citing the involvement of patients as key to the meeting's success.[33]

In both its strong emphasis on consumer participation and the absence of commercial participation, the forum's vision embodied the ideals of the international community health movement. The 1978 Declaration of Alma-Ata, for example, states that "people have a right and duty to participate individually and collectively in the planning and implementation of their health care."[34] Subsequent WHO documents, notably the 1986 Ottawa Charter for Health Promotion and the 1991 Sundsvall Statement on Supportive Environments for Health, reinforce the themes of strengthened community participation and empowerment through full information and funding support.[35] Sociologist Deena White writes that the community health movement's mandate – the coordination of health systems in the public interest and engaging consumers in health policy – was part of a strategy developed in the 1960s and 1970s to push back against the excessive use of technologies in health. She observes that engaging countervailing forces was a way to curtail rising costs inherent in the medical establishment's professional ambitions: "In this context, the community health approach was seen to hold promise for a more rational health care system that valued the expressed interests of patients and potential service users above competing professional interests such as high-technology work environments or intensive therapies."[36]

White cites two examples: Quebec CLSCs (community-based health centres, introduced in 1971 and run jointly by local governments and community action groups), and a project in Oregon (known as the Oregon plan) intended to gain community support for service rationing. In both cases, the project failed to empower lay actors. White interprets the failure as evidence that health administrators are actually the ones empowered: they tightly control consultations and public representation, making claims of democracy and public choice largely illusory; at the same time, public consultations reduce the uncertainty of public response to a novel initiative, while involving lay members on a decision-making board spreads the responsibility of "delicate decisions" to include the community.[37]

The strategy of engaging consumers to push back against commercial interests is consistent with the pharmaceutical industry's exclusion from the forum planning structure, which could only have been a deliberate decision. Judith Erola attended the forum as a delegate and the president of the Pharmaceutical Manufacturers Association of Canada, and when I asked her about the industry's absence as an official partner, she laughed and replied, "Well, no one invited us! I think, for me, I was very careful to not go in where it would be seen as an intrusion, or where you were not particularly welcome." Nonetheless, engaging patients as a countervailing force against excessive high-tech interventions and the attendant costs of intensive therapies assumes that patients are not drawn to such interventions, a questionable premise in the case of cancer patients, and especially, as medical anthropologist Patricia Kaufert observes, the middle-class women who dominated the breast cancer movement.[38]

In the months leading up to the national forum in November 1993, the issue of pharma funding surfaced among the members of the patients' subcommittee. A draft working paper on networking produced by a subset of the SAN Subcommittee members in August 1993 includes drug manufacturers in a list of possible funding sources for developing a national "survivor-directed, independent" network of breast cancer groups. On another front, the subcommittee had decided to mount a number of projects, including a photo exhibit portraying a woman who had died of breast cancer in each of the provinces and territories. This project reprised one in the United States, where a nationwide coalition of American groups had used a photo exhibit as a focal point at their first national rally the previous spring. The forum's budget did not include the estimated $5,000 needed to mount such a project. Health Canada was prepared to contribute half of the money (the exhibit included messages from the government leaders in each of the provinces and territories) but said that the patients' subcommittee would have to find matching funds. With the conference only a few months away, Pat Kelly proposed approaching a pharmaceutical company. I vehemently opposed the idea and was surprised that most other members of the subcommittee agreed with Pat, the vice-chair, and had no objection to asking a drug company for money to support the project. As chair of the subcommittee, however, I was responsible for the budget and exercised veto power, a decision some felt was undemocratic. With the conference date looming, Health Canada organized a series of phone calls and a meeting in which pharma funding was ruled out; Pat approached a clothing designer, who agreed to donate the money needed. Pat recalls:

> I had been down to see how the National Breast Cancer Coalition was doing its meetings in Washington – and ... I had seen this photo exhibit down there [funded by Bristol-Myers Squibb]; and then we got things rolling up here. And I thought, "Let's find out if Bristol-Myers Squibb can do something for us" ...
>
> But it never really went anywhere because you said, "No, we're not taking any pharma funding." I thought, "Why the hell not?" The US [activists] did it, and they're certainly not in bed with – I would never imagine them to be sort of an astroturf group.[39]

At the time, my prior experience as a journalist in the feminist and consumer rights movements was more influential in shaping my view than any understanding of drug company influence in medicine in general, or breast cancer in particular. Like others in the movement, I was still learning about the medical power systems, but I saw the forum as a critical moment for patient organizations to establish credibility among established players. Industry support of a project dedicated to patients and their supporters would be especially odd, I thought, given the industry's absence as a sponsor in the conference as a whole. In retrospect, arguments on both sides at this point presaged the divisions that would later rupture the movement; at the same time, they reflect the on-the-fly discourses of activists who were still relatively new to disease group advocacy and to the potential trade-offs of industry alliances.[40]

How Funding Shaped Post-forum Structures

The national forum's success, in particular, the central role accorded to patients, catalyzed women who participated to return home and start their own survivor-directed groups, which began to develop on a provincial and regional basis. Meanwhile, Health Canada set up a special national fund, the Canadian Breast Cancer Initiative, to address problems identified at the parliamentary hearings and the forum. The fund provided $25 million over five years to support breast cancer research and education, and to support projects of various kinds. Although the bulk of the money ($20 million) went to a dedicated breast cancer research fund, smaller initiatives included five regional information projects and a national infrastructure of local and regional grassroots groups with a central coordinating organization (the Canadian Breast Cancer Network). The latter was to serve as an information centre and would provide an advocacy voice for breast cancer survivors in Canada.[41]

All these organizations had varied mandates, and their cultures of action evolved over time. I focus, however, on the network of organizations most directly flowing from the parliamentary hearings and forum process, whose central mandates included community-based education, support, and advocacy (with various definitions as to what these terms mean), because the struggle over pharma funding was most significant in these groups. Over time, the stance each group took vis-à-vis the pharmaceutical industry became part of its identity within the movement.[42]

Initially, regional and local groups reflected the needs and resources of the patients involved. On the east coast, for example, patients who had been attending a support group for women with breast cancer decided, as Kathleen, one of the cofounders, put it, that "[they were] really interested in trying to make some changes in the system. [They wanted to] bring some issues to the attention of the government, or the Department of Health or the hospital, or whatever."

In 1994, they founded Breast Cancer Action Nova Scotia to improve services by raising awareness of the needs of people in the community affected by breast cancer. At first, the group "didn't need anything in terms of funding," said Kathleen, "because we weren't really doing any work! We were meeting, we would write letters to the [provincial] minister of health, or we had the minister of health come and speak with us. We might write a letter to the newspaper. That was more the type of thing that we were doing."

As the group established itself, organizations and agencies with health-related interests began to approach them to collaborate on small educational projects: two workshops on breast cancer and the environment, a patients' needs assessment, and another to assess the breast health needs of women of African heritage in the region. These provided the group with project funding, raised its profile, and established its local credibility.

Pat and Anne, who had already initiated the Alliance of Breast Cancer Survivors and the Breast Cancer Support Network for Ontario Project, conceived of an organization that would provide centralized resources to the many support groups the latter project had spawned. Their ambitious goal was to provide telephone support and treatment information by and for women in Ontario with breast cancer. They envisioned a woman-run centre housed in an attractive walk-in space in downtown Toronto, with a lending library, a 1-800 phone number, and materials tailored to under-served subgroups, including cultural communities, rural women, lesbians, and the disabled. When they approached the Ontario government for funding, "we got a grant of $25,000 just to write the proposal!" Pat exclaimed when I talked to her in 2007; "those were the old days." In June 1995, with a start-up grant of $200,000 in hand, they launched Willow.

Despite the flurry of government grants that became available as breast cancer gained political capital, the proliferation of organizations and the demands on them raised concerns about staffing and long-term sustain-

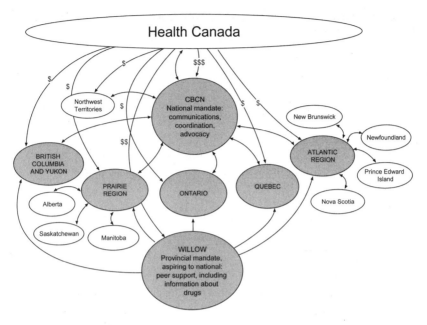

FIGURE 1 Breast cancer group structure, mid- and late 1990s

ability. Pat was project director of the Breast Cancer Support Network for Ontario Project:

> Women would complain, "You're not organizing us into meetings often enough" ... We were getting this pressure, "when this ends, we want a clearinghouse. We want to be able to stay connected and have these training sessions [in how to run support groups]." You know, you have $200,000 for two years. The expectations were so high that it was just sort of crippling.

The structure of groups at that point had begun to take the shape depicted in Figure 1. Although every group engaged in local fundraising efforts, the overall picture reflected the influence of the federal government: the Canadian Breast Cancer Network (CBCN), located in the capital (Ottawa), a dense network of support in the richest and most populous province, and regional structures that mapped onto the five information projects funded through the Canadian Breast Cancer Initiative.

Internal Discourses about Pharma-Funding Overtures

Women active at the time recall the post-forum period as a turning point for overtures from drug companies. "It was about then that the pharmaceutical companies started recognizing us because of the Montreal forum – there was such a high profile," Pat says. Burlington Breast Cancer Support Services, the local group she had cofounded, began to receive calls from the pharma companies. These offers of funding came just as the groups were under pressures to expand and they provoked anguished discussions. Sarah Spinks, a member of the Alliance of Breast Cancer Survivors (ABCS), explains that the discussions took place at a time when the group was undergoing rapid growth, which created pressures to find more funds:

> We began to feel we needed a professionally led support group. People were so sick, we were having trouble keeping people in the group – they were scared off by the really sick women. We felt we needed a skilled facilitator. We eventually did hire one, and it helped. We needed to get ahead, to work harder. [The discussion about pharma money] was at the moment when we needed money for things like that.

Another pressure point that led members of the ABCS to discuss pharma funding was the group's ambition to become an advocacy force for cancer prevention. Members were "very, very keen" on making breast cancer prevention a priority, says Sarah, and they particularly wanted to draw attention to the potential causal relationship between environmental contaminants and breast cancer. Lack of resources held them back; nonetheless, members were almost unanimous in their opposition to taking funds from the industry. Sue recalls, "We went to the discussion table over it. We really struggled with it." Ultimately, those who argued against accepting pharma funding prevailed. She explains:

> We wanted to be unbiased, and there's no such thing as a free lunch. And why, if we're trying to be the voice of the community, why should we taint this voice with money from a private interest? I mean, we were quite happy taking government money, but you know, that didn't seem as compromising for us; if we could get our hands on government money

that was fine ... But amongst it, rightly or wrongly, was the notion that these people [working at pharmaceutical companies] are in this industry to make money out of cancer. And although many of us had taken the drugs that they were selling, and therefore may or may not be alive if we hadn't, we didn't think that had a place in what we were trying to do as a survivor organization. And that was the voice that continued.

At Willow, which had geared up after receiving its $200,000 grant, the board meetings became a site of intense debates about pharma funding. The new board was a mix of breast cancer survivors (50 percent, as mandated by the group's charter), women's health activists, high-profile women from the entertainment and media worlds, and women with connections to business. In June 1995, as they headed toward a splashy launch at the Royal York Hotel in Toronto, tensions ran high. Cofounder Pat, who had been hired as Willow's executive director once the group received the grant money, recalls:

When we were doing publicity for the launch, we were sending out faxes by hand. And that's when the pharmaceutical companies started coming in and saying, "Oh, this is a fabulous event, do you have sponsorship?" ... And this one guy approached us and he said, "You know, this is a really important event and we'd like to help sponsor it." And [his company] gave us – twenty [thousand]? – maybe five thousand dollars ... And it was about the same time that Taxol was just coming out.[43]

The group's minutes from September 1995 corroborate the amount as $5,000, received from the French pharmaceutical company Rhône-Poulenc (now Sanofi-Aventis), which had developed Taxotere, a competitor to Bristol-Myers Squibb's Taxol. Throughout that fall, Anne recalls, the issue of corporate funding was "the hot button with Willow." Anne describes herself as being part of a subset of the inaugural board that had strong opinions against pharma funding:[44]

Some of the more high-powered women on the board and their connections were talking up sources of money with people they knew in industry, and [in] the banking world as well. The CIBC was a big backer of Willow in the early days. And Home Depot also gave a lot of money and in-kind service. But one of the board members felt very strongly that we should pay attention to an overture that had been made by Procter & Gamble. Somebody [from the company] approached her and asked her to go take it to the board. And that was sort of the beginning of the demise.

Procter & Gamble had offered to train workers for the organization's 1-800 line, and the company became a case in point at the board meetings for discussions about the ethics of industry funding. A few years earlier, an American journalist had written an exposé critical of the company's business and environmental practices, prompting some Canadian environmental groups to organize a boycott of its products.[45] An initial discussion at Willow was framed generally as "the ethical practices of large companies with whom we may choose to do business."[46]

In November 1995, Anne called another meeting to discuss ethical issues related to fundraising in more depth. Board members were encouraged to read the book about Procter & Gamble in preparation, and Anne drew from work she had done in the women's health movement to present a critical history of the pharmaceutical industry's harms to women. She gave examples of women's health groups in Canada and the United States that did not take money from drug companies, emphasizing their belief that accepting pharma funds would compromise their ability to speak critically about industry practices. She gave other examples of groups that were open to pharma funding. In the end, the board agreed it would "view each case individually, paying particular attention to pharmaceutical companies."[47]

At Breast Cancer Action Montreal (BCAM), the year 1995 also saw a series of industry overtures that prompted internal debate. The first came in January. The San Francisco–based biotech company Genentech, which was recruiting patients in the United States and Canada for clinical trials for the new breast cancer treatment Herceptin (trastuzumab), sponsored a meeting for activists near Washington, DC. BCAM was invited to the meeting through its informal links to the California-based group Breast Cancer Action, which was convinced the drug had value. Borrowing a page from AIDS activists, Breast Cancer Action had demanded that the company make the drug available on a compassionate basis to women who might benefit from it. Genentech rejected the request, prompting Breast Cancer Action to demonstrate at the company's headquarters in December 1994. The company responded by inviting representatives from several activist groups to meet to air their concerns; the company would pay the costs of the meeting. Montreal was one of the Canadian sites for clinical trials and with encouragement from the American organization, in January 1995, BCAM sent a representative to Washington and, in April 1995, to a subsequent follow-up to the meeting in San Antonio.[48]

An entry in the board minutes in the following months suggests misgivings about the decision, and an internal call for the group to begin thinking about a policy: "What is [our] stand on flying off on drug company junkets?" Board members saw the interaction with Genentech as different from using pharmaceutical company grants to run organizational programs; rather, the purpose was to address a difference of perspective between activists and company representatives – arguably, exactly the type of policy consultation the group was established to promote. Nonetheless, the meetings were held in high-end hotels, complete with pricey meals; being guests in this corporate environment highlighted the financial and power differences between the group and the industry, as well as the contradiction between dining out on company largesse while attempting to speak for patients on drug policy questions.

The Genentech encounters were not an isolated case for BCAM; the May board minutes record a discussion of three overtures from different pharmaceutical companies in the previous month. One, described in detail and more unsettling than the Genentech meetings (which were at least fairly transparent in purpose), involved a visit to the group's office by a woman who said she was representing "a client," but wouldn't reveal who the client was. A series of leading questions suggested that she wanted to galvanize the group to lobby to have the drug Taxotere (docetaxel) included on the provincial drug formulary as a treatment for breast cancer. When the visitor repeatedly refused to say whom she represented, she was asked to leave the office.

Several factors helped heighten BCAM's wariness toward the pharmaceutical industry and reinforced its commitment to discussing drug harms as well as benefits. In early 1994, the group found itself at the centre of a political storm that implicated a local surgeon in a high-profile research fraud case involving breast cancer clinical trials. Deena Dlusy-Apel, who was on the board at the time, recalls:

> It's such a demystification process! ... And it also makes you very, very cautious. It makes you want to tell everybody that, if they're going to be in a [research] protocol, to make sure that they are in the best protocol available to them. And also, of course, we started finding out that the drug companies were the ones funding a lot of these things [clinical trials]. And what were they trying to find out? How to sell more pills! More chemicals! And we found out that they were the same ones making the chemicals that were poisoning us in the first place. So it was just an ongoing revelation of information.

Added to the clinical trials fraud, Breast Cancer Action Montreal had begun to share office space in January 1995 with the women's health advocacy group, DES Action Canada, which had worked for over a decade to educate the public about diethylstilbestrol (DES) and its effects, including an elevated risk of breast cancer in DES mothers. DES Action continued to pressure the federal government for stronger drug safety regulations, and BCAM's informal affiliation with the older group helped shape its early policy stances on pharmaceutical issues. Indeed, across groups, the arguments of advocates opposed to pharma funding drew in large part from the 1980s feminist critique of the pharmaceutical industry and deployed a coherent discourse to support this position. By contrast, the initial arguments of those defending industry funding remained superficial (e.g., "Why not?" or "Other groups do it") and lacked an ethical edge.

Industry overtures and the debates they engendered were not unique to Canada and were certainly part of the American movement's experience. As mentioned, Bristol-Myers Squibb supported the US national advocacy organization's photo exhibit, and Genentech hosted two national meetings for advocacy groups while conducting clinical trials for Herceptin. Despite the extensive documentation of the US movement, however, accounts chronicling the relationship to the pharmaceutical industry are spotty.[49] Those that exist suggest that relationships with big pharma began about the same time as they did in Canada and aroused similar internal debates. American anthropologist Mary K. Anglin provides two instructive accounts based on an ethnographic study she began in 1992 of a grassroots group in Northern California she identifies with the pseudonym "NORCAL."[50] She describes a series of meetings between representatives from the breast cancer group and Bristol-Myers Squibb (makers of Taxol), Burroughs Wellcome (makers of Navelbine), and Genentech (makers of Herceptin). The meetings, which included an expensive dinner, were formative for that group's discourse on the ethics of pharma funding. The first took place in 1993, when Taxol was about to be released and when the Clinton administration was attempting health care reform. Although ostensibly organized to review research proposals and data on experimental treatments for breast cancer, Anglin says the meetings "became forums in which drug companies instead discussed 'health care reform' and the problems it created for industry."[51]

In an apparent attempt to sway the group against the US administration's proposal to introduce a Canadian-style, single-payer insurance system, the representative from Bristol-Myers Squibb told members that drugs like Taxol would not be available in a Canadian model of health care. At one meeting, when an activist challenged the company's agenda-shifting tactics, the drug company reps threatened to withdraw their commitment to the breast cancer community. The activist backed away from her challenge and the meeting continued. The activists concluded that in buying them dinner, the company had "bought our silence" – or at least purchased the company's right to have first say in a discussion. Determined that they should set the agenda of such meetings, they resolved to accept "no more meals." Subsequent meetings with Burroughs Wellcome and Genentech reinforced the group's disillusionment about the possibility of breast cancer groups negotiating as equal partners with big pharma. Viewed from a Canadian perspective, Anglin's account underlines the pharmaceutical industry's preference for the (then) American status quo of privately funded health care over a Canadian-style system. The account also foreshadowed the attraction breast cancer advocacy groups would hold for individual companies as they brought new, more costly breast cancer treatments to market.

Advocacy Discourse on Tamoxifen and Taxol Drug Trials

In 1991, tamoxifen was widely accepted as the standard hormonal treatment drug for breast cancer. Based on the drug's treatment success, Canadian and American researchers launched a large US-Canada clinical trial, the BCPT, designed to study tamoxifen's potential as a way to prevent breast cancer. At the same time, Taxol and Herceptin, two new treatments for breast cancer, were in the drug treatment pipeline and nearing clinical trials. The introduction of new treatments, along with the study to test a cancer treatment drug as a preventive, gave the newly formed groups a chance to shape the discursive construction of these technologies. What balance of risks and benefits were their members prepared to accept? The confluence of patient activism and novel treatment approaches (both Taxol and Herceptin had different mechanisms of action than the existing therapies) also opened up new marketing opportunities for the companies. As these American experiences suggest, the result was a dance in which each partner could be caught off-guard by the other's moves. In Canada, this potential to surprise is seen in two early advocacy efforts: the first centred on the clinical trial to test tamoxifen as a preventive, and the second on gaining access to Taxol.

The research group behind the BCPT, the highly regarded Pittsburgh-based National Surgical Adjuvant Breast and Bowel Project, had been conducting clinical trials to study treatments for breast cancer for decades. Although the prevention trial seemed poised for success, with significant backing from the US-based National Cancer Institute and many experts in the cancer research and policy fields, a feminist women's health organization based in Washington, DC, the National Women's Health Network (NWHN), developed a strong critique, led by physician Adriane Fugh-Berman, arguing that the study subjected healthy women to unacceptable risk.[52] The broader principle, the NWHN argued, was that public health interventions demand a higher level of safety than do treatment interventions because they are administered to large populations of healthy people, most of whom would never become sick from the disease in question. A woman given tamoxifen to treat cancer, by contrast, is known to be at risk of dying of the cancer, and this fact allows a greater tolerance for harm from the treatment. As Fugh-Berman put it, "You wouldn't normally jump off the roof of your house, but if your house is on fire, you might."[53]

Some prominent members of the scholarly and drug policy communities questioned the trial for reasons much like those of the NWHN activists. At the parliamentary hearings, the tamoxifen prevention study elicited support, ambivalence, and opposition from both researchers and members of breast cancer groups. In 1993, Breast Cancer Action Montreal and the ABCS entered the fray; each sponsored a large public panel discussion featuring Adriane Fugh-Berman and two local health professionals. Their goal was to promote public discourse about the trial's ethical and medical controversies.

For the two groups, sponsorship of the events was consistent with their commitment to environmental advocacy, which they had articulated in statements of concern about the lack of research and policies to understand and address the causes of breast cancer and the largely unexplained rise in rates. In publicly targeting a high-profile international project, however, the groups were taking a bold step, asserting their willingness to question mainstream scientific opinion and values. They argued that researchers and cancer policy makers were prepared to invest money studying cancer prevention using a pill – and one with known toxic, even fatal, side effects – while underfunding research into causes of the disease. In publicly bringing these concerns to the fore, the groups directly challenged a host of powerful actors: the research group that had designed and spearheaded the study; local practitioner-researchers recruiting volunteers; the US National Cancer Institute, which approved and funded the trial; and AstraZeneca, the maker of Nolvadex (tamoxifen), which provided the research team with the drug and stood to see its potential market expand by 29 million women in the United States alone if the study demonstrated a preventive benefit from tamoxifen.[54]

The drug Taxol inspired the ABCS to undertake a different type of advocacy project. Taxol had an unusual history, dating back to 1964 when a US National Cancer Institute research program discovered that taxol, an extract from the bark of the Pacific yew tree, had anticancer properties. The discovery languished for decades because the compound was naturally occurring and could not be patented. Promising Phase 2 clinical trial results were first reported in 1989. In order to move taxol to market, the US government gave the American pharmaceutical company Bristol-Myers Squibb exclusive rights to provide the extract from Pacific yew trees under a 1991 agreement. The company developed a semisynthetic method of production that made it patentable, and in 1994 taxol became Taxol. The US Food and Drug Administration (FDA) approved Taxol to treat metastatic ovarian cancer in 1992; in April 1994, the agency approved the drug in the United States as a second-line treatment for metastatic breast cancer (i.e., to be used if standard chemotherapy treatment fails).[55]

Taxol was being studied in clinical trials in Canada to treat ovarian cancer at the time of the parliamentary hearings on breast cancer and was creating a buzz as an exciting new cancer treatment. In testimony to the subcommittee, Dr. Joe Pater, the director of clinical trials at the National Cancer Institute of Canada, cited the drug as an example of how publicity about new treatments could misinform the public: "We're doing a randomized trial [of Taxol] in ovarian cancer, not breast cancer ... The exaggeration [in the media] as to the potential benefit of this drug makes it very difficult to explain to patients that it's not going to cure their cancer. It might cause it to go into regression."[56]

By 1994, clinical trials to study Taxol as a treatment for metastatic breast cancer were underway in Canada, and the ABCS decided to lobby the provincial government to include the drug on its formulary for patients suffering from advanced breast cancer. Sue Groves, who was on the board at that time, recalls:

> We had a board member, a lovely woman, who had liver mets [metastasis] and she was on Taxol ... She had young children. It was really giving her a lease, not on – there wasn't a belief [among members of the group] that she was going to survive – but there was certainly a quality of life that she was experiencing which we as survivors and nonsurvivors were incredibly impressed by; ... Taxol kind of broke some barriers for women living with metastatic disease. It was easier to tolerate. I mean it wasn't a cakewalk, but ... it was certainly easier to tolerate than Adriamycin.

The group's favourable impression of Taxol was compounded when the affected board member introduced the others to a second woman with advanced breast cancer whom she had befriended. The latter, a lecturer at York University in Toronto, was able to return to work after she began taking the drug. The board's members found it "amazing" to see two women doing so well, said Sue. They thought, "Not only are these women living longer, they are actually able to live their lives!" Inspired, they became critical of restrictions on the drug's access:

> So we then became *really* pissed off that only a certain number of women were able to get access to this drug because it was only being funded through certain [research] protocols. And so ... we went to the provincial Parliament. And we had a question raised in the House, and it was "Please, can this be looked at?"

Sue remembers the Ontario Parliament giving the Taxol access question "pretty short shrift," but the group had also organized a press conference, and media coverage was extensive. "And, eventually, the Taxol bar was lifted," said Sue, though she was uncertain how significant the group's efforts were in the outcome.[57]

Pat Kelly, no longer active in the ABCS but involved in several other breast cancer groups, suggests that the pharmaceutical industry was a player in the Taxol lobby. In an interview I conducted with her in 2007, she told me she first heard about the lobby when a representative from Taxol's manufacturer, Bristol-Myers Squibb, approached her and said she was working with the professor from York University. The drug rep thought that, given the extent of Pat's involvement in the breast cancer movement, she should know about this case. "It turned out that she had been paying for [Taxol] herself for about two years," Pat says. "It was the only way she could get the drug. And she had very advanced breast cancer, and she was continuing to be quite functional. She was teaching and, I mean, it was one of those Lazarus sorts of stories."

Sue, however, had no recollection of the representative from Bristol-Myers Squibb: "So whether or not there was any backdoor engineering from pharma, I don't know," said Sue. I really can't say that there was; it certainly didn't feel like it at the time, but I was much more innocent then. It was the very beginnings, in terms of our community."

Pat cited another reason for believing Taxol should be available to Canadian patients with breast cancer: it was being prescribed in the United States. Along with her activism in community groups, she was updating a handbook about breast cancer for patients with an oncologist from her local cancer treatment centre, and she asked him what he intended to write about Taxol. He didn't want to mention the drug because it wasn't available in Canada and he had no experience using it with patients. "Don't raise expectations," he cautioned. "It's not out there." Pat recalls:

> And I said, "Well wait a minute. If they're using it in the US" ... You know, this is the time of the whole Krever Inquiry [into the contamination of Canada's blood system] where ... the US Red Cross had been screening for HIV/AIDS for almost a year before Canada started screening. And the Krever Inquiry statement was "You can't ignore standard of care in another country." So I thought, "How can we say that we're going to apply this [principle] in screening for blood, but we're not going to apply that to clinical practice?"
>
> So that really got me, I think it was a true disparity ... We didn't think we could afford to screen [blood for HIV/AIDS]. Well, it turned out we couldn't afford not to ... [And Taxol] represented a dramatic shift in the way we had been treating breast cancer previously; so this was a whole new gold standard for treatment.[58]

Pat's argument invoking the Krever Inquiry to establish an ethical principle in favour of drug access bears close attention because a similar discourse later formed the basis for drug treatment lobbies by patient organizations. Reading Justice Krever's recommendations, I would not interpret anything in them to imply that Canada is obliged to adopt a standard of care implemented in other countries; on the contrary, the recommendations explicitly state that Canada should make its own regulatory decisions about blood products. Referencing the move to international harmonization, Justice Krever welcomes the potential benefits of international collaborations as standardized formats for submitting information, sharing information on product reviews, and inspections based on good manufacturing practices. He then adds this caveat:

> The Bureau of Biologics and Radiopharmaceuticals must, however, retain the authority to make the licensing decisions for Canada. It must also retain the authority and the ability to conduct its own inspections and lot-by-lot reviews of biological drugs, particularly blood products.[59]

Krever's report, in fact, stresses the need for regulatory safety above all. Recommendation 2e states, "The goal of the blood supply system must be to supply safe therapies to persons who need them. The principle of safety must transcend other principles and policies."[60] In his emphasis on safety, Justice Krever places the blood supply service firmly within the purview of the public health system – an area of medicine concerned with disease prevention and the maintenance of good health rather than disease treatment. The report states:

> The safety of the blood supply is an aspect of public health, and, therefore, the blood supply system must be governed by the public health philosophy, which rejects the view that complete knowledge of a potential health hazard is a prerequisite for action.
>
> The balancing of the risks and benefits of taking action should be dependent not only on the likelihood of the risk materializing but also on the severity of the effect if the risk does materialize, on the number of persons who could be affected, and on the ease of implementing protective or preventive measures. The more severe the potential effect, the lower the threshold should be for taking action.[61]

I concur with Pat's claim that we couldn't afford not to screen the blood supply for the two viruses; I differ with her extension of the same logic to approving new drug treatments. The point underlying Justice Krever's analysis is essentially the same one that Fugh-Berman made in her argument against using tamoxifen for the prevention of breast cancer: public health has different historical and philosophical roots than the medical treatment of disease. Maintaining a secure blood supply is comparable to maintaining a safe water supply; it is not analogous to deciding on whether or not to adopt a new drug into practice. The logic of Pat's analogy, which compares the urgency of adopting new practices to improved safety in the blood system despite gaps in scientific knowledge can't simply be transposed to the adoption of new medications, which pose safety risks of their own.

Structural Cracks Portend a Major Rift

In several groups, the pharma-funding issue fractured the board. Anne

Rochon Ford of Willow recalls discussions during successive board meetings becoming increasingly heated, with the tenor of the discussions about pharma funding following a pattern:

> The nature of it was always this one person in particular coming forward and presenting [the issue] like this was a no-brainer – "Why would we *not* take their money?" [She would make] exactly the kinds of statements that get raised over and over and over again, like "All money is dirty money; why can't we just put it to clean use?" or "Pharma is no different from banks or any other big corporations; why do we make a distinction?" ... And it just escalated and escalated.

Eventually, feeling more and more isolated, Anne resigned. She says:

> You know [with the stresses of getting the organization up and running] it wouldn't have taken much for us to kind of fall apart and for some of us to just walk out, which is what ended up happening. I walked out of a meeting and basically never came back ... The pharma-funding issue was the line in the sand that I wasn't prepared to go past. I disagreed with too many people on the board. And at that point, if I recall correctly, it was a majority who was then [saying], "Let's go for it."

A similar tension was felt in the ABCS's meetings, though in this case the dynamics were reversed. Sarah remembers Pat as the group's outlier on the issue:

> We were very skeptical of working with the pharmas; we were very opposed to it, except for Pat. She was much more keen on [us taking pharma funding] because we needed money. She felt – and she was right on this point – that if we were going to be an organization that made a difference, we were going to have to push harder.
>
> I was very aware of that issue [conflicts of interest] and very suspicious ... We had several discussions – long discussions. There was a lot of concern about it because we thought we might need to say things the companies didn't like. We thought, "Holy moly, this could be very problematic!" ... It was the advocacy we were worried about, that we would

look tainted if we took it – and of course, if we took it, we would have to be open.

In the end, all of the board members opposed the industry as a source of funding except for Pat, who left the ABCS about this time to work on starting Willow. The remaining members of the ABCS chose to proceed frugally, without paid staff. "Our credo was 'Don't spend it if you don't have it,'" says Sue. "The only time we got money was when someone died ... And because we didn't have a very big investment in spending money, we didn't owe anything to anybody."

What began as a minor, intermittent dilemma for the groups to resolve internally was taking on larger dimensions, soon to be exacerbated by new government policies about the funding of advocacy groups.

External Pressures to Accept Pharma Funds

In the early 1990s, Liberal member of Parliament John Bryden took up the cause of restricting grants and charitable status in the nonprofit sector, arguing that Revenue Canada should revoke the charitable status of those organizations that obviously exist primarily to lobby the government or the public.[62] In 1996, Revenue Canada made administrative changes to the reporting requirements for groups with charitable status, including stricter monitoring for compliance. Taken at face value, claims that groups designated "charitable" and "nonprofit" should have some accountability to the public were not without merit or public appeal – the donations they received were, after all, subsidized in part by the taxpayer. Many working in civil society organizations, however, felt the call for greater scrutiny allowed governments to selectively shut down legitimate debate.

At the same time that their advocacy role was being curtailed, civil society groups were being recast as cheap service providers who were left, as one critic observed, with "more responsibility but no voice."[63] Bryden in his report on Canada's charities expressed a different concern. Taking note that governments were now offloading to charities the social services they traditionally supplied, he worried that these groups had no oversight to ensure they met adequate performance standards.[64] Again, the face validity of this observation obscures the central questions of which parties were benefiting, and at whose expense. The purpose of offloading was to downsize government and save money by eliminating the jobs of salaried, unionized professionals who had previously provided these services and who could be held accountable as employees. The suggestion that community workers, who were often volunteers or only modestly reimbursed, should fill the resulting service gap while submitting to external surveillance to ensure quality standards reflects both the move to exploitative work conditions and the subtle control over civil society resistance and pressure for social change.[65]

Internal debates about pharma funding within breast cancer groups were thus held against a backdrop of government advocacy chill, added pressures to provide professional-level community services, and a culture of surveillance – all of which undermined the previous relationship of trust and collaboration the groups had built with the government. The Women's Advisory Committee of PMAC (Pharmaceutical Manufacturers Association of Canada), meanwhile, was encouraging its member companies to provide funds to women's health organizations in the community; this was done, Judith Erola emphasized, "as a very much no-strings-attached sort of thing."

In health policy, the early to mid-1990s was a period of rapid transition in two key areas: single-payer health care and pharmaceutical policy. Canada's single-payer health care system came under increasing strain as the federal government struggled to bring its deficit under control while coping with rising medical costs; Canada abandoned compulsory licensing and curtailed the generic drug industry in return for an industry promise of more research and development spending by the brand-name pharmaceutical companies, and took steps to reduce drug review times. The new anticancer agents that began to emerge from the pipelines of pharmaceutical and biotech companies carried with them price tags previously unseen. In Canada, a five-year course of tamoxifen, with its many generics, was still priced at about $11.30 per month, or $680 for the full five years; Taxol rang in at about $14,000 for a full course, and Herceptin, which was still in clinical trials, would eventually tally about $8,000 a month. These prices were already causing sticker shock in the patchwork of private insurers and provincial governments, which had to decide whether to include these new drugs on their formularies. How the growing community of breast cancer organizations would respond was still to be seen.

The free trade agreements opened the door for private American management firms to take over public health care services in Canada, including hospitals, though the Canada Health Act's requirement for public administration was a disincentive to such purchases. The agreements themselves may have been less important than the public discourse about health care that was part of the FTA and NAFTA era, which depicted health care less as a shared responsibility serving the public interest than a business. Seen through this lens, Canada's national debt and the fragile economy in the early 1990s were the result of Canadians living beyond their means and misusing the health care system – a claim that drew attention away from the real inefficiencies of the hospital-based, curative approach to health.[66]

In 1993, the Liberal Party regained power federally but adapted the neoliberal agenda the Progressive Conservatives had put in place. They recognized that the public remained committed to the health care system (once the centrepiece of their policy achievements) and used the stealth tactic of reducing transfer payments to the provinces rather than overt attacks. The reduced transfer payments cascaded through the system: hospital budgets were cut and patients were sent home sooner to be cared for by unpaid family members; casual employees were used to supplement full-time, unionized staff in nursing, cleaning, and food services; and traditional ideals of volunteerism were invoked to shift the burden of support, care, and fundraising onto community organizations, businesses, families, and individuals. News stories about hospital deficits and opinion pieces in the largely conservative mainstream media reinforced the claim that managers of health care institutions should adopt a competition-based business model, even though the single-payer system had repeatedly been shown to be more economical to administer than a privatized system.[67]

Despite pressures to erode single-payer health care, the flaws in the free-market argument also encouraged resistance from many actors within the system. The signs of struggle within the breast cancer movement over pharma funding bore elements of the contrasting public responses to these radical systemic changes. Calls for a greater emphasis on prevention, a cautious approach to new treatments, and a stance independent from the pharmaceutical industry resonated with the public health goals of disease prevention and a universally available care system based on need

and treatment effectiveness. Demands that more money be spent on finding a breast cancer cure, policies to make new treatments rapidly available,
and the acceptance of pharmaceutical company funds were more consistent
with a curative model of health, with free-market economics, and with
a neoliberal ideal of small government, economic growth, and business
norms of operation. At this point, however, the groups had not clearly
incorporated neoliberal discourse into their cultures of action.

The federal government's embrace of free-market ideology revived the
rhetoric of drug lag, recasting drug safety regulations as impediments to
efficiency, economic development, and making life-saving treatments
available to patients. In 1994, the Liberal government introduced the
Regulatory Efficiency Act (Bill C-62) to "modernize" and "streamline" the
bureaucracy under the rationale of controlling the federal budget; the US
government introduced a similar reform the same year, singling out the
FDA as a target.[68] Todd Weiler, a lawyer who worked on drafting Bill C-62,
described the proposed Canadian legislation as a mere procedural change
"to improve the way in which Canada regulates risk,"[69] but critics accused
the government of a covert agenda that would sacrifice the safety of ordinary Canadians to profit business elites. In the end, the act died on the
order paper.[70]

The spirit of regulatory efficiency was nonetheless already guiding
changes to the drug regulatory system. In 1992, as a strategy for speeding
drug approvals, Canada introduced the use of expert advisory committees
(i.e., contract reviewers) to conduct the first review of New Drug Submissions.[71] Opponents of the committees argued that outside reviewers
had only one or two days of training and were poorly supervised, or they
were consultants with conflicts of interest because they both conducted
tests and prepared submissions for industry.[72] In 1995, the Therapeutic
Products Directorate adopted another controversial program, cost recovery, following a trend within federal departments to charge user fees for
its services. Fees charged to the pharmaceutical industry were expected to
reach $40 million per year, raising fears that the companies could pressure
the government to reciprocate with faster approval times, which could in
turn compromise safety – a charge the Health Protection Branch "vehemently denied."[73]

Government funding cuts and pressures to take on more responsibilities were obvious contributors to stresses within the groups; the gradual shifts in discourses about health care, pharmaceutical policy, and safety were additional, more subtle, forces that began to fragment the movement. By the middle of the decade, the boards of numerous groups had articulated arguments in favour of and against pharma funding (see Table 1). None of the groups had actual experience working with drug companies on an ongoing basis, however, and the discourse in favour of pharma funding, despite having vocal adherents, was still sketchy and ethically weak. A competing discourse drew from the women's health community's experience in the previous two decades and was grounded in an understanding of pharmaceutical marketing techniques, but outside research to support these arguments was limited.

TABLE 1
Early 1990s discourses about pharma funding

Discourses in favour	Discourse against
Mutual benefit	
It's a win-win exchange: good PR for the company and money for us to provide services.	The exchange is profoundly unequal. Pharma's "win" goes beyond PR to promoting new product lines to a captive target audience, which has potential downsides for the group, including subtle pressure to give biased information about the company's product, a distortion of the group's priorities in favour of the company's, and loss of reputation if the group is perceived to be in pharma's pocket.
The need justifies the end	
Yes. Fundraising is hard work. We need the money for our services, and we can't afford to be purists. All money is dirty; pharma money is no different, but we can put it to clean use.	No. Pharma money is tempting because it's easiest, but other companies might donate without compromising the group's basic purpose and ethical values. Members and potential collaborators need to trust us to put patients' needs first; an obvious conflict of interest puts our ability to do that in doubt. Some companies that sell cancer treatments have marketed improperly tested drugs that have caused harm to many women. Some produce pesticides that may contribute to cancer; others have been fined for dumping chemicals in the environment, or cited for poor employment practices or other human rights breaches.

▶

Discourses in favour	Discourse against
Our members would support it	
Most women don't care where the money comes from, they just want help; if we refuse pharma money, we're turning our backs on their need.	Don't assume indifference – canvass your members to find out how members feel about the group taking industry funds. Some may not care, especially when facing a life-threatening disease, but they may simply have not given the question much thought. Make the topic one for discussion and learning.
It's strings-free	
What's the problem? The money is strings-free. The company's representatives seem sincere, and the company gave to us before and never asked for anything.	Strings can be invisible; a company's donations are targeted to groups whose purpose is related to their product lines, so the group can expect to be promoting sales in some way. The employees who contact the group may sincerely want to help the organization, but the company is beholden to shareholders and is obliged to try to make a profit. A no-strings agreement now doesn't preclude the company making later demands on the group to provide recognition to the company or to silence criticism.
It's the norm	
Other groups do it; why shouldn't we?	You can't serve two masters; choosing to put patients' needs first shows leadership that others may follow

Sources: Author interviews; Anne Rochon Ford, *A Different Prescription: Considerations for Women's Health Groups Contemplating Funding from the Pharmaceutical Industry* (Toronto: National Network on Environments and Women's Health, 1990).

4

Advocacy Redefined

During the breast cancer movement's first five years, local groups had enough novelty on their side to garner community support and money from various provincial programs and foundations, while the national group had funding from the five-year Canadian Breast Cancer Initiative. To the extent that pharma funding was discussed, it was a back-burner issue that surfaced periodically when a particular situation prompted internal discussion. Between late 1996 and 2001, however, the community split into two camps, staking out opposing positions on the question of pharma funding. I call this the contestation period. Debates that had taken place within the confines of board meetings were formalized and moved into public forums as conference debates and prescriptive documents. Groups formulated these competing perspectives against a backdrop of continued neoliberalization, which reshaped federal health care and pharmaceutical policies, and redefined civil society advocacy.

Government and Policy Actors

Throughout the latter part of the 1990s, international trade agreements continued to reshape national policies in Canada, including the regulation of pharmaceuticals. In 1998, the federal government reviewed and decided to renew the 1993 law that had abolished compulsory licensing and set up the Patented Medicine Prices Review Board.[1] Broad-based concerns about the health care system prompted the establishment of two large inquiries: a Royal Commission headed by former Saskatchewan premier Roy Romanow and a Senate inquiry chaired by Senator Michael

Kirby with cochair Marjory LeBreton.[2] Pharmaceutical policy was a dominant theme in both reports, in part because drug costs were among the fastest-rising costs in health care but also because pharmaceutical policy in Canada is a patchwork that lacks the coherence of health care policy in general and cries out for attention.[3] Complicating this picture was the pressure on Canada to align its pharmaceutical policies with standards set by the International Conference on Harmonisation (ICH), a regulatory unit formed in 1990 by the pharmaceutical companies and governments in the United States, the European Union, and Japan to provide a transnational regulatory framework for drug approvals and post-market reporting of adverse reactions. (In October 2015, the ICH rebranded itself as the International Council for Harmonisation of Technical Requirements for Pharmaceuticals for Human Use, an organizational change designed in part to expand the membership, involving more drug regulators.) The ICH, a product of globalization, divided pharmaceutical policy analysts. Proponents accept its ostensible purpose – to serve the public by freeing up new funds for drug development and by making drugs available to patients more quickly. Critics argue that safety standards have been compromised and that a more likely motive is to maintain the industry's competitive position in the marketplace.[4]

The federal government under the Liberal Party of Jean Chrétien continued the move begun under the Conservative regime of Prime Minister Brian Mulroney, away from the welfare state and toward a trade-based, neoliberal governance model. The reconfigured Canadian state placed increasing constraints on the growing patient-group movement. Finance Minister Paul Martin had included a promise to review the federal government's policies on interest groups in his 1994 budget speech and, the next year, following the Treasury Board's review, he announced in the House of Commons that "our approach to interest group funding will change."[5] Some groups would be moved to a matching funds policy, others stripped of their core funding altogether. Rachel Laforest, a scholar who specializes in the study of interest groups and social movements, cites this era as an all-time low in the state's relationship with the nonprofit sector in Canada, precipitating a crisis of identity and confidence.[6] Breast cancer groups, despite having been singled out as important additions to the policy community, soon felt the impact of these cuts. In July 1996, the board minutes of Breast Cancer Action Montreal noted, "Government funding [is] very tight and getting tighter. Governments are very cautious about giving, especially to new groups. Core operating funds are practically impossible to get from governments and foundations." By the end of the 1990s, the elimination of core funding had severely restricted the ability of health and social justice public interest groups to participate in policy debate.[7]

At the same time, says Laforest, after a period of cutbacks, governments at all levels began to see the importance of interest groups to policy and began mentioning the sector in speeches. As the economy improved in the late 1990s, the Chrétien government recognized that the drastic cuts to social programs in the 1996 budget had badly damaged its relationship with the nonprofit sector. In an effort at restoration, the Liberals began to borrow discourses and policies from Tony Blair's Labour Party government in the United Kingdom, including Blair's model of the social investment state (SIS). Under an SIS regime, state spending is acceptable when programs have perceived payback potential. Policy areas in which the Chrétien government saw this potential for future return included investments in technology and innovation for health care and the environment. Thus, under an SIS regime, groups that raise money for research into new health care technologies, or that promote the use of these technologies once developed, might well merit government funding; groups critical of these priorities and products would be a tougher sell and might be seen as impeding economic growth.[8]

A new program, the five-year, $90-million Voluntary Sector Initiative (VSI), extended the concept of public-private policy making and service delivery "partnerships" beyond business to the voluntary sector, but favoured organizations that posed no challenge the state. The state's role in these partnerships is described as "steering, not rowing."[9] The VSI's five-year process of government dialogue with the voluntary sector culminated in the Voluntary Sector Accord, signed in 2001.[10] The accord was adapted from a novel policy instrument developed by New Labour to facilitate constructive relationships between the government and nonprofit groups. Canada's accord is much more ambivalent than its UK counterpart, however.

The Department of Finance took a cautious approach, which contributed to the accord's failure to address two key issues: the right of groups to engage in advocacy, and their claim to legitimately receive tax-funded grants.

New government programs redefined the concept of advocacy to mean evidence-based policy consultations with the state, while delegitimizing confrontational tactics that made claims on the state. "Toolkits" and funding programs encouraged the voluntary sector to develop management skills and build capacity in the areas of policy research and evidence-based expertise, which the government needed. Organizations that adopted this mainstream, professionalized model of advocacy were invited to collaborate in policy development and were sometimes held up as models for other voluntary organizations to follow. By comparison, organizations that used mobilization tactics and media campaigns were neither funded nor included in consultations, thus encouraging conservative, nonconflictual strategies. Furthermore, a series of seemingly unrelated federal regulations all acted to constrain advocacy.[11]

Examining Canada's SIS state program through a feminist lens, political scientist Alexandra Dobrowolsky concludes that the focus on service delivery further squeezed the women's movement, which neoliberal cuts had already diminished. By funding groups that were uncritical of government policies, and those whose members volunteered time to provide education and support, federal SIS programs were tailored to starve out the more activist residue of the women's movement while encouraging those groups engaged in the service work that paid professionals had largely performed in the welfare state. For breast cancer groups that looked to the feminist women's health movement as a model, these policy changes did not augur well.

Two Meetings Define the Divide

In November 1996, a conference on breast cancer advocacy injected substance into the previously anemic arguments in favour of collaborations between grassroots groups and the pharmaceutical industry. Titled "Together to an End," the conference took place in the picturesque lakeside city of Orillia, Ontario, and was billed in the executive summary of the conference report as the first of its kind since the 1993 Health Canada–sponsored National Forum on Breast Cancer. Although the meeting was smaller than the forum, with about a hundred participants, attendees included many of the same members of grassroots organizations who had attended the meeting in Montreal. Pat Kelly, who had left Willow during the lead-up to the group's launch, helped organize the meeting. Additional participants included women from new groups that had sprung up since, and several prominent representatives from the health policy, medical, and media spheres. Among the latter was William Hryniuk, an oncologist and former CEO of the Hamilton Regional Cancer Centre, Monique Bégin, former minister of health in the Trudeau government, and André Picard, health columnist at the *Globe and Mail*.

Sponsorship was markedly different from the forum, however. Health Canada, which had been the main organizer and funder of the forum, made only a minor contribution, supporting delegates from vulnerable populations. Funding came primarily from the pharmaceutical industry, including (most prominently, as listed on the acknowledgements page), Bristol-Myers Squibb, Zeneca Pharma, Eli Lilly, Rhône-Poulenc Rorer Canada, and (given lesser billing) Amgen Canada, Biomira Inc., Glaxo Wellcome, Pharmacia & Upjohn, and the Pharmaceutical Manufacturers Association of Canada (PMAC).[12]

Each of the lead sponsors had a major breast cancer drug either on the market or in the pipeline, as follows: Bristol-Myers Squibb (Taxol), Zeneca Pharma (Nolvadex [tamoxifen] and Arimidex), Eli Lilly (Evista), and Rhône-Poulenc Rorer (Taxotere). Of the other sponsors, Amgen Canada marketed Neupogen, Eprex, and Aranesp; the Edmonton-based Biomira had a breast cancer vaccine in the pipeline; Glaxo Wellcome made the anti-nausea drug Zofran (ondanestron), used to alleviate chemotherapy-induced nausea and vomiting; and Pharmacia & Upjohn made Aromasin, used to treat advanced breast cancer in patients whose disease has progressed after treatment with tamoxifen. Pharmacia & Upjohn also made Ellence, a drug in the same class as Adriamycin, used as a component in adjuvant therapy.

Judith Erola, then president of PMAC, explains the background to the pharmaceutical industry's sponsorship of the conference.

Judith: That was a natural outgrowth, if you will, of my early work with them, and then slowly I think we developed a good relationship with the breast cancer people and with industry. And I encouraged our companies to do that sort of thing. So that took place, but it took place rather slowly, because I think everybody was very wary.

Sharon: Do you mean the groups or the companies?

Judith: The groups *and* the companies. No, neither side was interested in seeing some kind of a scandal, where somebody was paying somebody to do something. It had to be done strictly above board and [be] effective without strings. So that took a while to build that kind of trust and to make sure that all the rules were followed.

Rather than presenting a preset program, the conference used Open Space Technology, a conference approach in which participants at a meeting set the agenda by posting topics they want to discuss and seeing who shows up.[13] Twenty-five issues arose from this process, and the conference report summarized the discussion generated at each session.[14] I looked with particular interest at the accounts of four sessions that addressed issues confronting breast cancer groups engaged in treatment advocacy.[15]

One stated, central purpose of the conference was the formation of a national advocacy organization. Two sessions, titled "Addressing the Conflict about a National (Advocacy) Organization" and "Empowerment for Common Action: A National Advocacy Group?" featured this theme. These discussions were fraught because the Canadian Breast Cancer Network (CBCN), the government-funded group that had emerged from the national forum, already had a mandate to advocate for patients in the national arena. Members of the CBCN's board attended the sessions and defended the group's ability to speak for the community. Champions of a new structure advanced the claim that the breast cancer community needed an organization devoted 100 percent to advocacy – an assumption that challenged the CBCN's legitimacy on two counts. First, in addition to advocacy, the CBCN served as communication central for local and regional groups, providing them with information, workshops, and other support. Second, as a registered charitable organization, tax law limited the group's advocacy expenses to 10 percent of its donated receipts, while its government funding was (under new government practices) increasingly tied to service work. The summary report of this session noted that some participants felt they were "walking on eggshells" during the discussion because an underlying tension suggested philosophical divisions within the community. "Speaking with one voice" was difficult, if not impossible, and the report framed this overt lack of agreement as especially problematic for advocacy, because "as soon as the voice is divided, governments, decision-making organizations 'get away with murder.'"[16] This call for a unified voice – even while acknowledging the community is divided – raises the important question of how, in a democratic system, an advocacy organization should best address genuine differences within its ranks.[17]

One faction at the meeting thus redefined the community's advocacy needs, arguing for an organization dedicated exclusively to advocacy that would neither solicit charitable donations nor apply for government grants. The new organization would be separate from the CBCN, though the CBCN could be a member. The proposed structure was based on the claim that government funding could silence a group – because a "breast cancer advocacy group will need to challenge government."[18] Implicitly, this discourse called for a restructured community, divided into two sectors: the service-oriented groups, which could seek government funds and solicit tax-deductible donations; and an advocacy coalition, which, like the conference itself, might be more appropriately funded by the pharmaceutical industry. The logic framed governments as the key targets for patient-driven advocacy and meant that the main conflict of interest for breast cancer groups lay in funding from government, not from industry.

These two sessions, then, used discourse to build support for a patient group–pharma alliance devoted to advocacy. The arguments aligned with the circulating rhetoric that reoriented public funding of civil society groups toward service. They also took an oblique shot at the consumer and feminist health communities' conflict-of-interest critique of industry-funded organizations and their dependence on industry funding.

A session titled "Guidelines for Corporate/Industry Working w/Breast Cancer Groups" seized this prickly nettle directly. It recommended forming a patient-driven consumer information service funded by industry and staffed by credible, independent experts. The session advanced four claims to support collaborations between the pharmaceutical industry and consumer-driven health groups as agreed on by the twenty participants:

- Industry wants good relationships with such groups.
- Current guidelines for collaboration are implicit and are being operationalized, but are not systemic.
- Health groups want timely access to the most appropriate treatments/care.
- Health groups can work with industry to create appropriate information/educational materials.[19]

Based on these claims, PMAC (the industry lobby organization) would convene a meeting to determine the future guidelines and the (yet to be created) national coalition would develop a position statement on working with industry.[20]

Apart from the pharmaceutical industry and the health and patient groups, key actors in the proposed advocacy coalition were the "credible, independent experts" who would assemble and disseminate knowledge about breast cancer therapeutics. The meeting notes provide examples of such organizations, including the BC-based Therapeutics Initiative, Cochrane (the UK-based initiative promoting evidence-based medicine), and Ralph Nader's consumer advocacy groups. None of these organizations was represented at the conference; indeed, this aspect of the proposal embodies several incongruities. Technology assessment organizations like the Therapeutics Initiative at the University of British Columbia and the organizations under Ralph Nader's umbrella have the science-driven objective of accurately weighing and publicizing the risks and benefits of health technologies, not the consumer- or industry-driven objective of "timely access"; furthermore, they define their independence in terms of strict separation from government, and from the industries whose products and services they are set up to evaluate.[21] The proposal, which argues that industry not only will fund the organizations' advocacy and educational activities but also set the central advocacy goal as "timely access," thus posits a through-the-looking-glass construction of the consumer protection models it purports to emulate. Imagine a meeting convened and funded by the Automobile Manufacturers Association giving rise to *Unsafe at Any Speed*, Ralph Nader's iconic book savaging the American automobile industry for ignoring known scientific principles in order to save costs in building its cars.[22]

A session on how to reduce breast cancer mortality in the next ten years highlighted the potential link between access to treatment drugs and breast cancer survival. One of the oncologist researchers who had testified at the parliamentary hearings, Dr. William Hryniuk, convened this session, at which he presented evidence to demonstrate that Canada lagged behind California in its breast cancer mortality rates. He proposed that the difference could be attributed to patients in California receiving more aggressive adjuvant chemotherapy, including high-dose chemotherapy with stem cell rescue. Within Canada, he further stated, disparities among provinces in breast cancer mortality rates were also striking, with British Columbia showing the best rates of survival. These interprovincial differences, he said, were likely the result of variance in the uptake of new treatments and perhaps also regional differences in the adoption of screening.

The session summary goes on to postulate that US-Canada treatment differences may be linked to systemic differences in the way health care is organized and administered: California's approach is commercialized and treats health care as a commodity, whereas Canada's universal health care system is government-run. The provincial health ministries in Canada are both the insurer and the direct agent of the legislature, a conflict of interest that protects the ministry from lawsuits; in the US system, by contrast, the courts and the legislature are said to protect the rights of the patient as a consumer. The consequence for patients is framed as a paradox: access to health care is deemed a right in Canada, yet life-saving breast cancer treatment is unevenly applied, breast cancer patients lack full access to the cancer specialists and treatments they require, and the patient has no recourse for her complaints; in the United States, access to treatment is not deemed to be a right, but the courts and legislatures nonetheless protect those rights. The performance of the California system is characterized as "superior," in sharp contrast to the health outcomes in Canada, characterized as "poor."[23]

These arguments are presented as hypothetical ("interprovincial variation is *probably* not due to under reporting or differences in disease virulence or incidence ... the *most likely* explanation for the variation *may be* that ... advances [in systemic adjuvant therapy] were unevenly applied to the women with breast cancer in the various provinces"[24]). A preliminary survey is cited as evidence that Canadian breast cancer patients have access to only about 25 percent of the oncologists and new drug treatments they require; the session summary proposes that an inventory be immediately undertaken to establish the percentage of breast cancer patients receiving (or having access to) screening mammography and the various types of chemotherapy, including cytotoxic and hormonal treatments, Taxol, anti-nausea drugs, and high-dose chemotherapy with stem cell rescue.

The logic of this framing upends several assumptions in the discourse of feminist health advocates, consumer protection advocates, and public health professionals: the problem for patients is not overtreatment and toxic side effects of drugs, but rather undertreatment and lack of access to new drugs. Consumer rights are defined in terms of the right to sue to gain access to these novel treatments, rather than universal access to safe, affordable medications shown to extend the patient's life or improve its quality. (The fact that cancer treatments are unaffordable for many Americans is not addressed, nor is the fact that lawsuits are a costly and emotionally draining way to exercise one's rights.) Private health delivery is argued as more able to provide access to new drugs – and is therefore more just – than a single-payer system. And the actors in need of a vigilant watchdog group are the government ministries and regulatory agencies that limit corporate power, not the pharmaceutical industry, or government agencies that bend to corporate interests. The prime target of patients' and consumers' advocacy groups should thus be government agencies that deny patients access to new drugs.

To improve the mortality statistics of breast cancer patients in Canada, one proposed solution was to revert to an entirely privatized system, but this was judged unlikely to be accepted. Another possibility was to create a national volunteer advocacy coalition to continuously lobby the provincial and federal governments for improved outcomes; "Such a coalition could be vigilant to ensure that the needed life-saving treatments would be continuously available in the future."[25]

Taken together, these four sessions moved well past the "we need the money, so why not?" justification of pharma funding and elaborated a complex discourse in favour of pharma-funded groups: they would pressure federal and provincial governments for timely access to new treatments, which in turn would reduce breast cancer mortality; eliminate regional inequities; and advance patients' rights. In the years that followed, these interlocking claims would resurface in the arguments of actors who favour industry funding as a source of revenue for patient groups. From an organizational perspective, the analysis argued for separating the patient-group community into service groups (largely funded by governments and tax-supported donations) and pharma-funded advocacy groups guided by an ethical code. Advocacy groups would speak with one voice, targeting government regulators and funders with the message that patients need faster, easier access to new therapies.

Women's Health Activists Regroup and Go Public

As this new discourse was being shaped, groups with roots in the women's health movement were also mobilizing to address the PHANGO (pharma-funded NGO) phenomenon head-on. In May 1997, women's health activist Anne Rochon Ford, who was executive director of a Toronto-based, federally funded women's health organization, held a public panel discussion in Toronto titled "Ethical Issues in Women's Health: The Delicate Business of Funding from Drug Companies." The discussion brought the discourse on the issue of pharma funding out of the inner sanctum of group meetings and aired it publicly before an audience of about sixty people. The meeting also took a step toward broadening the feminist perspective on pharma funding to include that of women with life-threatening illnesses.

Three of the speakers opposed groups taking funds from pharmaceutical companies: health activist Barbara Mintzes, physician Joel Lexchin, and Harriet Simand of DES Action Canada. The fourth, Darien Taylor, cofounder of the Toronto HIV/AIDS group Voices of Positive Women, argued that particular characteristics of AIDS differentiated members of her organization from those in more established feminist health organizations. First, they knew their disease was fatal and they depended on drugs for their survival. In addition, she said, the personal situations of the HIV-positive women were often dire; they were "marginalized, stigmatized, isolated, poor, suffering physically and emotionally."[26] Voices of Positive Women could not afford to support all these needs without financial help, which the industry was willing to provide. Implicit in the group's rationale for turning to the pharmaceutical industry for funds is the fact that government programs were *not* supporting these needs, or certainly not adequately. The social safety net was now much more loosely knit, and those most in need of assistance – in this case, people suffering from a stigmatizing, fatal disease – were called on to find funding for many of the support services they needed.

Ford had been active in a few breast cancer organizations and understood well the developing discourse on pharma funding. She explained to me in an interview:

> I had been hearing over and over and over the same phrases [that continued] to come up in talking about [pharma funding]. And often things would just not go very far in terms of talking them through and figuring out all that was behind [the differences]. And so the hope for that evening was to try and get a little bit more nuance to the discussion and not have it just be a "You're wrong, I'm right" kind of focus.
>
> Which [is what] things often end up being in organizations where you don't have a lot of time and your board only meets monthly and you've got to make hard decisions under pressure because "This company wants to give us money and if we don't take it by next week, 'There it goes, we've lost it.'"

She saw Darien Taylor as "a perfect sort of defender" of pharma funding because Taylor had given the issue a lot of thought and was not just presenting a knee-jerk rationale for acceptance. Taylor explained that HIV/ AIDS activists had worked closely with the pharmaceutical industry to promote research into new drugs and to ensure that women volunteered for clinical trials, while at the same time exerting pressure on the companies to make still-experimental drugs available to them. The other three speakers emphasized the need for extreme vigilance in dealing with an industry that actively strives to shape the way the public and physicians think about health. In doing so, they argued, the industry often misrepresents the potential benefits of their products in order to encourage a dependence on marketable technologies (e.g., the promise that hormonal pills enable women to "stay young").

All four speakers agreed that a mechanism was needed to distance the groups from an industry funder. They offered two proposals: a central, neutral body that would collect money from the pharmaceutical industry and distribute the funds among community-based health groups according to fair criteria and with the identity of donor companies kept anonymous; or a compulsory tax on drug companies' profits used to create a fund that distributed monies back into the community. Either mechanism would have to ensure that groups critical of the industry were not left to fend for themselves. Ideally, such a structure would reduce the likelihood of other groups absorbing and disseminating a biased understanding about drugs.

Ford felt that the panel struck a chord. In 2007, reflecting on the event, she told me, "We had a pretty good turnout, and I could tell by the enthusiasm of the people in the audience that this is something that was really needed, that people wanted to understand. Because ... on a completely superficial level, to most people it looks like, 'Well, why wouldn't you?' 'Why wouldn't you take the money,' right?"

The panel's proposals for structural change drew from an assumption that the public needs constant reminders of the remedy/poison duality that the pharmaceutical industry and patients alike are reluctant to acknowledge; yet both moral and health imperatives demand that the poison side be confronted. Implicit in the recommendations was a critique of the drug companies themselves. An account of the panel in the DES Action Canada newsletter reminded readers that Eli Lilly had yet to compensate the DES daughters and sons in Canada who were harmed when their physicians prescribed the drug to their mothers: "If the drug companies are serious about their role as good corporate citizens, then you would expect them to redress situations of marketed drugs that turned out to be harmful, rather than only providing token funding to groups which will not be critical of the industry."[27]

After the panel event, Anne Rochon Ford decided to move the discussion still further into the public sphere, using the debate as the basis of a booklet directed to women's health groups. *A Different Prescription: Considerations for Women's Health Groups Contemplating Funding from the Pharmaceutical Industry* put the commonly heard arguments for and against taking pharma funding in a critical framework.[28] Assessing the booklet's impact a decade later, Ford reflected that she received more thanks for it than for anything else she had ever written: "People sent emails and notes to me saying, 'This is exactly what we needed.' Or, 'We had a board meeting last night. I was the only person arguing this and I lost, but boy, I sure appreciated your [booklet]' – that kind of thing ... So I think it's good to have that tool out there."

Barbara Mintzes took the discussion to an international audience the same year in a booklet written for Health Action International (HAI). *Blurring the Boundaries: New Trends in Drug Promotion* discusses the pharmaceutical industry's covert use of promotional strategies, including the sponsorship of patient groups. Although much of her research was Europe based, the section on patient groups drew numerous examples from Canada. Mintzes found evidence that drug companies selectively sponsored patient groups as part of a carefully thought-through product-promotion strategy. When Glaxo Canada launched Imitrex (sumatritan), a new treatment for migraines, for example, the company found a patient group that had been dormant, gave it substantial grants, and held public meetings in the group's name, although the meetings were actually organized by Glaxo as part of a prelaunch promotional campaign. John Martens, a pharmacist responsible for patient education in British Columbia at Glaxo who later worked for the independent research organization Therapeutics Initiative, told Mintzes that when the organization protested the company's heavy-handed involvement, Glaxo simply found another organization to fund:

> "What companies would do and I was actually part of the process, is create a demand for a product before it was actually released," states Martens. "We went around to various communities and organized public health education seminars on migraines and that topic was really popular ... We held these seminars right across Canada."
>
> They actually charged $5 for the seminars, Martins explained, a marketing tactic designed to deflect suspicions that the event was being funded by a pharmaceutical company. Global sales for sumatritan in 1995 were US$600 million, which explains Glaxo's intense promotion to "carve a niche in the migraine market" for its product.[29]

Mintzes already had concerns about drug companies' funding of patient groups, based on having seen industry-funded groups distribute biased and promotional information. These concerns grew when her research turned up reports in the pharmaceutical marketing literature about new organizations that pharmaceutical companies had formed as part of a marketing campaign to launch a new drug. Critiquing alliances between patient groups and pharmaceutical companies is a balancing act, Mintzes told me in an interview, because the organizations often do provide an important service to patients:

> There are groups that have been started by people who have been affected by a horrible disease and who then have provided support and information and, basically, a service to other people who have also been affected. And they've come out of their experience and made it something positive in the sense of helping others to go through a similar thing. And that's a crucial, important side of patient groups ... I think the criticism of the industry funding of patient groups is totally necessary and [so] I always try to separate that critique from the sides that are positive.

This separation can be difficult to achieve, as the San Francisco–based breast cancer group Breast Cancer Action discovered. In 1998–99, concerned about corporate ties within the community, its board developed a formal donations policy on corporate contributions and tried at the same time to start a public discourse about the issue. Barbara Brenner, who became the executive director of Breast Cancer Action in 1995, was instrumental in initiating the policy.

> *Barbara:* [In 1994] the board had a very clear statement that "we cannot be bought." And it wasn't that pharmaceutical companies were flooding us with money ... But members of the board were very clear that it would be okay to take pharma money and it wouldn't affect our position.
>
> *Sharon:* What was the meaning of that statement?
>
> *Barbara:* The meaning was that we were going to say what needed to be said. We were going to tell people what was going on with treatments or real prevention, no matter who gave us money. I think that was the premise of that statement. People really believed it, and I think they acted consistently with it.

The board had periodic internal conversations about whether it was appropriate to accept funds from drug companies, but the issue was not seen as pressing. The group had received small grants from pharma companies, including $1,000 from Genentech, which Breast Cancer Action requested to cover the costs of a meeting the group held to discuss clinical trials that Genentech was conducting for its new breast cancer treatment, Herceptin. Although they continued to revisit the question occasionally and continued to say, "We can't be bought," nothing really changed until 1998, when what Barbara calls "a great controversy" erupted, prompting the group to formulate a formal "no pharma money" policy.

> We struggled with this for about a year, at the board level – not with what we should do, but how we should say it. Should we have a more detailed policy? Should we actually start to say no? Should we openly say no? And at that point, Genentech sent us another cheque for $1,000 and we sent it back.

The controversial event in question involved an article that another cancer group in the Bay area published in its newsletter, discussing funding from corporations as a move that could potentially contradict the organization's raison d'être. The article sparked an internal exchange among the leaders of several local groups, one of whom felt that her organization had been unfairly criticized. The discussion escalated and culminated with a passionate letter written by prominent environmental and cancer activist Sandra Steingraber, arguing against corporate funding.

> And basically her message was "Silence is the sound of money talking." I then shared [the letter] with my board president and said, "It seems to me it's time for us to look at this again. This the best articulation we're likely to see of an argument for taking a strong policy position, and we should just decide if we're going to do it."

The ensuing internal discussion led to the adoption of a policy stating that the organization would not accept money from any company that profits from cancer (e.g., drug companies and cancer treatment centres) or contributes to the cancer epidemic in any way the organization knew of (e.g., tobacco companies).

> Not because the money's bad and not only because we need people to trust what we say, but we're working in alliance across issues, and people [in other organizations] have to know that you're trustworthy. And that's very hard to achieve if you're taking money from the industry.

After adopting its corporate donations policy, Breast Cancer Action published a series of articles in its newsletter, explaining the group's decision and the reasons for it. The group's decision to move the discussion into the public arena was "not made willy-nilly," Barbara explains, but was an attempt "to have a conversation that's really important to the movement," prompted by an event within the movement:

> And people responded in very interesting ways. There were people who wrote to us and said, "Are you people out of your goddamn minds?" And then there were the people who wrote to us and said, "If I had a million dollars, I'd give it to you!" Now, unfortunately, nobody with a million dollars has found their way to us, so we're still struggling [*laughs*]. But there are many people who believe that we're doing the right thing.

Although the discussion within Breast Cancer Action's membership led to a clear position, the group was unable to persuade those groups that were taking money from the industry to engage in a public debate on the issue. The discourse thus became one of critique on one side and silence on the other. When Breast Cancer Action adopted its policy, the board decided the group would not be a member of any coalition that accepted money from pharma or other corporations that its policy ruled out, which meant resigning its membership in the national coalition, which did accept pharma funding. The corporate funding issue thus became a defining one for this group's identity and reconfigured alliances within the American movement. Few other breast cancer groups had, or went on to adopt, a "no pharma funding" policy, so Breast Cancer Action found itself relatively isolated within the breast cancer community; it redirected its energies toward pursuing ties with organizations that shared its perspective on corporate funding, including feminist health groups, environmental groups, consumer protection groups, and a few breast cancer groups such as the Massachusetts Breast Cancer Coalition and Breast Cancer Action Montreal.

An Industry Strategy Takes Shape

At the same time that the debate about pharma funding was dividing the grassroots advocacy community, a new discourse on the potential value of alliances between the industry and patient groups was gaining currency inside the pharmaceutical industry itself. The industry began to recognize patient groups as influential actors worthy of attention, and also as a foreign territory in need of special navigational tools. This recognition is clear from a wave of conference presentations, books, reports, and journal articles that began to appear in the late 1990s and early 2000s, featuring case studies of successful alliances and typologies of the forms they could take. The format, venue, institutional origin, and geopolitical provenance of the documents varied, but the overlap in content and the tenor of these documents are striking.

In 1999, for example, Eric Rule from the global professional services and accountancy firm PricewaterhouseCoopers and a consultant, Hayley Chapman, addressed a Toronto-based corporate think tank with a talk titled "Alliances between Disease-Specific Non-profit Organizations and Private-Sector Pharmaceutical Companies."[30] In England, former industry insider Fred Mills drew on seventeen years of experience as head of a UK-based consultancy firm with leading pharmaceutical companies as clients to publish the book *Patient Groups and the Global Pharmaceutical Industry: The Growing Importance of Working Directly with the Consumer.*[31] At the 2000 world conference of the Public Relations Society of America, AstraZeneca's Karen Miller gave a talk titled "Patient Advocacy: Leveraging the Newest Dimension of Health Care Public Relations."[32] In 2001, the monthly industry magazine *Pharmaceutical Executive* published "For Love of the Game," profiling an organization for patients with multiple myeloma founded by a former pharmaceutical industry employee diagnosed with the disease.[33]

This wave of publications and talks signalled a shift in how the industry viewed relationships between pharmaceutical companies and nonprofit organizations. The alliances were redefined from mere goodwill charity gestures to important components of a company's business plan. Karen Miller's presentation, for example, challenges the myth that industry alliances with patients' associations are a one-way street, with all the benefits flowing to the nonprofit. Rule and Chapman likewise state, "Traditionally the relationship has been based on sponsorship but now pharmaceutical companies are ensuring that the partnership is tied to business objectives."[34] Although AIDS organizations are recognized as the game changers in patient advocacy, and patient groups in the United States are seen as global leaders in organized lobbying, the documents collectively take note of the diversity of diseases now represented and the range of countries in which political advocacy by patient groups has become a fixture. Rule and Chapman's Canadian study found that very different forces drove the industry and nonprofit sectors to form such alliances. Nonprofit groups were looking for sources of income in the face of government cutbacks and stiff competition among the ever-growing field of charities, whereas companies were under pressure of increased competition in their own sector, both from generics and from other major brands launching similar products within therapeutic categories. The industry was also facing the financial pressures of rising overhead costs and declining profit margins. According to the study's findings, government intervention in the industry was increasing, but so was customer power, along with a demand for choice.[35]

For companies that managed to develop successful partnerships, these changes presented opportunities, industry leaders argued, and heading their list of potential benefits was faster drug approvals. Advocates' knowledge of the patients' perspective, the ability of their groups to function as information hubs, and the shared goals such groups have with the industry – especially the desire for new, successful drugs – are critical assets. As the *Pharmaceutical Executive* article noted, "'The industry is starting to see that we [patient groups] are the link for getting information about their products and clinical trials to the patient communities,' says [Kathy] Giusti. 'They realize that link can really speed the drug's approval process. That's the driving factor for the pharma industry.'"[36]

If faster drug approvals were the gold ring for the industry, patient groups had the potential to help industry achieve a host of other corporate goals. These included increasing the industry's influence with governments, improving a particular company's image, providing the company with access to new markets, and gaining access to data. Groups could increase pre-market awareness in targeted patient groups, set the stage for "reimbursement issues and lobbying activities," establish a "reliable/credible vehicle for product information distribution;" provide "firsthand insight into needs, issues, concerns and trends of target customers;" and form a bridge to "key community leaders who influence national policy, research, drug approval and care delivery."[37] Yet another source noted that groups could "recruit patients into clinical trials, reinforce patient decisions to try a drug, boost product sales, and build compliance."[38]

Various documents make the point that the two sectors have different cultures and each side must understand the other if an alliance is to work. Trust, communication, and cultural compatibility were identified as among the keys to workable relationships, said one.[39] Another observed that failed partnerships were, unfortunately, perhaps more common than successful ones; its authors recommended clear terms of engagement, mutually defined project goals and objectives, and an incremental approach that allows the parties to develop trust and understanding.[40] Open communication and established boundaries were deemed more important than written agreements, and several documents emphasize that, ideally, each party should have the ability to terminate the agreement at will.

In his book-length analysis, UK industry consultant Fred Mills discusses legal and ethical "restraining forces," including legal restrictions on organizations with charitable status and "the issue of retaining their independence, being unbiased and avoiding the perception that sponsorship equals ownership by the drug company."[41] Mills's references to breast cancer organizations are sparse, but his discussion of legal and ethical obstacles closely parallels the discourses in the groups I studied, suggesting that these concerns have resonance across disease groups and national boundaries. He notes: "Many countries are now developing a set of criteria to guide NGOs in forming relationships with pharmaceutical companies. Although these differ in detail from country to country, they are all similar in their broad aims, which comprise equity, transparency and mutual benefit."[42]

Pharmaceutical companies have been known to take the "unsophisticated and simplistic" view that "the NGO could be given some money and would then campaign on behalf of the company's product(s)," says Mills.[43] This approach, he asserts, is now discredited, and most companies act with greater "transparency and altruism." And although Mills is optimistic that groups and industry can form relationships that meet the necessary ethical standards, he is sympathetic to the idea of independently administered blind trusts, with the money coming from the pharmaceutical industry and other sources. Such a fund, he says, "would appeal to the philanthropic motives of the pharmaceutical industry, since this type of solution offers a means to maintain a high degree of credibility, to contribute to community life and to avoid any suggestion that they are directly or indirectly buying the services of a patient group."[44]

Collectively, the documents discussed in this chapter identify patient-group alliances with the pharmaceutical industry as a complex area of emerging knowledge that the main actors are struggling to master and shape. The near-simultaneous appearance of so many prescriptive documents, both for and against this hybrid phenomenon, signals a fertile stage of discourse. The construct I have dubbed the PHANGO is no longer a novelty, but neither is it normalized. Insiders on each side of the debate recognize the PHANGO as a powerful but ethically contentious instrument to drive policy. Each seeks to elaborate a normative discourse and to disseminate its tenets to a broader community.

5

The Movement Fractures over Pharma Funding

In the grassroots period, pharma funding to Canadian patient groups involved awards of between $1,000 and $5,000 for single projects, and decisions on both sides were made in the absence of formal policies. In the contestation period, larger sums of money came into play, particularly in alliances with the national or umbrella organizations, while awards to smaller regional groups began to take on a pattern. Amounts are difficult to document, but in some cases, contributions were in the hundreds of thousands of dollars.[1] Groups began to adopt formal policies, and some initiated public discussions. Two groups that engaged in partnership arrangements were Willow and the Canadian Breast Cancer Network, giving rise to internal tensions.

"Upstairs, Downstairs" Tensions at Willow

The early years of Willow, those predating and immediately after the organization's official launch in June 1995, were marked by tumultuous board discussions about pharma funding and other questions related to the group's identity. The launch of the organization was premature, according to several accounts, not only because the board was struggling with the corporate funding issue but because Willow was not yet ready to provide the telephone support and information services that were its central purpose. Anne Rochon Ford, one of the founding members, left in the fall after the 1995 launch, in part because she felt the board was moving to accept funds from drug companies; Pat Kelly (who had been the executive director) left in the wake of an unrelated disagreement.

In late 1995, a new executive director began setting up a telephone peer-support and information service. She hired several women, including "Virginia," to train and supervise the breast cancer survivors who volunteered to staff the phones. Using a detailed training manual, the trainers taught the volunteer peer counsellors to respond to questions from the public with sympathy, in a nondirective manner, and with unbiased facts. The paid trainers also took many calls themselves, which gave them a feel for the community concerns and ensured a core of peer counsellors when volunteer staffing fell short. Members of Willow's board of directors, all of whom were volunteers, had no part in the phone service or daily running of the organization but set policy and took care of the finances. By the organization's bylaws, half of the board members had to have had breast cancer; the other half were sought out because of their high profile, connections, and fundraising potential. The paid executive director acted as the liaison between the "upstairs" board and the "downstairs" staff and volunteers.

For ten years, Virginia remained at Willow, where she saw a reinvigorated struggle over pharma funding play out over an extended time span. Once the phone lines became operational, the staff members training the phone volunteers with breast cancer became passionate voices against pharma funding. As Virginia recalls, the new executive director agreed with this position, which, despite the contrary views of some board members, was eventually put in writing:

> Within two years of my working at [the organization], we had a written policy of not taking pharmaceutical funding. And I remember the board and staff weekend meeting where the wording of that policy was thrashed out.
>
> And it was not necessarily something that everyone agreed on, but the majority certainly agreed at that time – the staff being the most vociferous around *not* taking this money. And [around] not doing forward planning that would put us in debt, so that we would have to consider it [pharma funding] in the future. It was a very, *very* important part of who we were at Willow.

Board members, who were responsible for keeping the organization afloat financially and who in many cases had been sought out because of their contacts and fundraising abilities, could be more pragmatic. The staff's commitment to the group's independence from the industry was visceral and rooted in their responsibility for maintaining the quality of information given to the public over the phones. Virginia elaborates on her role as a peer counsellor:

> I had contact with women every day who phoned asking for information and peer support in their breast cancer journey. And a large portion of the conversation was discussion around treatment. Our mandate was to *not* tell them what to do. And we were very strict about that, Sharon, really strict! And we were good at being strict. But what we were there to do was to answer their questions *honestly*.
>
> I can't stress strongly enough how *unbiased* our delivery of support needed to be; because, as you know, these women were vulnerable, they – a great many of them want somebody to tell them what to do. And sometimes they'd rather have another survivor tell them what to do than a physician ... So that's what made our position even more important to be clean on [i.e., impartial] – because we *shouldn't* be telling them what to do. And we shouldn't be *implying* that we know, or be tainted by anything that would even suggest that we had associations with anything. Because I saw – and this is very purist of me – I saw organizations like Willow as being the *only* safe place for survivors to go to get support that was agenda-less, that didn't have a back-speak to it.

Virginia's work as a Willow staff member brought her into contact with the wider community, including industry representatives. For her, the written policy provided a shield from their overtures:

> In the beginning, because it was public at Willow that we didn't take money, and we *were* public, we said, "We don't." And as a spokesperson at Willow, I said it often, that we don't take pharma funding. And when I was at events then, promoting Willow on community tables – sometimes you'd be at something like a hospital show, or the College of Physicians and Surgeons of Ontario, or something like that – and a large proportion of the exhibitors at those things are pharmaceutical companies. And there

would *always* be cards left on my table when I wasn't there. Or people would approach me – AstraZeneca, *all* of those big names – and say, "You know, we'd love to help you out." And I'd just say, because I felt comfortable saying it, "Thank you but no thank you. We don't take pharma funding." And some of them would say, "Why? Why wouldn't you take pharma funding? Why? It's a win-win situation!"

It was like going to the disco in the '70s and the irritating guy coming up and asking you to dance – "Why *don't* you want to dance?" You know, it was the same kind of thing: "Well, because I don't choose to. These are the reasons, read my lips." But some of them were very persistent. They would say, "Well, we're in negotiations with [the group in] Burlington" or "We're in ...," you know, to make it seem like there was something wrong with you because you were looking a gift horse in the mouth.

By 2000, the executive director had changed several times, and Virginia began to notice a subtle shift in the organizational culture on the question of pharma funding:

Virginia: The makeup of the board became more corporate-oriented. And that's where the change really happened. But as far as I know, it didn't make any difference to the actual online support and what we taught our volunteers to say and do, and not say and do.

Sharon: You mean corporate in the sense that they were from the corporate world?

Virginia: Yes, from the corporate world. Nothing wrong with that; as I said, I've lived in the corporate world myself. So it's not like I felt that they were the antichrist or anything. It was that they looked at the organization from a very corporate point of view. And remember that we're dealing with a nonprofit, and that sometimes the thinking was around "Well, what are the results here?" "What's our profit on this [activity]?" in other words. And "How can we make the books balance?" What changed, in my mind – and this is purely subjective – was a greater preoccupation with how Willow looked in the community and who Willow was associated with, rather than the ground work, what was happening in the trenches.

In Virginia's perception, the organizational structure created a divide between the organization's board and its staff. As the organization grew, the issue of funding from the pharmaceutical sector was a fracture line:

> To use corporate-speak, we were losing our market share because more and more services were being provided elsewhere for breast cancer survivors ... And I think the shift was that two things happened at the same time. What came first? In my mind, it was the change in the makeup of the board. The board started attracting, one after another – so-and-so referred so-and-so, and so-and-so came on the board – so the makeup of the board became more women who came from a corporate world, came from a fundraising mentality that did not have the same ethical values, or – I don't mean that they were immoral – they were just different from those that we had started with.
>
> And at the same time, the persistent knocking at the door from the pharmaceuticals: it was a question of "Well, why not? Why shouldn't we?" ... So it was the two things happening. The pharmaceuticals were always knocking at our door, but the door was being answered now by the people who didn't see anything wrong with that.

Just as problematic to Virginia as the shift in the culture of the board members who brought in money was an absence on the board of survivors who would raise ethical flags at board meetings.

> *Virginia:* We had these go-get-'em women [on the board] who would bust their ass for Willow; I mean, many of them worked hours and hours to do stuff. But it wasn't tempered by the kind of survivor that would – that could – bring a voice to the board that would show the other ethical sides of it. And it was difficult getting breast cancer survivors to go on the board at Willow. It was very hard; very, very hard.
>
> *Sharon:* Why do you think that was?
>
> *Virginia:* I think that the kind of [survivors] who were interested in Willow were often women that just wanted to be in the trenches and do the phone work ... My feeling was often, even with a survivor peer-support volunteer, that people sometimes wanted to volunteer

in a breast cancer community group for a period of time and then, once they moved on in their treatment, they wanted to leave it behind.

And a lot of these corporate women did it because they truly believed that this was a thing that they should do – some of them had sisters-in-law or [other] people that they'd lost in their lives. None of them were survivors. But they had an attachment to the issue ... And they worked tirelessly to bring money in. And some of them got tired and said, "Okay, well, why am I busting my ass to do this when I think it's okay just to take this money from pharmaceuticals? Why wouldn't we? I don't get it."

The written prohibition against taking money from pharmaceutical companies began to erode, Virginia recalls, not by discussion or an overt, formal decision, but when the rules were bent for a highly successful annual fundraising event, Eat to the Beat – the brainchild of two board members from the corporate culture.

Virginia: It's an eating extravaganza. And volunteer chefs from all over town, from all kinds of different restaurants and catering services, come. They have a table, and they serve samples of their food. And they donate their time and all of the food ... It was the single largest fundraising project of Willow. I mean, it brought in, at one time, over a third of our operating budget in one event. So [it was] very, very dicey. [Was the] weather bad that year? You know, if there was something that happened, it was really risky, Sharon. But it never bombed ...

Now, the way they evolved with it was, in the beginning it led [i.e., it was independent of Willow]; it stood for itself. These women that ran it had a separate committee, the Eat to the Beat committee. And they would get people to donate ... [The board members] went around finding this stuff, they worked really hard. Then they started to get a bit nervous about this. So, as we know, fundraising events have a lifespan. And because they wanted to pre-empt the loss of income from finding stuff, they went looking for corporate funding of the event so that they would know from the get-go that, whatever

they took at the door, they would have a certain amount aside
to cover costs.

This was very, very careful spending, and a beautifully run
fundraising event, without question – very ethical. But then they
started looking around for headliner sponsors. So it would be –
the headline sponsor would be in for $50,000.

Sharon: Hmm!

Virginia: And that's where they caught the pharmaceuticals. That was
the first time the pharmaceuticals came in and started funding. And
initially they said, "Well, it's an Eat to the Beat function. It's not
really direct funding to [Willow]."

And I think after the first year of them doing that, that's when they
changed the funding policy. Because [the staff] were saying, "You
know what? You're breaking the rules here. Don't we have a funding
policy? You know, I'm a little uncomfortable with this." And that's
when they said, "Okay, well, we'll relieve your discomfort and change
the policy." [*Both laugh.*] ... And the only rule with the headline
sponsorship was that you didn't have two pharmaceuticals vying for
the same position, or two banks ... So that's how they got in. It was,
sort of, "Well, [our company will] just give you some [money]." At
first, they were buying tables at the event. And then it was a headline
sponsor thing.

Realizing the board was about to change the policy, the staff made a
last-ditch bid to intervene.

Virginia: During the time when we knew that it was on the cards to
be changed, we got wind of this, as staff, and we asked to present to
the board on it because we felt that maybe they hadn't had enough
information. We were still in that twilight zone where we thought,
"Maybe these people can be convinced that is not a good thing for
the integrity of a so-called unbiased organization." And a couple
of us sent memos containing a lot of the criteria and saying, "Can
we come and make a presentation to a board meeting ...?"

[Because] although Willow maintained a 50:50 survivor–non-
survivor ratio, many of the survivors on the board were not women

in the trenches. I mean, they had their own experience with breast cancer but were not necessarily *au fait* with the community feel, or had not been active volunteers in the community. And so perhaps, we thought, maybe they haven't got the understanding of how this might affect our community – which was very naive of us. And they refused to take a presentation from us.

Sharon: Wow.

Virginia: So we knew at that point it was done and dusted.

Once the policy was changed, Willow entered into an agreement with AstraZeneca, which the staff asked to see, but they were refused on the grounds that the agreement was privileged information. "Which did nothing to make any of us feel particularly confident about what that arrangement was," said Virginia. "If it's open and honest, why can't we see it?"[2]

The power to acquire, transmit, or block knowledge was central to the dispute between the board and staff. The staff prided themselves on their knowledge of "the community feel," which informed their ability to provide a needed impartial service to "knowledge-hungry" patients facing treatment decisions. The board knew the state of the organization's finances, the community of potential funders, and the terms of agreement with a particular company. For Virginia, the ethical dilemma that pharma funding posed at Willow was intimately tied to the organization's pledge to give unbiased information in its peer-support service to a particular demographic.

> *Virginia:* We're talking with a population now that is, you know, a baby boom population, women that are hungry for information, that look for stuff, that aren't going to trust everything their doctor says. And in a sense, to me, although these are perhaps more well-informed people, it also leaves them vulnerable to an insidious form of persuasion. Am I making sense?
>
> *Sharon:* Yes. And how much of that was your analysis and thinking, and how much of it was part of the training that Willow developed over the years?
>
> *Virginia:* Well, in the beginning, that was exactly what Willow said it would be ... The training manuals said that all the way through. You

know, "We will not give advice." "We will not be tainted" ... and even after Willow started taking pharma funding ... that was made abundantly clear. I mean, you can't control everything; you might get a peer-support volunteer who decides that the be-all and end-all advice is to take Adriamycin. But if she was heard saying something like that, she'd have been yanked pretty fast. We had a pretty high bar with the screening on the volunteers over the ten years I was with Willow; [the bar] was very high, very high. And they were watched.

Virginia's reasoning that the obsessive knowledge seeking of the stereotypical baby boomer patient was vulnerable to biased knowledge – which informed her argument against the use of pharma funding for a health information service – contrasts with the counterargument cited by proponents of pharma-funded information. In the latter case, today's well-educated, knowledge-seeking patient is far too savvy to be fooled by advertising hype, and efforts to protect her from misleading claims are framed as condescending. She needs, demands, and has a right to information from all possible sources, including pharma. In a carefully reasoned counterargument to this "logic of choice," Annemarie Mol, a science and technology studies scholar based in the Netherlands, elaborates on the idea of patient vulnerability. She refutes the premise that sick patients are autonomous individuals who want choice above all, or that they are in a position to make choices that will improve their health. What the sick want above all, she argues, is care: help in understanding what is possible and how to achieve it.[3]

The CBCN's Board Splinters

About the same time that the tension over pharma funding divided the staff and board members at Willow, the board members of a second group found themselves internally at odds over the same issue. The Canadian Breast Cancer Network (CBCN), established with support from the federal government in 1994, the year after the national forum, was designed to provide information for local and regional breast cancer groups and to speak nationally on behalf of breast cancer survivors (I was a member of the CBCN's founding board of directors). From 1995 to 1999, the group relied primarily on a five-year commitment of federal government funds. The group was then told that this money would be gradually phased out and the organization would have to become financially self-supporting.

In 1999, Ortho Biotech, a biotech subsidiary of Johnson & Johnson, was marketing a drug called Eprex and invited the CBCN to enter into a partnership arrangement.[4] It was a federal election year and Karen deKoning, the CBCN's newly elected president, decided the group should lobby to have its funding renewed. She was also eager to move the group into environmental advocacy on cancer prevention. None of the federal money could be used to support advocacy, but the biotech company was more than willing to fill this gap. The board voted to accept the money. The company provided an "unrestricted educational grant" of $65,000 for three advocacy workshops, to be held at sites across the country; $25,000 for an event known as Breakfast on the Hill, with women parliamentarians; and additional funds for a special advocacy issue of the organization's newsletter. This initial arrangement had no written contract and the money was to have no strings attached. The company made several after-the-fact demands, but overall the group's board was pleased: the workshops were well subscribed, participants' evaluations were favourable, and the organization recruited twenty new members to its advocacy committee.

In early 2001, Ortho Biotech's community relations director proposed a second round of funding, this time over a period of three years. The money would support more advocacy workshops and a needs assessment survey of the group's members. This time, however, the company wanted a written agreement specifying that the workshops would include information on anemia (anemia was the main indication for the company's biologic therapy, Eprex). Anemia can be a side effect of cytotoxic chemotherapy drugs used to treat breast cancer, and Ortho Biotech hoped to have chemotherapy-induced anemia approved as an additional indication for its drug. As well, the company had a list of other requests: it wanted to supply questions to be inserted in the needs assessment questionnaire, to send a representative to the group's annual general meeting and other events, and to be thanked for its financial support on the group's website, in its newsletters, and in other publications. This proposal split the board.

At $75,000 to $100,000 annually for three years, the money was significant. For the most part, the funding could be used for purposes agreeable to the group. A few members, however, including Karen, balked at the demand for reciprocal benefits. Negotiations and discussions continued for several months, with special meetings of the executive, conference calls, revised contracts, and lavish lunches and dinners with the company's representatives. Karen attempted to remove or modify the troubling demands, whereas the company ratcheted them up. New requests included promoting a web-based decision tool for patients that included an anemia assessment questionnaire, participating in and endorsing Anemia Awareness Week, recruiting the group's members to a study of anemia and fatigue, publishing articles about anemia and fatigue in its newsletters, and cohosting, with the company, a reception for survivors at an upcoming international breast cancer conference. From the perspective of consumer education, the company's pairing of anemia and fatigue hinted at the trouble to come: fatigue is a much broader, subjective concept than anemia, and no regulatory agency had approved Eprex to treat fatigue.

Karen strongly opposed the contract:

> To me it was like we might as well put a big sign up on our website, "We're now promoting Eprex." The drug wasn't actually mentioned, but all this information about anemia – there was only one reason to do that, as far as I was concerned. It wasn't just [that] they said, "This is information that women need to know" – and some of that was okay – but when you got down to it, it was all about drugs that in a roundabout way they were promoting. So that was when we did the survey with the board.

In a survey conducted in October 2001, each board member voted on the components of a new draft partnership agreement. The majority rejected the most blatantly promotional items and accepted others, but on every item, views were divided. Opponents to the contract had three main concerns: the CBCN could be perceived as working for Ortho Biotech and would lose credibility; the name of the company's drug might come up at the workshops, which would contravene a commitment the organization had not to promote specific drugs; and the group could lose control of the organization by focusing excessively on one issue among the many that concerned its membership. (Absent from this list of concerns was the possibility that the drug might prove harmful – a significant oversight, as later events would show.) Defenders countered that the organization would be providing a much-needed service – that patients were upset because doctors didn't talk to them about anemia and fatigue; that the offer would improve the CBCN's shaky finances; and that the company's representatives had proven themselves trustworthy.

Board relations became bitterly factionalized, and the question of the partnership remained an open sore. The president felt that the contract was tantamount to selling out the organization; the vice-president felt that the organization's very existence was in jeopardy and that this partnership, on balance, was an excellent opportunity to secure the group's future by working with a company that cared about patients. Soon after, the president's two-year term expired and the vice-president assumed the presidency, as per the organization's bylaws. Within a few months, the new president signed a three-year agreement with Ortho Biotech, one which included most of the disputed terms. Karen resigned, and two board members subsequently did likewise in support. In her letter of resignation, Karen noted that she believed the company's representative had cut her "out of the loop" while she was president by not returning her calls, dealing instead with the sympathetic vice-president and biding her time until Karen's term as president expired. Looking back, Karen felt she had been naive:

I'd never been president of an organization at the national level, and I didn't realize [a company] could be nice and court you and give you what you wanted – which was money to do advocacy [on prevention and the environment] – and then come back at you with their own agenda. I should have known better. So I blame myself, in some respects, for getting involved and then having to fight a battle the second year.

An additional factor, however, was the less-than-ideal funding arrangement with Health Canada:

We always had trouble getting our funding from the government on time, and we were dependent on [Health Canada] for operating [funds]; they were always a couple of months late. Once we had to shut down the office for a short time and we had to let a couple of staff go because we just didn't have the money to pay them. So when [Ortho Biotech] offered us all this big money, the lights with the board went off all over the place. They didn't look at it from an ethical standpoint, as [in] what taking money from [Ortho Biotech] and doing what they wanted would do to our reputation or our image. All they thought about it was, "It's money. Let's take it and run." But there were strings attached as to what that money was going to go for.

Soon after she left the CBCN, Karen was instrumental in merging two cancer organizations: the Breast Cancer Prevention Coalition, of which she was a member, and the Saunders-Matthey Foundation for Breast Cancer Research, started by Ray Matthey after he lost both his daughter and wife to breast cancer. Karen and Ray cochaired the newly formed Saunders-Matthey Cancer Prevention Coalition until Matthey's death, when she became its chair. The organization subsequently became a foundation and continues to fund research on the primary prevention of cancer. The CBCN continued its relationship with Ortho Biotech and (as per its contract) cohosted a reception with the company at an international breast cancer conference in 2002. Lynn, a board member who later resigned as well, characterized Ortho Biotech's behaviour as "really unethical": "I think they gave the [international conference] something like $110,000, a *huge* amount of money ... and they were doing such outrageous things, taking the board [of the CBCN] out to dinner, just spending money left, right, and centre. That was really bad."

Jean Wilson, a member from a regional breast cancer group that belonged to the CBCN, also recalls Ortho Biotech's involvement with the umbrella organization as a bitter learning experience for the community:

At the conference in Victoria, Ortho Biotech kept announcing that there was going to be this big workshop on anemia. One of our members was at the conference and could hardly wait for that; and when she went, she was so disappointed because they simply told them about the one drug, not even about all the medical ways, but just about their own drug.

One other member of the CBCN's board resigned in support of Karen, but the majority remained. "Hanna," one of the latter, told me she was pleased, on several levels, with the relationships the group had with Ortho Biotech. First, the company had provided money at a time when funding from Health Canada had been unreliable, and second, the money enabled the CBCN to produce a diary and appointment book in English and French that pulled together information from different sources, which she describes as a neat decision-making aid for patients undergoing treatment.

In October 2001, the CBCN's board of directors adopted a set of guidelines for entering into corporate partnerships. It described nine expectations that would be fulfilled by any partnership agreement the organization entered into, including that the partnership would benefit breast cancer survivors; that it would be compatible with the CBCN's goals and meet the organization's social and ethical obligations; that it would avoid endorsing specific products and treatments; and that the organization would be prepared to disclose publicly any responsibilities it had to the partnering corporation. The CBCN subsequently entered into relationships with other pharmaceutical companies and continues to do so today.

A Pharma Compromise

Regional organizations also had overtures from the pharmaceutical industry, though at a more modest level of funding. By 1997, Breast Cancer Action Nova Scotia had moved beyond writing letters to the editor. Its priorities were to promote awareness of breast cancer and of the needs of community members affected by the disease. For a while, projects and events evolved in tandem with the group's gradually expanding financial and human resources. In addition to collaborating with other organizations to conduct workshops and breast cancer–related needs assessments, the group was part of a provincial task force on cancer care and vocally protested a shortage of oncologists at the local cancer clinic; four new medical oncologists were subsequently hired. Established agencies paid for collaborative projects, individuals gave small personal donations, and when a member died, the group sometimes received several thousand dollars in legacy donations.

One particular project, however, began modestly but unexpectedly mushroomed, exerting pressure on the group to seek ongoing money for a salary. Kathleen Barclay recalls this as the first time the group discussed pharma funding. In December 1996, Paula Leaman, a web-savvy board member, launched a website describing the group and its activities. Within the site she incorporated the Breast Cancer Action Nova Scotia Discussion Forum, an online interactive space where patients could post questions and raise cancer-related issues, and then discuss them with one another. The Discussion Forum was easy to use and the website's inclusion of it made the Forum one of the first such online discussion sites for breast cancer patients anywhere. Within a few years, recalls Kathleen, the hits on the group's site exploded: in 1997, the year after its launch, postings numbered one or two messages a month; by April 1998, the site received 5,611 hits a month, accelerating to 18,917 a year later. Local women logged on to talk, but so did women from the four corners of the globe. This small regional group of volunteers had inadvertently spawned an international phenomenon.

For the group's board, however, the success of the website's Discussion Forum created internal tensions. The work to maintain it outstripped the group's volunteer person power, and its cyberspace profile began to overwhelm the organization's hands-on presence in the local community. Kathleen explains:

> There were a few years there where we just – we couldn't keep up. The Discussion Forum really started to dominate the group, which caused some big issues in the group. And we needed some money because Paula just could not stay on top of all the work that it was generating ... And one of the things that, right from the beginning ... made Paula so busy was moderating it to make sure that it wasn't being spammed ... If people came on and said, "Oh, the miracle drug!" we would take that off. We had a policy that "you can't come here and just say whatever you want to say" ... If someone said, "The cure for cancer is blah, blah, blah," it would come off. Or, "You should read my book!" – we would always take that off.

Kathleen recalls the group discussing, in 2000, pharma funding to support the website. Based on a consensual understanding about its purpose, and with strong leadership from the website administrator, members began to articulate a policy that defined the Discussion Forum as outside the reach of pharma funding:

> The Discussion Forum was very much Paula's baby, [and] she was very against [pharma funding]. She would say, "Newly diagnosed people come here, they don't want, they don't need to be seeing AstraZeneca, and this and that, dominating the site." One of the reasons the site is so popular is because it is women talking to women. It's very noncommercial and it's very grassroots. It's a safe place. And that was really important, especially to Paula. And, of course, we all agreed; we all went along with her. That's exactly the presence that we wanted to have.
>
> But it did make it a lot more difficult to find funding. Because, yeah, it would have probably been a lot easier if we would have been happy to [accept a corporate sponsor]; we probably could have found people interested in funding it.

In addition to the supportive messages to those newly diagnosed or suffering a relapse, the Discussion Forum was a rich source of lay knowledge about living with breast cancer. Experiences with treatments, including drug treatments, were a common theme of shared understanding among forum participants. Like the peer support given at Willow, these exchanges were not about giving advice. Rose explains:

> It tends to be more like, "My doctor's prescribed Taxotere; I've been taking it for three weeks and my fingernails have gotten all thick and smelly, and you know ..." [*Sharon laughs*], "what do I do about this, has anybody else ever had this happen?" And somebody else will – with any luck, quite a few people will write in and say, "Omigod yes, isn't it disgusting! I wore white gloves to bed at night with hand cream!" Or something like that. It's about side effects of drugs, like, "Did your joints ache with Arimidex?" And you'll get eighty responses saying, "Omigod! Did they ever!"

A participant from Florida took the informal exchange of patients' knowledge a step further. Her oncologist had prescribed the drug tamoxifen but had not warned her about its many side effects affecting quality of life, such as hot flashes, weight gain, and loss of libido. She prepared a questionnaire asking women taking tamoxifen what side effects they suffered, and what information their physician had provided about side effects when prescribing the drug. Paula created a web page for the questionnaire, and two hundred women taking tamoxifen responded, frequently citing unexpected side effects from the drug. The woman who initiated the survey compiled the responses into a report, posted it on the Discussion Forum, and sent it to cancer specialists.

The survey validated the position of board members who wanted the website to remain pharma-free. Says Kathleen:

> I think it was a pretty common thought among our board members that the pharmaceutical industry was part of the problem. And so why would we take money from them? And I think a lot of people felt it would make us unlikely to speak out. For example, the survey about tamoxifen was cool, it really was! [The woman from Florida decided,] "I'm pissed off and I'm going to find out [about the side effects and the information doctors give to patients,] and I'm going to interview all these people." And I guess there was some thought [of], "You know, if we were taking money from – who makes tamoxifen? It's AstraZeneca, isn't it? – then would we feel completely at ease being critical about tamoxifen?"

Kathleen, who saw herself as one of the more outspoken members, didn't believe pharma funding had to silence critique. "Frankly, I don't have an issue with that," she told me. "If I take your money, it doesn't mean I'm not going to say anything ... I don't think that has to be the case." For some board members, however, a national breast cancer fundraising organization, the Canadian Breast Cancer Foundation (CBCF), was a more palatable source of funding. The CBCF holds an annual breast cancer run in locations across Canada every October, raising millions of dollars each year, and disperses a portion of the money raised in each community to local organizations and projects. Yet, said Kathleen, even this source met with mixed reaction within the board:

The whole pharmaceutical issue was really a topic of conversation. There were people on our board that were against taking money from the CBCF because *it* gets money from pharmaceutical companies. So it was a big issue at our board. We discussed it quite a lot actually. Then we had a couple of members draw up a policy, and our policy in the end – because we all couldn't agree – was that we would look at it on a case-by-case basis, which really wasn't much of a policy! [*Laughs.*] But we were not going to get consensus on it.

In the end, the group applied to the CBCF for funds to hire a website administrator to maintain and moderate the Discussion Forum. At the same time, board members concluded they needed an office and a part-time paid person on staff to carry out the day-to-day work at the local and regional levels and to apply for grants, as Kathleen explains:

Because we had grown a little bit and were more involved, and a lot of it was through the website, but through many other avenues also. And often we would be asked, "Oh, we need a board member to sit on such and such a committee, we need ..." you know, representation here and there. And we didn't have people who could do that. Either people were not wanting to get that involved, or they worked full time and they just couldn't do those kinds of things.

Kathleen had just ended a contract teaching job, and in early 2001 the group hired her one day a week for six months to write grant applications. Her request to the CBCF to support the Discussion Forum succeeded; so did an application to Health Canada for a grant to develop the Atlantic Breast Cancer Network, a regional network of breast cancer groups and resources.

Despite a lack of consensus within the organization, the group avoided the kind of crisis over pharma funding that had divided the CBCN and Willow. They achieved this with a case-by-case policy and agreement that the Discussion Forum would stay pharma-free. At this point, too, the group was still fairly small, with a simple structure and (as yet) no office. The new funding meant they could pay the website administrator, hire Kathleen part-time, and delegate the rest of the work to the volunteer board.

Out West: Better Partners than Government

Another regional group, Breast Cancer Action Manitoba, began as a support group and grew gradually in response to local needs, much like Breast Cancer Action Nova Scotia, minus its Discussion Forum. Following the National Forum on Breast Cancer, the group started a newsletter and began to undertake community-focused advocacy projects to meet local needs, including a post–breast surgery aqua class. With funding from the CBCF, the group saw this service expand from its location in Winnipeg to more than a dozen smaller centres. The group's first experience with funding from a pharmaceutical company was for the newsletter. Jean, an early member of the group who was still active when I interviewed her in 2007, recalls the decision in the mid-1990s as uncontroversial and unproblematic for the group, in part because the company seemed indifferent to the project:

> I don't even remember which drug company funded us – but they never, ever lifted the phone to say anything about our publication. We acknowledged the contribution every time we published – we publish quarterly. And we mailed them a copy, but we never heard – I mean, they just accepted it. And the particular rep [who approved the funding] left. Then after that they didn't fund us; they said they were looking in a different direction. But it ... was strictly an educational grant with no strings attached, and there *were* no strings attached.

The group subsequently received funding for a series of three conferences, designed as a vehicle for women to share their knowledge with one another. A member had been frustrated in her encounters with the medical system because she didn't always understand what her doctors were saying, Jean recalls,

> so she wanted a conference where we really talked about all of the things ... but in a really secure atmosphere when it's just us. We could talk about it *all*, and get information ... So we had three conferences that were *for* people with breast cancer, *by* people with breast cancer. We called them "Together." They were *very* successful!

For the first conference, in 2000, the small organizing group took a broad approach and developed a list of potential funders, large and small:

So we started as big as we could; we tried Health Canada, who totally, totally led us astray and made us very bitter. We were working with a specific person, and we submitted about three drafts and followed their guidelines and made the changes, and certainly they were all honest; but, as you know, you have to have a slant, and this was "capacity building." Anyway, after we did that one, we submitted the final [draft], and we were simply told it didn't fall under their criteria – that they didn't fund conferences.

Adding insult to injury, Breast Cancer Action Manitoba Support and Advocacy West later discovered that a project funded out of the same competition was investigated for the misuse of public funds, including trips to the Caribbean. Says Jean:

And when that broke, we were so furious that they had turned us down. I mean, they'd been so incredibly nitpicky anyway with all the wording, and then to turn us down totally and abruptly after leading us on, and to find out they had just carelessly funded this [other project] without any checks and balances at all!

Members from a number of groups echoed the theme of inconsistent communications and insensitivity within federal government granting agencies, which had once been viewed as sympathetic allies. The anger generated helped create a positive environment in the community toward pharmaceutical companies, which were generally receptive and straight-forward. In the end, all three of Breast Cancer Action Manitoba's conferences – which drew about three hundred participants each – received most of their funding from the CBCF, some local foundations, and a handful of pharmaceutical companies. The companies made no effort to intervene to influence the conference programming, says Jean: "The first [conference], I know some of the drug companies said they would like someone there, since they were [supporting] it, and we said, 'No, it's only for survivors, so no.' And I don't think they ever had a rep there at the other two."

The Outliers: "No Pharma Funding"

Breast Cancer Action Montreal (BCAM), a local but high-profile organization, took a different stance. In 2001, the board members discussed a booklet that CBCN had published with funding from Janssen-Ortho, the parent of the company that sold the antianemia drug Eprex, and decided to adopt a corporate contributions (donations) policy. Janine O'Leary Cobb, who had been active in the 1980s and early 1990s on women's health issues related to menopause, was president of BCAM at this time and drew from her past experience to lead the group's discussion. "I think I just saw so much of the bad side of the pharma companies going to the [international and North American] menopause meetings – there was obviously so much money floating around that it turned me off," she says. "I became cynical hearing the kinds of claims they would make."

To prepare for their discussion on a formal policy, she and the other women on the BCAM board read Anne Rochon Ford's booklet, *A Different Prescription*. They also read the corporate donations policy that the San Francisco group Breast Cancer Action adopted in 1999 and borrowed much of its wording. They reasoned that the policy was needed to avoid real or perceived conflicts of interest that could undermine its credibility and political legitimacy as a group that speaks publicly about breast cancer prevention, diagnosis, and treatment. The policy would also serve to maintain the integrity of BCAM's information service. The principles guiding the corporate fundraising strategy read, in part, that the group "will not accept financial support from corporate entities whose products or services are known ... to include cancer diagnosis or treatment," and went on to specify that this included pharmaceutical companies, biotech companies, private cancer diagnosis and treatment facilities, and "companies that develop and market cancer-related technology."[5] In keeping with the group's educational work on environmental links to cancer and its advocacy to eliminate environmental carcinogens, the policy also precluded any association with companies known to endanger environmental or occupational health through a disregard for environmental or workplace regulations.

BCAM went public with its policy, posting it prominently on its website and with a notice in its newsletter.

Adopting a formal policy was good for the group for both pragmatic and political reasons, Janine reflected in a 2007 interview:

> I think it's important for people who look at our website to see the policy. It's important for when we're looking for speakers or organizing events to be able to show them the policy. The fact that it's down there in black and white, on the one hand, explains why we're such a small group, and explains why we can't afford to pay a lot of money for speakers or those sorts of things.
>
> And I think most people have a grudging respect for that kind of integrity – it's certainly rare enough. And I just find it unbelievable that so many groups, particularly breast cancer groups, believe that they are not influenced! I don't know how they can serve two masters like that.

Within the group, the decision itself was not controversial, though details took some time to hammer out. Maychai Brown, the group's former administrative secretary, newly hired at the time the board adopted the policy, recalls that maintaining the integrity of BCAM's information service was one reason for the group's stand against taking pharmaceutical funds, but a greater concern was that such money would undermine the credibility of its advocacy and education work, which was often critical of the status quo. She explains:

> We were ... concerned about taking funds from any group that was in some way profiting from breast cancer. We said we wouldn't take money from pharmaceutical companies because ... we might subtly be swayed by whatever medications they were making. We would feel that "we are getting money from them, and we can't bite their hand" ... That implies a *conscious* decision [that we would promote their products] ... but it was more of a worry that sort of unconsciously we would be swayed. Also, since we'd been fairly critical of certain preventative pharmaceuticals, [we thought,] "How can we then turn around and take money from *any* pharmaceutical [company]?" Because it opens us up to criticism that we're hypocritical.

For the board members, the policy became a badge of integrity that distinguished BCAM from the breast cancer organizations that now do accept pharma funding. "Cassie," who joined the board in 2000, shortly before the policy was adopted, agreed that the policy is a point of pride and group identity:

> We all agree on [the policy]. A few people are tougher, but we all have the same position. We all feel the same way. I certainly do – although some people express themselves in a way that sounds more hardline. You have to be clear and clean, it's a matter of integrity ... I can be proud to be in such a group.

After BCAM adopted its policy, overtures from the pharmaceutical industry were rare. Maychai – from her vantage point running the office – recalls very few in her tenure, although she does remember one invitation to sit on a consumer advisory committee. "I just tend to dismiss them," she says. "I say, 'No, I'm sorry, that doesn't interest us because we have a policy.' And they don't go further, and we don't explain. But I can tell you, it doesn't happen often at all – maybe three times since I've worked here, [so] in six years."

As in the United States, moving the critical discourse about pharma funding into the public arena proved divisive in the group's relations with the larger movement community. BCAM, like Breast Cancer Action, belonged to a national umbrella organization, in this case the CBCN. For several years around the time of adopting the policy, BCAM tried to bring the CBCN, and other groups and agencies, around to its way of thinking on issues related to pharmaceuticals and pharma funding. In these efforts, the group not only promoted the idea that breast cancer organizations should resist funding from drug companies but also raised alarms about "the growing influence of the pharmaceutical industry in dictating [health] policy."[6] One letter, sent to the CBCN, presented the umbrella organization's board with counterarguments to what BCAM saw as the national organization's developing closeness to the industry. In early 2001, BCAM sent a copy of its newly minted corporate donations policy to the national group but received no response. The group also wrote to other CBCN member organizations, urging them to oppose the national group's use of pharmaceutical money, an initiative that isolated the local group from other members.

A year later, BCAM learned that members of the CBCN's board had participated in an industry-funded public panel that presented direct-to-consumer advertising (DTCA) of drugs as an important form of consumer education. In response, the local group decided "to inform [the national group's] board members about the issues" surrounding DTCA by sending a package of information critical of advertising drugs to the public.[7] Canada had long had a ban on such advertising, a policy the industry was trying to overturn. McMaster University, in Hamilton, Ontario, became another target of the group's protests, after the university's president announced its decision to accept funding from Eli Lilly Canada to establish a chair in women's health. BCAM sent a letter in July 2000 that recalled Eli Lilly's manufacturing and marketing of diethylstilbestrol (DES), the company's refusal to acknowledge the adverse effects on the women who took it and on their children, and the corporation's resistance to offering recompense to those harmed or at risk because of the drug. In accepting money from Eli Lilly, the letter continued, the university lent support to the company's questionable claim of being committed to the pursuit of women's health. In yet another protest, the group wrote to convey its outrage when a provincial agency that had the mandate of disseminating breast cancer information throughout the region published a full-page advertisement in its bulletin, announcing that three pharmaceutical companies (Roche, Zeneca, and Novartis) had sponsored the agency's bulletin.[8]

These actions solidified the group's identity as an organization critical of alliances with the pharmaceutical industry. The stance distanced BCAM from the breast cancer community while strengthening its ties with the women's health movement, with its discourse of disease prevention and drug safety and effectiveness.

In 1999, the Alliance of Breast Cancer Survivors (ABCS), the Toronto advocacy group whose members agreed that pharma funding could compromise its ability to speak out, closed its doors. The group's hard line against pharma funding, combined with the federal government's unwillingness to fund a group that made advocacy its priority, made its demise inevitable, says Sue Groves:

Because, how long can you get volunteers? You can't run an effective organization entirely on a volunteer basis. I feel that very strongly ... any organization needs somebody on the payroll just to keep things ticking over. And the ABCS didn't have that. And couldn't find anywhere that would provide funding that would allow them to do what they wanted to do ... We did get government money for one particular project, but it had nothing to do with advocacy. It was about diversity. But we couldn't use it for anything else, unfortunately.

One may wonder why a "no pharma funding" policy forced the ABCS to fold when BCAM, with the same determination to remain independent, continued into the new century. An important contributing factor may have been the location of the two groups, the first in Ontario and the second in Quebec. Sociologist Deena White describes the two provinces as at opposite extremes in their subscription to neoliberalism. Unlike most other Canadian provinces in the neoliberal era, Quebec encouraged its civil society organizations to maintain a culture of collective identity, and to oppose the individualist, competitive model of organization promoted in other provinces, and most particularly in Ontario. Furthermore, the Quebec government did not abandon its collaborative local partnerships with civil society organizations and even took steps to protect the autonomy of these organizations and their advocacy role. As of 2007, the provincial government was BCAM's largest single source of revenue, at $15,000 annually, which gave the group the financial base for a small office and part-time administrator. This was not contract-for-services funding; in theory, at least, the organization could spend the money as it pleased. The office administrator believed an implicit assumption of the grant was that she would provide an information service to the community. Since the community already had several good cancer information services, Maychai stayed on top of their offerings, listened sympathetically to callers, and directed them to the agency that seemed most appropriate. By 2015, the group's annual provincial funding had increased to $62,000; along with the additional funding from donations and project grants, the group was able to hire a full-time executive director and several project staff.[9]

A New Style of Pharma-Funded Advocacy Emerges

A new Canadian cancer organization, the Cancer Advocacy Coalition of Canada (CACC), held its launch in 2000, backed almost entirely by unrestricted educational grants from pharmaceutical companies. The CACC brought the question of pharma funding into the public arena, albeit inadvertently.

Following the meeting Together to an End, Pat Kelly gathered advocates from various patient cancer groups and health professionals working in the cancer field to form an organization. The CACC was dedicated exclusively to cancer advocacy for all types of cancer, not just breast cancer. The impetus was the session at the Together to an End conference titled "How Can We Reduce Breast Cancer Mortality in the Next Ten Years?" at which an oncologist who was a delegate at the meeting presented data showing provincial disparities in survival rates of women with breast cancer. Pat recalls,

> He presented this data that showed – and this [was] in '96 – women in British Columbia who were treated for breast cancer in a five-year period had a 27 percent improvement in overall survival [over those in] Ontario ... And what was going on was that in BC ... they never limited what the treatment options were that they offered women. They had an organized system. They were more aggressive. They offered the full range of treatment options. They were more aggressive in providing women with information about that. And women tended to make choices for more aggressive treatment.

A recommendation at the Together to an End conference session was to form "a national volunteer coalition to continuously lobby the provincial and federal governments for improvements in outcomes," and the CACC set out to do precisely this, by addressing provincial disparities.[10] One of the coalition's vehicles was an annual report card that rated provinces on various aspects of their performance in treating cancer.

Beth Kapusta, another early member of this group, had been diagnosed with Hodgkin's lymphoma while still a university student. She heard a radio interview in which Pat Kelly talked about her experience with the cancer system and was impressed:

> I sought her out, and I found her. I said, "Look, I'm really interested in your approach to the larger systems problems; is there anything I can do?" And she was having a meeting a couple of weeks from then, and I became involved because there was a kind of passion, an alignment [in our perspectives] of wanting to change things at a systems level.

As a member of the CACC, Beth designed and wrote the organization's first report card. When the group tried to gather the data, however, it found that provincial data sets were insufficient for meaningful comparisons. The lack of comparative data thus became an advocacy issue and was a featured article in *Cancer Care in Canada*, a magazine that the organization used to launch its advocacy efforts, in the fall of 2000. As a whole, the publication's dozen or so short articles were a collective call to action to deal with a mounting crisis in cancer care in Canada. A statement on the back cover explained that donations to the CACC were not tax deductible because, in order to maintain its unrestricted ability to engage in advocacy, the organization had opted not to apply for charitable status.[11] Whereas cancer organizations set up as charities are limited by law to spending only a small percent of their donations on advocacy, the CACC could direct its entire annual budget to advocacy. The organization's funding, continued the back-cover statement, came from annual membership fees and unrestricted educational grants from corporations; however, the fact that the corporations were drug companies was not specified. I asked Beth about the origins of the organization's pharma sponsorship. How did it come about? Did the companies approach them, or vice versa? She explains:

> Well, we approached everybody. But pharma was really the only industry that would fund that kind of work. And, at that point, we were purely doing advocacy, so there was no possibility of getting charitable status. So very quickly you get into the kind of contradiction game. If you want to do pure advocacy work, you don't really have any other option.

Articles in the group's publication reprised two prominent themes from the Together to an End session on reducing cancer mortality: that Canada lagged behind the United States in providing patients with the latest treatments, and that patients had a right to choose these treatments. An article on breast cancer treatments titled "New Chemotherapy Regimen out of Reach for Canadian Women" compared the rapid adoption in the United States of a new chemotherapy treatment as the standard of care with the much different situation in Canada.[12] The treatment in question was the combination known as AC+T (Adriamycin and cyclophosphamide plus Taxol) as an adjuvant treatment for women whose breast cancer was node-positive (i.e., stage 2). The article quoted Brian Leyland-Jones, an oncologist then based at McGill University, as saying that American oncologists considered AC+T to be "the single most significant advance in the treatment of breast cancer in the past 20 years."[13] AC+T was adopted as the new standard of care in the United States after preliminary results of a clinical trial were presented at a meeting of cancer specialists in 1998. Canadian breast cancer survivors who had followed the American case applied pressure on the Canadian government and, the article suggests, may have contributed to the government's decision, in April 2000, to approve Taxol (paclitaxel) as an adjuvant therapy for early-stage breast cancer. The article noted that, because provincial governments had not yet decided whether to include AC+T in their treatment guidelines, only a very few Canadian women could gain access to AC+T, through clinical trials.

In the United States, however, opinions were far from unanimous on whether the rapid embrace of AC+T was in the best interest of patients – a fact not mentioned in the article. In November 2000, the US tax-funded health research agency, the National Institutes of Health, held a consensus conference to review the evidence on various adjuvant treatments for breast cancer. The resulting report acknowledged the value of taxanes (Taxol [paclitaxel] and Taxotere [docetaxel]) in treating metastatic (i.e., advanced) breast cancer, but summed up the evidence for adjuvant use as follows:

> Several studies have explored the clinical utility of adding these drugs to standard doxorubicin/cyclophosphamide [AC] treatment programs in

the adjuvant treatment of node-positive, localized breast cancer. Although a number of such trials have completed accrual and others remain in progress, currently available data are inconclusive and do not permit definitive recommendations regarding the impact of taxanes on either relapse-free or overall survival. There is no evidence to support the use of taxanes in node-negative breast cancer outside the setting of a clinical trial.[14]

For American physician and historian Barron Lerner, the haste with which American oncologists adopted AC+T as standard treatment reflected a cultural predilection in the United States to accept a corporate model for medicine and to welcome aggressive treatments for breast cancer. In 2001, he wrote:

> This desire for potent chemotherapy was recently demonstrated when a new combination of drugs – Adriamycin, cyclophosphamide, and paclitaxel (Taxol) – became the treatment of choice for breast cancer based largely on one presentation made at an oncology meeting and a marketing campaign by Taxol's manufacturer, Bristol-Myers Squibb.[15]

The CACC thus accurately presented AC+T as a "treatment of choice" in the United States at the time; by Lerner's account, however, this status was the result of clever marketing and culturally embedded attitudes, not superior performance as demonstrated by scientific evidence. The claim that data available in 2000 qualified AC+T as a significant advance in treatment for breast cancer, or one that a health care system prioritizing benefit to patients should adopt, was thus unconvincing. By 2014, clinical trial results for AC+T as an adjuvant treatment regimen found that the combination did improve disease-free survival and overall survival, but at the cost of significant risks from Taxol, including nerve damage, muscle and joint pain, and potentially fatal hypersensitivity reactions.[16]

In an interview, I asked cancer researcher Victor Ling, president and scientific director of the Terry Fox Research Institute in Vancouver, his views on drug access lobbies based on international comparisons.

Dr. Ling: I think some patients will advocate or agitate for newer drugs, even experimental drugs, that are not available to them in this country but are available to [patients] in other countries. But, in Canada, because we have a publicly funded health care system, we have to have very strict guidelines and criteria as to what the public system will pay for. It can't just be guided by special interest groups, or by political influence, or by advertising. People who really want to go to other countries to have other treatments, if they can afford it, they will do that. We all know that people have gone to other countries to undergo what one might consider questionable procedures. And no matter how much they agitate for it, I don't think the Canadian government, or the Canadian public, should pay for those kinds of procedures if they do not meet the standards for approved drugs.

In a one-page feature on cancer and the law, the CACC's magazine suggested conditions that would give patients a right to new treatments. A brief article attributed to McGill bioethicist Margaret Somerville highlighted three points from Canadian court decisions related to the question of whether Canadians have a right to "the best cancer treatments": first, that a treatment not available in Canada could still be termed a "standard treatment" if it was standard in another country that had "comparable health care;" second, a treatment could not be deemed medically unnecessary based on "cost alone"; and third, physicians have a primary duty to care for an individual patient, not to save resources for others.[17] Together these claims might suggest that patients could not, in law, be denied treatments available elsewhere, particularly on the basis of high cost. But the full complexity of the courts' decisions could not be explained in a one-page feature. Canada's health care system and the US system may be comparable in some respects (in the range of services provided, they are more like one another than they are to systems in low-income countries), but in many other ways they are a study in contrasts. And saying "cost alone" can't be used to rule out a treatment does not imply that cost can't be considered. On the third point, the physician's well-recognized obligation to do the best for each patient does not obliterate responsibilities physicians have to society – in particular, the responsibility to promote "equitable access to health care resources" and to "use health care resources prudently."[18]

A complementary article featured the case of Quebec lawyer Barry Stein, who went to New York for treatment of metastatic colon cancer because his doctor said the delay to receive treatment in Montreal would be unreasonable.[19] When the provincial insurance plan refused to reimburse the costs of his treatment, he sued and won. Like the synthesis of court decisions, this capsule summary of a case feeds a narrative that Canadians are being deprived life-saving treatments because the system skimps on costs. (Stein lived and went on to found a national advocacy group for patients with colon cancer.) Although the case would give any thoughtful person pause, one selected example, stripped of detail, is no basis for policy change.

Notably too, an article on why people with cancer in British Columbia appear to do better than their counterparts in other provinces makes no mention of more aggressive treatments; rather, extensive quotations from Dr. Jack Chritchley, a vice-president of the BC Cancer Agency, stressed organizational aspects of the province's system, including integration of the phases of cancer care, from early detection through treatment, support services, and rehabilitation.[20] Other systemic features that he highlighted were regularly updated, standardized guidelines to promote regional uniformity in the standard of care, and a range of counselling, support, and education services, including school-based programs to teach children about healthy lifestyles. The claim that breast cancer mortality was lower in that province because of a more aggressive use of chemotherapy appears in a small separate sidebar to this two-page feature, and cites a 1998 book critical of Canada's health care system by journalist and health writer Lisa Priest.[21]

A Media Challenge

Whether these articles alone would have pushed the CACC's launch into the media headlines is uncertain. Just before the magazine went to press, however, an American cancer association published data on cancer mortality in American states from the North American Association of Central

Cancer Registries and included data on Canadian provinces from Canadian registries.[22] This gave the organization a hook that guaranteed media coverage. As Pat Kelly explains, "All the Canadian provinces were piled up on the bottom of the list. We had fifty-two reporting agencies and ... in terms of outcome data ... the Canadian provinces were the worst."

The CACC's report card, and the Canada-US comparison in particular, caused a media sensation when it was released on September 25, 2000, though coverage was not universally positive.[23] Journalists covering the story consulted cancer epidemiologists who challenged the interpretation that linked differences in cancer mortality primarily to underspending on cancer treatments; far more important than treatments in accounting for cancer mortality rates, they said, were smoking, diet, and other regionally variable causes of the proportions of people *diagnosed* with cancer. Utah, for example, which topped the list for survival rates, has a large Mormon population, and Mormons, whose religion proscribes tobacco and alcohol use, as well as certain sexual behaviours, have a low incidence of cancers related to smoking, to drinking alcohol, and (in women) to multiple sexual partners and to few or no pregnancies.[24] Some news stories questioned the claim that US cancer mortality rates were lower than those in Canada. Erich Kliewer, director of epidemiology at CancerCare Manitoba, told a *Winnipeg Free Press* reporter that he used the data set on which the CACC based its assertion to do his own calculations and concluded that Canada's cancer survival rates were slightly *better* than those in the United States; a story in the *Hamilton Spectator* also asserted that Canada's mortality rates "are actually a fraction better here than they are south of the border." In a similar vein, Richard Schabas, head of preventive oncology at Cancer Care Ontario, told Helen Branswell of the Canadian Press that the regional differences reflected a well-known east-to-west gradient, with better survival rates on the western part of the continent, in both Canada and the United States.[25] Throughout the news stories, quotations from members of the CACC continued the theme put forward in the session that Dr. Hryniuk convened at the 1996 conference: that patients were dying needlessly because they were being denied new, effective therapies available to American cancer patients.[26]

This thesis was challenged again, the following January, in an American cancer journal. In two linked articles, the *Journal of the National Cancer*

Institute (*JNCI*) used the CACC's campaign to highlight the perils of comparing international data when the systems of data gathering and statistical analysis are not standardized. Cancer data is not collected the same way in the two countries, said three Canadian experts – Barbara Whylie of the Canadian Cancer Society, BC cancer epidemiologist Mary McBride, and Don Carlow, a physician and CEO of the Canadian Association of Provincial Cancer Registries. Variations in cancer mortality rates are generally small in North America, said McBride, but they are complicated by variations in cancer incidence rates linked to community demographics such as age and socioeconomic status.[27] When I interviewed Pat Kelly in 2007, she defended the report card's critique:

> Afterward, when it was attacked, when we took this and published it, the media went ape-shit with it, as you can imagine; because ... what we were saying was, "This is evidence, when you benchmark us against seemingly the best in the world and the worst, we're not doing so well; and we're so proud of all of our cancer data" ... So that was our first foray, and that was funded by the pharmaceutical industry.

Although media follow-up heaped skepticism on the organization's conclusions about the quality of cancer care in the United States, McBride acknowledged in one of the *JNCI* articles that the myriad sources of information now available to the public put an extra onus of responsibility on researchers and the media to convey the meaning of cancer data accurately and adequately. In a similar vein, Don Carlow insisted the criticisms of the Canadian system were unfair, but that administrators of cancer databases had to do more to explain their findings, while moving to systems that would make cancer statistics easier to compare across national borders. Pat Kelly, in her remarks to the *JNCI* reporter, welcomed these signs of attitude change on the part of systems administrators. She said the group aimed to raise the issue of variations in cancer treatment and mortality in a time of transition, in which patients wanted to regain a sense of control over treatment decisions. The lack of adequate data was one of the barriers it had faced. Calling the analysis "a 'quick and dirty' description of cancer mortality rates in the United States and Canada that is intended to raise questions," she added, "I'm not saying we did an outstanding job by any means given the barriers we had to overcome."[28] At the same time, the sheer volume of media stories about variations in cancer mortality injected the CACC's explanation, highlighting treatment variations, into the popular discourse.

In November 2000, two months after the CACC released its analysis, the controversy over the CACC's comparison of Canada-US cancer mortality rates gained an even higher profile. CBC's *Marketplace*, a weekly consumer rights television program, ran a feature that prominently highlighted the CACC and made much of the fact that the organization was funded by the pharmaceutical industry. A transcript posted on the program's website of past shows captures the episode's critical tone:

> The group swept into the media spotlight in the fall of 2000 when it released a controversial study on cancer deaths. The coalition is advocating faster approval of costly cancer treatments. It also wants governments to cover expensive new drugs.
>
> What the media did not report was where the group was getting its money from.[29]

Interviewed on the program, Pat Kelly acknowledged that the organization was almost entirely funded with money from the pharmaceutical industry. Beth Kapusta describes feeling set up by the program:

Beth: Their thesis was that we were this well-heeled advocacy organization that was running on all this pharma funding. They were looking for a big kind of opulent, excessive expression of it, and I was doing this work out of my office on the second floor of my little house in Toronto. It was a very seat-of-the-pants kind of operation. They had no evidence for any of the accusations that they were levelling. But they started with a very adamant thesis that we were this dark force of patients doing the mouthpiece work of pharma.

Sharon: But it was a pharma-funded group, wasn't it?

Beth: Absolutely! But there was no interference. We had strict guidelines to accept only unrestricted educational grants and a principle of no sponsor interference written into all the agreements.

When I spoke to Beth in 2008, she stated unequivocally that the industry partners did not dictate or influence the content of the CACC's work:

> They wouldn't be funding it if they didn't have a vested interest, but it's whether they have a *direct* influence that I think is more the issue ... I think the biggest criticism that's been levelled against organizations that take pharma money is that they're somehow extensions of the minds of pharma. Pharma may see that there's a long-term interest in having patient groups educated and funded and arguing for broader access to treatment. But it's more that kind of grey zone of – it happens to be an area where patients have the same long-term interest. It may not even be an exact alignment of interests, but that the pharmas see it as an investment in having a voice that will support their long-term goals.
>
> There's no question in my mind that pharma is highly self-interested. But I've never experienced editorial interference where I've been asked to change a fact or realign content, or to do anything that offended me.

Beth and Pat both agreed with the claim that patients and the industry share an interest in drug development and the rapid uptake of new products. Beth describes herself as fundamentally a pragmatist who owes her life to drugs. Although she felt it was important to have multiple sponsors for a project, she was impatient with those who used the pharma-funding issue as a "crowbar":

> I tend to ... focus on the outcome. You can pull apart the politics of anything and it will crumble ... Pharma became this unfortunate armature for fractiousness ... I know how hard all patient groups work for their funding – it's really hard!

Shortly after the launch of the CACC, Pat Kelly joined a new coalition of patient groups that wanted to speed the approval of new drugs at Health Canada, Best Medicines Coalition, a group also funded by the pharmaceutical industry.

> *Pat:* And the Cancer Advocacy Coalition led to the Best Medicines Coalition conference. Because one of the things [that] surfaced was

how long it took. Waiting times for drugs were longer in Canada, at that point, for Health Canada to approve than anywhere in the G8. You know, the Health Products and Food Branch was taking 600 days to approve a Herceptin or something. And the FDA [Food and Drug Administration] had just started a fast-track program for oncology agents.

And Louise Binder [a prominent Canadian AIDS activist] was out there and had asked me to come to this conference that she organized on the reform of Canada's drug review system. And I think the Herceptin book had just been published; and so, anyway [*wryly*], I got involved with pulling together, again, another group.[30]

As with the CACC, the main advocacy target of Best Medicines Coalition was not the pharmaceutical industry but Health Canada's Health Products and Food Branch. The BMC's goal was to get the federal agency to meet its performance targets for new cancer agents; to this end, says Pat Kelly, the coalition members worked with, not against, senior bureaucrats.

Pat: We actually worked quite closely with staff from Health Canada to identify the primary obstacles for them meeting their performance targets of 180 days from submission to approval. At that time, the only way a company could submit a drug for review was by paper submission – no electronic submissions. Huge tractor trailers full of documents would back up into loading bays at Tunney's Pasture [the site of Health Canada's offices in Ottawa], and they had to be unloaded into offices by hand, under security. This was a problem for reviewers, and Health Canada said they had a huge problem staffing the review positions – the pay was not enough to attract qualified people. [And] while the pharma industry was required to pay for the review process as a way of subsidizing costs, Treasury Board routinely clawed back the industry funding, leaving Health Canada without resources to [meet its] benchmarks. Working with Health Canada staff, we identified the "ask" to elected officials to be "Stop the claw backs," rather than blaming Health Canada. The senior bureaucrat we dealt with was Bob Peterson [director general of the Therapeutic Products Directorate]. He came and spoke at the conference, and it was considered a major pivot in building relationships between advocates and Health Canada on this issue. The waiting time for drug approvals changed significantly after that.[31]

Health Canada at the time was undergoing a major restructuring, and the Health Products and Food Branch (a rebranding of the Health Protection Branch), which is responsible for drug regulation, was a focal point of the department's new vision. The branch wanted to recover from 1990s setbacks, including low morale inflicted by massive budget cuts and the loss of its reputation from the tainted-blood tragedy. The new management had hired top-tier scientists from the academic community and, based on the belief that the public had unrealistic expectations that regulations could guarantee safety from fraud and health hazards, was "shifting from a regulatory model to a 'risk management' model."[32]

Advocates of this model argue that risk is inevitable and the goal should therefore be to maximize benefits and minimize risks; critics point out that the government's plan to speed up the regulatory process for drug approvals (part of a strategy called "smart regulations"), was explicitly designed, as laid out in government documents, to spur innovation and economic growth, and to reduce the administrative burden on business, a vision in which health benefits can become secondary. This was the view held by members of Women and Health Protection, a group to which I belonged; other members included Anne Rochon Ford, Barbara Mintzes, and Joel Lexchin. In his 2016 book, *Private Profits vs. Public Policy*, Lexchin says of the trend toward deregulation of drug approvals at Health Canada in the late 1990s and early 2000s: "While health was not ignored, the emphasis was clearly on creating a business-friendly environment."[33]

Best Medicines Coalition, with its focus on faster approval times, was thus in step with the government's renewed vision for a risk management approach to drug approvals.

> *Pat:* If chemotherapy is only curative once, there ought to be a sense of urgency to get it right ... And this is where I want to make the distinction – I'm only talking about cancer drugs. Because I don't

know about anything else, for one thing; but again, it goes back to that sense of urgency.

Sharon: Well, I don't know that fast is necessarily better.

Pat: Well, it's not fast [enough] ... With cancer you get one shot at getting it right ... So for me, Joel [Lexchin]'s argument about, "We need to be cautious because there can be harm done" – for the most part, with the new cancer agents, these are people for whom there aren't, there is no other option available to them! And so, we're holding back on something for this group of people who may benefit from it, but who certainly can't be harmed by it.

Pat's emphasis on the urgency of having access to new treatments that might be curative captures a reality of the cancer patient's dilemma. Once cancer has metastasized, it is considered fatal; thus, if a beneficial drug is stuck in the pipeline, a patient may lose her chance to benefit. As the example of high-dose chemotherapy shows, however, an emphasis on rapid access may undermine the need to "get it right." Drugs can severely compromise a patients' quality of life while providing no survival benefit, or even shortening life. The anti-AIDS drug AZT, while not fraudulent, was overhyped and did not meet activist expectations as the harbinger of a cure. Over time, AIDS treatment activists concluded that patients are better served by solid basic research than by rapid access to drugs with debilitating side effects and uncertain or modest benefits.[34]

As in the early AIDS movement, people with advanced cancer are predisposed to demand a potion to treat their problem and are inclined to try whatever seems promising. Patient-led access lobbies tap into a cultural belief in optimism as a strategy for coping with and beating a cancer diagnosis. The presumption that new treatments give patients a reason to think positively is also deeply embedded. Clinical trial results show the gains for breast cancer patients from cytotoxic chemotherapy are typically modest: less than a 5 percent improvement in survival time, and no more than a one year net gain in survival time. Even more sobering, the small gains shown in research protocols can disappear or be greatly diminished when a drug is used in real-world settings, largely because the typical cancer patient is older and sicker than those selected for clinical trials.[35] For women who are responsive to estrogen and who are therefore candidates for tamoxifen or other anti-hormonal treatment, the potential life extension may be somewhat greater, depending on the woman's risk of mortality, based on the assessment of her tumour and other factors.[36] A study of patients who underwent chemotherapy found, however, that they believed the potential benefit was roughly twice what the evidence demonstrated, a misperception that seems to belie the myth of the informed patient. Indeed, the American surgeon Atul Gawande points to research showing that patients with metastatic cancer who saw a palliative care specialist stopped chemotherapy sooner than those who had the usual oncology care; they also suffered less depression and lived 25 percent longer.[37] He notes, too, that the statistical curve of survival probabilities for a particular terminal illness almost always has a long tail, representing the very few patients who beat the odds. What's wrong, he asks, rhetorically, with a patient hoping that she will be the exception to the rule? Gawande continues:

> Nothing, it seems to me, unless it means we have failed to prepare for the outcome that's vastly more probable. The trouble is that we've built our medical system and culture around the long tail. We've created a multi-trillion dollar edifice for dispensing the medical equivalent of lottery tickets – and have only the rudiments of a system to prepare patients for the near certainly that those tickets will not win. Hope is not a plan, but hope is our plan.[38]

Patient advocates who make access to new drugs the focus of their advocacy are in effect promoting the culture of the long tail, a status quo system that serves the lucky few and leaves many patients in the lurch in their final months.

This is not to say that pharma partners script the access lobbies it funds. Pharmaceutical companies seek out and financially support patients and organizations whose pre-existing beliefs and advocacy goals coincide with their own – and these aren't hard to find. Numerous studies of breast cancer patients conducted since adjuvant chemotherapy for breast cancer was introduced in the late 1980s have found that the majority of breast cancer patients would accept the risks and toxicity of chemotherapy for an improvement in survival of 1 percent or less.[39] The authors of a 2005 study suggest that the bar for benefits deemed acceptable may have dropped over time; almost half the participants in their research said a gain of 0.1 percent, or even *one day*, would justify undergoing chemotherapy.[40] Pharma-funded access advocacy ensures these patients' voices are heard; those troubled by the gaps in service Gawande points to may simply find that companies that were once happy to fund them have now changed their priorities.

The PHANGO: From Contestation to Normalization

The contestation period reflects a shift within the pharmaceutical industry from the sporadic, small grants to patient groups of the grassroots period to a practice of long-term alliances and larger grants given to groups that share the industry's perspective. Whereas in the grassroots period groups responded to industry overtures with a degree of confusion and debated the issue internally based on past experiences and knowledge (or lack thereof), in the contestation period, the discourse within groups begins to take formal shape with the production of documents and debates in public venues. Within the industry, the norms for ethical and successful relationships were likewise formalized, with the discussion and codification of best practices. Industry documents, books and conference presentations show that the how-to of funding organizations began to develop as a valued area of expertise in the organizations.

The contrasting discourses within breast cancer organizations that favour or oppose pharma funding began to restructure the community itself, as the issue became one basis on which groups and activist leaders formed or severed allegiances. These group allegiances cross disease boundaries; patient organizations and patients interested in advocacy began to regroup into coalitions defined not by disease but by their understanding of the ethics of pharma funding and whether such funding would expand or limit the community's access to medications.

At the core of the contestation are different understandings of the risks and benefits of cancer medications, of patients' rights regarding medications, and of advocacy (see Table 2). Do rights revolve around rapid access to new medications, regardless of price? Or are rights regarding medications defined in terms of safety, protection from fraudulent claims, and equitable, sustainable access to a limited basket of treatments that fall within the system's budgetary constraints? Can these contrasting perspectives be balanced? How is "truth" about a drug's risks, benefits, and monetary value determined? What is advocacy? Who gets to engage in it? And how should such work be funded?

The developing discursive claim that patients have a right to new medical treatments coincides with the industry adopting a systematic approach to funding patient organizations. The strategy was designed to advance corporate goals, and doing so meant investing relatively large sums of money over long periods. In three of the organizations discussed in this chapter – the Canadian Breast Cancer Network (CBCN), the Cancer Advocacy Coalition of Canada (CACC), and Best Medicines Coalition – pharma funding aligns with messages that promote faster drug approvals and adding drugs to formularies. Despite challenges from opponents, both the CBCN and the CACC mounted campaigns to promote awareness and acceptance of novel treatments for breast cancer patients.

The CBCN's agreement with Ortho Biotech to highlight anemia as a problem from which its members might suffer did not promote the company's drug Eprex directly. Rather, the promotional strategy was based on the same principles as what drug regulators and the industry call a "help-seeking ad." This type of campaign raises awareness of a condition and encourages those who might be suffering from it to seek medical help, just when the company is bombarding physicians with messages promoting the same drug for the condition in question. The CACC's campaign, by contrast, advanced on multiple fronts and positioned the group as an opinion leader in cancer policy. Its advocacy campaign was framed to raise the public's anxiety about the adequacy and accessibility of cancer treatments in Canada in general, and new chemotherapy treatments in particular.

While the contestation period was one of internal disruption for both the CBCN and Willow, by the end of the period, both groups had effectively converted to a funding model that includes pharma sponsorship as a stable source of funding. Notably, Willow began as a Toronto-based Ontario service but by the end of contestation period was expanding its service (and influence) to other provinces. These groups were arguably the two most important breast cancer organizations that emerged from the post-forum expansion: the CBCN because it remained the national coordinating body and advocacy voice for local and regional groups, and Willow because of its role in providing information to women making decisions about breast cancer treatments.

TABLE 2
Late 1990s discourses about pharma funding

Discourse in favour	Discourse against
Drug lag	
New treatments are not reaching cancer patients, thus contributing to needless deaths. Health and patient groups and the industry share a desire for patients to access treatments in a timely manner.	Drug lag is largely a myth that serves the industry; we need strong, unbiased regulatory agencies to ensure drugs are effective and safe, and should provide these agencies with the resources needed to do their job.
Main target for advocacy	
Government agencies are targeted for denying patients access to new drugs.	The pharmaceutical industry is targeted for bias in overpromoting drugs and withholding information about side effects.
Risk/benefit balance of new drugs	
The cautious approach makes no sense when a cancer patient has no other options; the patient may benefit but can't be harmed. The industry understands drugs better than anyone, and patient groups can work with companies to develop educational programs about drugs for patients.	Even sick patients run risks of harmful drug effects if they are given new drugs before side effects are known, and the industry record in acknowledging these harms is poor. Older drugs or nondrug treatments may be better. The industry misrepresents the potential benefits of their products and should not be allowed to "educate" the public about treatments.
Provision of social supports	
Very sick people need supports they are not getting, and pharma funding helps patient groups mount supportive programs.	Governments should repair frayed social safety nets to give sick, marginalized people the supports they need; industry is too self-interested to fund these programs. Nonprofit groups and sick people can provide valuable peer support and information that complements professional services.

▶

Discourse in favour	Discourse against
Single-payer health care	
A US-style commercialized approach to health removes cancer treatment and education from government, improves patients' access to services, and frees patients to sue treatment facilities if they are dissatisfied with a service.	A commercial system leaves too many uninsured. Single-payer is the best system to ensure equitable access to health resources and to use them most efficiently; the system should be strengthened with drugs brought under the single-payer umbrella.
Needed structural changes	
Distinguish groups that provide services from groups that engage in advocacy. Create a dedicated, pharma-funded advocacy coalition to confront government-funded agencies that control treatment access.	Put in place an impartial, neutral body to fund advocacy groups, using fair criteria that don't marginalize groups that critique government policies or industry practices.
Conflicts of interest	
Industry donates money to patient groups because companies want to be good corporate citizens. Implicit codes of conduct can be strengthened and made explicit and systemic. Exerting direct pressure is wrong, but this rarely happens; no one wants a scandal. Patients' and companies' interests overlap (e.g., ensuring patients know about new, potentially helpful drugs and have rapid, equal access to them; learning about clinical trials patients can enter). The real conflict of interest in patient-group advocacy is with government funding because provincial governments also fund provincial drug formularies and pay the salaries of health care providers and administrators; these government employees can't speak out against the system because they are part of it.	Pharma funding of patient advocacy groups is a conflict of interest because the companies have an obligation to shareholders to maximize profits, whereas patient organizations' first obligation is to patients. Industry funding will inevitably be part of a marketing plan, with influence that may be subtle and indirect. Patients' and companies' interests diverge on time needed to carefully assess new drugs, on unbiased information about benefits or harmful side effects, on pricing, and on nondrug remedies and disease prevention. Governments have an obligation to serve the public, and well-designed government funding can usefully support advocacy on behalf of less powerful interests. Donations from industry, if given at all, should be distributed through a neutral party.

6

Pharma Funding as the New Norm

Between 2002 and 2011, pharma funding became the norm among Canadian breast cancer organizations engaged in advocacy, with only a small number of groups resisting the practice wholly or in part. I call this the partnership period. Industry and the groups created discourses and practices that normalized industry–advocacy group partnerships, aligned them with government policies, and represented the alliances as mutually beneficial. Such partnerships were represented as a fact, albeit one with inherent risks. Proscriptive texts emphasized ways that groups and companies could configure their relationships to avoid the pitfalls, meet ethical standards, and construct enduring alliances. This jointly agreed-on platform became the basis for treatment advocacy projects (discussed in Chapter 7). Meanwhile, despite pressures to conform, and despite shrinking resources, a small subset of breast cancer organizations continued to resist pharma funding.

A Shift in the Drug Advocacy Discourse

Within the pharmaceutical industry, prescriptive documents produced in the partnership period no longer sought to convince companies that working with patient organizations could be beneficial; rather, they assumed the practice was accepted but encouraged companies to improve their game. One strategy proposed was to take a public relations company on board as a matchmaker: a PR firm with contacts throughout the corporate and nonprofit communities could help "introduce [a company] to the right partners," notes one article in the trade publication *Pharmaceutical*

Executive.[1] PR firms were also well placed to guide the industry to the sweet spots of mutual benefit for companies and patient groups – the foremost among these being access to expensive treatments. A twenty-year veteran of the PR firm Hill+Knowlton Strategies – both a former cancer patient and a one-time press agent for the FDA – explains that the "empowered patient" is central to these partnerships: "The middle ground [where pharma companies' and patient groups' interests meet] came about with baby boomers who, unlike older patients, felt they should be involved in their health care and should challenge physicians' decisions."[2] Such statements subtly shape the concept of the "empowered patient" as a boutique shopper, aware of the newest products and determined to get the latest treatment, regardless of cost or her physician's contrary advice.[3]

Post-2000, public relations companies began to produce documents of their own, establishing their reputations as knowledgeable, successful matchmakers integral to the success of a pharma company–patient-group partnership. Like pharmaceutical companies, many PR firms have a global reach, which allows them to conduct local surveys that help clients adapt core messages to conditions that vary nationally and regionally. Cohn & Wolfe, for example, has offices in Europe, Latin America, the Middle East, and North America, including three in Canada. In 2003, the company's Toronto office surveyed twenty Canadian organizations with experience working in partnership arrangements, including pharmaceutical companies and nonprofit organizations in the health sector. To "help its clients navigate the shifting landscape of partnerships," the survey asked about opportunities for success, as well as barriers and challenges.[4] A forty-page report distinguishes "challenging" (i.e., less successful) partnerships from those that worked and mapped emerging best practices. The appearance of such studies signified that brokering corporate-nonprofit partnerships was an expanding business opportunity and one in which public relations firms were jostling to establish themselves as leading actors. Cohn & Wolfe emphasized that the company had "more than 13 years of experience creating such partnerships."

In its report, Cohn & Wolfe affirm that corporations were adopting a more strategic approach to choosing partnerships. They were discarding "cheque book philanthropy" – also characterized as "spray and pray" – in favour of writing fewer but larger cheques, and seeking "two-way ...

reciprocal partnerships" that would satisfy "broader corporate goals, such as enhancing corporate reputation, obtaining assistance with government relations, or building a customer base."[5] These relationships were more likely to be ongoing than one-off; they were "multilayered," involving decisions made by committees representing more than one department within the company. Nonprofit organizations, by comparison, put ethical concerns at the forefront; their credibility was "their most valuable asset and they [didn't] want to jeopardize it." As part of this more engaged and, ideally, long-term type of relationship, companies and nonprofit groups alike developed tools for regular, honest communications, including written agreements or (because agreements could prove too rigid) looser documents. The latter might outline the principles of partnership and have a checklist to evaluate the potential partner on criteria such as ethical considerations, shared values and goals, credibility, and influence with – or access to – key stakeholders. All the companies in the survey wanted the groups to measure the impact of the program they were supporting by showing in advance that it had "put meaningful metrics in place": "not only do businesses want to know how a partnership will affect their bottom line; they also want to see the non-profit demonstrating a positive impact on those communities it serves."

In sum, to obtain corporate funding, groups were expected to develop projects with measurable benefits to both the business and the nonprofit partners. And in keeping with the values of the "knowledge economy" (an economy based on intellectual capabilities more than on physical labour or natural resources), corporate-nonprofit partnerships were understood to be an area of expertise in which actors on both sides had to become well versed if they were to successfully navigate its hazardous shoals.[6] In fact, the partnerships themselves are seen as sites of knowledge production and knowledge sharing that help both parties maintain a leadership edge in their respective communities.

Other industry publications reinforced the assertion that maximizing sales was not the only motive for working with patient groups. The attacks of some early AIDS groups on pharmaceutical companies taught the industry that patient groups had the potential to damage as well as enhance reputations. As the phenomenon of patient power spread to other diseases and conditions, the pharmaceutical sector recognized its collective interest in cultivating relationships with the patient-group sector and in demonstrating sensitivity to patients' needs. In this spirit, the company Novartis carefully managed its relationship with patients during the development and launch of Gleevec, an expensive treatment for a relatively rare cancer, chronic myelogenous leukemia (CML):

> The early example of AIDS patients transformed into activists against pharmaceutical enterprises who thought they had done a great thing in bringing the first AIDS drugs to market gave all of us at Novartis pause. We had to display our concern for CML patients; we had to show them that Novartis was doing all that it could to speed the production of ST1571 [i.e., Gleevec].[7]

Another article cites Karen Miller, AstraZeneca's director of ally development, who relates that when the company began marketing tamoxifen as a preventive, it made a mistake:

> [AstraZeneca] authorized an ad agency to develop patient education materials for Nolvadex (tamoxifen) before getting patient input. "By the time the materials were created we realized they contained wrong information," Miller says. "We learned our lesson. For Arimidex®, we worked with the advocates."[8]

Such articles depict the new millennium's "knowledgeable patient" as someone who monitors websites and knows when a promising new drug is in clinical trials, someone who merits industry respect and even fear. Pharmaceutical companies have an interest in understanding what patients and their organizations value, in building and maintaining their trust, and in shaping the knowledge of movement leaders about their products. The pharmaceutical research firm Best Practices, LLC, based in North Carolina, underlines the importance of knowledge as a reciprocal commodity in the partnership arrangement in a promotional text for its 2004 book *Patient Advocacy & Professional Organizations: Building Effective Relationships*. The company's website states: "By reaching patient advocacy groups and professional organizations, companies inform thought leaders, prepare the marketplace for upcoming products, impact policy, gather market intelligence, and gain valuable feedback from patients."[9] The advertisement characterizes patient-group relationships as essential to a company's marketing strategies and promises to spell out criteria for sorting through the large and confusing array of patient groups so that companies can "target efforts toward organizations with the greatest potential impact." One "key finding" for building successful relationships is the value of having a consolidated in-house unit responsible for interacting with the groups that it recommends be "housed in marketing or corporate affairs." Companies are also advised to develop criteria for ranking the groups by their "strategic importance."

As these texts demonstrate, the question of whether the partnerships are intrinsically beneficial to the industry was no longer a preoccupation; the central questions were how to make them succeed, to define what ethical standards they should meet, and to find the means to accomplish these two goals.

For an industry perspective on how drug companies in Canada saw the challenges of working with patient groups, I interviewed Steven Edwards, a representative from a multinational pharmaceutical company who was hired during the 2000–09 decade to work with patient organizations on behalf of the company's Canadian office. In our conversation, Edwards cited the headline-generating Vioxx scandal of 2004 as a game changer for the way he and others in the industry approached patient advocacy groups.[10] The scandal arose when Vioxx (rofecoxib), an anti-inflammatory drug often prescribed to control arthritis pain, was found to cause heart attacks, a risk that manufacturer Merck knew about but did not disclose to regulators for five years.

> *Steven Edwards:* And so the reputation of the industry had taken a serious hammering. I mean, to put it bluntly, the pharmaceutical industry was – people were looking at it with new eyes. And the whole concept of public relations and product public relations was transformed, I think, by the fallout from what happened there.
>
> I always felt anyway that good public relations had to be patient-centred. My senior managers also believed fervently that we as a company had to put patients at the heart of what we did. And product public relations was very much key to that, was a litmus

test to that. We had to reposition and rethink and redevelop all that we did here. Unlike traditional product public relations, which was all about product promotion, it should really be much more of a relationship-driven activity, taken in many ways outside of the mainstream of just promoting a product, much more around promoting mutually important things, like disease awareness, and sharing of information that's helpful on both sides.

Clinical trials information, for example: helping patient groups and patients be aware of our clinical trial programs so they could get on these trials and have an understanding of what was coming down our pipeline, because, particularly in the area of cancer, as you know, that's so important – to have the chance to get access to some of these new therapies. And so this was really the driving force behind the work that I was involved in ... Convincing senior commercial managers of the value of what we did was not easy because it didn't have an immediate commercial payoff. I had to work very hard to show them that there was good business sense behind what we did. And for people who are very dollar-driven, that wasn't easy ...

But we did have some good senior support from the head of the company. We had a very clear vision [about what] we wanted to be. We set out with a vision to become the company that patients trust. And if you believe in trust, you have to believe in a relationship strategy, because trust can only come through good relationship building ... And that means putting aside some of the narrower, if you like, the immediate kind of pressures of making sales and product promotion to really build trust, so that you can develop what I called a mutual platform, and so that you could understand "What is it when you are developing new therapies, what is it about that therapy that patients value most?" And very often it isn't the product itself, it's all the services that you put around the product – the information you make available, the support – those things are just as valuable as the raw product ... And you're not going to understand that unless you have the relationship with patient groups.

Within groups that had formed alliances with pharmaceutical companies, parallel discussions took place to identify strategies for success and to respond to ethical concerns. Pat Kelly, one of the activists who testified at the parliamentary hearings, played a lead role in advancing this discourse. In 2002, she completed a master's thesis titled "Begging Your Pardon: Exploring the Impacts of Pharmaceutical Industry Funding of Non-profit Organizations."[11] In it she examines the debate in Canada about pharma funding of nonprofit groups from her perspective as an advocate, a former cancer patient, cochair of the Support, Advocacy and Networking Subcommittee of the National Forum, and CEO of the pharma-funded Cancer Advocacy Coalition of Canada, which sponsored her thesis research. Her interviews with key informants from other organizations that received funding from the industry and those that didn't, with health policy journalists, and with representatives from two pharmaceutical companies that fund nonprofit organizations, provide a detailed picture of how participants in these alliances understand and address the ethical issues. "Begging Your Pardon" thus articulates the perspective of these actors at the outset of the partnership period on both their industry funding and their critics.

A recurring theme is a sense of grievance on the part of leaders within pharma-funded organizations who believe opponents of industry funding have attacked them unfairly; they are presumed guilty without evidence. Several who had agreed to appear on the *Marketplace* television program felt they had been set up and humiliated, to the detriment of their organizations. In Kelly's view, such tactics reflected a cultural malaise that linguistics professor Deborah Tannen has dubbed the "argument culture," a mode of interaction that fosters a "spirit of attack."[12]

Kelly agrees that groups whose purpose is to respond to the needs of people harmed by pharmaceutical products, or to advocate for primary prevention of disease, might understandably oppose pharma funding; however, she adds, they can't and shouldn't speak to the needs of people who depend on pharmaceuticals to treat their conditions. Doing so, when the groups targeted have a different purpose, "contravenes the democratic and social justice principles that NPOs [nonprofit organizations] share." She argues that such injustice is done when these groups "undermine public confidence in NPOs that have received funding from pharmaceutical sponsors, while at the same time these NPOs can and do clearly demonstrate accountability and transparency in relationships." Groups critical of pharma funding "may have a stake in manufacturing conflict and polarization," she suggests; by contrast, alliances between nonprofit organizations and the pharmaceutical industry strive to "foster the values of trust, collaboration, information sharing, horizontality, networking, negotiation, consensus and flexibility."[13]

Citing the Cancer Advocacy Coalition of Canada (CACC) as an example, Kelly locates the eye of the storm as the interest pharma-funded groups have in gaining access to new drug therapies:

> The intersection of interests between [our organization] and pharmaceutical sponsors is specifically in the area of timely access to evidence-based treatment and diagnostic therapies. As such, CACC members advocate for changes to the drug review system and to provincial formularies such that cancer patients will gain safe, efficient access to evidence-based therapies ... While the CACC does not limit advocacy efforts to improving access to drug treatments, it is because of the overlap of interests between the goals of [the organization] and the pharmaceutical industry that controversy arises.[14]

Her research found that nonprofit organizations had indeed collectively mobilized their resources to reduce federal and provincial barriers to accessing new drug treatments, acting for the "repressed interests" of patients and their families: "These advocacy efforts have arisen in response to both member demand and public expectations that NPO[s] act to serve as public champions, especially with regards to complex public health policy."[15]

Groups that refuse pharma funding but accept funds from the government are more than just privileged: their government funding is a conflict of interest that undermines their ability to criticize government policies, she argues, citing DES Action Canada, among other examples. The government's 10 percent rule limiting the amount of donated money registered charities can spend on advocacy is a further barrier for groups with charitable status that want to advocate on behalf of patients.

A central claim of Kelly's thesis is that pharma-funded patient organizations can and, in her experience, do function ethically and maintain arm's-length relationships from their industry sponsors. She dismisses the so-called astroturf groups as largely mythical but acknowledges that the label has tarnished the partnership concept. She was aware of only one patient organization in Canada that she would define as an astroturf group, that is, an industry-created organization that lobbies for corporate interests under the guise of being a community-based, public interest organization. I asked her to elaborate on the distinction she made between an astroturf group and one that received pharma funding but was not astroturf. She replied:

> Who starts the group? I think that's, that's probably fundamental to it. It's, "Where did this come from?" Was it a marketing objective, or a marketing strategy to promote a product? Or did it come because there was a gap in service? Or is it because there was a desire to have policy change that you couldn't change from an individual organizational point of view? Or because the existing organizations involved in that structure are providers?

She went on to discuss a structural difference between the Canadian and American health care systems that (as was argued in one session of the Together to an End conference) she believes limits the ability of health care workers in Canada to challenge government policy:

> I think one of the biggest challenges is that the cancer agencies or the professional organizations of nurses and radiation oncologists and therapists – who in the States are very influential – [are] employees of government here. So their hands are tied. As individuals, they can lobby candidates during an election. But they can't lobby government directly, because that's what their organizations [do] – their senior government officials meet with senior officials from the cancer agencies. And some cancer agencies, if not all, have restrictions on communications, so they can't really change the system from within. And they're reliant on external grassroots advocacy efforts, particularly as I think patients now are a pretty powerful voice, a compelling voice, for change. So that's the difference.

Participants in her study could cite only a few instances in which pharmaceutical companies committed "infractions," such as efforts to control editing of materials or to use logos inappropriately; with one exception, the organization resolved the conflict through discussions with the company in question.[16] Public opinion, she asserts, is moving to a position that supports these partnerships as a way that corporations can demonstrate social responsibility; indeed, a society that promotes capitalism, by extension, "promotes a social contract imposing an obligation [on corporations] to consider public interest."[17]

In their book *P®otest Inc.*, Peter Dauvergne and Genevieve LeBaron adopt a Gramscian analysis to argue against this view.[18] Social activists internalize corporate responsibility as a value, they contend, when they come to accept capitalism as the only viable economic order. As part of this internalization, the rules and customs of the powerful become "normal," and activists accept the corporate perspective that governments and citizens best leave justice to market forces. In this model of ethical practice, governments avoid using regulation to keep industry in line and instead encourage industry to practise voluntary social responsibility. When industry-funded NGOs endorse these voluntary initiatives and codes of conduct, they lend legitimacy to the claim that corporate self-regulation constitutes good governance. Although corporatized activism can do considerable good, these authors argue that working within a corporate frame forces them to adopt modest, measurable goals that are achievable, that facilitate consumerism, and that legitimize the disparities and injustices of capitalism.

Pat Kelly concludes, in "Begging Your Pardon," that the alliances between pharma companies and nonprofit groups in Canada have shown they can self-regulate and function accountably. She notes, however, that in 2002, both sectors lacked "broadly recognized best practices."[19] To defend themselves against media challenges and to maintain public trust, she proposes that groups and pharmaceutical companies alike should further develop "frameworks for principled relationship-building":

> Despite the growing trend of cross-sector partnerships, it is not enough to welcome the new hybrids with open arms. For those groups who choose to pursue corporate alliances, it will be necessary to clearly articulate the terms and the outcomes, and be prepared to develop effective, flexible self-regulating mechanisms. Distinct boundaries must be maintained to safeguard against the "Astroturf" phenomena that drives media

rhetoric and undermines public trust. Accountability and transparency in these transactions are the methods that will safeguard and justify public confidence.[20]

Guidelines for Partnerships

Given the response to calls from within the industry and from the community of pharma-funded groups for more systematic attention to ethical principles, the partnership period saw the development of formal guidelines for disclosure and accountability. Nonprofit organizations, the industry, and the federal government all created such documents.

Among nonprofit groups, the Canadian Breast Cancer Network (CBCN) introduced guidelines for corporate partnerships in October 2001, and the Campaign to Control Cancer, a group Pat Kelly cofounded in 2001, has a sponsorship agreement that it uses to spell out the terms under which it accepts funding from corporations. Both agreements include a clause saying the organization will not endorse or promote a particular product. The CBCN is a member of the Canadian Cancer Action Network (CCAN), an umbrella organization for cancer organizations in Canada, and now subscribes to the CCAN Code of Conduct Governing Corporate Funding.[21] Signing the code is optional for CCAN members; those that decide to adopt it are required to recommit on an annual basis. CCAN does not monitor adherence to the code, which outlines guiding principles and policies for both patient organizations and companies. For example, activities will be conducted in accordance with the interests of patients (a principle), and the organization will not endorse or promote individual products or services (a policy). The CCAN code goes on to specify that "advocacy activities, such as making patient submissions for drug reviews or petitioning governments to fund a particular drug, are not considered promotion because these activities are intended to improve access to the treatment, rather than recommend that it be prescribed. Similarly, providing educational information on available treatments is not considered promotion."[22]

On January 1, 2009, the lobby organization for the Canadian brand-name pharmaceutical industry responded to criticisms about conflicts of interest and lack of transparency, and issued *Rx&D Guidelines for Transparency in Stakeholder Funding*.[23] The new guidelines were framed particularly to apply to relationships with "patient groups, consumer groups, advocacy groups, associations of health care professionals and the not-for-profit business sector."[24] A preamble asserts that it is "natural" that the pharmaceutical industry should work together with stakeholder groups, given the range of their mutual interests; however, it stated, the industry realizes the potential in these relationships for real or perceived conflicts of interest and is therefore committed to "transparent, trustworthy and credible" relationships.[25] A statement of principles affirms the priority of the health and well-being of patients, the independence and integrity of stakeholders, the need to avoid conflicts of interest in interaction with stakeholders, the transparency of funding relationships, and the need for clearly delineated parameters for joint activities. Guidelines advise companies to voluntarily disclose lists of stakeholders to which they gave direct funding, to avoid joint activities designed to promote specific medications, and to avoid creating patient groups for the sole purpose of furthering market access. A set of interpretive guidelines, and of questions and answers, includes the specification that projects and agreements that began before January 1, 2009, would be grandfathered and that Rx&D would not ("for now") monitor companies or penalize those that did not comply. Furthermore, the guidelines for transparency in relationships that member companies had with physicians uses stronger wording than a section on relationships with patient groups, which uses conditional wording. A spokesperson for Rx&D explained that the organization could not enforce the terms of a company's relationship with a patient organization if that group was not prepared to be fully transparent.[26]

Beth Kapusta and Pat Kelly, two of the activists who had worked in alliances with drug companies using formal agreements, describe how they had experienced the partnership agreements working in practice. Beth had been involved in cancer activism for about eight years when I interviewed her, and had worked with several pharma-funded industry groups and projects, as well as participating on government-sponsored cancer committees and forums. Because the companies usually have a one- or two-year corporate plan, the nonprofit organization would usually meet with the company a year ahead of a project they were asking to have funded. Beth explains:

In the early days, I would help with [the organization's] fundraising, so
I would attend some of the [discussions with pharma]. And it was
really hard work to get money out of those people.

Sharon: [*surprised*] Oh really?

Beth: Oh, yeah, absolutely! You have to present yourself as a well-run
business. You have to show the kind of work that you're doing, and
that it's got accountability and coherence. It's tough work.

The groups she was involved with always obtained funding from more
than one source, to mitigate the tendency a funder might have to push a
point of view or product. And, she emphasizes, in none of these projects
had she ever been asked by a pharmaceutical company to do anything that
offended her sense of independence; in fact, she had "never been asked to
do anything by a pharma company."

Pat Kelly describes the logic model, a type of management tool that
was part of her organization's annual business plan, which she used to
communicate the structure and function of a proposed project to a potential
corporate funder.[27]

Pat: It's just a quick one-page charting that shows, "These are our
program areas, these are our targets, these are our messages, and
these are our outcomes." And it gives you a nice flow: "That's what
we're going to do for the next two years, and this is what we're
asking *you* for."

So they don't get to cherry-pick. [They don't get to say,] "Yes, I
want my name on your website, but I really don't want to fund a
meeting in Kakabeka Falls. We're not really interested in that." [We
tell them,] "You have to do the whole ball of wax. And you can do it
at different levels, but you don't get to say what part you can do or
don't do. We don't change what we're going to do based on your
involvement or your money. We just let you know, 'This is what
we think needs to be done in the next year or so.'" So that's what
they get.

Sharon: When you say the groups should make their agreements
public, what would a typical agreement be like?

Pat: Basically it says, "This explains who we are and what our values are. And this is what our project plan is going to be for this year. This is our track record. This is how we have influenced government. These are the metrics, the outcome of this group for the last three years. And this is what it costs." So you publish your financial statement, and you say to them, "This is what we're asking you for, and this is what you get in return for that."

The Federal Government Normalizes the Service-Advocacy Divide

Within Canada's federal government, the idea of alliances between non-profit cancer entities and the pharmaceutical industry also gained normative status during this period. In 2000, as part of its modernization process, the Health Products and Food Branch (formerly the Health Protection Branch) within Health Canada set up an Office of Consumer and Public Involvement (OCAPI), to improve transparency and accountability within the regulatory regime. The office, which initiated and organized public engagement activities for the branch, served two purposes: it responded to public pressure to demonstrate its commitment to public involvement, and it brought Canada in line with an international trend in high-income democracies to incorporate public input into drug evaluation and approval processes. Staff within OCAPI, many of whom had community organizing and activism backgrounds, believed strongly in the principle of public involvement. They saw their work as potentially revolutionary and ahead of parallel efforts undertaken in the drug regulatory agencies in other countries.[28]

In 2004, the Health Products and Food Branch released a four-year strategic plan, which had as one of five strategies "Improved Transparency, Openness and Accountability to Strengthen Public Trust and Stakeholder Relationships." The plan for carrying out this transparency strategy listed changes that would take place within the branch but, although industry, patient, and consumer organizations were cited as stakeholders, along with government, the document did not discuss the onus on patient and consumer groups, or industry, to conform to principles of transparency.[29] Those of us working in women's health and consumer protection groups noted, however, that many of the people OCAPI selected to assess real-world product effectiveness and risk were from organizations sponsored by the pharmaceutical industry; that, our groups argued, was a conflict of interest and should (at least) be transparent. In response, OCAPI developed a document titled the *Voluntary Statement of Information Form for Public Involvement* (*VSI-PI*), designed to "recognize the importance and value of openness and transparency in public involvement activities and decision-making processes." The form, which went through several iterations, asked a series of questions, including whether the individual or the organization to which she belongs has either a direct or indirect financial interest in "an organization or company likely to be affected by the outcome of this public involvement activity." From the time of its inception, in August 2004, the form was conceived as wholly voluntary to complete: an individual can decline to respond to any or all of the questions and still participate in the public involvement activity; or she can fill out the form and decline to give the Health Products and Food Branch permission to make the information public.[30] A draft policy statement on the *VSI-PI*, issued in August 2004, explained the reason for this apparent inconsistency. Any information about participants in a public consultation had to conform to the requirements of the federal Privacy Act. Specifically, "The Privacy Act stipulates that the information provided cannot be used by the Branch for any purpose other than that to which the participant consented and the information cannot be used unless the participant completes all or part of the information form and signs the consent portion."[31] Thus, although participants at public consultations concerning drug policy would be asked in the interests of transparency to declare whether they had received funding from one or more drug companies that might be affected by the policy under discussion, the Privacy Act requires the government to make disclosure of personal information voluntary. As government lawyers interpreted the law, corporate funding to a voluntary sector organization with which the individual is affiliated counts as personal information, even if that person is participating in a consultation process that could have an impact on the public's health.

Along with federal government policies that pushed civil society groups to service provision, prohibited them from using government funds to support advocacy, and sanctioned the use of "unrestricted educational grants" from the pharmaceutical industry for the same purpose, OCAPI's implementation of consumer involvement at the Health Products and

Food Branch helped normalize the PHANGO (pharma-funded NGO). The impact of these policies on cancer activism is seen most clearly in the Canadian Strategy for Cancer Control, also known as the Cancer Control Strategy, or simply the Cancer Strategy.

In 1999, the country's major cancer charities and provincial cancer agencies set up a cancer-control initiative, with logistical support from Health Canada. The goal was to develop a nationwide, coordinated, comprehensive master plan to improve the way all cancers were handled at all stages, from prevention to palliative care. The strategy would thus develop a systematic approach for cancer policies within the government but also in provincial screening programs, public education about cancer, treatment protocols, and community supports. Bringing all cancers under a single policy-development umbrella was to build on and, in time, supplant the Canadian Breast Cancer Initiative/Alliance, which had drawn breast cancer groups into policy circles. Health Canada hired Neil Berman to coordinate the various volunteer committees of the plan. He explains his role in an interview:

> There were just two of us [Health Canada staff] there, and then we started ... by engaging with all the stakeholders, in particular, the very high level leaders in the cancer sector. What I was tasked with was setting up all the committees, engaging with all the stakeholders, and preparing recommendations to the federal government ... The strategy was worked out by a staff of bureaucrats, very few of us, in Health Canada ... and about 700 to 800 volunteer staff – not just medical staff and researchers, but patients, survivors, volunteers and charities, et cetera. The strategy was set up formally in 2002.

The pharmaceutical industry was absent from the three-year intensive planning stage but was brought in once the strategy was formally launched, says Neil, who continued to play a coordinating role. He describes the reasoning and process for accepting industry funding.

> *Neil:* So the decision was that, yes, we should not ignore ... the private sector, or we should not keep them out of the Cancer Strategy completely ... What our [governing] council decided was that if the

pharmaceutical industry [should] say, "Yes, we're able to provide you some funding for your clinical guidelines group," then we do have some acceptance: "Okay, you can provide us [funding] for [that], just as a generic grant support." They can't insist on any outcomes or intellectual property [reverting] to them; it's just a free grant. And that's something that a lot of the cancer agencies in this country have accepted.

Sharon: Is that the same as an unrestricted educational grant?

Neil: Exactly, yes. And there could be agreement – they could say, "Oh, we'd really like to be told what your committee eventually decides on ..., just out of interest, as long as it's okay for you to provide [the decision] to our industry." So those kinds of collaborations are fine.

Two breast cancer activists whose engagement with breast cancer groups date back to the early 1990s assumed leadership positions in two organizations connected to the plan: Liz Whamond and Jack Shapiro co-chaired the Canadian Cancer Advocacy Network, which later changed its name to the Canadian Cancer Action Network (CCAN), and Pat Kelly chaired the Campaign to Control Cancer (C2CC).The two groups mirrored the service-advocacy dichotomy within patient groups that the government's stance against funding advocacy had created (see Figure 2). The need for a service group of patients in the Cancer Strategy arose because the strategy had a large number of committees developing action plans in different areas and each one needed volunteers who were either ex-patients or current patients or, in some cases, family or friends of patients. Neil Berman describes the process he followed in setting up the groups:

What I did was I got all the organizations to agree to combine into a network ... It was called at the time the Canadian Cancer Advocacy Network. And then I suggested that they call it something else, because the federal government is not allowed to provide any funding for an advocacy network. So I said, "Well, I can only have meetings for cancer patient networks. You can attend those meetings, and I can fund [the expenses]." And I set up the meetings a couple of times a year.

Early [on], the Canadian Cancer Advocacy Network tried to get me to try to obtain funding for them, because they wanted to do a lot of advocacy. And I had to give lots of lectures, explaining that the federal government cannot fund advocacy projects.

The CCAN was an umbrella group representing fifteen or so cancer organizations. Its function was to raise issues within the Cancer Control Strategy that were relevant to cancer patients and their families. Liz Whamond's account of why the group changed its name from the Advocacy Network to the Action Network concurs with Neil Berman's: "We wanted to take government money, and we couldn't do that with 'advocacy' in the name." She and her cochair then agreed they would not take pharma money despite this limiting what they could do:

> [We] have always wanted to avoid pharma funding. Now, that doesn't apply to our member organizations [groups representing breast cancer, prostate cancer, leukemia, et cetera]. Many – I would guess most – of our members do take pharma money. But at the higher level, we've said no. That makes the member organizations happy, because we're not in competition with them for funds ... Many organizations say, "They're unrestricted grants." They probably are, and probably in the case of most unrestricted educational grants they don't interfere; but you know if you speak out [against something they want], they will cut you off.

The second organization, the C2CC, is not embedded in the Cancer Strategy but undertakes advocacy on the plan's behalf; its main revenue stream is pharma funding. Pat Kelly, the founder of the C2CC, did not believe that pharma funding was a problem for a group whose mandate was to promote the broad goals of a national cancer strategy with a large cross-section of the cancer community behind it.

> *Pat:* Because what we're trying to advance is the strategy. It's already determined. You know, it's [the product of] seven hundred people working together over three years ... So it's not about drugs. It's about a comprehensive approach to controlling cancer that includes primary prevention ... And then it has the whole palliative care, end-of-life program that was developed by the Canadian Hospice

Palliative Care Association. So it plugged everybody in and said, "A rising tide lifts all ships."

Sharon: So what *are* they getting in return?

Pat: They get to be part of the Canadian Strategy for Cancer Control, same as anybody else.

Sharon: They get their name on the ...

Pat: Same as every other group. So, I hear what you're saying. You would assume if they're there, and they're fat and influential, they're going to demand return on their investment. They get what everybody else gets – better cancer control. They get their name on the list.

Beth Kapusta, who became involved in the strategy as part of the C2CC, felt a palpable tension between the pharma-funded advocates and those who opposed pharma funding:

There's always been a huge war between people within the community, between those who accept pharma funding, as if it were black and white. You know – the pharma-takers, and the sanctimonious ones on the other side who feel they've never been tarnished by that conflict. And the Cancer Control Strategy was a classic war of those oppositional views.

The C2CC took a lot of heat for its pharma funding, says Beth. She feels, however, that the patient groups that were part of CCAN were hamstrung by their own embeddedness within the plan itself.

Beth: It was seen by Health Canada that if the patient component was being funded by public dollars, that advocacy was not part of their activity menu. So even though you have patient representation, you don't really have an effective public voice.

Sharon: And that's because of the government's views on advocacy?

Beth: Yeah. And that was told in no uncertain terms to the patient groups like CCAN, the patient arm of the Cancer Strategy.

Sharon: So what did they expect CCAN to do?

Beth: They expected a kind of patient pool to provide a volunteer advisory service to confer credibility on the process.

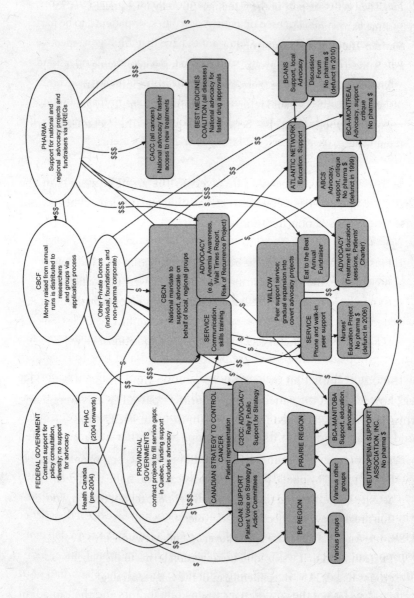

FIGURE 2 Group structure, 1999 to 2010: Funding sources divide service and advocacy

Neil Berman had a similar understanding of the role of the patient groups:

> One of the things I set up when I was working on the Cancer Control Strategy [addressed the fact that] we definitely needed patient survivors, or people who were focused on patient outcomes, or patients, to be part of our committees ... Because you want to have that kind of perspective when you're discussing things and making decisions: to understand what it is to be a patient – what would be the impacts, et cetera. And in all the committees across the cancer-control continuum that we set up ... we had to decide how we could find volunteers who are either ex-patients or current patients, or family or friends of patients.

I relayed to Neil that some people I had interviewed thought CCAN was ineffective because its members did not have their own budget.

> *Neil:* Well, they don't. And the only money I provided was to set up meetings. And even then, they said, "Oh, we need consultants or managers. We need to hire [them] to do advocacy work." And I said, "No, I can't apply for funding for that."

The Cancer Control Strategy thus reinforced a discourse that separates patient groups into those that are pharma funded and free to engage in advocacy and those that are government funded and assigned to service provision only. In contrast to those providing volunteer service to the Cancer Control Strategy, leaders in the pharma-funded advocacy group could build compensation into its budget, along with other advocacy-related expenses such as international conferences. As cochair of CCAN, Liz Whamond expressed her frustration at the resource inequality between the two groups. The C2CC had "huge machinery," including a company to handle logistics, she said, while she and her cochair "work off the corner of our desks." Nor could CCAN, unlike the C2CC, afford to send delegates to important policy meetings, like the Second International Cancer Control Congress, held in Rio de Janeiro in 2007, though the Canadian government was one of the conference's main contributors and the Canadian Strategy for Cancer Control was a topic on the program.

The federal government's embrace of corporate partnerships as a normalized means of supporting citizen advocacy complemented the parallel process that stripped civil society groups of government funding. As described in Chapter 3, the Liberal Party, which held power from 1993 to 2006, defunded civil society groups in its 1995 budget. Arguably, the Liberals had political as well as economic motives for weakening the civil society sector, which they did not overtly acknowledge. Many Liberal Party supporters opposed the free trade agreements that the government signed onto in the 1990s because they believed they undermined Canada's control of its social programs, including the health care system.[32] The party attempted to repair its damaged relations with this sector via its five-year Voluntary Sector Initiative, implemented in 2001, but unlike the earlier funding approach, the Voluntary Sector Initiative tied federal support of groups to the government's economic goals. When the Conservative Party took power in 2006, party strategists viewed the networks of civil society groups that various Liberal governments had funded over the years as a political threat. By consistently funding certain grassroots constituencies, they reasoned, the Liberals had cultivated "Liberal outrider organizations," whose members included "feminists, gay-rights activists, law professors, aboriginal leaders, environmentalists, etcetera" – groups that were assumed to be hostile to the Conservative ideology and agenda under Stephen Harper.[33] Tom Flanagan, a political scientist and adviser to Prime Minister Harper during the 2006 campaign, explained in a radio interview:

> Over decades, Liberals built up these kinds of organizations. It's partly a question of who gets money. It's also a matter of giving access: Who gets to have meetings with ministers? Defunding is part of it ... It's not something that's going to happen all at once, but I think we want to get back – I hope we'll get back – to more of a situation of neutrality where civil society organizations are expected to make it largely on their own resources.[34]

(Note that Flanagan's remarks refer to Conservative Party strategy under the Harper government. The "Red Tories," an influential contingent of members in the party's earlier guise as the Progressive Conservative Party, combined fiscal conservatism with a socially progressive agenda, including support of such causes as feminism and gay rights.[35])

Accordingly, in the partnership period, feminist organizations that had depended wholly or in large part on funding from the federal government had their funding sharply reduced or eliminated entirely, particularly if they had been involved in advocacy. This shift encountered resistance from many community organizations, as well as from Opposition parties in Parliament.[36] Several women's health groups critical of pharmaceutical companies lost funding that they had received through programs at Health Canada. DES Action Canada ceased operations in 2009; the Consumers' Association of Canada, a national consumer watchdog that had been an influential counterweight to corporate power since the 1950s, was crippled by the loss of its core government funding.[37] The Canadian Breast Cancer Network was threatened with defunding in 2008, but Opposition parties rallied to the organization's support and its grant was reinstated.

Resistance to Neoliberal Policies

To some extent, this environment of funding cutbacks simply continued the Liberal government's 1993 to 2005 starvation of government programs that were not in direct support of business or trade objectives. In 2004, for example, the federal government under Liberal prime minister Paul Martin launched a broad restructuring of regulatory policy called Smart Regulation, which promised to "streamline and speed up approval for new drugs, foods, biotechnology products ... [and] harmonize standards, especially between Canada and the United States."[38] After the 2006 federal election, which the Conservatives won, the restructuring process continued but under the name Cabinet Directive on Streamlining Regulation. Public consultations were held across the country on a draft directive. A government report on the consultation workshops took note of a split in responses to the proposal between consumer advocates and those from the business community. Summarizing the perspective of the nonprofit sector, the report notes:

> Participants from public advocacy groups worried that the Smart Regulation Initiative, and by implication the draft Directive, was being driven

by international trade considerations and North American integration, which they saw as a move toward deregulation and the lowest common denominator in protection for the environment, health and safety of Canadians.

Generally speaking, participants from the public advocacy sector felt strongly that the draft Directive subscribed to a business/*economy*-first paradigm.[39]

By contrast, the summary of testimony from business interests stated: "Many participants, primarily from the industry, business and natural resource sectors, expressed strong support for the overall approach of the draft Directive."[40]

The strategy, part of a ten-year plan to advance the country as an "innovative economy" on the world stage, gives lip service to health and public safety, but its main purpose is clearly to promote trade and innovation. In 2007, the federal government released a blueprint for modernizing drug regulation that it described as "proactive" and "enabling."[41] One aspect of the new model was a reformed drug regulatory system designed to bring Canada's review times in line with international benchmarked performance standards. Called progressive licensing, the new "life cycle" system of licensing was designed in part to speed up availability of new drugs; to this end it incorporated a lower standard for drug approvals. A second component was an improved system of post-marketing surveillance, to be achieved by numerous means, including collaboration with the FDA and other international drug review agencies.[42]

Even within the government, however, some actors strongly resisted applying the trade agenda to health and drugs. In 2004, a parliamentary committee released a report on the health aspects of prescription drugs, *Opening the Medicine Cabinet*, which made a series of recommendations on the questions of clinical trials, post-market surveillance, and direct-to-consumer advertising.[43] The report supported safety measures and openness over commercial interests in clinical trials. The report also stressed the need for independent information about drugs and expressed concern that industry promotion was contributing to inappropriate use of drugs and excess expenditures. It recommended major improvements in the reporting of adverse drug events, including heightened surveillance of drugs after licensing, with public disclosure of adverse-event reports. The report also recommended tightening the ban on direct-to-consumer advertising and enforcing violations.

On the broader question of health care, most Canadians – a proportion as high as 90 percent, according to one poll – continued to support the single-payer health system, despite a rhetoric of "unsustainability" from elites wanting tax cuts and a private system that would prioritize access on the basis of ability to pay.[44] In 2004, under Paul Martin's Liberal government, the federal government signed a health accord with the provinces and territories, an agreement designed to set national standards for health care and to provide stable funding.[45] While the government committed to a large transfer of funds to the provinces and mapped out its National Pharmaceuticals Strategy, it placed few conditions on the transfers, raising concerns about the lack of accountability when provinces violated the Canada Health Act by imposing user fees and extra billing, and transferring medicare to for-profits. Furthermore, when the health accord expired in March 2014, the ruling Conservative government opted not to renew it. According to the Canadian Health Coalition, this decision "will lead to 14 different health care systems. Access will depend on your ability to pay."[46] The Canadian Health Coalition also faulted the Harper government for major cuts to the Canada Health Transfer ($36 billion over ten years, to begin in 2017), elimination of the equalization portion of the Canada Health Transfer (an additional $16.5 billion in transfers over five years), and abandonment of the National Pharmaceuticals Strategy from the 2004 accord. The cost of new drugs to the system continued to make headlines in both Canada and the United States, with cancer drugs drawing particular attention.[47]

Within breast cancer organizations, pockets of resistance to the wave of pharma partnerships remained. Breast Cancer Action Montreal (BCAM), with its policy on corporate contributions adopted in 2001, made willingness to endorse the policy a prerequisite to joining the organization's board of directors or its small staff. The group also promoted its stand on pharma funding with a banner on its website. Increasingly isolated from the broader Canadian breast cancer movement, BCAM incorporated its lone-wolf position on pharma funding as part of a distinct identity: a commitment to promoting a carcinogen-free environment, opposition to pink marketing (using the breast cancer cause to market consumer products), and a willingness to adopt positions critical of drug promotion.[48]

In September 2001, BCAM became a member of Prevention First, a coalition of like-minded American and Canadian health organizations that testified in 1998 at an FDA hearing of the Breast Cancer Prevention Trial.[49] Groups in the new coalition had urged the FDA to refuse Astra-Zeneca's application to market Nolvadex (tamoxifen) to healthy women, and all were concerned about conflicts of interest involving the pharmaceutical industry. The coalition viewed itself as a counterforce to the advertising campaigns of pharmaceutical companies and identified itself as "a coalition of independent health organizations," to underline the fact that no member groups accepted funds from the industry. In mid-2001, the coalition was awarded a $200,000 grant for two years from the Goldberg Family Foundation, which enabled each of the member groups to hire a part-time staff member. Laura Shea began to work for BCAM in two areas: pharmaceutical policy, especially the insufficient attention regulatory agencies paid to adverse drug events, and promoting the precautionary principle as the best basis for policies governing the use of toxic substances to the environment. She organized film and speaker events to stimulate public discussion and wrote regular articles in the organization's newsletter. Issues discussed included the FDA's decision to add a "black box warning" to the label of tamoxifen, the Women's Health Initiative's finding that hormone replacement therapy increased the risks of breast cancer and heart attacks in older women, and the safety-focused recommendations of the parliamentary committee's report *Opening the Medicine Cabinet*.[50]

When the coalition's funding from the American foundation expired in 2003, Laura's status shifted to that of a volunteer and member of the board. Although she continued in this capacity for several years, she began full-time employment and had to restrict her involvement. Pharma funding and drug policies continued to preoccupy BCAM, however, as reflected in newsletter articles up to 2007.

Despite the unwillingness of most breast cancer organizations to eschew pharma funding, the split in the movement was not absolute. In some organizations that endorsed accepting funds from drug companies, the group structure was adapted to allow an expression of resistance to pharma funding. Within Breast Cancer Action Nova Scotia, the website administrator, Paula, continued to protect the Discussion Forum from the incursion of pharma funds until 2007, when the Canadian Breast Cancer Foundation discontinued its funding for that project. Paula's paid position was eliminated, and she left the organization. The group's Internet discussion group subsequently lost momentum and was abandoned in 2010.[51]

When Willow changed its policy to accept funds from the pharmaceutical industry in 2000, "Virginia," who was still a staff member, created a similar "no pharma funds" zone around a project of her own design, educating nurses about the concerns of women with breast cancer. She continued to work for Willow until 2006, when she and two other staff members were laid off. While she acknowledged that her "salary had to come from somewhere," and if the organization was accepting pharma money for its general operating funds, she could not remain "completely untainted," she tried to isolate her project from the group's pharma-funding policy:

> They [the executive director and board of Willow] knew I wouldn't take pharma funding for my program, so in a way there was some small part of me that felt that I was upholding what the [organization's] original beliefs were – which were still my beliefs – that we should not be taking money from pharmaceutical companies ... For a couple of years in a row [the program with nurses] got funding from the Canadian Breast Cancer Foundation for the second and third year, and then we got money from the Bank of Montreal for a year – that kept me going. And then, by default, I persuaded them to hang onto the teaching program and put it in core funding, so I wasn't dependent on an outside funder ... I made it quite clear that I wouldn't represent the program to a pharmaceutical [company], but that I would do what I could to try and bring somebody else on to fund it. And [the program] was a difficult sell to funders; it never got funded by an independent [sponsor] again after that.
>
> And I would say [to the executive director], "If I have to stand up in front of a classroom of nurses and tell them that I'm here by virtue of AstraZeneca, I'm going to throw up. I'm just not going to do it. So if you want to take the money, take it, but AstraZeneca or anybody else is not going to get their logo on my stuff. And I won't mention it." Whereas

when I was doing [the nurses' program] for Bank of Montreal or the CBCF [Canadian Breast Cancer Foundation], I would say very briefly at the beginning, "I'm here because the Canadian Breast Cancer Foundation gave me the money." Or "I'm here because Bank of Montreal gave us a grant." And that's it ... But that was something I was able to live with, and I wasn't prepared to head it up with a pharma name.

She saw the distinction as "a little bit like ethical investing":

And if you want to be completely pure about this, are you going to question every individual donor, where they got their money from? How far back do you want to go on this tree of money? And I guess that's how I learned to live with BMO [Bank of Montreal] money. I decided, "Okay, well, I think I don't want to know where BMO has its money invested" ... But the difference between that and pharma funding was [the pharmaceutical companies] had an immediate agenda [i.e., selling drugs to patients].

When "Virginia" was let go from her job, she did not know whether her stance against pharma funding was a contributing factor: "[The board's] argument against [the nurses' program] all the time was it should be self-funding. And at the end of it, how much incentive in getting rid of me was that I was a loudmouth that didn't fall into line, and how much of it was a purely fiscal decision?"

Even a "purely fiscal decision" can't be untangled from the issue of pharma funding, however, because Virginia had been unable to find an alternative sponsor for the project. The claim that the pharmaceutical sector was virtually the only industry willing to provide substantial funding for breast cancer projects is a consistent theme in the interviews with women who attempted to find alternative commercial sponsors when government funding dried up. And this claim resonates with the private sector shift in strategy for funding nonprofit groups; in the late 1990s, companies across the spectrum abandoned haphazard "good citizen" funding in favour of alliances with organizations that could benefit the company in some way.

By 2008, helped in no small part by government policies that left them few alternative sources of funding, groups that defined their role on behalf of patients as independent watchdogs vis-à-vis the pharmaceutical industry saw their power and numbers dwindle; the dominant advocacy voices for patients were pharma funded.[52]

Beneath a Community "at War," a Political Divide

As the debate about pharma funding among groups in Canada's breast cancer movement intensified, the split within the community appeared on the surface as an often bitterly personal, internecine competition for increasingly scarce funding. Less obvious were the connections to the tectonic plates realigning health policies to conform to a neoliberal world order. The charge that government funding of activism presents a conflict of interest while pharma funding of grassroots advocacy can be made ethical via agreements like the unrestricted educational grant glosses over several critical ways in which the new forms of governance rewrite the rules of activism. Welfare state governments recognize power and resource differences among social groups and assume that redressing these inequities is, in the long run, necessary for democracy. Protest and critique (within defined boundaries) are legitimate means of reducing social disparities. Providing government funds to groups with a social change agenda is, therefore, not a conflict of interest but a way for governments to support countervailing powers that would restrain market forces. Neoliberalism rewrites these assumptions to define the restraint of market forces as a social problem.[53]

PHANGOs are just one manifestation of activism funded by multinational corporations. In the past few decades, groups as disparate as Save the Children, Amnesty International, and the Sierra Club have all taken on corporate partners. In their analysis of the global move to corporatized activism, Peter Dauvergne and Genevieve LeBaron argue that although groups required to benchmark their accomplishments in the community to justify corporate grants may do some good, they inevitably set modest, achievable goals that fit within a corporate values frame. By designing strategies for ethical purchasing, they promote consumerism. Above all, they don't challenge the injustices of capitalism. The rewriting of goals within the patients' movement becomes apparent with close examination of particular projects, as we'll see in the next chapter.

7

Advocacy Groups and the Continuing Struggle over the Pharma-Funding Question

One is also quite aware that the bottom line of a pharmaceutical company of course is to improve share values and increase profits, not necessarily always for the best outcome for the patient. Not that they aren't interested [in the patient's outcome]; they are very much interested; because the best medicine will obviously make the best profit, et cetera. But sometimes, even though a medicine may not be more effective, it's promoted in a way that [makes it] seem better, so one should be careful about that. And being part of a provincial cancer agency, which is a publicly funded entity and not for profit, clearly we should not be interested in lining the pockets of pharma companies, we should be interested in what's best for our patients.

– VICTOR LING, SCIENTIFIC DIRECTOR OF THE TERRY FOX RESEARCH
INSTITUTE AND SCIENTIST WITH THE BC CANCER AGENCY

Anthropologist Emily Martin's account of pharmaceuticals as having complex personalities colourfully captures the idea of social construction as it applies to drugs. A drug is not just a chemical or biological entity; even before emerging from the lab, its remedy/poison duality will permeate the imagination of its discoverer, whose career may hinge on how his or her brainchild performs in animal tests and (assuming it clears that hurdle), in clinical trials. From there, an array of significant actors – company executives, the marketing team, clinical researchers, physicians, regulators, journalists, and patients – all have a hand in shaping a new treatment's developing personality as the drug journeys through its life cycle.

In this chapter, I examine three pharma-funded advocacy group projects and ask whether and how the funding helped construct the personalities of the drugs in question. A fourth project addressed a broader question, the issue of patients' rights, including what rights they have to access new treatment drugs.

Case 1: A Dance around EPO

The drug erythropoietin or EPO (brand names Epogen and Eprex) first appears in my chronology of Canada's breast cancer movement in 1991, at the parliamentary hearings. In her testimony, Sylvia Morrison cited her inability to access Epogen, an erythropoietin-stimulating agent (ESA), as one roadblock in her desperate attempt to gain access in Canada to the experimental treatment of high-dose chemotherapy. ESAs stimulate the production of red blood cells, and the drug's role in the complex but ultimately discredited high-dose chemo procedure was to combat anemia. A second drug, Neupogen, reduced the chance of death from infection, obviating the need for isolation and allowing for shorter hospital stays. Erythropoietin reappears later in my patient advocacy narrative under the name Eprex – the drug for anemia that Ortho Biotech was marketing in Canada when the company provided a large grant to the Canadian Breast Cancer Network (CBCN) for advocacy. Ortho Biotech sells erythropoietin as Epogen in the United States but as Eprex in Canada, which explains the name discrepancy.[1]

Erythropoietin has a complicated corporate and legal history. The American biotech company Amgen developed EPO in the 1980s and manufactures the drug, but Amgen was too small to market the product on a large scale so made a licensing agreement with Ortho Biotech, a subsidiary of Johnson & Johnson (also called Janssen-Ortho). The agreement gave Amgen the kidney dialysis market in the United States, whereas Ortho Biotech had the right to market to American cancer patients suffering from anemia and to the entire European market. A bitter territorial and legal dispute soon ensued over competition for the lucrative cancer patient market; post-2000, ESAs rose to be among the world's top-selling drugs, with combined sales of over $10 billion in 2006. Details of this corporate struggle – a case study in shady drug-marketing strategies – would be too long a digression here; nonetheless, the backstory is the sort one might want to consider before entering a partnership with one of the principals.[2]

As seen in Chapter 5, when Ortho Biotech provided funding to the CBCN for advocacy, the negotiations set off a dispute within the organization among the board members and ultimately led to the resignation of the president, Karen. From her perspective, the company wanted to push the boundaries of an unrestricted educational grant and to use the organization for product promotion. Group members who accepted the funding saw the company's conditions as justifiable; they believed telling patients about anemia and chemotherapy, and encouraging them to discuss potential remedies with their doctors, was a useful service and did not constitute drug promotion if they didn't specifically mention Eprex. At this time, Eprex had no clear poison side to its personality as a breast cancer therapy. On another front, however, EPO was emerging as being less than benign. ESAs were introduced into competitive cycling circles as blood-doping agents in the late 1980s, and their benefits proved spectacular (stimulating erythropoietin increases oxygen-carrying capacity, one of several mechanisms that likely account for the boost it gives to competitive athletes). As a means to cheat at sports, however, ESAs had a downside. An excess of red blood cells makes blood thick, sluggish, and prone to clot, conditions favourable to sudden death by heart attack or stroke. Also in the late 1980s, when ESAs were being tested in clinical trials in Europe, a cluster of eighteen elite cyclists in the Netherlands and Belgium died mysteriously, though use of ESAs was the suspected cause.[3]

Competitive cyclists clearly put their bodies under enormous duress, so even if ESAs caused these fatalities, it has no bearing on its significance for breast cancer patients. The use of EPO in oncology is littered with red flags of its own, however. First, the Food and Drug Administration (FDA) approved the agents to treat anemia in cancer patients in 1993 based on very little evidence. Johnson & Johnson submitted pooled data from numerous small studies and enrolled patients with various tumours. As Otis Webb Brawley, chief medical and scientific officer of the American Cancer Society, explains it, this was a time when the AIDS epidemic threatened America's blood banks, and "the prospect of finding a hormone that would induce the body to produce its own hemoglobin was enticing."[4] Although the pooled studies were the basis for approving ESAs for anemia in cancer patients, the researchers asked only whether the drugs "had the ability to prevent blood transfusions."[5] They did not ask about toxicity or the impact on disease progression or survival. Despite these omissions – critical questions to be answered, in Brawley's view, before the drug could be given to cancer patients – EPO gained approval because it was asked to clear one hurdle and succeeded: it prevented blood transfusions.[6]

In 2002, ESAs were linked to a small but significant number of cases of pure red cell aplasia, a life-threatening condition in which the body loses its ability to produce red blood cells on its own.[7] Research then began to accumulate that the drug actually *hastened* the death of cancer patients, in some cases by thromboembolic events but also perhaps by promoting tumour growth – a possibility the FDA had raised when the agency first licensed erythropoietin for cancer in 1993.[8] The initial evidence came from a clinical trial of patients with head and neck cancer that compared those given erythropoietin to a control group and found that the patients given erythropoietin died sooner.[9] Another clinical trial, involving 939 women with metastatic breast cancer who were undergoing chemotherapy, was undertaken with the expectation that those given Eprex would survive longer than those given a placebo.[10] Instead, after four months, the reverse was true, and the trial was terminated. The drug had two adverse effects: it promoted both tumour growth and fatal thrombotic events. Four additional trials, including one with non-small-cell lung cancer patients, yielded similar results; and two clinical trials published in 2006 showed that ESAs increased the risk of death from thromboembolic events in patients with chronic renal failure.[11]

Inadequate pre-market testing was not the only problem with ESAs. Both Amgen and Ortho Biotech had aggressively promoted the highly priced drugs, which the business press touted as a major therapeutic success story, as well as being a financial blockbuster for both Amgen and Ortho Biotech (Johnson & Johnson). This financial success was achieved by crossing the boundaries of legal promotion. In the United States, the FDA had approved ESAs for the limited purpose of reducing the number of blood transfusions required to treat severe anemia, either induced by chemotherapy or caused by the cancer itself; the drugs were not approved "to alleviate fatigue or weakness or to improve a patients' quality of life."[12] In Canada, approval was also confined to treating extreme anemia; any other uses would be considered "off-label prescribing" – a practice that is legal for a physician in treating a particular patient (on the grounds that physicians are free to exercise professional judgment in the best interest of their patients). Pharmaceutical companies, however, are prohibited from promoting off-label use of their products, since approval is based on evidence that a particular drug has benefits that outweigh the risks for the particular condition stated on the label.

Despite this limited indication, Johnson & Johnson used direct-to-consumer television ads in the United States to promote its product as a way to alleviate fatigue or to give cancer patients "strength for living."[13] The ads depicted chemo-weakened cancer patients who could make an omelette, run a B & B, or throw a grandson in the air after taking Procrit. According to Otis Webb Brawley, scientists at the FDA tried to stop the ads but "pro-industry attorneys appointed by the Bush administration to run the agency's top legal office blocked the scientists' efforts."[14] In May 2007, prompted by concerns about "hyperbolic advertising" on the part of the companies that make ESAs[15] and a rebate system instituted by the companies that allowed high-prescribing physicians to reap substantial profits,[16] the FDA convened an advisory committee to consider whether the drugs were overused. Testifying before the committee, a furious Otis Webb Brawley suggested erythropoietin was akin to "Miracle-Gro for cancer."[17]

The FDA responded by placing its highest level of safety alert, a black-boxed warning, on Amgen's two ESAs, Aranesp and Epogen, and on Ortho Biotech's Procrit. The black box typically signals a potentially fatal outcome. Health Canada, which does not use black-boxed warnings, issued a safety advisory about the medications on April 16, 2007, noting that the drugs were sold in Canada under the names Aranesp and Eprex.[18]

At the time the CBCN engaged in its relationship with Ortho Biotech, no published evidence showed the dangers of Eprex for cancer patients; neither did any evidence show their safety. Sudden deaths among cyclists were on the record, however, and the FDA had raised tumour promotion as a possibility as far back as 1993. Thus, while the CBCN had scant opportunity to be informed about these concerns, the companies making the drugs presumably were aware of them. To what extent did Ortho Biotech take advantage of the CBCN as a vehicle for promoting its product? In its second phase, the advocacy awareness project was clearly defined in the agreement with the organization to include discussions of anemia. And the materials the CBCN generated about anemia and chemotherapy also mentioned fatigue, an elision that could be interpreted as subtly broadening the indication in the minds of patients. Thus, in its efforts to remain viable, the CBCN may have inadvertently drawn attention to a drug that hastened the deaths of members who trusted the organization for information. Furthermore, I found no evidence that the organization actively warned patients of its dangers once the drug's dangers were documented.

In 2008, I interviewed "Hanna," a former CBCN board member, who had remained on the board after Karen deKoning's resignation. Hanna was pleased with the relationship the group had with Ortho Biotech on several levels. First, the company had provided money at a time when funding from Health Canada had been unreliable. Second, with the money the company provided, the CBCN was able to produce the diary and appointment book to help patients undergoing treatment make decisions. These may seem like benign aids to give to cancer patients, but the items could subtly support the company's promotional goals by encouraging patients to keep track of possible symptoms of disease progression and of drug side effects, such as fatigue, and encourage them to see their doctors at the first sign of problems.

Upon being asked if she had had any reservations about Ortho Biotech promoting one of its drugs for use with breast cancer patients at the time the group received funding, Hanna referred to having worked in a hospital setting where she saw the dangers of blood transfusions (a treatment for extreme anemia); she also emphasized her comfort with the relationship the group had with the company.

> *Hanna:* At no time did we have to, nor would we, endorse, okay? I
>   think, personally, Eprex was a good idea at the time.
> *Sharon:* It hasn't worked out very well, though.
> *Hanna:* It hasn't. But then again, if you look at blood transfusion, if
>   I had my druthers, I'd rather have Eprex than a blood transfusion. I
>   used to work in blood transfusion. It's not what they know that's in
>   it [the blood], it's what they don't know. And they had been using
>   [Eprex] for renal transplants and renal dialysis for years at this

particular point ... It's a choice out there what we believe; but we
would never endorse any product ... Other people assumed we did,
but that was their problem.

Sharon: Well, it's also a problem for the group if there's an appearance
of closeness.

Hanna: We've also learned through the years that people can think
what the heck they want. And if people are looking [for problems],
I mean, you could do that with any project. So if they want to think
it, fine.

Since the tainted-blood scandals of the 1980s, high-income countries, including Canada, have introduced measures to minimize the risk of infections from blood transfusions.[19] Although it's true that blood transfusions are never risk-free, Otis Webb Brawley argues that, for cancer patients, "transfusions should be given in place of ESAs whenever feasible, particularly to patients with metastatic disease. A patient with active disease is more likely to suffer tumor progression: the more tumor you have, the more tumor there is to stimulate."[20]

Case 2: A Dance for New Anti-hormonals

Estrogen is known to stimulate tumour growth in the majority of breast cancers (tumours classified as estrogen-receptor-positive, or ER+), and numerous breast cancer treatments that reduce estrogen exposure have been developed. The UK-based company AstraZeneca introduced the now-classic breast cancer treatment tamoxifen (brand name Nolvadex) in the 1970s. Initially, tamoxifen's success rested on the drug's dramatic reduction of the woman's chances of developing a second cancer in her cancer-free breast – a surrogate endpoint; by 1988, combined results of clinical trials showed that tamoxifen meets the higher standard of extending survival time.[21] Although tamoxifen has side effects that can be life-threatening, a 1998 study that weighed tamoxifen's reductions in mortality from breast cancer against increased mortality from endometrial cancer and/or blood clots (tamoxifen's known life-threatening side effects) found that the benefits far outweigh the risks.[22] Subsequent studies with longer follow-up (up to fifteen years) have affirmed tamoxifen's benefits for women diagnosed with early ER+ cancers and show that reductions in mortality continue even after medication is stopped.[23] These reductions are still greater if tamoxifen is continued for ten years rather than five.[24] There seems little doubt that the drug contributed significantly to the reduction in breast cancer mortality in high-income countries since the early 1990s. It might seem strange, then, that patient advocacy groups would focus their energies for a decade on a class of drugs designed to replace this reliable workhorse.

In the first half of the 2000–09 decade, AstraZeneca, Pfizer, and Novartis all had competing entries in a new class of breast cancer drugs known as aromatase inhibitors. AstraZeneca, the company that developed tamoxifen, developed the first aromatase inhibitor, Arimidex (anastrozole) and was ahead of the competition in generating clinical trial results; Novartis was not far behind, however, with its entry Femara (letrozole), while the third company, Pfizer, was close on the heels of its rivals with a large international study of Aromasin (exemestane). By 1995, all three drugs were in various stages in the process of passing through the drug approval process.[25]

Like tamoxifen, these drugs reduce a woman's exposure to her endogenous estrogen, but by a different mechanism. Whereas tamoxifen blocks the ability of circulating estrogen to enter the tumour, aromatase inhibitors are designed to eliminate the production of estrogen in postmenopausal women almost completely (they are not meant to treat premenopausal breast cancers). Theoretically, then, their effect in reducing breast cancer recurrence might be expected to exceed that of tamoxifen; however, side effects might be more severe than tamoxifen's. Given tamoxifen's extraordinary commercial success – by the late 1990s, the drug had become the bestselling anticancer treatment on the market – the prospect of an even better drug was generating excitement on the financial front. In Canada, because tamoxifen dates to the era when compulsory licensing was in effect, many generic versions were available throughout the 1990s; elsewhere, however, the expiry on AstraZeneca's patent on tamoxifen in 2002 was closely watched in business circles. In the global marketplace, to justify the anticipated higher price, the new class of drugs would have to demonstrate a significantly improved ratio of risk to benefit.

In the oncology literature, clinical trial results of the drugs caused both anticipation and controversy. The three studies mentioned above each had a similar design in which postmenopausal women with ER+ tumours were treated first with tamoxifen, then randomly switched to an aromatase inhibitor or to a comparison group of either tamoxifen or a placebo. By March 2004, when the early results of the third study appeared, each of the three novel drugs had been shown to significantly lower the risk of a recurrence compared with the standard treatment of a five-year course of tamoxifen. The early clinical trial results suggest that both Arimidex and Femara have fewer serious side effects than tamoxifen – neither causes endometrial cancer – though both weaken bones, raising the risk of fractures, osteoporosis, and joint pain.

These findings fell short of demonstrating the superiority of aromatase inhibitors over tamoxifen because all three trials had been halted before their intended completion date, on the grounds that withholding a more effective therapy would be unfair to women in the standard treatment group. The practice of stopping a trial early is based on ethical considerations (volunteers in a clinical trial should not be denied a treatment that is clearly superior to the one administered in the arm to which they are randomized), but the appropriate criteria for stopping a trial are hotly debated in the ethics literature. The use of surrogate endpoints is a particular concern, and all three trials of aromatase inhibitors used the surrogate endpoint of a cancer recurrence as the basis for stopping, rather than a true endpoint: improved overall survival and/or quality of life. Early stopping thus precluded gathering evidence of long-term benefits and toxic effects of the newer therapy compared with tamoxifen, leaving the most important questions unanswered. Do aromatase inhibitors reduce mortality, as tamoxifen has been shown to do? If they do, does their impact on mortality exceed that of tamoxifen? Did the prolongation of disease-free survival come at the expense of reduced quality of life? Without answers to these questions, the research and treatment communities were divided: enthusiasts of the new treatments eagerly recommended that the newer drugs be adopted into standard practice; more cautious voices argued that the results were early findings only and could not justify shifting standard practice away from a proven treatment like tamoxifen. Stephen Cannistra, a professor of medicine at Harvard University, cited the study of letrozole and tamoxifen as an example of where early stopping may have led to a misleading conclusion. Although the four-year disease-free survival rate favoured the letrozole group compared with placebo,

> there was no statistically significant difference in OS [overall survival], and the letrozole group experienced a greater frequency of osteoporosis, fractures, hot flashes, and myalgias. In addition, no patient received letrozole for more than 3 years, precluding any meaningful assessment of long-term toxicity or optimal duration of therapy. Although a QOL [quality of life] analysis was performed as part of this study, the results were not available at the time of the initial study publication.[26]

The ambiguous results of a trial interrupted prematurely may be frustrating to those in pursuit of answers, but one group of ethicists points out that most parties to a clinical trial benefit perversely from the early-stopping practice:

> For example, truncated trials that report a large treatment effect tend to be published in the most prestigious medical journals, which enhances the careers of the investigators and increases the likelihood that they will receive grants. Funding agencies have an interest in stopping trials early to minimize research costs. Pharmaceutical and for-profit sources that financially support trials are interested not only in controlling costs but also in the publicity and market share that result from reporting a trial stopped early for apparent benefit. Medical journals are interested in these trials because of publicity and citations, which result in increased journal impact factor, prestige, and advertising revenue. And patients and their advocates are motivated to stop a trial early when the experimental intervention is promising in order to hasten delivery of the intervention to clinical practice. All of these motives may affect investigators' decisions and encourage an inappropriately early stop to a trial.[27]

Yet the results of a trial that is stopped early are difficult to apply to clinical practice. An editorial published along with the study of Pfizer's Aromasin reflects on the dilemma of evaluating aromatase inhibitors given that trials for all three of the new drugs were stopped before meaningful results were available. Martine Piccart-Gebhart, a professor of oncology in Belgium, writes:

> The weaknesses of the [Coombes et al.] study are the immaturity of the data in terms of overall survival and safety ... Will the study show a survival benefit with longer follow-up? The answer is uncertain. The hazards of death could be disproportionate over time ... The results of these three trials at median follow-up of only 30 months does not allow us to conduct a useful risk-benefit analysis, which is an integral part of making appropriate treatment decisions. Although the short-term toxic effects of aromatase inhibitors have not been particularly worrisome ... the long-term consequences of estrogen deprivation in postmenopausal women remain a concern. Particular attention will need to be paid to bone and cardiovascular health, cognitive and sexual function, and quality of life ... Considering these three important trials, what should clinicians do? Many more years will be required to fine-tune the risk-benefit assessment of adjuvant aromatase inhibitors.[28]

And as Piccart-Gebhart predicted, assessing the three aromatase inhibitors in relation to tamoxifen and in relation to one another has proved to be a long-term project. As new clinical trial data emerge, reviews of the data from the three novel agents continue to generate controversy. One research team remarked on a "developing trend among oncologists to conclude that aromatase inhibitor adverse effects are rather inconsequential," despite evidence that 15 percent to 20 percent of participants in clinical trials discontinue the drugs because of toxic effects, including joint pain, vaginal dryness, loss of libido, hair loss, and cognitive impairments.[29] Two separate cost-effectiveness analyses disagreed on whether the gains that aromatase inhibitors offer in disease-free survival justify the substantial increase in cost over tamoxifen.[30]

Despite the uncertainty over their effects, in the regulatory sphere, all three drugs have gained marketing approval. In July 2004, Health Canada awarded AstraZeneca's Arimidex the status of NOC/c – meaning conditional approval – as a treatment for early breast cancer in postmenopausal women who had already been treated with tamoxifen. The acronym "NOC/c" stands for "notice of compliance with conditions," meaning that, on the basis of early clinical trial data, the drug meets the conditions for approval (i.e., safety and efficacy) and the company can begin marketing it for the specified indication; however, because the results are preliminary, the company must continue to monitor results and submit them to the agency. Novartis's Femara was awarded NOC/c status for extended adjuvant therapy on April 1, 2005, and on May 12, 2006, Pfizer's Aromasin gained NOC/c approval from Health Canada for early breast cancer after two to three years of tamoxifen therapy.[31]

Since AstraZeneca was one of the companies to support Willow once the organization dropped its ban on pharma partnerships, I asked "Virginia" if the group had engaged in any activities that might be seen as promoting the company's products. As with the decision to change the policy on pharma funding, she and other staff members were uneasy about the group's relationship with the company, but they were not privy to the discussions of the organization's board. She laughed at my question and replied:

> Funny you should ask ... And this is where the secrecy comes in. After AstraZeneca started negotiations with Willow, the organization took up a relationship with them through what they call "patient information sessions" ... There would be a patient forum [at] different places in the province. There would be a doctor and the executive director, I don't know who else. And it would be advertised in the community under a title like "hormonal treatments" or something like that, and would be promoted through the local hospital. Usually, the doctor would be a local doctor.
>
> And what we were given to understand was that these were sessions that were funded by AstraZeneca, but we never knew what Willow was doing or getting out of it. And when we questioned the executive director, she would say, "Well, I'm just there to represent Willow's services at these events, to balance it out" ... And so whether or not the doctor or any other pharma rep at that event was talking specifically about a specific drug, I cannot swear would be the case. But it was my understanding that [she] became very *au fait* with some of the products or product that were being promoted at the time ... So I can't say. I do know that the way it played out with us is she never told us what went on.

Nor, Virginia recalls with chagrin, could Willow's staff obtain details on trips the executive director made to international meetings:

She would end up at these international conferences as well, in Europe. I mean, we used to say, "Ah, Christ, she's off to the South of France again!" [*Both laugh.*] Totally pissed off, we were! The furthest we got anywhere was probably Sudbury or something. And this was this side of the coin. They would send her off on these things, and it was all pharma stuff. It was all pharma funded. It was a joyride. And I don't know that Willow ever actually saw a lot of money out of it ... Because we'd pore over the annual report and see whether or not we could find this money – what was in it for us? If we were getting blighted by this, where's the money? ... But we, there was never any real evidence of that, just these mysterious patient information sessions, and these trips to Europe to be the Canadian representative. And at these things, results of trials would be announced ...

So the answer to that question is yes, I think that there was a hand in. You know, this is around the time that there was competition. Tamoxifen was on the wane. And there was a competition for the estrogen-receptor-positive market [i.e., the aromatase inhibitors]. And yes, I think that that's what that was. But can I prove it?

Based on Virginia's (albeit incomplete) understanding, the format of the meetings in the province resembled information meetings about treatment options that AstraZeneca funded in regional groups across the country. In 2005, Breast Cancer Action Nova Scotia (BCANS) accepted an overture to participate in a public education evening. A local oncologist (whom some of the women in the group knew as their cancer specialist) approached the group to say AstraZeneca had invited him to give a public talk on breast cancer at the provincial art gallery. The company was sponsoring several such events in cities across the country and had hired a PR firm to book the venue and place advertisements. The group's role would be to take on some of the organizational and hosting responsibilities ("the scut work," as one board member put it). In exchange it would receive $1,000 of the total $5,000 the company had budgeted for the event. In accordance with the group's "case-by-case" policy, this offer went to the board. Rose recalls, "And we debated about that for quite a while! [*Laughs.*]

And then we decided, 'Well, okay, that's not compromising ... We're not endorsing their products, we're not giving them our blessing or anything.' And that sort of opened our eyes to something known as an 'unrestricted educational grant.'"

To ensure that BCANS was not in any way endorsing the company's products, the group set out certain conditions. It told the company that it would not mention the company's sponsorship in its introductory remarks; as well, it obtained assurances from the oncologist that he would be discussing *all* adjuvant therapy in his talk and that he would not make any specific references to AstraZeneca products. The group also told the company that it did not want it to have any brochures or signs on the site, and that AstraZeneca would not be acknowledged as sponsor in the program. BCANS's phone number appeared on the advertising so that the company would not have contact information of patients or family members who called. The event went smoothly, and members of BCANS were pleased that AstraZeneca remained totally uninvolved.

For BCANS's board members, receiving a share of the money was not the sole, or even the main, benefit of participating in the event. As part of the Atlantic Breast Cancer Network, a project funded with a federal government grant, the group was initiating a series of its own educational talks, organized in-house. When members of the public called the group for details of the evening, they could opt to have their name added to the group's own list for promoting events. The event also raised the group's profile, associating its name with a successful evening (about fifty people attended) at an attractive downtown venue.

The following year, a radiation oncologist who was well liked in the community approached BCANS and invited the group to participate in a similar event, with sponsorship from Pfizer. Once again, the board discussed the project and members agreed to go forward. "Cindy," the then-president, explains: "The board will want to know, 'What do they [Pfizer] expect in return?' And that would depend ... if they expected a lot in return, of course we would turn it down ... You know, we're very leery about taking pharmaceutical money and being associated with any pharmaceutical company." For this second event, two oncologists and a plastic surgeon shared the agenda. The session took place at the local cancer centre and drew 150 people.

Once again, the company paid all the costs, including the advertising, the audio-visuals, and an honorarium of about $500 each for two oncologists (the plastic surgeon was not paid). The radiation oncologist handled the communications with Pfizer and, as before, no mention was made at the event of the sponsoring company or its products. As was true of the previous information session, the board members involved in organizing the event saw the opportunity to expand the group's member base and reputation as more important than the direct financial payment from Pfizer of about $1,000.

When I asked BCANS' board members about the industry's motives for giving the group funds for an event where it had no publicity, they were perplexed. "Meredith" commented, "It would be nice if we knew exactly what pharma wanted from us." Rose speculated, "I guess it looks good on their bottom line to say, 'We gave money to BCANS; so maybe they are getting some good PR out of it with their stockholders.'"

Despite the competitive environment of new-drug sweepstakes, all three companies had a common interest in gaining awareness and clinical acceptance of aromatase inhibitors as better than tamoxifen. A public information session at which an oncologist would talk to patients about adjuvant therapies for breast cancer – especially new developments – could thus serve the interests of all three competitors, even if no specific brand names were highlighted. Indeed, surveys of physicians have shown that they want unbranded information to give to their patients.[32]

The state of scientific uncertainty that came from stopping the three trials early provided an ideal environment for companies to engage other actors in a process that would emphasize the potential benefits of the drugs and minimize their risks. As Harvard medical oncologist Stephen Cannistra argues, the existence of ambiguous research results sets the stage for treatment recommendations based on "our ignorance of the future" rather than our "certainty of the present," and on "hope that these therapies might have led to a survival advantage" rather than on "the facts" that would have been available if the studies in question had run their course to maturity.[33] Importantly from the perspective of patient activism, a typical way of dealing with such scientific uncertainty in medicine, Cannistra says, is to punt the decision to the patient with a discussion of treatment options:

The implication is that patients will know the right answer, despite the fact that their physicians do not know how the new treatment will affect important measures of clinical outcome. In this regard, it is legitimate to consider whether the results of the letrozole ... [trial] might unfairly tantalize patients with the prospect of prolonged PFS [progression-free survival], in the absence of a known survival benefit, and with the possibility of treatment-related toxicity.[34]

In other words, informing patient organizations of a promising new treatment option for their disease builds on the construct of the modern patient as knowledgeable and informed, while systematically ensuring ignorance of the key facts. Cannistra asks:

What patient would easily refuse the prospect of prolonged progression-free or disease-free survival under these circumstances, and how many would be able to understand the uncertain and oftentimes tenuous relationship between PFS [progression-free survival], OS [overall survival], and QOL [quality of life], when data regarding these important outcomes do not exist as a result of early study closure?"[35]

A "patient information session" in the wake of clinical trials that were stopped early begins to make sense as a marketing strategy. Even the most cautious presentation of the science to a lay audience is unlikely to include a discussion of surrogate endpoints or debates about clinical trial stopping rules. And caution can be a challenging attitude to maintain when medical research hints at an important advance. Cancer researcher Victor Ling, scientific director of the Terry Fox Research Institute, describes the temptation to embrace promising early trial results:

Anybody who does research knows that preliminary results can lead one astray. Let's say you start a trial: sometimes the first few handfuls of patients give you really great results. Then, when you get to the hundredth or thousandth patient, you find out that it's not as good as you thought and, actually, it's not a very good drug at all because, statistically, things do happen. So sometimes we [scientists] get led up the garden path by our enthusiasm, based on preliminary results.

I think it's always dangerous for anybody to promote [a treatment] before the final result is actually known. I can understand why some patient groups are impatient to promote certain new drugs, because obviously they want to get a good thing into the hands of patients as soon as possible. It's a laudable goal. But, on the other hand, it's not laudable if they want to circumvent a careful scientific approach to evaluating a new drug or a new procedure ... And sometimes that happens.[36]

The treatment information sessions for patients raise ethical issues on another count; namely, such events could circumvent restrictions intended to control the venues in which drug companies can ethically communicate drug trial information. Because inappropriate use of prescription drugs can harm the user's health and even cause death, claims about these products are controlled, with the particular safeguards dependent on the means of communication. We have seen in Chapter 1 that drug advertising is controlled by legislation and that, historically, Canadian legislation specifies that advertising of pharmaceuticals be directed to health care providers, not to consumers. Examples of promotion that is permitted include drug ads in medical journals, materials that drug reps give to physicians, and materials the companies produce for health-care providers to give to patients. The Pharmaceutical Advertising Advisory Board, or PAAB, an entity nominally independent of the industry (its board includes industry members), is set up to review these materials. While the PAAB has no legislative authority, all member companies of Innovative Medicines Canada (formerly Rx&D) have agreed to submit all advertising material to the PAAB for pre-clearance and to abide by PAAB rulings; and all medical journals have agreed not to run ads unless they have been cleared by the PAAB.[37]

Canadian law prohibits direct-to-consumer advertising, or DTCA, although in 1996 the government relaxed the rules to allow unbranded "help-seeking" or "see your doctor" ads, which mention a condition but not a manufacturer or a drug meant to treat it. In 2000, a second Health Canada policy shift extended eligibility to branded "reminder" advertisements, which mention a drug but not the condition it is meant to treat. Health Canada is responsible for monitoring these ads.[38]

Both these systems – Health Canada's regulatory authority over DTCA and the PAAB's non-legislated mandate to review drug advertising materials – are meant to ensure that the information about drugs that reaches patients is accurate and balanced.[39] If advertising is taken to mean any communication intended to stimulate sales, the treatment information events that patients' organizations sponsored in relation to aromatase inhibitors could be seen as a novel approach to directly reaching a highly interested consumer base and seeding interest in a new drug treatment. The events, with their unbranded information about a new approach to treatment, thus resemble "see-your-doctor" ads, paid for by a company with a vested interest in selling a drug. Yet accountability is lacking, since neither of the existing oversight systems tracks whether such events responsibly relay this information.

On July 14, 2004, AstraZeneca publicly announced Health Canada's approval of Arimidex. The press release began: "Marking the first major treatment advance since tamoxifen's introduction over 25 years ago, Canada's leading oncologists and breast cancer patient support and advocacy groups gathered to applaud a new era in treatment for early breast cancer. Women have the best chance of cure at this stage of disease."

The breathless tone continued through the rest of the press release, with enthusiastic quotations from three Canadian oncologists, the executive directors of Willow and the CBCN, and a patient from British Columbia. Neither of the women speaking on behalf of organizations endorsed the product outright; rather, they enthused more generally about dramatic advances in the treatment of the disease, better options, the importance of investing in research, and the value of patients participating in clinical trials. The patient who was quoted as an individual, by contrast, came out full square for Arimidex, expressing thanks that she was "given the opportunity" to take the drug.

If a drug company pushed a group too far, however, it could meet with resistance. "Meredith," a member of Breast Cancer Action Nova Scotia's board, recounts a post-event overture from AstraZeneca that was less than comfortable for the group: "Now AstraZeneca thinks they can ask us for things on a regular basis. They've come up with a website that promotes [the drug] Arimidex that's very warm. They wanted [the group] to link our website to theirs. We said 'No, let's step back.'"

Pfizer and AstraZeneca's local patient awareness events weren't the only pharma-funded projects that highlighted aromatase inhibitors in the patient community. In September 2007, the CBCN announced on its website a survey "led by" the CBCN and conducted by the professional polling company Ipsos Reid. "Despite ... the wealth of resources available," the announcement stated, the survey had found that "only one in 10 women surveyed are aware of their risk of relapse after five years of tamoxifen treatment." The web announcement had links to a series of additional resources: a more detailed press release; a one-page summary of the survey's finding, with three questions women were urged to "ask your doctor"; and a video posted on YouTube. The questions, adapted to the woman's stage of treatment, asked about "risk," "next steps," and "options." The video took the form of an extended piece of news reportage, including a series of clips: first of the CBCN's president, then of a woman who had completed tamoxifen treatment but was not aware she was still at risk of a relapse, and finally of an oncologist who mentioned the option of taking an aromatase inhibitor.

The resource package characterized women's lack of knowledge about their risk of post-tamoxifen relapse as alarming. Each component underlined the importance of women speaking to their physician, using terms like "essential" and "strongly recommend." A medical oncologist quoted in the one-page summary referred to current treatment guidelines, "such as those from Cancer Care Ontario." These guidelines, she said, "reinforce that modern post-surgical (adjuvant) therapy options such as aromatase inhibitors, including extended therapy beyond five years, can save lives."

The professionalism of the package was striking and had all the hallmarks of a help-seeking ad, the type of direct-to-consumer advertisement that discusses a medical condition but omits the brand name of the product the company wants to promote. None of the materials names a drug, but they emphasize the risk of a recurrence and urge the viewer to "ask your doctor" for more information about available remedies. Such ads are typically used when a pharmaceutical company is heavily promoting a newly approved product to physicians. Help-seeking ads are meant to increase the volume of patients making doctor visits who specifically ask what remedy the doctor might happen to have for the very condition for which the new drug is approved. Like the patient information sessions, the questionnaire and video package fall into the ambiguous zone between information and advertising that the government created when it relaxed the prohibition against DTCA in 1996 and allowed "ask your doctor" ads. Although Health Canada now considers such ads legal, the information in them should be accurate and balanced. Furthermore, a brand name company sponsoring an ad of this type in a magazine or on television would be required to submit the ad to PAAB for review.[40]

The survey and YouTube video struck me as another innovative way for a company to engage patient groups while stretching the already elastic DTCA regulations. The same content in a television ad sponsored by a drug company would clearly have fallen under Health Canada's regulatory purview and a complaint to the agency would have triggered a review. Whether the implied urgency and the allusion to saving lives would have passed the review is uncertain, and Health Canada rarely enforces this law. Nonetheless, Canada's Food and Drugs Act states, "No person shall ... advertise any drug in a manner ... likely to create an erroneous impression regarding its merit or safety,"[41] which seems inclusive of communications from nonprofit groups.

Another advantage from the company's perspective is that the group is able to target the precise population the company wants to reach, and at considerably less cost than nationwide media ads. And a patient-directed breast cancer group – if it appears to be independent of the company making the product – is probably a more trusted source for patients than the company making the product. The Canadian Breast Cancer Network's web page did not identify a drug company as a sponsor. Instead, it credited the survey as sponsored by the Canadian Breast Cancer Foundation, the national organization that raises funds for breast cancer research and community-based projects. Puzzled, I asked CBCN's executive director if a drug company had sponsored the initiative. She confirmed that Novartis – the company that makes the aromatase inhibitor Femara – had paid for what she called the Risk of Recurrence project.[42]

This was two years after Health Canada had given conditional approval, in April 2005, to Novartis's drug Femara as a follow-up therapy for women who had taken tamoxifen for five years. Understanding of the drug's long-term benefits and side effects compared with tamoxifen remained a grey area, however, and not all provinces had placed Femara on their drug formularies, though Ontario had. Given this discrepancy in provincial formulary approvals, the group may have been used as a vehicle for what drug policy analysts call "whipsawing" – using the availability of an expensive new drug on one province's insurance formulary as a lever to force other provinces to add it to theirs.[43]

Researcher Victor Ling, who serves on the executive of the BC Cancer Agency, emphasizes that changes like the Internet altered the patient-physician interaction so that patients today have much more influence on treatment decisions than they did twenty or thirty years ago. Although not aware of any actual pharma-funded cancer-patient advocacy initiatives, he can imagine a scenario that, in his view, would put the group in a conflict of interest.

> *Dr. Ling:* If enough patients advocate, let's say, for a particular drug that is currently not on the [formulary] list ... it could politically influence the Ministry of Health to approve it. So I'm sure that if a company wanted to use that route as a way of influencing a decision – that would be a possible way.
>
> *Sharon:* You mean, basically get the patients to pressure the provincial ...
>
> *Dr. Ling:* No, I would not say in any obvious way; I mean, in any of these situations, the company can provide information, education. And as I say, sometimes a new drug may be equivalent to or not much better than an older drug, or not *really* better – not enough for the formulary to change; but the company can position it in a way that it's the newest and the latest thing. And you know how we are all sucked in by advertising – I mean, not just for drugs but for everything in life! [*Laughs.*] That could influence the patient group, and that could cost the system more – sometimes, quite a bit more.
>
> It's challenging for people who are trying to manage drug costs and manage care costs, because they may be seen as the bad guy [who is] not wanting to give patients what they think is best for them. Perhaps what is not always appreciated is that sometimes experts

know that the data for a new drug isn't robust enough. It may be fine experimentally, such as using it in a clinical trial. But to prescribe it on a regular basis – the evidence may not be at that level yet.

As aromatase inhibitors gained wider use as a therapy, the importance of iatrogenic joint pain as a serious quality-of-life problem for the patient became increasingly apparent. Rose, a BCANS board member, describes a tension between the patients' perspective on side effects and that of physicians' as it manifested in discussions on the group's Discussion Forum:

And [you'll hear] lots of moaning and complaining about how doctors never tell you about the side effects of drugs. And it's supposedly because then you'll get them, you'll psych yourself into getting them, if you know what they are. And so sometimes [patients] look at it as a conspiracy to hide the possible side effects and not tell you the whole picture so you can make an informed decision. Like, "For the little tiny bit of additional protection I'm going to get from this drug, am I willing to put up with not being able to walk up the stairs?" There's that kind of conversation on the Discussion Forum. And here [at the office] too, for that matter! ... On an education night, drinking tea and eating cookies, moaning and bitching about drug companies, it's not unusual! [*Laughs.*]

Indeed, research shows that as many as half of all patients taking aromatase inhibitors experience joint pain, with an estimated 20 percent becoming "noncompliant" (i.e., ceasing to take the medication) as a result. Drug companies and many professionals in the cancer care system view noncompliance as a serious problem. For the patient exercising her right to choose quality of life over a chance of modest extension of life, it may not be.[44]

I asked "Hanna," who had been on the CBCN's executive at the time of the Ipsos Reid survey, about the group's decision to undertake the Risk of Recurrence project. As she describes the initiative, the CBCN's board saw the project as assisting physicians in getting the word out about an important new therapeutic development.

Hanna: People weren't aware of it ... And this new drug was so much more effective [than tamoxifen] in stopping a recurrence.

Sharon: And this was one that a patient would take after five years on tamoxifen?

Hanna: Yes. And we did do some advocacy around that because people didn't realize [it was an option] ... but if you have all the physicians informed and the patients are informed that they need to explore this, [our message was,] "Ask your doc about it, it's important." And it is important ... Nobody wants that [coming] back again. If you've got something you can take ... for the people [whose tumours are estrogen-receptor-positive], where you can say, "This is really going to decrease your chances of the ugly coming back," they had to know about it.

The different cancer centres attacked this [in] different ways. Letters went out to all the patients that they could find, which [tracking down patients] is not an easy task. And the docs would have to comb through all the records. There were information sessions on it [saying], "This is what's here; as a patient, you have to think about whether you want to do this or not." Some did, some didn't. But it was like, "Holy crap, this thing really worked. How are we going to let our patients know?" ...

And that's why we did the video. [We thought], "If we can get out there, [get] people just go and ask" ... And it was important [as] part of this "informed patient" approach ... It's unique for a drug to be that good. And it was not that tamoxifen was bad, it's just that this one was so much better. And ... to have a drug that would do that, and to prove it was doing it? I say, "Bring it on;" because I've had a recurrence, and a recurrence is not a pleasant thing to go through.[45]

I could not share Hanna's enthusiasm for aromatase inhibitors, considering the still-preliminary status of the evidence and the relatively small (albeit statistically significant) advantage these expensive new drugs conferred. When I suggested that a group receiving funds from the manufacturer might inadvertently convey an overly positive view of that company's product, Hanna disagreed. Ultimately, she countered, an oncologist prescribes the drug:

In cancer care, any of the drugs that are prescribed are given according to clinical practice guidelines that have been developed by the individual cancer agencies. The guidelines include [details on] informed consent and [making patients aware of] the side effects. And I've been in on conversations with people, and sat in with them, and, at least in this place [the hospital where she worked], they are well informed. Very well informed.

Despite the new treatments that have been approved in the past decade, tamoxifen's long track record with benefits demonstrated in long-term clinical trials, as well the availability of lower-priced generics, make it the treatment of choice for ER+ breast cancers, according to Dr. Susan Love in the 2015 edition of her popular book for breast cancer patients.[46] Indeed, new data favourable to tamoxifen continues to emerge: an overview of five clinical trial results published in 2014 showed that, in three out of the five studies, a ten-year rather than a five-year course of tamoxifen provided modest gains in survival and a lower risk of recurrence in the second breast compared with a five-year course of treatment.[47] The finding prompted the American Society of Clinical Oncology (ASCO) to recommend that all ER+ patients, regardless of menopausal status, be offered tamoxifen treatment for up to ten years, rather than the previous standard of five. For postmenopausal women, sequential use of tamoxifen and an aromatase inhibitor was an alternative option, provided that the aromatase inhibitor is not prescribed for more than five years. This limitation was because of inadequate data on long-term use. Contrary to the CBCN's advocacy materials, however, the authors of the updated ASCO guidelines concluded that, in choosing to extend endocrine therapy for postmenopausal therapy beyond five years, "it is not known which strategy [i.e., tamoxifen or an aromatase inhibitor] is preferred."[48] Since the two treatments have different adverse-event profiles, the individual patient's tolerance for one or the other was left as the deciding factor.

With aromatase inhibitors, as with ESAs, competition among companies for the lucrative breast cancer market appeared to form the backstory to the funding overtures to breast cancer groups. On some issues, though, major drug companies share the same advocacy goals. The third case study illustrates just such a project.

Case 3: A Dance for Formulary Funding

In 2008, the CBCN published a forty-six page report on wait times for cancer diagnosis and treatments, which on its second page acknowledged support from the GlaxoSmithKline Foundation. The first half of the report examines and compares wait times to breast cancer diagnosis, surgery, radiation treatment, and chemotherapy in each province and territory, a discussion that corresponds to the usual meaning of "wait times." Another section of the report, however, stretches this conventional meaning to encompass drug availability – that is, drug approval times and the inclusion of drugs on formularies. A section on the wait times for drug approval and availability frames the interval between a company's submission to the regulator for approval and the time that the drug is put on all the provincial and territorial formularies as a wait time for patients. Nowhere does the discussion mention that this interval is a critical wait time for the drug companies, since they cannot begin marketing a drug until it gains regulatory approval; similarly, sales will be limited if insurance plans "wait" to cover the drug (to receive more information from ongoing clinical trials, for example, or in the hope of negotiating a better price). Indeed, the report argues that the wait time for a drug actually begins when the company submits its drug for approval. The discussion of wait times is highly critical of the federal government processes for approval and of the provinces and territories for delaying formulary inclusion because of costs, noting that the total time elapsed from when the manufacturer first applied to Health Canada to its inclusion on a provincial or local formulary could be between three and five years, or longer.

One criticism the report makes is that cancer drugs are typically approved in the United States and Britain before they are approved in Canada; the authors don't mention that drug companies usually apply for approval first in the United States for strategic reasons: the market in the United States is huge, the United States stands alone among wealthy nations in having no price controls on pharmaceutical drugs, and FDA approval is a crucial hurdle in getting a drug to market. A 2014 study comparing Canadian drug approval times with those in the United States and Europe concludes that the main reason by far for slower approval times in Canada is the delay on the part of drug companies in submitting their drugs for review in Canada.[49] (For advocates of faster drug reviews, this reality provides an opportunity for Canada to expedite its own review times. Pat Kelly notes that the fact that most pharmaceutical companies invest in much larger markets before coming to the smaller Canadian market "means drugs have been reviewed by scientific review boards in the EU/UK/France/Japan, et cetera, and often these review boards include Canadian researchers; but Canada has always stood by its 'sovereign' authority position, a duplication of effort and costs. It seems there is much room for collaboration and efficiency on this front."[50])

The CBCN's wait-time report is entirely uncritical of drug companies for their drug pricing practices and nowhere mentions misleading drug promotion practices, or that drug treatments may in fact shorten some patients' lives while extending others. The latter reality was most dramatically seen with high-dose chemotherapy, (post-)menopausal hormone therapy, and Eprex; however, even drugs like tamoxifen and Herceptin, with demonstrated benefits overall, are toxic for a subset of patients and sometimes have fatal outcomes.

The implicit assumption in the CBCN's report is that patient-group advocacy should focus on having new drugs approved and put on formularies as quickly as possible – as opposed to focusing on drug safety, efficacy, price, or the reliability of information provided to physicians, patients, and the public; nor should the groups consider nondrug approaches to living with cancer, advocate the judicious use of medical resources (to limit iatrogenic harms, distribute benefits for maximum effect, and ensure long-term system sustainability), or promote measures to prevent cancer. The type of rich ethical debate about surrogate endpoints, clinical trial stopping rules, and rising drug prices – all concerns that aromatase inhibitors have stimulated in the medical literature – is entirely missing; instead, the report reinforces the discourse that equates longer life with access to new drugs. It states, "As new targeted and biologic medications that will actually save lives become available, women will be denied access to them."

When the CBCN's wait-time report was published, GlaxoSmithKline (GSK), the corporate arm of the project's sponsoring foundation, had a new, targeted biologic breast cancer drug, Tykerb (lapatinib), in clinical trials. Tykerb was designed to treat women with HER2-positive cancers, the same subpopulation now treated with Herceptin. In a clinical trial, Tykerb was shown to improve time-to-disease progression by four months in women with HER2-positive cancers when used in combination with another drug, capecitabine, made by Hoffmann-La Roche under the brand name Xeloda.[51] Time-to-disease progression is a surrogate endpoint for drug efficacy and does not actually demonstrate that a drug extends survival time. Compared with Xeloda alone, the addition of Tykerb provided an expected gain of 0.12 quality-adjusted life years or QALYs. (A QALY adjusts time gained from a treatment to take quality of life into account.) The trial showed that the drug combination met the minimal standard of effectiveness and relative safety. On this basis, in 2009 and 2010 various national regulatory agencies, including the FDA in the United States, the National Institute for Health and Care Excellence in the United Kingdom, and Health Canada, approved Tykerb in combination with Xeloda to treat women whose disease had progressed on Herceptin; that is, GSK could legally market Tykerb for this indication.[52]

Insurance coverage of the drugs was another matter. In the oncology literature, the approval of Tykerb was accompanied by several cost-effectiveness analyses, which concluded that the drug's modest benefits did not warrant its price tag. One study put the cost at US$2,900 a month – an estimated $19,630 over a patient's lifetime and $166,113 per quality-adjusted life years gained. The CBCN's report does not mention Tykerb by name but advances the argument that delays in the regulatory approval and formulary funding of "new targeted and biologic medications" – a generic description that applies to Tykerb – are detrimental to breast cancer patients. The document outlines an advocacy strategy under which the CBCN will "work collaboratively with other concerned organizations to ensure that breast cancer issues, including wait times and drug availability, remain high on the public agenda." Nowhere does the document discuss the implications for the health care system of funding high-cost treatments with unproven or modest benefit.[53]

An example of just such advocacy occurred in late 2009. On December 18, a story in the national *Globe and Mail* described the plight of a woman who had rapidly advancing metastatic cancer; her oncologist had recommended Xeloda + Tykerb as a treatment of last resort.[54] GlaxoSmithKline offered the woman Tykerb under its compassionate access program, but the Ontario government refused to cover Xeloda's $800-per-month cost to patients under its Exceptional Access Program because the Xeloda + Tykerb combination was not on its drug formulary. GlaxoSmithKline had submitted its application to the province's Committee to Evaluate Drugs in July 2009, but the province was still studying the proposal – a delay of five-plus months.

In an information email to its mailing list in January 2010, the CBCN described the advocacy it undertook to convince the Ontario government to fund Xeloda so that the patient could receive the capecitabine (Xeloda) + lapatinib (Tykerb) combination treatment without charge. Prompted by the *Globe and Mail* story, the CBCN wrote to the Ontario Committee to Evaluate Drugs and the Ontario Minister of Health, urging it to approve Xeloda + Tykerb for inclusion on the province's formulary. The organization also orchestrated a campaign among its online communities, asking member organizations and individuals to do the same. In late December, the Ontario government approved the drug combination for formulary inclusion. The CBCN's January 2010 email to its list concludes:

> Health Canada approved this combination of drugs, *which is saving lives.* Surely the Ontario Committee to Evaluate Drugs (CED) process should have *put saving lives ahead of additional evaluation* and approved it immediately. This combination of medications is prescribed for patients with advanced or metastatic breast cancer as a last resort. Time is of the essence for these breast cancer patients ...
>
> The Ontario CED approval of these drugs is an important step in progress for Canadian women currently suffering from metastatic breast cancer. By approving this combination of drugs, it gives women with breast cancer and their physicians more treatment options ... but more action is needed. We believe, *in conjunction with the International Federation of Pharmaceutical Manufacturers & Associations*, that each patient should receive the treatment that is best tailored to their profile instead of being *denied access to potentially life-saving drugs that are not yet approved.* (Emphasis added)

One cannot know exactly what influence the group's efforts contributed to the Ontario government's decision to have the new drug combination placed on the provincial formulary, but a national newspaper story along with a national campaign by patient organizations during the Christmas season would be hard to ignore (the CBCN characterized the decision makers who delayed the decision as showing a lack of compassion). The international debate as to whether the treatment was cost-effective is not acknowledged; indeed, the appropriate stance of governmental decision-making bodies is presented as little more than to rubber stamp new drugs.

Of particular note is the CBCN's identification of Xeloda + Tykerb as a *life-saving* drug combination, even though the clinical trial results had actually shown improved time-to-disease progression. Indeed, it is widely agreed that advanced breast cancer is not presently curable, though treatments may extend life and/or alleviate symptoms; in describing Xeloda + Tykerb as life-saving, the CBCN's communication to its members thus reconstructs scientific knowledge about the disease in its advanced form (asserting that metastatic breast cancer *can* be cured, with new drugs), redefines the conventional meaning of clinical trial results (a surrogate endpoint is used as a measure of efficacy), and adopts the consumerist language of "treatment options" as an underlying ethical principle for medical decision making. The communication to members also overtly aligns the organization's policy position on treatment access with that of the International Federation of Pharmaceutical Manufacturers & Associations, the global umbrella organization that represents the interests of the brand-name pharmaceutical companies.

Whether GlaxoSmithKline had direct participation in the CBCN's report other than funding is not evident from reading the report; three years after its publication, however, the CBCN hosted a webcast sponsored by the same company, in which GlaxoSmithKline took a direct and leading role. "Understanding the Healthcare Environment in Canada and Atlantic Canada" was webcast as a service to the CBCN's east coast members and had two presenters, both GSK employees. The webcast identifies one as the company's national reimbursement strategist, specialty care, with previous work for the company in stakeholder relations, government relations, and market access; the other is the company's director of external affairs in Quebec and Atlantic Canada. Under the anodyne title "Understanding the Healthcare Environment," the webcast explains in detail the drug regulatory process in Canada and the drug reimbursement practices in the four Atlantic provinces. Claims include the assertion that "all patients are not treated equally"; more specifically, "Access to cancer treatments is: variable, not universal, not portable, not comprehensive and not always publicly administered." The language is carefully keyed to the Canada Health Act, implying that access to cancer drugs violates all five tenets of the act – though orally administered drugs like Xeloda do not technically fall under the act. The solution advanced to correct these "inequities" is faster drug approvals and full coverage of new breast cancer treatment drugs by all provinces and territories.

The final section of the webcast presents advocacy by patients and physicians as the key to influencing the "scientific and bureaucratic road-block" in the health care environment. The webcast lists audiences for groups to target with their advocacy, including the provincial ombuds-man, human rights offices, members of the legislature, the Premier's Office, and key ministries such as Health and Status of Women. The detailed outline for advocacy provides a twelve-point action plan, with advice such as "develop and implement contact plan: key decision makers, political staff in MOH [Ministry of Health], Premier's Office, civil servants and cham-pions inside government public service."

The webcast thus used the regional network of breast cancer organiz-ations to expose breast cancer patients to an advocacy plan, developed and presented by a pharmaceutical company, that framed the discourse about access to new cancer drugs in terms advantageous to the industry. The presentation reiterates the now-familiar discourse of rapid access to new drugs as the central issue for improving breast cancer survival. Key sources for the presentation are the annual report card of the pharma-funded group the Cancer Advocacy Coalition of Canada, a publication on drug access by the conservative think tank the Fraser Institute titled *Access De-layed, Access Denied*, and a 2009 report by the Canadian Cancer Society titled *Optimizing Access to Cancer Drugs for Canadians*.[55]

The Cancer Society's report echoes the concerns of the CBCN's wait-time report, Cancer Advocacy Coalition of Canada's annual report cards, and the Fraser Institute's *Access Denied*: first, that coverage for cancer drugs is unequal across the country's provinces and territories, as well as within a single jurisdiction (the latter depends on whether an individual has private insurance and, if so, the terms of that coverage), and second, that the costs of the newer cancer drugs are "prohibitive to all but the wealthiest Canadians."[56] The evidence that pharmaceutical companies bear much responsibility for access inequities by overpricing their products and playing provinces against one another is hinted at only once, in a single sentence on the last page of the report that states that the "twin drivers of spiralling drug costs – utilization and prices – must be examined to ensure that Canadians receive value for money today and so that future generations can continue to afford a high quality drug funding system."[57]

The CBCN's wait-time report raises a central question: How important are wait times for new drug treatments for the health of breast cancer patients? In a November 2016 news analysis, CBC health journalist Kelly Crowe suggests the Fraser Institute's "historic fascination with wait times" warrants scrutiny from both an ideological and methodological perspective. "Every year for more than two decades [the institute] has published a gloomy report about wait times for health care," she writes. The institute's founder, Michael Walker, initiated the first report in 1992 after expressing his criticism of the Canadian health care system three years earlier, saying that the system prevents high-income Canadians from purchasing higher standard health care equipment and service. Competitive markets would improve Canadian's well-being, he argued. The institute's wait-time reports are based on a short survey sent annually to a mailing list of thousands of the country's doctors, asking them to estimate how long their patients wait for care, and the response rate is consistently only about 20 percent. Health policy analysts view the reports as methodologically flawed ("an abomination" in the words of Saskatoon-based health policy consultant Steven Lewis). Although some patients undoubtedly do experience unreasonable waits, the policy analysts Crowe spoke to recommended in-depth analyses of those cases to understand how the public system could be reorganized to address the problems, rather than installing a parallel system of private health insurance.[58]

The CBCN's report thus draws on three sources that echo the neoliberal claim that patients' interests are best served by rapid access to new pharmaceuticals. Omitted is the substantial evidence for the competing discourse, which supports careful drug reviews, less dependence on toxic treatments for those with late-stage disease, and prudent use of health care funds to maintain a sustainable system that aims to provide treatment to all Canadians on the basis of need. Whether this selective use of available evidence is a coincidence is discussed in the final chapter. First, however, let's look at a fourth advocacy project, one that reflects on the related matter of patients' rights: When we get sick, do we have a *right* to particular medications, or to gain access to services within a particular time frame?

Case 4: A Dance for Rights

In June 2003, at the invitation of the Ontario-based breast cancer organization Willow, a dozen women from breast cancer groups across Canada attended an advocacy workshop in Ottawa. The invitation was extended by the then-president of Willow, and the workshop was funded by AstraZeneca, which had established an ongoing relationship with the organization's executive director. At the end of the workshop, a committee was struck. The committee's goal was to develop a patients' bill, or charter, of rights (both terms were used), a project that continued for four years. This reconstruction is based on conversations with five women who were part of the project at different points in its development, and on my own intervention as a member of the breast cancer community.

Kathleen Barclay, who attended the workshop, told me that the plan to create a patients' bill of rights had not been clearly articulated to participants in advance. Nor was the charter mentioned on the first day of the meeting; instead, the women took part in brainstorming sessions at which they discussed the coverage, care, and access to treatment and support in their home provinces. These discussions highlighted the regional variability in treatments and services. Although everyone knew such disparities existed – they are often the focus of news stories, and leaders within a group would invariably know of patients who had been given conflicting treatment recommendations from different doctors – the inconsistencies across provinces were nonetheless eye-opening.

When the Ontario-based organizer and executive director of Willow introduced the idea of the patients' rights charter on the second day, participants had mixed reactions. For one woman, the proposal was a surprise, but a tool that seemed interesting as a way to address regional treatment inequities. She had seen first-hand the stress and confusion of a patient who lived in another province at the time of diagnosis and came home to be treated, only to have the team of local specialists recommend a different treatment plan than the one that had been proposed when she was diagnosed. For Kathleen, however, the lack of transparency raised the spectre of a hidden agenda:

> The bottom line is, we got there, and it was clear that it was already decided what was going to come out of this meeting, it was the breast cancer patients' charter of rights ... It just really turned me off, because no one said when we were invited, "Oh, we're going to be working on a breast cancer patients' charter of rights." It was billed as an advocacy workshop [i.e., more broadly, with no specific outcome]. It was all kind of predetermined ... It felt just a little off ... Like, why do you need my opinion? Just do what you want to do.

Kathleen was not alone in feeling that disclosure about the purpose of the meeting was inadequate at the outset. A representative from the CBCN also described the meeting as being "not what we signed on for" and "one of these meetings where the outcome had been predetermined." Following the workshop, the CBCN's board concluded that developing a patients' charter was a waste of time and money and withdrew its participation. This lack of support eventually proved to be a major hurdle for the project.

The fact that the charter was to be sponsored by a pharmaceutical company *was* disclosed to participants, who differed in how they reacted to this arrangement. One woman, who was initially wary of AstraZeneca's involvement, observed that drug company representatives were not part of any of the discussions; she quickly felt assured that the company would not interfere. For Kathleen, however, the drug company had an obvious and potentially compromising presence:

> We all had our lovely little gift baskets from AstraZeneca. Now, I'm not saying I don't like a gift basket, who doesn't? And they were lovely – all these young women who are the PR [public relations staff] for AstraZeneca are very lovely and friendly and showed me a great time ... But really, is the drug company trying to get us to advocate a patients'

charter of rights to be telling women that they are entitled to get whatever drugs they want or need, no matter how expensive it is? Is it going to bankrupt our health care system? I think it's a complicated issue. The whole thing didn't sit well with me. It was just a bit too complex, and I don't feel like those issues were addressed.

I asked Kathleen if the questions were raised. She explains:

> Some people raised those kinds of issues. I raised [the fact] that I didn't like that I had come there, and why would we *as a group* not be deciding what kind of efforts we want? Because my understanding was that ... we, as a group, would talk about our experiences. And we would say, "You know, maybe *this* would be a very good thing."
>
> But no, it was "*This* [is] what [is] going to be done." Well, then, why wasn't that said up front? It was a little bizarre. I didn't think it was the way to do things ... If you're going to bring all these people together, maybe we have some ideas – maybe we have something that is better than what AstraZeneca came up with! I don't think it was appropriate for them to be steering people quite so much. [*Laughs.*]

Kathleen's discomfort was about process; she didn't take a hard line against pharma funding per se:

> I don't feel that because someone gives you money that you have to toe any kind of line. And I have never, ever seen – when I think of other groups I know that take pharmaceutical money in the form of un-restricted educational grants – I think there are ways that you can do it without compromising yourself. I'm not saying you should, but there are things that are needed, and if you can't find the money anywhere else – which I think is ridiculous, that we *can't* find the money anywhere else – I'm not sure I'm against it in certain circumstances. You know, if something needs to be done, it needs to be done!

What did bother her was her feeling that she was silenced when she questioned the preset agenda:

I brought up that I really didn't like this, and I felt that nobody wanted to hear that. You know, that I shouldn't be saying that. And I'm very much the type of person that [thinks], "Why shouldn't I say it? It's a perfectly legitimate question." There's no way I should feel like I'm being rude – just because you gave me shampoo? It comes back to that whole thing – just because someone gives you money, I don't feel that gives them the right to tell you what to say. It gives them the right to never give you money again if they don't want to.

The workshop concluded with the creation of a working group made up of women who supported the idea of the charter (the group never had a formal name, so I refer to it as "the working group"). Kathleen and the CBCN representative were among those who withdrew because they viewed the agenda as predetermined. Another participant withdrew because she didn't think the proposed document would have any teeth. Jean Wilson and Lynn Macdonald, neither of whom had attended the workshop, joined the working group soon afterward, when participants from each of their local communities sought someone to take their place. Thus, a six-person committee emerged from the initial meeting, with regional representation as a major criterion for inclusion; members came from breast cancer organizations located in provinces from the east coast to the west. The project was nearing its end when I began my field research, and three of the six members of the group at that time agreed to be interviewed.[59]

Clearly, some of the more critical workshop participants selected themselves out of the project when the objections they raised were glossed over; these concerns resurfaced later to dog the project. Members of the six-person working group who carried the project forward may also have had misgivings, but these were overridden by their awareness of regional inconsistencies in services for women with breast cancer and a sense that such disparities were unjust. The injustice charge arises when treatment differences are interpreted as specialists in one region lagging behind the latest research, or reining in their budgets to the detriment of patients. Australian oncologist Ranjana Srivastava has another perspective. Differences in the way the same condition is treated – from region to region, or from one specialist to another – often do not reflect inequalities, she says, but are the result of confusion in the field when no single approach has been shown to be superior to others. Srivastava argues that patients would be less frustrated by contradictory opinions among medical experts if physicians were more willing to admit that often the data are murky.[60] She believes clinical practice would benefit if both physicians and patients learned to accept that much of modern medical knowledge is uncertain. The workshop, however, seemed to frame inconsistencies in practice as evidence of injustices to be countered with advocacy. As Jean put it, the workshop discussions reinforced and enriched her local knowledge of disparities in services, which in turn provided the foundation for a charter of rights for patients:

> As a support group, we saw the same thing that they saw at Willow. Sometimes – not through carelessness or lack of understanding – there [are] huge differences in the treatment and in your options, in how everything happens. So we were aware of this ...
>
> [Our provincial cancer care organization] feels the same way. Sometimes [staff] are contacted by women, and of course they become aware of the differences. So when Willow contacted them ... the person who went to the first, original meetings thought, "Okay, this [project to create a charter] is a good thing!"

The charter was to address these disparities at two levels: for the individual patient in conversations with her medical team, and at the societal level, as an advocacy tool the patient community could use to press for policy changes. An oncologist who worked with the group underlined the utility of the charter of rights as a tool for communication between a patient and her doctor. As one member of the working group explains his contribution, he saw the need to get the standard of care synchronized across Canada, and having a document in the hands of each newly diagnosed patient was a way to advance this goal. The charter would help a patient understand the kinds of questions she could ask the doctor at her appointment, questions about the kinds of resources she could tap into for support, and how long it should be until she had surgery.

Shortly after the initial meeting, the working group began having regular discussions by conference call and email. The member from Quebec had been instrumental in developing a breast cancer patients' rights charter in her province, and the Quebec document served as a starting point for the group's discussions. They talked about what it meant to have quality care and timely care, and what was different from province to province. Based on their discussions, they modified the Quebec document, showed their revised draft to the medical specialist who made suggestions about what to add or take out, and so on, through an iterative process of discussion, consultation, and wordsmithing. Lynn, who became the working group's chair, recalls AstraZeneca as being very much in the background during this period. The company had hired a public relations and communications company, Courtney Rainey Group, to handle the logistics of setting up teleconferences every two or three weeks. "We were really almost unaware that AstraZeneca was sponsoring the project at this point," Lynn recalls. As the group's point person with Courtney Rainey, Lynn found the arrangement "very professional." She felt reassured that the company kept the pharmaceutical sponsor at a distance. In addition, the group's contact at Courtney Rainey enthusiastically supported the project and maintained regular contact with the working group.

By late fall 2003, the working group felt ready to send what Lynn calls "a more or less finished draft" out to other organizations across the country in order to "test out the waters locally and get some feedback." To the dismay of the working group, not everyone agreed with the draft charter. Indeed, objections from the community precipitated an unanticipated crisis within the group and generated a delay of almost a year. Three objections stood out. First, virtually all hospitals have patients' charters, so why create another one? A second argument (which was raised at the workshop) was that the charter wouldn't have any teeth. The third concern was that the project was sponsored by a pharmaceutical company.

The first objection stemmed from the fact that patients' charters and patients' bills of rights have been a growth industry both in Canada and internationally since the 1990s. In addition to the charters in many hospitals, provincial governments across Canada have introduced bills at various times to articulate patients' rights and responsibilities; a few countries, notably France and the United Kingdom, have national charters. The plan to develop another charter or bill of rights for patients in Canada thus raised the question, why invest time and resources to produce yet another? Furthermore, once produced, what claim to legitimacy would this charter have over others?[61]

A related concern was that the working group was an ad hoc structure of volunteers created for the sole purpose of developing a patients' charter. Once the document was ready, new patients would make use of it only if an organization or agency made a point of promoting it. The working group members I interviewed had hoped the Canadian Breast Cancer Network, as the community's national voice, would take ownership of the charter; however; the national group withdrew from the project at the outset and declined to be the host organization. In part this was because the president of the CBCN at the time thought existing hospital charters were sufficient; but other reasons, discussed below, came into play as well.

The objection that the charter would have no teeth is a common response to such documents. Statements of patients' rights vary in content and in force. The majority are voluntary guidelines that assert policies based on moral maxims such as "the right to participate in decisions affecting care," and "the right to individual dignity and privacy." These assertions may be backed up by institutional mechanisms for filing complaints, such as an ombudsman. Less common are documents that assert entitlements to goods and services (e.g., limits on waiting times or a right to particular medical tests or treatments). When included, such rights are tied to structural and economic constraints. In Canada, numerous attempts to enshrine patients' entitlements in law have been unsuccessful, according to Lauren Vogel, who analyzed the scope of patients' rights laws and documents in a series of articles in the *Canadian Medical Association Journal*: bills in Alberta and Ontario were defeated, and a provincial health council in Nova Scotia rejected the idea of a charter of patients' rights as legally too complicated. A section of Quebec's *Loi sur les services de santé et les services sociaux* (Act concerning health and social services), passed in 1990, includes a statement of patients' entitlements, both moral and material, but material rights are restricted to those that the individual's chosen institution has the resources to provide. Significantly, the initial version of the patients' rights charter included material rights as well as moral rights, in particular, the right to certain medications; the final document included only moral rights.[62]

The working group struggled with the question of what a breast cancer patient could do if she felt the rights spelled out in the document were not being respected or met; they could not think of an agency to which the patient could appeal to give the document force, or even a way of reaching patients before they made their treatment decisions. Lynn explains:

> If a woman was diagnosed, and the standard of care wasn't being met, what recourse did she have to have that corrected? You know, we didn't solve that. That was, I think, one of the faults of the charter, that it didn't develop a mechanism – aside from the Canadian Cancer Society information line – but everybody recognized that that wasn't the ideal way to go. And also, the political landscape had changed in terms of services being offered to women. Increasingly, women's [hospital stays for] surgeries became shorter and shorter, and women were being discharged so fast that there was no way, if you had a [hospital] visiting program, that you could get through to people [to give them a copy of the charter] before they were even out of hospital.

A third objection to the document related to pharma sponsorship and to the question of material entitlements, in particular, to two mutually reinforcing claims included in a draft of the document circulated to other groups in late 2003 and early 2004. Section I, Item 2 asserted that patients have "the right to the highest standard of care ... regardless of cost" and Section I, Item 8 made the claim, "You have the right to have all costs associated with your breast cancer diagnosis and treatment covered under medicare." In fact, neither of these claims corresponded to the realities of Canada's health care system. For one thing, the treatment guarantees under the Medical Care Act and the Canada Health Act, which define medicare in Canada, have always recognized fiscal limitations. Second, medicare does not include specific coverage of pharmaceutical drugs except for hospitalized patients, an omission that policy makers have grappled with since the Medical Care Act was introduced in 1966. Medicare does, however, cover essential treatments and procedures carried out in a hospital. Because older, cytotoxic cancer drugs have been administered by infusion in-hospital, they have in fact been covered. More and more, however, cancer drugs are available in pill or capsule form, to be self-administered at home by the patient. The coverage of these drugs becomes a case-by-case negotiated decision under provincial formularies and private drug plans. Worth noting, then, is a glossary of terms in the draft document that included the term "adjuvant treatment," illustrated with two examples: tamoxifen and Arimidex – both drugs made by AstraZeneca, the project's sponsor. Tamoxifen had by then been for many years an approved adjuvant treatment in Canada, but because it was in pill form, it would not be defined as a hospital-based procedure. At the time the draft patients' rights document was circulated, in late 2003 to early 2004, Health Canada had not yet approved Arimidex as an adjuvant therapy for breast cancer.[63]

Thus, embedded within the generally uncontroversial claims to moral rights, the draft document included a number of material claims that are part of a contested discourse on the direction of Canadian health policy. As a lobbying tool, the charter could conceivably be used to rally patients to demand rights they did not have in law. As Kathleen suggested, this may have been the company's intention when the original advocacy workshop was convened. Kathleen was not the working group's main critic on this count, however; I was. To my surprise, I discovered in the course of my interviews that a letter I had written and long since forgotten about had disrupted the work of the working group, stalling the project for over a year.

In February 2004 (three years before I began my interviews), I received the draft copy of the patients' rights charter, which the working group circulated to obtain reaction from the community. The letter came to me from the CBCN. I was one of many breast cancer survivors across the country on the national group's large email list, and the document reached me in a routine mailing; I was also on the founding board of the CBCN, which was established after the National Forum on Breast Cancer, so took a personal interest in the organization's ongoing work. At the time I received the draft copy of the charter, I was not aware of the working group's existence, and I mistakenly assumed the document had originated with the CBCN. Alarmed by the contents, particularly the way (in draft form) access to medications were framed as a right, I responded to the request for input with a letter, which I emailed to the CBCN. Unaware that the CBCN had effectively withdrawn from the project, I framed my objections as if that group and its board were responsible for drafting the document.

My central argument was that, in encouraging breast cancer patients to demand that all aspects of their breast cancer treatments be covered under Canada's medicare system, regardless of cost, the group was promoting an unrealistic sense of entitlement and abdicating its educational role (as I saw it) of encouraging patients to critically evaluate costs and treatments. I further claimed that the pharmaceutical industry "stands to benefit far more than patients from a document that claims patients have a right to disregard treatment costs." I urged the CBCN not to risk losing credibility as an organization engaged in health policy advocacy work by releasing the document in its present form, and I asked whether a pharmaceutical company had funded the project and contributed to framing the document. The group's executive director (whom I knew) responded in a friendly email, pointing out that the group was "not the lead player in the project" and would itself be discussing issues related to the project at an upcoming board meeting. She added that she had forwarded my email to Willow, the lead organization, and to others who were directly involved. By this indirect route, my letter found its way to the working group, whose members neither responded to the points I had raised nor acknowledged receipt of the letter.

I am prone to writing letters, many of which disappear into a void, and by the time I began my research, I had forgotten about this particular missive. In our interviews, Lynn and Jean were clearly uncertain about how to broach the topic with me; I too was uncomfortable when it became clear that, from their perspective, my actions had stalled for a year a project to which they had committed hours of volunteer time because they believed it would be valuable to patients. As Lynn told me, "I mean, this isn't said in a blaming way, but [your letter] just stopped things cold in its tracks. Things sort of puttered along for the next year ... But anyway, we kept [going] along, and we had phone calls every so often, discussing what would be the next steps." During this period, a mood of discouragement settled on the group. Jean believed that my letter was the main reason the CBCN would not provide a home for the charter ("our biggest failure"), more important than the belief of the CBCN's then-president that hospital-based patients' charters were sufficient. Like many of the women I spoke to who were open to drug company partnerships under certain conditions, Jean was far from a cheerleader for the industry; indeed, she told me she agreed with most of the points I had raised in my letter. She supported wholeheartedly my point that public funding should be restricted to drugs and procedures shown to have tangible benefits to patients, as well as my contention that patient groups should be challenging some of the price tags on these drugs. She cited the concessions Canada made when it signed the Free Trade Agreement in 1987, effectively ending the system of compulsory licensing, as a low point in Canada's political history.

Learning that my letter had disrupted the group's process disturbed me for a reason that went beyond an awkward autoethnographic moment: I realized I had been shut out of an important conversation. Unlike the disagreement within the National Forum on Breast Cancer's subcommittee about having Bristol-Myers Squibb fund the photo exhibit, which was acknowledged head-on (albeit as a side issue to the main task of mounting the forum), I was unaware of the impact my letter had had. Instead of discussing the matter with me and other members of the broader community, members of the working group had discussed the letter's contents among themselves and with "James," the sponsoring drug company's representative.

> *Lynn:* I explained to him the sensitivities [about pharma funding]. In fact, he saw your letter. And I said, "This is the kind of thing that we want to be very cautious about."
> *Sharon:* What did he say about the letter? Did he comment on it?
> *Lynn:* He said, "You just have to deal with it." But it wasn't that easy to do.

This, to me, indicates a profound dysfunction within the community. Rather than survivor-run organizations serving as a venue for members to openly discuss their differing perspectives, the pharmaceutical industry had become an arbiter of ethical concerns deemed too sensitive to be discussed among activists, even when they agree on many counts.

The executive director of Willow, who had organized the project, eventually reignited the women's passion. In late 2005, she brought the working group members together for a face-to-face meeting in Toronto that broke the psychological stasis that criticisms from the community had created. Stella Kyriakides, a prominent activist from the European breast cancer community, was an invited guest at the meeting. A clinical psychologist by training, Kyriakides became active as an organizer, writer, and speaker on breast cancer issues after her own diagnosis and in 2006 was elected to the Parliament in Cyprus. She was a member and eventually president of the executive board of Europa Donna, a coalition of European breast cancer organizations that has participated in a decade-long effort to create a Europe-wide bill of rights for cancer patients. A 2014 document, signed by forty-one authors, provides details of a proposed bill of rights intended to "underpin equitable access to an optimal standard of care for Europe's citizens."[64] Several pharmaceutical companies, their branches, or affiliates – Sanofi Oncology, Bayer, and Bristol-Myers Squibb Foundation – are among the funders acknowledged, and the document includes such statements as, "The European patient should have: Rapid access to the latest innovations in diagnosis and treatment for the individual cancer patient following relevant regulatory approval."[65] However, the proposal appears to be aspirational rather than legally binding in its intent.

Listening to Kyriakides describe her early activism in Cyprus, a much smaller country than Canada, the Canadian women were spellbound. Breast cancer had not even been on the political agenda in Cyprus but, through Europa Donna, European women had together developed a cohesive vision to shape their advocacy and bring it to their Parliaments. By contrast, Canadian advocates seemed to lack a common focus. Jean described the meeting with Kyriakides as a turning point:

Jean: Everyone had a certain amount of hesitancy. We knew [the charter] was a good goal. We understood it, because breast cancer is the [particular] cancer we understand. We didn't want to be seen as thinking our cancer was more important than anybody else's. But ... it was hard enough to get the breast cancer groups together – we had no way of dealing with *all* the cancer groups. We were having a hard enough time keeping it coherent, representing everyone across the country. I think in our hearts we had doubts about how to proceed in the most ethical manner possible. And she was so clear. She said, "You want to arrive at the right decision. Who are you? You are breast cancer advocates. Do this wholeheartedly! Only good can come from that. This can grow wider, but it has to grow well from here."

It really helped us. It helped us to erase our doubts and to focus and to go right ahead, strongly. Because I thought, "Of course she's right." And I said to someone at the meeting, "You know what? Medicare started [small] in Saskatchewan. Of course this is right. This can be bigger, but we must do our job well, this is our step, the step *we're* able to take."

Despite the success of the November 2005 meeting that same fall, several changes transpired that troubled members of the working group. In each instance, the pharmaceutical company exerted pressure in a way they viewed as "not right," despite the actions having no bearing on the charter's actual content.

In September 2005, the working group was making changes to address the critical feedback from various external sources in order to finalize the charter. The pharmaceutical company hired an activist who was also a professional writer and included her in a face-to-face meeting, where she helped draft the changes and finalize the document. Other members of the group did not realize until later that the company was paying her. Jean explains:

She kept saying, "Well, I'll work with the Courtney Rainey personnel to help with this and this" ... But it was *much* later that we found out, and never officially, that she was in fact being *paid* to do it, which made her an employee! Well, that did not sit well with us ... We weren't being paid by AstraZeneca. And I don't know if she was being paid by them or by Courtney Rainey – it was never clear. But we didn't think it was right that it was happening without our knowledge. And that's just a small point. But we *so* wanted to make sure it was all straightforward and above board so it could pass any scrutiny. That was critical to us ... because we just needed it to be so transparent.

Later that fall, AstraZeneca replaced Courtney Rainey Group with a different PR firm, National Public Relations, without consulting with the working group. This distressed the group's members because they had established a congenial working relationship with Courtney Rainey; losing the company's logistical support seemed like another setback just when they had renewed their focus. Furthermore, rather than working with the newly hired company, the group found itself suddenly in a direct working relationship with James, an AstraZeneca employee responsible for patient liaison. Members of the working group describe James as "very hands-on." Lynn reflects on how the events of this transition period struck her, in her role as the group's chair:

We had never, ever, dealt with AstraZeneca in any way up to that point. The company was sort of in the background, but we didn't know anything about it. So all of a sudden James starts organizing and changing the phone calls, and calling me. He said to me, "Look, we've let Courtney Rainey go, and we've got to hire our own PR firm, and that will take ..." [and] he gave me a timeline; I think it was until basically the end of March, to get the new PR company in place.

This was just a few months before the official launch of the charter, in May 2006, at a national conference of breast cancer research called Reasons for Hope. Lynn recalls:

So I think that was an adjustment for all of us; but at that point we were so determined to finish it that we put up with perhaps more than we would have otherwise. Although James, I have to say, I have a very warm spot in my heart for him because he was a nice guy, but he was like a bull in a china shop because he took such a hands-on role. That's never happened to me. Usually, it's been the leader of the breast cancer group that's taken on the [lead] role. To my mind, he never should have been on the teleconferences.

Jean reinforced these sentiments.

> *Jean:* When they changed public relations groups, we were very
> uncomfortable with James's hands-on attitude. And there were
> several times where he said he would phone someone, and I voiced
> this [discomfort] clearly. I said, "I think Lynn should be the one to
> phone. Lynn's the head of our group, she's chairing our group." You
> know [*laughs in exasperation*], "It's not appropriate!"
> *Sharon:* And he would agree?
> *Jean:* Well, he would just keep trying to change things! He would say,
> "Well, is it agreeable if I contact so-and-so?"

The working group members' understanding about what was appropriate behaviour for the pharmaceutical company hinged on their belief that the project's funding was awarded as an "unrestricted educational grant," a term with which most advocates were familiar, though not everyone agreed on its meaning. Those I interviewed took the term to mean that the company would provide funding for a project, the broad lines of which both parties concurred with at the outset (i.e., a patients' rights charter), but the group would make all the ongoing project decisions. As the May launch date of the charter approached, tension escalated over the divergent understandings that the working group and AstraZeneca had of the unrestricted educational grant. Before a final prelaunch meeting, the draft document had included the acknowledgment "Supported by an unrestricted educational grant from AstraZeneca Canada," but working group members arrived at the meeting to find this phrase had been removed from the document circulated for final approval. Jean recalls the meeting in Mississauga, which included James:

> He [James] had removed the language about an [unrestricted] educational
> grant ... And of course we were shocked. We said, "No, no, this has to go
> back in!" And he said, "But it doesn't matter, and our lawyers are not
> comfortable with this" ...
> And that's when I – one of the few times I spoke up (because I've always
> felt that I'm a better soldier than I am a general). Anyway, I said to him,

"No, no, do you realize that all this work is for nothing, the charter will mean *nothing*, without that? People will simply be suspicious, this will be an AstraZeneca 'something,' it will not represent people with breast cancer."

Members of the group were genuinely perplexed by the removal of the mention of the unrestricted educational grant because, despite James's intervention in their operations, they felt that he and the company's previous representatives had not interfered with the most important aspect of the charter, its content:

Jean: I said [to James], "You haven't interfered – why would you be afraid to say that?" And certainly there was a lot of [discussion] ... there was no doubt that in that room there wasn't a single person that would let that go by.

Sharon: Why do you think their lawyers were uncomfortable? Did he say?

Jean: Nope. He just said that they had said, "Oh, remove that." But, of course, we were firm. And he didn't fight us on it when he saw that it would mean that the work would have gone for nothing and the charter would become meaningless if it was an AstraZeneca charter.

And I spoke frankly, I said, "You know, most of us have a real distrust for working with large companies, especially drug companies. We don't want to be seen as pawns, and we are not puppets to have our strings pulled." And I said, "So the fact that you *have* done this in a way that could be documented [to show] that you were not directing things, it doesn't matter! Without that wording people will suspect, and rightly so, and it just will make it meaningless."

And I think he understood what we were saying. I think he thought that we were being a bit overly fussy about it. But I think that he got it anyway. Whether or not he agreed, *we* all agreed and [felt certain] that there would be literally hundreds and perhaps thousands of individual people who had breast cancer who would agree [with our perspective]. So it was never brought up again.

The charter launch took place in Montreal at Reasons for Hope, the conference the Canadian Breast Cancer Research Alliance held every two to three years to showcase Canadian research on breast cancer. The conferences were geared to researchers, but the support of advocates was viewed as vital to maintaining public support for the research fund; breast cancer patient organizations across the country were thus provided with one or two free entrance passes.

The launch was held at the end of an afternoon in the break before supper and was attended by a smattering of journalists and the several dozen women with breast cancer who were at the conference (I was one of them, though at the time, I knew nothing about the charter's history and had forgotten about the letter I had written several years before). Once again, the members of working group felt that James was too visible and engaged – he greeted people at the door and shook their hands, introducing himself as being from AstraZeneca. He did not, however, sit at the speakers' table or address the audience or the press during the actual launch. At the ceremony, several members of the working group and an oncologist who had been supportive of the group's efforts gave short speeches, describing the purpose of the charter, how it was developed, and the hopes they had that Canadian breast cancer patients would take ownership of the document and use it to learn about and assert their rights. Printed copies of the charter in French and English were available, and a table of hors d'oeuvres encouraged people to linger while members of the working group spoke to the press.

Lynn recalls the launch with some discomfort. James had been recently transferred to Canada from the company's offices abroad before being assigned to the file, and she attributed his high visibility to his lack of understanding of the political tensions within the Canadian breast cancer community: "It bothered me, frankly, that AstraZeneca was there, and so blatantly in public sight. As you know, this [pharma sponsorship] is a very hot issue, and it was like throwing it in people's faces." I asked Lynn if she had talked to him beforehand about his role. "Oh, yeah," she replied, "yeah. But he had no idea what we were talking about, and what I was talking about." Lynn also thought the new PR firm had some responsibility for reining James in, "because they should have known that if you've got an unrestricted educational grant, the PR firm takes a much larger role."

By the time the charter was launched, the CBCN had a new president. In a final attempt to bring the CBCN on board as the charter's home, the working group members agreed to have James approach the CBCN's executive director. She was sufficiently receptive to prepare a proposal – a three-year plan that would have involved AstraZeneca providing the CBCN with financing for a different project. To Jean's chagrin, James balked and terminated the negotiations:

> Certainly, he has the right to turn them down flat about financing, because that's what *he* does. But he brought it to us and told us that it happened ... he turned them down flat before he told *us* he was turning them down flat. So that felt reasonably autocratic, you know ... I don't know. It's up to us! ... If [AstraZeneca] turned it down, I think we should assist the CBCN in finding somebody [to fund its project]... We care about the charter!

Another member of the working group was more sympathetic to James's impatience with the CBCN, given that the national group had been un-supportive during the charter's development and cut off communications. In addition, the collective mood in the Canadian breast cancer movement at that time was fragmented and contentious, in this advocate's view. A lot of projects were competing for attention and funding, making it hard to rally national support for any one project, particularly one like the charter, which did not have immediate, tangible benefits for patients and had critics within the movement.

Once the charter had been launched, the working group experienced another frustrating lull, which Lynn and Jean attributed to various factors. Lynn had health setbacks that drained her energy and absorbed much of her time. The originator of the project, from Willow, took the reins at another cancer organization, and the member from Quebec retired from her activist organization. James (who everyone agreed was "a doer" despite his intrusive style) returned to his home abroad. Neither his replacement nor the new PR firm took any initiative to contact the group. The few re-maining members of the group were left in limbo. Without funds or clear

direction, they returned to the demands of their local-regional organizations, where the charter was low priority compared with the day-to-day
pressures of running these groups. With the continuation of funding
cuts, the local organizations were strapped for funds and volunteers were
hard to recruit; the few core members were suffering from burnout and
didn't have the energy to put into an extra project that seemed less immediate and concrete.

The ad hoc working group now needed an organization to take
ownership of the document so that newly diagnosed women would be
aware of it and so that its advocacy potential could be realized. The two
most logical organizations to house and promote the document were
Willow, the group that spearheaded it, and the CBCN, as the national voice
for breast cancer patients; but neither wanted to adopt this role.

The working group's frustration over being absent from the negotiations
with the CBCN illustrates a larger dilemma posed by the drug company's
sponsorship. Throughout the project's history were instances in which
AstraZeneca, the two public relations companies, and Willow (as the lead
group on the project) guided the process in directions that members of
the working group did not fully support or understand. In retrospect, the
problems dated back to the workshop, where several key participants had
viewed the project as artificially imposed, rather than as a solution that
sprang organically from the workshop discussions. Perhaps, mused one
of the working group members, if the goal of the workshop had been
transparent when they were invited, if they had been given documentation
from the European charter project to review in advance, they would not
have felt surprised or ambushed on the second day. Lacking the chance to
shape the project's origins, workshop members were divided from the
outset and these divisions festered.

This lack of control extended to other decisions, such as paying an
activist who they thought was volunteering to edit the charter, the switch
in PR firms, and James's sudden appearance a few months before the
launch and his disappearance soon afterward. A year after the charter's
launch, Jean remained puzzled by James's role:

> Well, I just think [AstraZeneca] brought this guy in to tie down some
> loose details and maybe to extract themselves from some community

projects. I mean, I could be mistaken. But he came over, he pushed this [the charter] through – he *certainly* seemed to get exceedingly involved – and then he was gone! [*Sharon:* Hmm ...] So, I cannot tell. I don't know their corporate philosophy for this year, you know?

In mid-2007, more than a year after the launch of the charter, members of the working group were not certain whether AstraZeneca was still a player. Lynn was beginning to regain strength after a hospitalization and was ready to re-engage in activist work but was hesitant about the charter.

Lynn: In some ways, I feel it's so remote now.
Sharon: Well, it does seem a bit adrift. You're not meeting actively with
  your group now, are you? Or talking; you're not making plans?
Lynn: No. Whoever replaced James is not making himself that visible
  ... I was supposed to talk to him, and he was supposed to call me and
  he didn't. So I called him and I emailed him. He'd be the person
  who'd have to make a commitment to get us organized.

Jean, however, felt it was now up to the working group to take charge and move the project forward. She was encouraged that several other nationwide cancer organizations – a lung cancer and a colorectal cancer group – had adapted the charter, giving credit to the working group as their starting point.

Even more encouraging, in the spring of 2008, Jean was able to claim, with satisfaction, that the charter produced by the working group had served as a model tool endorsed by an action group of the Canadian Strategy for Cancer Control, the national initiative to combat cancer in Canada. The action group, which was responsible for ensuring the patient's perspective was not lost and for improving the quality of life for cancer patients and their families, had endorsed the idea of a cancer patients' charter modelled on the one developed by the working group and had presented a modified document at a series of cross-Canada workshops. As Jean writes in the newsletter of her regional breast cancer group,

Our wish at the time of the launch ... was to encourage other cancer groups to develop a charter adapted to their needs and finally to have enough groups on board to be able to pressure the federal government with the tool to force them to act on our behalf and assure us of national standards. Now the federal process is backing this national team to develop a cancer patients' charter based on our document.

It appeared that the charter would have a home after all, vindicating the working group's years of effort.

Despite Jean's satisfaction with the outcome, it's clear that AstraZeneca was the guiding partner in this dance until the company disengaged, and that the grant was anything but unrestricted. The preset agenda was at odds with the understanding and goals of the participants who joined the project, and the company repeatedly took control of the process, leaving participants baffled and upset. They finally succeeded in passing the document on to an organization willing to own it, but only after their relationship with the pharmaceutical company had died from the latter's neglect.

Power and Knowledge

All four projects would seem to be efforts to rally patient organizations behind demands that would support the industry's goal of instilling a discourse that shapes patients' (and the public's) understanding of drug policy debates. Each of the projects means one thing to the group but has quite another meaning when viewed through the lens of drug regulations and drug marketing. The industry's marketing goals can run contrary to patients' best interests, a disparity seen most starkly in Ortho Biotech's drug Eprex, which earned billions for the company but proved detrimental to cancer patients in clinical trials. Jean, who knew the squeeze the umbrella group was experiencing when its government support was cut back, sympathized with the CBCN's decision to enter into an agreement with the company, but in retrospect the partnership troubled her:

> I think it's widely known that the CBCN was totally taken in by Ortho Biotech ... In the end, it made it look as if the CBCN was supporting this new drug that they were doing to help people with anemia ... And, of course, since then there's been a lot of literature that these kinds of drugs interfere with the chemotherapy. So this was a very bitter [lesson], and the CBCN was played horribly.

Jean's reflection recalls Foucault's argument that "truth" at any point in history is the result of power and knowledge struggles that are enacted through daily practices. What is the true meaning for patients of Eprex, aromatase inhibitors, wait times, and patients' rights? In each of the four cases, the group's understanding of what appears best for its community is no match for a drug company's knowledge about its own drug and the nuances of the regulatory process. In every case, the fiction of an "unrestricted educational grant" provides a distracting cover while a PR firm provides sophisticated strategies for packaging the message the industry wants to deploy.

Several activists who were generally accepting of pharma funding acknowledged that the dominant discourse had important gaps. Beth Kapusta observed that the absence of patients who were standing up and lobbying for lower drug costs or asking for clearer information about how drug prices are determined left "a huge gap in the critical spectrum." When I asked her about the lack of representation for patients' interests when those interests were not aligned with those of the pharmaceutical industry, she went on to say of drug policy, "That stuff is really hard!" She had recently joined a committee that was examining the ethical issues underlying access to therapies:

> And I'm a bright, university-educated, quick study on most things, but when I look at the whole domain of ... ethics and of the societal obligation to provide treatment, I feel like I'm in over my head. It's not something that can be taken lightly ... It's a complicated subject – I don't really know how to answer your question because it's a much more nuanced issue than I could rhyme off the top of my head. There are so many interrelated factors having to do with the shape of our health care system, and our expectations as patients.
>
> I don't even know if I believe we should be investing the amount of money that we're investing in these therapies, because in the end we can't afford them as a society, so why would we develop them? It's kind of like giving R&D money to Rolls-Royce to make a hybrid car. Well, yeah, but most people can't afford to buy one, and is [the investment] in the best interest of society? Because at that level, you have to look at the balance of things.

Beth didn't suggest that the silences on crucial topics were the result of industry funding. Others did, however. Kathleen describes the awkward feeling of disapproval in the room when she spoke her mind about the workshop's preset agenda, and numerous others concluded that their groups could not to accept fund from the industry because "you don't bite the hand that feeds you."

Conclusion

THE FIGHT FOR MEDICINE'S SOUL

The Medical Commons and the Allure of Privatization

Canada's medical system treats health care as part of the Canadian commons – resources that belong to and benefit the entire community. For decades, advocates of publicly funded health insurance have argued that excluding drugs from the services that medicare covers was a political misjudgement and that bringing pharmaceuticals into the health care commons with a national plan would serve the goals of equity and better health outcomes, as well as the economies of bulk purchasing. It's my belief that the pharmaceutical industry succeeded in co-opting Canada's breast cancer movement by encouraging leaders to view drugs as free-market commodities; to do so, they adapted well-honed methods that have been used to build relationships with physicians. In harnessing breast cancer groups and the patient advocacy movement, the industry has covertly advanced a policy agenda that one analyst calls "neoliberal pharmaceutical science." Rather than fostering public debate about the best way to provide those drugs that patients truly need, the alliances confuse a discourse that is crucial if Canada is to sustain its health care commons and that is even more critical if the system's reach is to be expanded to include pharmaceuticals.

If this analysis is correct, the breast cancer movement in Canada has failed in the idealistic goal that Rabinow and other advocates of bio-citizenship foresaw for patient groups – that of keeping medical science honest. Rather than providing a check on the self-interest that tempts actors in the system to stray from medicine's main goal – alleviating suffering – patient organizations have themselves been led astray. Instead of critiquing marketing strategies that distort the truth about a drug's benefits or risks, high prices, unpublished results of clinical trials, or strategies that offer drugs as the sole antidote to illness, PHANGOs – pharma-funded NGOs – protest government regulation of drugs, heartless bureaucrats, and perceived barriers to accessing novel treatments of uncertain value. From both a scientific and an ethical perspective, these advocacy goals are misplaced. The research evidence doesn't support the claims on which they are based, and marketing pharmaceuticals as profit-generating commodities following a capitalist model is inconsistent with the public interest. Corporatized advocacy, however, rests on this consumerist model of medicine.

Many establishment actors, including physicians, researchers, and editors of medical journals, are convinced that our current approach to developing, assessing, and prescribing pharmaceuticals is so dysfunctional the public interest is no longer being served. They have called on the public to support their struggle to hold medicine to higher principles than the marketplace, perhaps by removing drug development and marketing from the corporate sector. If patient organizations hope to be credible actors in these debates, their leaders must confront the ways in which pharma support undermines their capacity to provide patients a voice.

Signs of Co-optation: Three Losses that Undermine Democratic Process

Three types of losses suggest that the movement's leaders didn't guide the movement's evolution to pharma funding; rather, the federal government reversed long-standing policies to support community-based advocacy, and in parallel, the pharmaceutical industry actively undertook a process of co-optation, using techniques proven effective in its relationships with physicians. One loss was discursive, a second was structural, and a third was a loss of agency.

Patient organizations are potentially valuable arenas for exchanging discourses among patients and those who share their lives. Given the inherent diversity of values and experiences among women, and the extent of uncertainty in health and medical science, competing understandings of reality are inevitable, but these differences can be a source of creative debate. Had the breast cancer movement's early mix of perspectives been sustained, the groups could have been centres for productive exchange. Over time, the promise and risks of drugs might have been reconciled through a process that integrated members' experiences with the research evidence that documents both benefits and harms. Instead, a discourse of hope (often bordering on hype) gained ground within the movement and critiques were dismissed as self-interested attacks.

Structural changes were a second sign of co-optation. Members who argued that the movement should remain independent of the pharmaceutical industry were silenced or removed from key spots within organizations. Organizations, likewise, disappeared or were marginalized if their leaders rejected pharma support. This process of pharma-critic attrition/ exclusion and pharma-booster augmentation gradually aligned the movement almost uniformly with a deregulatory agenda and an acceptance of spiralling prices. The separation of the organizations' advocacy and service functions was another structural loss. Pharma-funded groups with no dues-paying members and that performed no services in the community used the federal government's tightened restrictions on advocacy to claim the advocacy role as their own, forfeiting community and political legitimacy in the process.

Loss of agency was evident in many of the narratives in preceding chapters as leaders surrendered decision-making control within their own organizations. This occurred despite conscious efforts to retain independence through resistance and to erect structural barriers against influence. Rather than working from their strengths – grassroots knowledge and a common interest in a system that works for patients – groups began sponsoring projects with hidden policy backstories far removed from their personal experiences. Out of their depth, they relied on industry representatives and public relations firms paid by the industry to brief them about regulatory issues.

Within each organization and in the movement as a whole, this transformation was gradual, aided by the turnover inevitable in a cancer patient organization: some members die, others recover and decide to put cancer behind them, while new members know less and less about the organization's history as time goes on. This organic turnover can't account for the extent to which the movement began to see its interests through the industry's eyes, however. That change came about through well-tested strategies, systematically deployed.

Anatomy of a Takeover: New Partners, Old Moves

Irish researcher Orla O'Donovan posits co-optation as an incremental process in which rigorous past standards are gradually and imperceptibly abandoned, then forgotten, as new practices and discourses take root and come to feel natural. Gradually, through successive compromises, groups experience "shifts in tacit understandings that may take place over time."[1] O'Donovan's analysis captures the broad strokes of the transformation within Canada's breast cancer movement. The evolution in this movement, although incremental, was not passive. The federal government set the stage with its focus on trade, deregulation, and a restructured civil society. This rapidly changing, sometimes hostile environment left breast cancer groups with a diminished mandate and financially adrift – internal stresses that pitted activists and groups against one another. The pharmaceutical industry astutely exploited the disarray.

Stung by the confrontational tactics of the early AIDS movement, the pharmaceutical industry took a highly strategic approach, wooing breast cancer groups with techniques that closely mimic those deployed in its seduction of physicians. These include the gradual development of personal relationships, beginning with small gifts and free meals. Analysts of the physician–sales rep relationship find that offering "food, flattery and friendship" engenders positive feelings that lay the groundwork for cozy working relationships and a desire to reciprocate, even when the gifts are small tokens like coffee and notepads.[2] Other industry methods used to cultivate support in the physician community are the singling out and training of people the industry calls "thought leaders," or "key opinion leaders," funding meetings and travel, and providing money awarded as unrestricted educational grants for medical education and research. Also familiar from the industry's repertoire for seducing physicians are PR firms that craft communications strategies and formulate claims focusing on drugs as agents of hope and voluntary codes of professional ethics with no oversight or penalties.

These techniques work. Research documenting their success with physicians now extends back several decades. They seed and sustain misleading myths; fuel demand for new, unproven treatments; keep drug prices high; and broaden prescription practices to include large groups of individuals (e.g., those classified as high risk or showing mild or ambiguous symptoms) in whom new drugs have not been tested and may do more harm than good. Because the techniques depend on basic principles of human psychology, patients are no less likely than physicians to succumb to them.[3]

Women in my study who participated in pharma-funded events attended dinners at expensive restaurants. Recalling an Astra-Zeneca financed dinner she attended in Ottawa, one woman described it as "unbelievable! ... We probably drank enough wine to finance [our organization] for a year!" In her tenure as president of the Canadian Breast Cancer Network (CBCN), Karen was fêted at lunches and dinners for which Ortho Biotech picked up the tab:

> They were very cordial to deal with. As a matter of fact, I remember we had a workshop in Toronto ... And they must have dropped over $1,000 on dinner [for] the full board. They ordered wine by the bottle, and ... [one of the pharma reps] said, would we like her to order for us? So she ordered an authentic twelve-course Chinese dinner ... Money was no object when they wined and dined you. Everything was first class and no holds barred.

These examples mimic the methods the industry had developed in the previous decades to woo physicians. And just as the dance with physicians is a tango with two partners, so is the pharmaceutical industry's relationship with patient advocates. The industry chooses the music and decides which groups would make suitable partners; the group decides whether or not to dance.

Among physicians, "product champions," also known as "key opinion leaders" (KOLs) or "thought leaders," are at the pinnacle of the industry's relationship building. These terms designate physicians whom pharmaceutical companies pay to speak at medical conferences, dinners, grand rounds, and other ostensibly educational events. Industry guidebooks and articles outline the techniques the pharmaceutical industry uses to create physician thought leaders: a company's marketing staff choose recruits based on physicians' views about its latest drug and their potential to influence peers. They build relationships with them, then groom them with media training, advice on public speaking, and prefabricated lecture materials, which KOLs can use to communicate "appropriate" messages (e.g., slide sets and articles favourable to the company's drug).[4]

The similarity of strategies at work in the patient advocacy movement is striking. The requirement to include the "patients' point of view" has become *de rigueur* on research review panels, ethics committees, health policy conference programs, drug policy committees, and the like, creating an enormous demand within the system for patient advocates. In theory, the patient representatives draw on their experience as patients to enrich the discussion. In reality, an invited conference talk requires significant preparation, as do research and policy meetings, which typically require reviewing voluminous technical files sent in advance. Some understanding of health policy and science is helpful, if not necessary, to engage meaningfully. Even a self-labelled "quick study" like Beth acknowledged that, on joining a new drug policy committee, "I feel like I'm in over my head."

Beyond the specialized content knowledge, advocacy engagement at the national or international level requires money for travel. Media savviness and public-speaking ability are additional aids to success and for which training is an asset. The same agencies now clamouring for patient representatives, including government regulatory bodies, sometimes provide modest funding to train patients or bring them to meetings that the agencies themselves sponsor, but they do not support the groups' advocacy-related projects and operational expenses. Patient organizations may thus obtain funding from health-related government offices or health technology review agencies, to send a delegate to specific committee meetings and events where patients are viewed as "stakeholders," but the funding does not provide salaries or fund efforts to prepare for meetings or to keep abreast of drug policy day to day.[5]

Experience in other jurisdictions suggests that industry training projects help companies select and groom articulate, well-briefed patients or former patients, filling these voids in much the same way that the industry supports the continuing medical education lectures that physicians must attend to maintain their licences.[6] In June 2014, for example, the UK company Pharmaphorum published the thirty-two-page report *Patient Opinion Leaders: The New KOLs for Pharma?* The publication likens selected patient advocates to physician-KOLs, adopting the term "patient opinion leaders" (POLs), who the report identifies as patients who challenge "physicians, payers and pharma companies to see things from their perspective" and who use social media to develop "impressive online followings."[7]

The deployment of these methods, familiar to health professionals who know them from their own milieu, is raising concerns that industry-funded advocacy may distort public policies to the detriment of patients. In one striking instance, the World Health Organization in 2007 sponsored public consultations to gather public input into a draft global strategy on neglected diseases. In briefs that sometimes used identical phrasing, fourteen advocacy groups argued in favour of strong intellectual property protections, the same position as the pharmaceutical industry. Noting that eleven of the groups received funding from various pharmaceutical companies, representatives from health agencies in four South Asian countries wondered, in a letter to the *Lancet*, if the hearings had been "hijacked by pharma." In a more recent, much-discussed case in the United States, the Food and Drug Administration (FDA) approved the drug Addyi (flibanserin) as a treatment to increase female sexual desire, overruling its own clinical reviewers. Evidence that the drug actually enhanced sexual desire was weak, while evidence of potential harm was significant: in clinical trials, flibanserin showed dangerous interactions with alcohol and other drugs. After the FDA twice refused the company's application, manufacturer Sprout Pharmaceuticals helped launch and fund an advocacy campaign, called Even the Score, to promote flibanserin on the company's third application. An Even the Score letter campaign and testimony from Even the Score supporters at the advisory committee meeting charged the FDA with sex discrimination on the grounds that women lacked a Viagra-type drug. To the dismay of many drug policy analysts, committee members voted eighteen to six in favour of approval, which the FDA granted in August 2015.[8]

I found two tiers of pharma engagement in the training of POLs. At the first level, companies fund patient organizations to host in-person or online advocacy-training sessions, which are open to all members of the organization who are interested in advocacy. Industry liaisons may attend these workshops, where they can observe which advocates present themselves well and are favourable toward drugs and the pharmaceutical industry. They also learn who is critical of pharma. At a second level, advocates chosen as POLs receive intensive training and go on to participate on decision-making panels and as featured speakers at conferences. They enjoy such nonmonetary perks as travel, the media spotlight, and collegial relationships with prominent physicians, researchers, and policy makers; they may also have paid positions within their organization, thanks to pharmaceutical company grants to the group. The implicit Faustian bargain is that they will not publicly critique the industry's products, prices, or practices. And since the drug company, not the group's members, chooses POLs, these "patient representatives" may not be the individuals the community would choose to speak on their behalf.

The North Carolina company Best Practices, LLC, in a slide presentation promoting the company's publication *Collaborating with Patient Advocacy Groups to Educate the Marketplace*, advises companies to recognize that the advocacy landscape is dynamic: "Some groups will be friendly, some groups may prove hostile."[9] Companies should "positively reach out to activist groups to understand their perspectives" and create a "topographical map" of the advocacy landscape as an aid to strategic planning. "Spot common ground" between the company and the advocacy group, the presentation advises. Within an organization, "work through group members who are identified as being 'the most reasonable.'" Such advice supports Karen's impression that in Ortho Biotech's overtures to the CBCN, the company representative identified her as a barrier to their goals and chose instead to work with the more "reasonable" (i.e., industry-sympathetic) vice-president; similarly, the strategy of selectively nurturing relationships is consistent with the recollection "Virginia" had that board turnover and a new executive director at the reins were events critical to Willow scrapping its policy against pharma funding.

For a physician, being a KOL can be a lucrative way to augment his or her income, but physicians who have worked as KOLs say that, at least initially, the biggest incentive is not the money but the ego boost and the opportunity to make professional contacts. Jerome Kassirer, who spent several years in the 1970s as a KOL, says, "To this day, I remember how important I felt to be chosen."[10] Like other KOLs, however, Kassirer describes an ego-deflating "aha" moment when the hidden strings became visible and he dropped to earth, poorer but wiser. The same can happen with POLs. Liz Whamond told me of her decision to attend an international meeting as a board member of the CBCN, travelling at Ortho Biotech's expense:

> I did go. Karen was organizing things with Ortho Biotech. I wish now I never had. It was the first and last time I ever did it. They didn't request that I do anything [in return]. I just didn't feel good about it ... You don't bite the hand that feeds you, or if you do, they won't fund you the next time you ask for money.

Another strategy borrowed from the physician relationship-building arsenal is the negotiation of meanings. Pharma-sponsored conferences, workshops, and gifts were an integral part of the strategy for building relationships with Canadian breast cancer patient groups. These encounters became sites for the subtle redefinition of concepts and assumptions central to the health system. Terms like "wait time," "treatment of choice," and "patients' rights" were invested with meanings favourable to the industry, and these meanings gained currency within the groups themselves.

One example is "unrestricted educational grants" (UREGs), a corporate term drug companies use to label funds they give to individuals and organizations for projects that ostensibly meet two criteria: the project is educational, and the company has no say in the agenda. In Canada, there are grounds to believe that unrestricted educational grants from the pharmaceutical industry are a significant source of funding for family physicians' continuing medical education (CME), the many educational events that doctors must attend each year to maintain their licences.[11] The practice is controversial, in Canada as elsewhere, with US estimates of annual grants in the tens of billions (the industry considers the figures confidential).[12] Despite the hands-off claim regarding content of these events, researchers have found that drug companies and the private firms providing medical education subtly influence the content of these supposedly independent events. A sponsoring company may suggest a topic or speaker, or provide graphics and other materials that discuss unapproved uses of its drugs.[13] Even given the evidence that such events embed drug-marketing messages that affect prescribing practices, medical schools and hospitals go along with the system because they don't want to give up the support.[14] Faced with evidence of bias in industry-funded medical education and materials, voices within the profession in Canada have begun to call for an end to pharma-funded CME and are casting about for alternative models of funding; France, for example, funds CME with a 1.6 percent tax levied on the industry.[15]

Members I interviewed from breast cancer PHANGOs cited the UREG as the vehicle under which funding was given. And yet, the industry sponsor's influence was so much in evidence at the CBCN's antianemia project that the president resigned in protest; likewise, several participants sensed a hidden agenda at the workshop AstraZeneca funded as a prelude to the patients' rights charter project. As is the case among physicians, some leaders of patient advocacy groups, especially those who said they had never felt any pressure from the industry, took the term at face value and felt reassured that the company would not ask anything in return for the money. Rose, of Breast Cancer Action Nova Scotia (BCANS), describes the group's initial experience in collaborating with a pharma-funded speaker event: "That sort of opened our eyes to something known as an 'unrestricted educational grant.'" The same group received a government grant to hire someone to raise funds for them. Rose recalls:

> He thought we were crazy not to go after the unrestricted educational grants. And he got us a lot of unrestricted educational grants, small amounts for various projects that we want to do. So I think we're a lot more open to that, but again it would have to be no strings attached. Luckily, a lot of them [drug companies] seem okay with that. They don't expect you to stick their logo everywhere if they give you money.

The paid fundraiser, who was hired on a federal grant designed both to provide new graduates with work experience and to move grassroots organizations to self-sufficiency, had an incentive to view pharma UREGs uncritically, since he had no vested interest in the organization and his job was to bring in money. However, "Meredith," from the same group, felt that accepting a number of small UREGs from one particular company slowly gave the company a toehold in the group's affairs. To Virginia, based on her experience at Willow, the very term "unrestricted educational grant" was a joke: "What is that? Give me a break! It's like, 'I've given my son an unrestricted educational grant to go to university, but if spends his money on drugs and drink, I'm pulling it!' [*Laughs.*]"

Rather than having a fixed meaning, then, the term "unrestricted educational grant" lends itself to multiple interpretations. In the terminology of science and technology studies, the UREG is a boundary object, something that permits actors from different sectors to collaborate across boundaries, because it can be invested with multiple meanings. The various sectors involved may negotiate the meaning of the object over the course of the collaboration, as "James" and members of the working group on the patients' rights charter did when the latter insisted on retaining the UREG designation on the patients' charter. Depending on how these negotiations evolve, the boundary object may enable the parties to work together or it may be a source of tension. Within the groups, the meanings that key decision makers assigned to the UREG were critical in determining whether a PHANGO relationship would succeed or fail. Usually they succeeded. As the less powerful partner, the groups paid for these successes in various ways, including the loss of members who held out for a stricter interpretation of the term, the loss of decision-making autonomy, and the loss of credibility within the community.[16]

Situating PHANGOs in a Historically Embedded Discourse

Pharmaceutical policy is arguably the hottest area of debate in contemporary medicine. In the past decade, over a dozen books and scores of articles have documented a crisis in medicine that puts the pharmaceutical industry squarely at the centre.[17] Among those sounding the alarm are respected, high-profile members of the medical establishment – past and present editors of prestigious mainstream medical journals, professors at Ivy League universities, researchers who conduct systematic reviews of drug trials, and former industry insiders. They refer to many instances where the distortion of information has made it impossible for physicians and their patients to trust the published information about drug treatments.

In Western medicine, ethical principles going back at least to the Hippocratic Oath stress the obligation of healers to put patients' needs ahead of profit. By contrast, the first obligation of pharmaceutical companies, like all corporations, is to their shareholders. Regulations were meant to ensure that pharmaceutical companies play by medicine's rules, not those of the market. The cries of alarm coming from distinguished physicians are because regulations like those in the Kefauver-Harris Amendments, which tried to square the circle, haven't worked. In the United States, the Department of Justice in recent years has fined major pharmaceutical companies billions of dollars for bribery and fraud. Leading the pack of delinquents have been Pfizer and GlaxoSmithKline. Pfizer agreed in 2009 to pay $2.3 billion in fraud charges for illegally promoting four of its drugs, while GlaxoSmithKline, charged with failing to report safety data (for the anti-diabetic drug Avandia) and for off-label promotion (for the antidepressant drugs Paxil and Wellbutrin), agreed in 2012 to pay $3 billion. There are grounds to believe that these two cases are just the tip of a large iceberg. As American law professor Kevin Outterson commented, drug companies "keep getting caught doing similar things." In 2009, he notes, twenty-five major companies, eight of which ranked in the top ten global pharmaceutical companies, were under "corporate integrity agreements," which require the company to submit to five years of independent monitoring. The cases have not abated since Outterson's tally. The consumer rights advocacy group Public Citizen documented seventy-four settlements and court judgments in the United States between November 2010 and July 2012, totalling $10.2 billion; more recent cases have been settled as well, among them Johnson & Johnson and subsidiaries, $2.2 billion for off-label marketing and kickbacks to doctors and pharmacists (November 2013), and Novartis, for kickbacks, false claims, and illegal promotion (November 2015 and October 2016).[18]

Neither the fines nor the agreements seem to deter drug companies from their pattern of misbehaviour, Outterson adds, which suggests that the industry simply writes off the fines as the cost of doing business. How can one explain such persistent criminality? Ben Goldacre, a physician based at Oxford University, argues in his book *Bad Pharma* that physicians, researchers, and those employed in the pharmaceutical industry are trapped inside a system with perverse incentives to put profits ahead of health. Jillian Clare Kohler, a political scientist who directs a World Health Organization collaborating centre at the University of Toronto that studies good governance and transparency in medicines, asserts in an essay co-written with two colleagues that "the pharmaceutical system is susceptible to fraud and corruption" for reasons that include the profit potential in the sale of pharmaceuticals, the vulnerability of patients to opportunism, and the fact that suppliers (including, but not only, drug manufacturers) are "profit maximizers." If fraud, corruption, and other criminal behaviours are as endemic to the present-day pharmaceutical industry, as Outterson, Goldacre, Kohler, and other authors claim (and the evidence is compelling), patient advocates need to understand the impact of industry misconduct on the communities they represent. They need to join with other concerned parties to correct the system weaknesses standing in the way of safe, effective drugs coming to market at affordable prices. And they need to ask whether their alliances with the industry are to the net benefit of patients.[19]

As leaders in patient organizations partake of pharma's food, flattery, and friendship, can they avoid being part of the same system? Can they hope to insulate their organizations from pharma's unethical practices with voluntary codes and negotiated agreements? Most authors who have written critically about big pharma in contemporary medicine in the past decade include pharma-funded patient organizations as part the problem, precisely because they consistently advocate uncritically for faster access to new drugs. Howard Brody, a physician and ethicist at the University of Texas, positions patient organizations in a multilayered system of actors with interacting parts, each implicated in unethical industry practices in different but complementary ways.[20] Individual physicians receiving gifts from drug reps comprise one level, physicians attending pharma-funded CME courses are another, and medical professional organizations are a third. His six other levels are patient organizations with industry funding, industry advertising aimed at consumers, industry support of medical journals, industry-funded medical research and KOLs, industry lobbying of government, and industry influence on the drug regulator.

In their relationships with the industry, each of these actors has some power, says Brody, and a central ethical question in medicine is "How can [each actor] use their power ethically and responsibly?"[21] He sees the answer to this question coming from fine-grained analyses at each level of "exactly who has power over what and in what circumstances." In my examination of the PHANGO-industry dyad, patient organizations were repeatedly outmanoeuvred as the industry played its hand, using well-honed strategies culled from decades of prior experience gaming the system. When patient-group leaders explained when and why it was ethically justifiable to accept pharma funding, they tended to take a narrow view, framing the issue strictly within their own organization's needs and experience. Many voiced a general mistrust of big corporations but lacked familiarity with the practices embedded in the pharmaceutical industry culture. They turned (justifiably) against those in government who had cut them loose, but failed to seek out potential allies who are struggling against the same neoliberal injustices.

Patient groups need to take stock of where their power lies and how best to use it. Although they lack the enormous financial resources of the pharmaceutical industry, these organizations have assets that the industry covets, most notably the trust of patients and the sympathetic support of wider publics. This trust gives them privileged access to the experiences and concerns of patients and the moral authority – indeed the responsibility – to advance these interests in the public sphere. This means staying close to the community's experience, while understanding the larger system and challenging its shortcomings.

From a patient's perspective, high-dose chemo and EPO (the drug erythropoietin) for breast cancer patients serve as cautionary tales against the single-minded pursuit of access to new treatments. Access advocacy nonetheless remains the focus of much patient advocacy, which points to a puzzling gap in my analysis: the origin of the multilayered discourse that justifies the pharmaceutical industry and patient groups working together to promote rapid access to new drugs. The cluster of ideas that came up repeatedly in my interviews with advocates not only runs counter to scientific evidence but seemed to spring full-blown from the long-forgotten Together to an End conference. Curiously, one finds the same statements repeated by patient advocacy groups in the United States, Europe, Australia, and New Zealand. Where did this discourse come from?

In a 2014 analysis of what he calls "neoliberal pharmaceutical science," political economist Edward Nik-Khah provides what I believe is the answer. He details a chapter in the history of the modern pharmaceutical industry, going back five decades to when the industry was still smarting from the

1962 Kefauver-Harris Amendments to the US Federal Food, Drug, and Cosmetic Act.[22] As explained in Chapter 1, the amendments were a response to the thalidomide disaster, high prescription drug prices, and misleading advertising – practices that tarnished the industry's early promise of revolutionizing medicine with an output of wonder drugs. For the first time, laws required drug manufacturers to provide proof that their drugs were effective before approval, and gave the government the power to restrict advertising. Based on a study of historical documents, Nik-Khah shows that, in the 1970s, an influential group of free-market economists with ties to the Chicago School of Economics targeted the Kefauver-Harris Amendments, with the goal of creating a market-friendly, deregulated pharmaceutical industry.[23]

As part of a strategy to reverse the amendments, in December 1972, they held a conference designed to attack the FDA and the 1962 amendments from all sides by forging relations with the pharmaceutical industry and generating antiregulation arguments. The meeting, held at the University of Chicago's Center for Policy Study, was called the "International Conference on the Regulation of the Introduction of New Pharmaceuticals." Major drug companies funded the meeting, and senior members of the companies presented papers; no contrary voices were included. A theme that arose from the conference was that the public had been misled about the need for drug regulation: far from serving the public interest, regulations were "keeping valuable and potentially useful drugs from the market." The health of consumers, speakers claimed, was best served by making drugs available quickly and by giving the industry responsibility for education about drugs.[24]

Conference organizers knew that the weight of public opinion supported the opposing views of reformers like Ralph Nader and his colleague Sidney Wolfe of the consumer rights advocacy group Public Citizen.[25] The conference team also met resistance from the academic community. The meeting's blatant ideological character alarmed the newly appointed director of the Center for Policy Studies, under whose auspices the meeting was organized, and a book compilation of the conference papers received scathing reviews from the scientific community. If they were to achieve their goals, the Chicago School economists had to find ways both to counter the popular desire for strict government regulation of the industry and to answer scholarly critics.[26]

They turned to Louis Lasagna, a physician and clinical pharmacologist who had testified at the Kefauver hearings where he caught the attention of some of the economists who had planned the conference. Lasagna had a reputation as a fierce proponent of clinical trials, but he had reservations about the FDA, reservations that grew throughout the 1960s to become strongly critical. By 1971, he had reversed his championing of clinical trials as a means of providing scientific answers on drug safety and efficacy, and claimed instead that medicine was inherently too uncertain and value-laden for science to yield definitive answers. Drug treatment decisions should therefore be turned over to patients, who could make decisions based on their own values. He ridiculed concerns about industry marketing publications that masqueraded as scientific journals and charged instead that the FDA was acting as a Soviet-style thought police.[27]

Still following Nik-Khah's account, in 1976, Lasagna established the Tufts Center for the Study of Drug Development (Tufts CSDD, or CSDD for short) to conduct research on pharmaceuticals in concert with pharmaceutical companies, with industry funding, and on the understanding that industry data would be kept confidential. The CSDD was housed at Tufts University, lending credibility to its activities. These included generating arguments for use in policy debates; studying legal, economic, and scientific issues; advising pharmaceutical firms on ways to commercialize research; and devising ways to change the public's "misconceptions" about drugs. Over the next decades, from his base in the CSDD, Lasagna developed and tested his ideas. To reinforce antiregulatory drug policy proposals, he set up in different countries think-tanks of like-minded scholars – including Canada's Fraser Institute – which issued reports with similar arguments, while scholars published journal articles repeating the same assertions, an "echo chamber" strategy developed by the tobacco industry to counter critical scrutiny.

Enduring memes that came out of the CSDD thought factory were "drug lag" and "$800 million pill."[28] The former claimed that patients were being denied access to drugs because of bureaucratic inertia; the latter claimed that price controls on drugs would put a halt to new drug development because drugs are so expensive to develop (in a November 2014 study out of Tufts, the CSDD's estimated cost of developing a new drug had ballooned from US$800 million to US$2.68 billion[29]). By the end of the 1970s, the CSDD was an influential force, and Lasagna was the leading advocate for "neoliberal clinical science."[30] When the political climate shifted in the 1980s to support neoliberal policies, Lasagna was ready to advance a set of free-market arguments for the development and sale of pharmaceuticals.

At this point, Nik-Khah's narrative intersects with my own. One idea Lasagna and his Chicago School colleagues embraced was to remove power over drug regulation from regulators and scientists and return "power to the people" in the area of drug availability and use.[31] Determining the best drug regimen to treat a sick patient "was just too 'complex' a question for scientists to answer," and such decisions were best left to the market: to patients.[32] The latter, Lasagna argued in 1976, "probably would not welcome such responsibility, but nevertheless should be forced to assume it."[33] And even though doctors and patients would inevitably make some mistakes in judgment that might cause harm to others, the cumulative effect of such errors, said Lasagna, would fall far short of the harm drug regulations do.[34]

Many – probably the majority – of health practitioners and drug policy scholars sought to strengthen the regulatory regime that was put in place in 1962. Like health activists in the public sphere in the 1970s, they were in four-square opposition to the discourses that Lasagna crafted at the CSDD. My research suggests, however, that the emergence of the AIDS movement in the 1980s, the breast cancer movement in the 1990s, and the plethora of subsequent patient advocacy groups that formed in their wake provided the CSDD a perfect opportunity for advancing this anti-regulatory position within a crucial subset of the wider public: a new generation of patients suffering from life-threatening or debilitating diseases who had gained, or demanded, participant status on a wide range of decision-making bodies. Under the identity banner of the "smart, informed baby boomer who takes control," fuelled by medicine's "messages of hope," and seduced by antiregulatory, antigovernment tropes, such groups embraced "patient power" demands for rapid access to the latest, high-priced drugs. The PHANGOs I studied accepted, and sometimes promoted, both the discourse of drug lag and of the $800 million pill, making them de facto participants in the echo chamber strategy that the Chicago School and the CSDD used to popularize their version of pharmaceutical science.

Nothing in my conversations with activists suggested they were aware of the deep roots of their rhetoric in Lasagna's grand vision of a pharmaceutical policy based not on regulatory science but on markets; yet, I believe the two sets of discourses coincide too exactly and that their content is too far removed from the evidence for the resemblance to be coincidental. Participants in my research spoke of bean-counting bureaucrats and the need for consumer choice; they used pharmaceutical company grants to create or commission performance report cards for the provinces, comparing their performance using "metrics" like breast cancer survival rates and wait times for breast cancer treatment to hold governments to account. Nik-Khah characterizes such audit activities as a means of controlling government regulatory bodies. With dozens of advocates saying essentially the same thing in different venues, the effect is to enlarge the echo chamber while isolating through exclusion those who question or voice dissent.

Adding to the echo effect, the campaigns and discourses of pharma-funded patient groups elsewhere closely resemble those in Canada. In Europe in 2006, for example, a consortium of doctors, nurses, and patient groups launched a pan-European cancer campaign, Cancer United, initially funded entirely by Roche, the world's largest maker of cancer drugs. The central message, backed by a study that Roche also funded, from the Stockholm-based Karolinska Institute, was that cancer survival rates differed among European countries and that cancer patients needed rapid access to new innovative cancer therapies – or patient survival would suffer.[35] The ensuing debate in the press and in specialist cancer journals resembled the uproar in Canada when the industry-funded Cancer Advocacy Coalition of Canada launched its campaign claiming cancer survival rates in Canada were worse than in the United States and similarly attributed the discrepancy to lack of access to new cancer drugs. Journalists and cancer specialists roundly criticized Cancer United for lack of transparency about Roche's sponsorship, with cancer epidemiologists citing major flaws in the research methodology. They pointed out that the study included twelve countries that did not even have cancer registries and therefore lacked survival data, and that the data from countries included was too old (dating from the 1990s) to reflect the effects of drugs discussed in the research, most of which had not been approved until 2000 or later. The methodology used, said one analyst, could "draw your attention to something strange" (i.e., regional discrepancies) but did not provide the basis for causal interpretations. In fact, she argued, with few exceptions, cancer survival depends on timely, high-quality surgery and radiation, not on drugs. In many European countries, cancers were being detected late, and the countries lacked the infrastructure for specialized oncology and co-ordinated cancer care – more plausible system inadequacies to explain intercountry survival differences than access to the latest drugs.[36]

Credibility at Risk

Outterson, Goldacre, and other critics of corporate misconduct in medicine are proposing nothing less than revolutionary change. Patient groups can be part of this revolution, or they can stand – as most now do – with the pharmaceutical industry. Those who warn of a moral crisis in the pharmaceutical industry and the medical profession invariably conclude that the vast majority of individuals working in these sectors are good people trapped in a bad system. I believe the same is true of those active in the patients' movement.

Patient groups are still able to sway the media, the public, and politicians through their advocacy campaigns – no doubt a heady experience. Nonetheless, the groups have lost credibility among those concerned about medicine's increasing corporatization. As far back as 2004, Marcia Angell, a Harvard-based physician and former editor-in-chief of the *New England Journal of Medicine*, characterized the sponsorship of patient advocacy groups as "another form of marketing disguised as education."[37] In his book *How We Do Harm*, Otis Webb Brawley, the chief medical and scientific officer of the American Cancer Society, an advocate for patients from poor, underserved communities and an outspoken critic of profit-driven care, writes, "Patient groups get money from the drug and device companies ... because they push the envelope, making claims so outrageous that even special interests dare not make them."[38] Peter Gøtzsche, writing from a European vantage point, asserts that patient organizations "are often sponsored by industry and often support industry's marketing goals rather than taking care of patients' interests." Patient organizations, he argues, should protest "the blatant abuse of patients in industry-sponsored trials" or take the industry to task when it shirks its duty, spelled out in the Declaration of Helsinki, to make the results of clinical trials publicly available. Drug pricing is another area of "total failure," says Gøtzsche: patient groups "complain loudly when national bodies have decided a drug is too expensive to be used ... whereas I have never heard any patient organization complain that the price was too high and that the drug company should lower it." Gøtzsche challenges patient organizations to "consider carefully whether they find it ethically acceptable to receive money that has been partly earned by crimes that are harmful to patients."[39]

Goldacre describes patient groups as a "murky and disappointing corner in ... direct-to-consumer marketing."[40] He interprets the alignment between patient group and industry positions as the result of the industry choosing to fund groups with views that already support its goals, resulting in a sector whose output is clearly biased and sometimes "frankly ugly."[41] Like Gøtzsche, Goldacre decries the propensity of patient organizations to launch vicious attacks on agencies like the United Kingdom's National Institute for Health and Care Excellence for taking its job of cost control seriously, while the same groups remain silent when drug companies launch "hugely expensive, marginally beneficial treatments."[42] These harsh assessments correspond with much of my analysis, but they overlook the painful internal struggles that went on in so many groups and the sophisticated, covert strategies that industry actors deployed to refashion the groups as extensions of the echo chamber complex.

These same strategies have captured many smart, established players with significantly more resources at their disposal than patient groups, including physicians, medical researchers, and journal editors. If these individuals – among the most powerful and respected members of society – can't outmanoeuvre big pharma, what are the odds that a patient group can do so? From this vantage point, I see no great shame that so many grassroots organizations have followed the well-trodden path of commercialized medicine. For groups to ignore how far afield they have strayed from their mandate, however, would be a grave mistake. Even worse would be to continue collaborations that erode their credibility, endanger the lives of patients they purport to represent, and leave their communities without a voice that can bring the full range of patients' collective experiences, needs, and values to the table. To do this they need to nurture meaningful, long-term connections with their communities.

Given the divided perspectives among patients, this may seem an impossible task. A first step could be what David Hess has called a "dissensus conference" – a play on the conventional meetings designed to arrive at consensus.[43] A dissensus conference is designed to bring together dominant and subordinate networks with competing views in a scientific field to debate issues on a level playing field. My analysis suggests that the division within the patient community is not entirely the creation of industry; the uncertainty of much medical practice, the diverse values of a heterogeneous population, the multifaceted nature of drugs, and the changing risk tolerance along the well-sick continuum all provide fodder for the current polarization. Disentangling true differences in perspective from industry-driven truthiness would bring contentious issues and their causes into relief. Policy makers could then weigh the arguments, choose among them, or construct compromise positions. This prospect should not be an excuse for policy inaction; policy makers are paid to make decisions that may displease some. What is important is that the spectrum of patients' views be articulated and made visible to the broader public so that the basis for decisions is transparent, democratic, and authentic.

Viable, stable communities require secure, independent funding, which, as one activist has pointed out, "has to come from somewhere." Given funding autonomy, groups that view industry communication as a plus might continue to engage with industry partners while remaining outside the echo chamber. Ideally, the funds patient organizations need would come from the community itself; however, Canada's current tax policies hobble fundraising efforts by restricting the charitable status of groups that conduct advocacy. In any case, fundraising drives are time-consuming and the field is too crowded for community organizations to rely on runs, charity concerts, and volunteers (many of whom are coping with life-threatening illness) for their core operations. If politicians, policy makers, researchers, and health practitioners are serious when they say they believe patients' voices are vital to their decisions, they will support the creation of a funding source so that patient and health consumer groups can rebuild their infrastructures as independent organizations. A familiar fallback suggestion has been to ask, or require, pharmaceutical companies to pay into a central, independent repository, creating a fund that would support groups with a good track record of giving evidence-based information to the public. This idea has been floated for decades, but the industry has not taken it up, which should be no surprise. Why would a profit-driven industry fund groups whose mission should be, in part, to challenge corporate excess and malfeasance?

An alternative is to look to governments, which have a responsibility to promote their citizens' health, or to health insurers, which have a vested interest in doing so (unlike pharmaceutical companies, which have a vested interest in promoting illness). Provincial health budgets are one potential source of funding for patient groups, given the amount spent on health care in Canada – $228 billion in 2016 – which is intended to be spent in the interests of patients.[44] In Germany, health insurers pay a small percentage per year per individual insured to support the self-help, information, and lobbying of health consumer groups.[45] In Canada, with its mix of private health insurers and provincial governments that act as health insurers and also deliver health programs, the German model might well work. Both private and public insurers feel the crush of insatiable patient demands, and an informed, independent patient community could save funds while improving health programs. With a noncommercial source of funding, patient groups could advocate (as they once did) for a broad range of patients' needs, including restrictions on carcinogenic environmental toxins, exercise programs adapted to their needs, better emotional supports, home care, and palliative care.

To keep on top of treatment issues, patient organizations might, as the AIDS community has done, select a corps of members who would maintain two-way communication with their community, learning from its members' experiences while keeping them informed of important issues on the drug policy and research fronts, and generating debate.[46] In concert with like-minded researchers, they could support myth-busting campaigns, aimed at putting to rest what Morris Barer, Robert Evans, and colleagues term "health care zombies," those false ideas that seem common sense but have embarrassingly little support from the research and yet refuse to die.[47] In keeping with Canada's tradition of seeing health care as part of the commons, independent patient organizations could take advocacy stances we have rarely seen from patient-led organizations – for example, hastening needed change in the area of clinical trials, demanding that the results of clinical trials become publicly available, and speaking out against unethical practices like ghostwritten journal articles, clinical trials conducted as a marketing strategy (sometimes called "seeding trials"), and studies of "me too" drugs. They might advocate against exorbitantly high prices and rally community support to break what two drug researchers have called the "market spiral pricing" of drugs.[48] Why should patients participate in clinical trials to provide data on drugs that they, or the system on which they depend, cannot afford? They could join the groups presently advocating for a national pharmacare program, administered by an agency committed to maintaining the system for future generations. Such an agency would have the muscle to bargain for reasonable prices and the support from the patient community to pay for drugs on a selective basis.

Perhaps not all patient organizations would endorse such an agenda, but given the opportunity to come to dissensus, the secret war could become an open dialogue.

Appendix

ORGANIZATIONS AND THEIR MEMBERS

Only those organizations and individuals mentioned in the text are listed; names in quotation marks are pseudonyms. (Note that the breast cancer community in Canada continues to evolve, and recent years have seen a major restructuring that has affected some of the groups in the narrative of this book. In 2015, Breast Cancer Action Montreal broadened its mandate to become Breast Cancer Action Québec; in March 2016, the Canadian Breast Cancer Foundation (CBCF) and Willow announced they would merge under the banner of the CBCF; in May 2016, the Burlington Breast Cancer Support Services disbanded and announced plans to resurface as Burlington's Cancer Wellness Foundation; and in the fall of 2016, the CBCF merged with the Canadian Cancer Society.)

Breast Cancer Movement (Canada): Organizations and Affiliated Members

Alliance of Breast Cancer Survivors (ABCS): Patricia (Pat) Kelly and Anne Rochon Ford, cofounders; Sarah Spinks and Sue Groves, members

Breast Cancer Action Manitoba: Jean Wilson, board member

Breast Cancer Action Montreal (BCAM): Carolyn Gibson Badger and Sharon Batt, cofounders; Janine O'Leary Cobb, (former) president; Maychai Brown, (former) administrative secretary; "Cassie" and Deena Dlusy-Apel, board members

Breast Cancer Action Nova Scotia (BCANS): "Cindy," (former) president of the board; Paula Leaman, board member, website creator and

administrator, staff member; Kathleen Barclay, cofounder, board
member, and later staff member; "Meredith," board member; Rose
Bechtel, board member (deceased)

Breast Cancer Research and Education Fund: Paula McPherson, founder

Breast Cancer Support Network for Ontario Project: Patricia (Pat) Kelly
and Anne Rochon Ford, cofounders

Burlington Breast Cancer Support Services: Patricia (Pat) Kelly and Barb
Sullivan, cofounders; Sylvia Morrison, member

Campaign to Control Cancer (C2CC): Patricia (Pat) Kelly, cofounder
and CEO; William Hryniuk, oncologist and board member; Beth
Kapusta, board member

Canadian Breast Cancer Network (CBCN): Karen deKoning, president,
1999–2000 (resigned in 2001); "Hanna," board member; and Lynn
MacDonald, board member (deceased)

Canadian Cancer Action Network (CCAN), formerly the Canadian
Cancer Advocacy Network: Liz Whamond, cochair, with Jack Shapiro

Canadian Strategy for Cancer Control: Neil Berman, scientist at Health
Canada, coordinator of the strategy

Je sais/I know: Marcella Tardif, cofounder

Willow: Patricia (Pat) Kelly and Anne Rochon Ford, cofounders;
"Virginia," staff member

Working Group, patients' rights charter: Lynn Macdonald, chair
(deceased); and Jean Wilson, member

Other Canadian Organizations

A Friend Indeed (menopause newsletter): Janine O'Leary Cobb, founder
and editor

Best Medicines Coalition (BMC): Patricia (Pat) Kelly, cofounder

Canadian Health Coalition

Consumers' Association of Canada (CAC): Wendy Armstrong, former
member of the CAC National Health Council and past president of
the CAC affiliate in Alberta

DES Action Canada: Harriet Simand and Shirley Simand, cofounders of
DES Action Canada

Neutropenia Support Association: Lorna Stevens, founder

Pharmaceutical Manufacturers Association of Canada (PMAC) (later
Rx&D; now Innovative Medicines Canada): Judith Erola, president,
1989–98; Leonora Marks, director of publications; Gordon Postlewaite,
director of university and scientific affairs

Support, Advocacy and Networking (SAN) Subcommittee of the
National Forum on Breast Cancer (1993): Sharon Batt and Patricia
(Pat) Kelly

Vancouver Women's Health Collective: Barbara Mintzes, former staff
member

Voices of Positive Women: Darien Taylor, board member

American and European Organizations

Breast Cancer Action: Barbara Brenner, former executive director
(deceased)

Health Action International (HAI): Barbara Mintzes, former staff
member

National Women's Health Network: Adriane Fugh-Berman, former
board member

Prevention First: Breast Cancer Action, Breast Cancer Action Montreal,
members

Other Actors

"James": AstraZeneca representative and liaison with the Working
Group on Patients' Rights

Joel Lexchin: emergency-room physician and pharmaceutical policy
critic

Michèle Brill-Edwards: physician, former senior drug reviewer at
Canada's Department of Health

Steven Edwards: employed in a public relations role with a multinational
drug company

Victor Ling: cancer researcher; president and scientific director of the
Terry Fox Research Institute and Distinguished Scientist with the BC
Cancer Agency

Notes

Introduction: The Secret War among Patient Groups

1 For an exchange about conflicts of interest within Alzheimer's groups in the United Kingdom and Canada, see Iain Chalmers, "The Alzheimer's Society, Drug Manufacturers, and Public Trust," *BMJ* 335 (2007): 400; Neil Hunt, "Alzheimer's Society Replies to Iain Chalmers," *BMJ* 335 (2007): 541. For three additional comments, published online, see Iain Chalmers's response to Neil Hunt; Linda Furlini recounting her experiences with pharma funding and the Alzheimer Society of Canada; and Scott Dudgeon of the Alzheimer Society of Canada responding to Furlini – all at www.bmj.com/content/335/7619/541.2/rapid-responses.

For references to ruptures in the breast cancer movement over funding from the industry in the United States and Europe respectively, see Mary K. Anglin, "Working from the Inside Out: Implications of Breast Cancer Activism for Biomedical Policies and Practices," *Social Science & Medicine* 44 (1997): 1403–15; Barbara Brenner, "Sister Support: Women Create a Breast Cancer Movement," in *Breast Cancer: Society Shapes an Epidemic*, ed. Anne S. Kasper and Susan J. Ferguson (New York: St. Martin's Press, 2000), 325–53; and Ned Stafford, "MEPs Shun Cancer Advocacy Group Because of Industry Funding," *BMJ* 336 (2008): 980.

For scholarly analyses that discuss varied stances toward industry funding among groups in specific locales, see Orla O'Donovan, "Corporate Colonization of Health Activism? Irish Health Advocacy Organizations' Modes of Engagement with Pharmaceutical Corporations," *International Journal of Health Services* 37 (2007): 711–33; Janine Barbot, "How to Build an 'Active' Patient? The Work of AIDS Associations in France," *Social Science & Medicine* 62, 3 (2006): 538–51; and Steven Epstein, *Impure Science: AIDS, Activism, and the Politics of Knowledge* (Berkeley: University of California Press, 1996), 299–300.

2 Epstein's *Impure Science* documents the AIDS movement in the United States from 1981 to 1995. For an account of the Canadian movement, see Ann Silversides, *AIDS Activist: Michael Lynch and the Politics of Community* (Toronto: Between the Lines, 2003).

3 See Howard Brody, *Hooked: Ethics, the Medical Profession, and the Pharmaceutical Industry* (Lanham, MD: Rowman and Littlefield, 2007), esp. 23–40.

4 These examples are from Peter Dauvergne and Genevieve LeBaron, *P®otest Inc.: The Corporatization of Activism* (Cambridge, UK: Polity, 2014), 26 and 32.

5 Bank-organized NGOs, donor-organized NGOs, government-organized NGOs, quasi-autonomous NGOs, and business-friendly NGOs respectively.

6 William F. Fisher, "Doing Good? The Politics and Anti-politics of NGO Practices," *Annual Review of Anthropology* 26 (1997): 439–64; see esp. 448–49.

7 Steven Epstein, "Patient Groups and Health Movements," in *The Handbook of Science and Technology Studies*, 3rd ed., ed. Edward J. Hackett, Olga Amsterdamska, Michael Lynch, and Judy Wajcman (Cambridge, MA: MIT Press, 2008), 522.

8 For a discussion of astroturf groups, see Sharon Beder, "Public Relations' Role in Manufacturing Artificial Grass Roots Coalitions," *Public Relations Quarterly* 43 (July 1998): 21–23. Orla O'Donovan, in a 2007 analysis of patient groups in Ireland and their relationships with the pharmaceutical industry, found a growing tendency for groups to see pharmaceutical companies as their allies, but the opinions groups had about the companies diverged; she cautions against concluding that pharma funding necessarily means the groups are colonized. See O'Donovan, "Corporate Colonization."

9 Fisher, "Doing Good?" 449.

10 Its prevalence in patients' movements has been well documented, notably by Samantha King in *Pink Ribbons, Inc.: Breast Cancer and the Politics of Philanthropy* (Minneapolis: University of Minnesota Press, 2006), and by Lisa Ann Richey and Stefano Ponte in *Brand Aid: Shopping Well to Save the World* (Minneapolis: University of Minnesota Press, 2011). The latter book analyzes the Global Fund to Fight AIDS, Tuberculosis and Malaria.

11 For a discussion of critical STS, see Sergio Sismondo, "Science and Technology Studies and an Engaged Program," in Hackett et al., *Handbook of Science and Technology*.

12 Philip Mirowski and Esther-Mirjam Sent, "The Commercialization of Science and the Response of STS," in Hackett et al., *Handbook of Science and Technology*, 626.

13 O'Donovan, "Corporate Colonization," 713.

14 For discussions of STS as a framework for studying patient organizations and health movements, see Epstein, "Patient Groups" and *Impure Science*. David J. Hess, "If You're

Thinking of Living in STS: A Guide for the Perplexed," in *Cyborgs and Citadels: Anthropological Interventions in Emerging Science and Technologies*, ed. Joseph Dumit (Santa Fe, NM: School of American Research, 1997), 143–64, provides a history of STS.

STS researchers who have studied patient groups and health movements include Phil Brown and Stephen Zavetoski, "Social Movements in Health: An Introduction," *Sociology of Health & Illness* 26, 6 (2004): 679–94; Carlos Novas, "Genetic Advocacy Groups, Science and Biovalue: Creating Political Economies of Hope," in *New Genetics, New Identities*, ed. Paul Atkinson, Peter Glasner, and Helen Greenslade (New York: Routledge, 2005), 11–27; David J. Hess, "Technology- and Product-Oriented Movements: Approximating Social Movement Studies and Science and Technology Studies," *Science, Technology, & Human Values* 30 (2005): 515–35; Nikolas Rose, *The Politics of Life Itself: Biomedicine, Power and Subjectivity in the 21st Century* (Princeton, NJ: Princeton University Press, 2007); Epstein, "Patient Groups" and *Impure Science*; and David J. Hess, Steve Breyman, Nancy Campbell, and Brian Martin, "Science, Technology, and Social Movements," in Hackett et al., *Handbook of Science and Technology*, 473–98.

15 On "Drugs into Bodies," see Epstein, *Impure Science*, chap. 6 (208–34).

16 Epstein, *Impure Science*, details the pressure AIDS activists put on the FDA to speed up access to new drugs. Other analyses of the FDA's transformation in the Reagan era reinforce the claim that parts of the AIDS activists' agenda coincided with the push by neoliberal governments and corporations toward relaxing safety regulations and speeding new pharmaceuticals to market. See, for example, Philip J. Hilts, *Protecting America's Health: The FDA, Business, and One Hundred Years of Regulation* (New York: Knopf, 2003); John Abraham and Courtney Davis, "Deficits, Expectations and Paradigms in British and American Drug Safety Assessments: Prising Open the Black Box of Regulatory Science," *Science, Technology, & Human Values* 32 (2007): 399–431; and Mirowski and Sent, "Commercialization of Science."

17 Epstein, *Impure Science*, 223.

18 Epstein, "Patient Groups," 534.

19 See Margaret Lock, "The Tempering of Medical Anthropology: Troubling Natural Categories," *Medical Anthropology Quarterly* 15 (2001): 478–92, on embodied knowledge.

20 See Martin Delaney, "AIDS Activism and the Pharmaceutical Industry," in *Ethics and the Pharmaceutical Industry*, ed. Michael A. Sontoro and Thomas M. Gorry (Cambridge, UK: Cambridge University Press, 2005), and Ann Silversides, "The AIDS Gravy Train: Pharma People Are Always so Gosh-darn Nice," *Daily Xtra!* December 16, 1999.

21 Epstein, "Patient Groups," 522 and 523.

22 I refer here to the drugs developed by mainstream researchers and companies with the goal of gaining approval for marketing through the government regulatory system. Demands by individual patients for access to "alternative" treatments have a long history among cancer patients; see, for example, Max Gerson, *A Cancer Therapy: Results of Fifty Cases & the Cure of Advanced Cancer by Diet Therapy*, 5th ed. (1958; repr., Bonita, CA: Gerson Institute, 1990), and Ralph W. Moss, *Cancer Therapy: The Independent Consumer's Guide to Non-toxic Treatment & Prevention* (New York: Equinox Press, 1992). See Epstein, *Impure Science*, on the first wave of the AIDS activist movement. See Gregg Gonsalves, Mark Harrington, and David A. Kessler, "Don't Weaken the FDA's Drug Approval Process," *New York Times*, June 9, 2015, for the op-ed in which two AIDS activists and a former FDA commissioner advocate for a rigorous process of drug approvals.

23 Abby L. Wilkerson, *Diagnosis: Difference: The Moral Authority of Medicine* (Ithaca, NY: Cornell University Press, 1998).

24 See Margrit Shildrick, *Leaky Bodies and Boundaries: Feminism, Postmodernism and (Bio)Ethics* (London: Routledge, 1998), and Wilkerson, *Diagnosis: Difference*. Marina Morrow, "'Our Bodies Our Selves' in Context: Reflections on the Women's Health Movement in Canada," in *Women's Health in Canada: Critical Perspectives on Theory and Policy*, ed. Colleen Varcoe (Toronto: University of Toronto Press, 2007), 33–63, provides an overview of women's health activism in Canada as manifested in three successive waves of the women's movement.

25 See Jacques Derrida, "Plato's Pharmacy," in *Dissemination*, trans. Barbara Johnson (Chicago: University of Chicago Press, 1981), 61–172; Donna Haraway, "A Manifesto for Cyborgs: Science, Technology, and Socialist Feminism in the 1980s," *Socialist Review* 80 (1985): 65–107; and Margaret Lock and Patricia Kaufert, "Introduction," in *Pragmatic Women and Body Politics*, ed. Margaret Lock and Patricia Kaufert (Cambridge: Cambridge University Press, 1998), 1–27. Lock and Kaufert emphasize that analysts need to recognize women's agency in navigating medical technologies.

26 Epstein, *Impure Science*, 194.

27 Ibid., 327.

28 For critical analyses of loosening of pharmaceutical policies under neoliberal regimes, see Courtney Davis and John Abraham, *Unhealthy Pharmaceutical Regulation: Innovation, Politics and Promissory Science* (New York: Palgrave Macmillan, 2013), and Orla O'Donovan and Kathy Glavanis-Grantham, *Power, Politics and Pharmaceuticals*, ed. Kathy Glavanis-Grantham (Cork, Ireland: Cork University Press, 2008).

29 David Hess, "Neoliberalism and the History of STS Theory: Toward a Reflexive Sociology," *Social Epistemology* 27, 2 (2013): 178. For a discussion of the tension the

term "neoliberalism" evokes among academics, see Kevin Ward and Kim England, "Introduction: Reading Neoliberalization," in *Neoliberalization: States, Networks, Peoples*, ed. Keven Ward and Kim England (Malden, MA: Blackwell, 2007).

30 See Ward and England, "Introduction: Reading Neoliberalization," on neoliberalization and the importance of qualitative analyses to assess changes.

31 Kelly Moore, Daniel Lee Kleinman, David J. Hess, and Scott Frickel, "Science and Neoliberal Globalization: A Political Sociological Approach," *Theory and Society* 40 (2011): 527.

32 Roger-Pol Droit and Thomas Ferenczi, "The Left Hand and the Right Hand of the State" [interview with Pierre Bourdieu], *Variant* 32 (2008), reprinted from *Le Monde*, January 14, 1992.

33 Pierre Bourdieu, "Neo-liberalism, the Utopia (Becoming a Reality) of Unlimited Exploitation," in *Acts of Resistance: Against the Tyranny of the Market*, trans. Richard Nice (New York: New Press, 1998): 102, emphasis in original.

34 Hans Löfgren, "Pharmaceuticals and the Consumer Movement: The Ambivalences of 'Patient Power,'" *Australian Health Review* 28, 2 (2004): 229.

35 Joshua M. Sharfstein, "Banishing 'Stakeholders,'" *Milbank Quarterly* 94, 3 (2016): 476–79.

36 On the "risk society," see Ulrich Beck, *Risk Society: Towards a New Modernity* (New York: Sage, 1992); Anthony Giddens, "Risk and Responsibility," *Modern Law Review* 62, 1 (1999): 1–10; and Löfgren, "Pharmaceuticals and the Consumer Movement."

37 See Miriam Catherine Smith, *A Civil Society? Collective Actors in Canadian Political Life* (Peterborough, ON: Broadview Press, 2005), 142, on the implications of re-envisioning social movement organizations, interest groups, and advocacy organizations as part of a voluntary sector. Feminist scholars who have analyzed the impact of neoliberalism on feminism in Canada include Sylvia Bashevkin, *Women on the Defensive: Living through Conservative Times* (Toronto: University of Toronto Press, 1998); Alexandra Dobrowolsky, "The Chrétien Legacy and Women: Changing Policy Priorities with Little Cause for Celebration," *Review of Constitutional Studies* 9 (2004): 171–98; Judy Fudge and Brenda Cossman, "Conclusion: Privatization, Polarization and Policy: Feminism and the Future," in *Privatization, Law, and the Challenge to Feminism*, ed. Judy Fudge and Brenda Cossman (Toronto: University of Toronto Press, 2002), 403–20; Wendy McKeen, *Money in Their Own Name: The Feminist Voice in the Poverty Debate in Canada* (Toronto: University of Toronto Press, 2004); and Miriam Smith, *A Civil Society?*

38 See Adriana Petryna, *Life Exposed: Biological Citizenship after Chernobyl* (Princeton, NJ: Princeton University Press, 2003), for an ethnography of post-Chernobyl survivors and the concept of biological citizenship. See Paul Rabinow, "The Third

Culture," *History of the Human Sciences* 7, 2 (1994): 53–64, on the cultural tension between science and humanism and the potential of patient groups to bridge the divide. On biosociality, see Paul Rabinow, "Artificiality and Enlightenment: From Sociobiology to Biosociality," in *Essays on the Anthropology of Reason*, ed. Paul Rabinow (Princeton, NJ: Princeton University Press, 1996), 91–111.

39 Rose, *Politics of Life Itself*; and Nikolas Rose and Carlos Novas, "Biological Citizenship," in *Global Assemblages: Technology, Politics and Ethics as Anthropological Problems*, ed. Stephen J. Collier (Malden, MA: Blackwell, 2005), 439–63.

40 Thomas Lemke, "Patient Organizations as Biosocial Communities? Conceptual Clarifications and Critical Remarks," in *The Public Shaping of Medical Research: Patient Associations, Health Movements, and Biomedicine*, ed. Peter Wehling, Willy Viehöver, and Sophia Koenen (Abingdon, Oxon, UK: Routledge, 2015), 200.

41 For critical assessments of biosociality, see Lemke, "Patient Organizations"; Margaret Lock, "Biosociality and Susceptibility Genes: A Cautionary Tale," in *Biosocialities, Genetics and the Social Sciences: Making Biologies and Identities*, ed. Sahra Gibbon and Carlos Novas (London: Routledge, 2007), 56–78; Alexandra Plows and Paula Boddington, "Troubles with Biocitizenship? Duties, Responsibilities, Identity," *Genomics, Society and Policy* 2, 3 (2006): 115–35; Rabinow, "Third Culture."

42 Epstein, "Patient Groups," 509.

43 See Epstein, "Patient Groups." His four other dimensions are the constitution of the group (the pathways by which groups emerge), social organization (size, geography, degree of formal structure, etc.), militancy and oppositionality (tactics used and the extent to which they challenge the status quo), and the group's goals.

44 Two of the earliest documentations of the pharma-funding phenomenon are Barbara Mintzes, *Blurring the Boundaries: New Trends in Drug Promotion* (Amsterdam: HAI-Europe, 1998), and Fred Mills, *Patient Groups and the Global Pharmaceutical Industry: The Growing Importance of Working Directly with the Consumer* (London: Urch, 2000). Mintzes critically assesses pharma's interest in patient groups as a method of drug promotion used to circumvent regulations. Mills's book, published in the United Kingdom and aimed at the industry, frames the ethical dilemmas of the alliances as surmountable, using transparent, honest policies and contractual relationships.

45 Articles that raise concerns about the lack of transparency of groups' funding include Sophie Arie and Chris Mahoney, "Should Patient Groups Be More Transparent about Their Funding?" *BMJ* 349 (2014): g5892; Douglas E. Ball, Klara Tisocki, and Andrew Herxheimer, "Advertising and Disclosure of Funding on Patient Organization Web-sites: A Cross-Sectional Survey," *BMC Public Health* 6 (2006), 201, doi: 10.1186/1471-2458-6-201; Cinzia Colombo, Paola Mosconi, Walter Villani, and Silvio Garattini, "Patient Organizations' Funding from Pharmaceutical Companies: Is Disclosure

Clear, Complete and Accessible to the Public? An Italian Survey," *PLoS One* 7 (2012): e34974; Michael Day, "UK Drug Companies Must Disclose Funding of Patients' Groups," *BMJ* 332 (2006): 69; Andrew Herxheimer, "Relationships between the Pharmaceutical Industry and Patients' Organisations," *BMJ* 326 (2003): 1208–10; Jenny Hirst, "Charities and Patient Groups Should Declare Interest," *BMJ* 326 (2003): 1211; Hans Löfgren and Agnes Vitry, "Health Consumer Groups and the Pharmaceutical Industry: Is Transparency the Answer?" in *Democratizing Health: Consumer Groups in the Policy Process*, ed. Hans Löfgren, Evelyne de Leeuw, and Michael Leahy (Northampton, MA: Edward Elgar, 2011), 239–54; Paola Mosconi, "Industry Funding of Patients' Support Groups: Declaration of Competing Interests Is Rare in Italian Breast Cancer Associations," *BMJ* 327 (2003): 344; Sheila M. Rothman, Victoria H. Raveis, Anne Friedman, and David J. Rothman, "Health Advocacy Organizations and the Pharmaceutical Industry: An Analysis of Disclosure Practices," *American Journal of Public Health* 101 (2011): 602–9.

Studies that detail the differences among groups in France include Barbot, "How to Build an 'Active' Patient?"; in Finland, Elina Hemminki, Hanna K. Toiviainen, and Lauri Vuorenkoski, "Co-operation between Patient Organisations and the Drug Industry in Finland," *Social Science & Medicine* 70 (2010): 1171–75; in the United Kingdom, Kathryn Jones, "In Whose Interest? Relationships between Health Consumer Groups and the Pharmaceutical Industry in the UK," *Sociology of Heath & Illness* 30, 6 (2008): 929–43; and in Ireland, O'Donovan, "Corporate Colonization."

46 Rob Baggott and Rudolf Forster, "Health Consumer and Patients' Organizations in Europe: Towards a Comparative Analysis," *Health Expectations* 11 (2008): 90.
47 Paul C. Hébert and Matthew Stanbrook, "The Federal Government's Abandonment of Health," *Canadian Medical Association Journal* 182 (2010): e809.
48 Janice E. Graham, "Harbinger of Hope or Commodity Fetishism: Re-cognizing Dementia in an Age of Therapeutic Agents," *International Psychogeriatrics* 13 (2001): 131 and 133.
49 Alastair Kent, "Should Patient Groups Accept Money from Drug Companies? Yes," *BMJ* 334 (2007): 934. For a discussion of discourses and how they define how groups understand reality, see Adele Clarke, *Situational Analysis: Grounded Theory after the Postmodern Turn* (Thousand Oaks, CA: Sage, 2005), 148–51.
50 Barbara Mintzes, "Should Patient Groups Accept Money from Drug Companies? No," *BMJ* 334 (2007): 935.
51 See O'Donovan, "Corporate Colonization," and Epstein, "Patient Groups."
52 Epstein, "Patient Groups."
53 See Robert Kleidman, "Volunteer Activism and Professionalism," *Social Problems* 41 (1994): 257–76, on professionalism taking different paths. John D. McCarthy and

Mayer N. Zald, "Resource Mobilization and Social Movements: A Partial Theory," *American Journal of Sociology* 82 (1977): 1212–41, theorize the structural dimensions affecting the trajectory of groups as they mature; Sheryl Burt Ruzek and Julie Becker, "The Women's Health Movement in the United States: From Grass Roots Activism to Professional Agendas," *Journal of the American Medical Women's Association* 54 (1999): 4–8, apply a similar analysis to distinguish grassroots and mainstream feminist organizations in the United States.

54 See O'Donovan, "Corporate Colonization."

55 For an assessment of neoliberalism's impact on civil society groups in Canada, see Miriam Smith, *A Civil Society?* Rachel Laforest, a professor of policy studies who specializes in interest groups and social movements, argues that the federal government's redefined relationship to voluntary organizations created a false dichotomy between individual and group representation that weakens Canadian democracy; see Rachel Laforest, "Rerouting Political Representation: Is Canada's Social Infrastructure in Crisis?" *British Journal of Canadian Studies* 25, 2 (2012): 181–97, and by the same author, *Voluntary Sector Relations and the State: Building New Relations* (Vancouver: UBC Press, 2011), and "Governance and the Voluntary Sector: Rethinking the Contours of Advocacy," *International Journal of Canadian Studies* 31 (2004): 185–203.

56 On the importance of understanding technologies from the perspective of users, see Nelly Oudshoorn and Trevor Pinch, eds., *How Users Matter: The Co-construction of Users and Technologies* (Cambridge, MA: MIT Press, 2004).

57 Scholarly analyses of the breast cancer movement that are particularly relevant to this work include Patricia Kaufert, "Women, Resistance and the Breast Cancer Movement," in Lock and Kaufert, *Pragmatic Women*, 287–309, on the early breast cancer movement in North America; Barron H. Lerner, *The Breast Cancer Wars: Hope, Fear, and the Pursuit of a Cure in Twentieth-Century America* (New York: Oxford University Press, 2001), on the cultural history of breast cancer in America; and Barron H. Lerner, "Patient, Public Activist: Rose Kushner's Attack on Chemotherapy," *Bulletin of the History of Medicine* 81 (2007): 224–40, on the work of the early American activist Rose Kushner; Patricia Radin, "'To Me, It's My Life': Medical Communication, Trust, and Activism in Cyberspace," *Social Science & Medicine* 62 (2006): 591–601, on the internal culture of a Canadian online support group; Mary K. Anglin, "Working from the Inside Out: Implications of Breast Cancer Activism for Biomedical Policies and Practices," *Social Science & Medicine* 44 (1997): 1403–15; Mary K. Anglin, "'You and *What* Army?' US Breast Cancer Treatment Activism and Big Pharma" (paper presented at the annual meeting of CASCA, Vancouver, May 2009); Brenner, "Sister Support," and Rothman et al., "Health Advocacy

Organizations," on pharma funding in the American breast cancer movement; and Mosconi, "Industry Funding of Patients' Support Groups," on the ubiquity of pharma funding in breast cancer groups in Italy and their lack of transparency.

58 Sjaak van der Geest, Susan Reynolds Whyte, and Anita Hardon, "The Anthropology of Pharmaceuticals: A Biographical Approach," *Annual Review of Anthropology* 25 (1996): 153–78, introduce the idea of drugs as social and cultural phenomena with social lives; Susan Reynolds Whyte, Sjaak van der Geest, and Anita Hardon, *The Social Lives of Medicines* (Cambridge: Cambridge University Press, 2002), expand on the role anthropologists can play in studying drug policy.

59 Alastair Matheson, "Corporate Science and the Husbandry of Scientific and Medical Knowledge by the Pharmaceutical Industry," *BioSocieties* 3 (2008): 358–59.

60 Readers familiar with Michel Foucault's two methodological approaches, genealogy and archaeology, will recognize his influence in the analytic use of periods. For a discussion of genealogy in qualitative research, see Clarke, *Situational Analysis*, 262–64; on genealogical research and periodization in health movements and patient groups, see Epstein, *Impure Science*, 357–58, and "Patient Groups," 525.

61 Keith G. Banting and Kathy L. Brock produced an important series of edited volumes on the role of Canada's nonprofit organizations and public policy: Keith Banting, ed., *The Non-profit Sector in Canada: Roles and Relationships* (Montreal: McGill-Queen's University Press, 2000); Kathy L. Brock, ed., *Delicate Dances: Public Policy and the Nonprofit Sector* (Montreal: McGill-Queen's University Press, 2003); Kathy L. Brock and Keith G. Banting, *The Non-profit Sector and Government in a New Century* (Montreal: McGill-Queen's University Press, 2001); Kathy L. Brock and Keith G. Banting, eds., *The Nonprofit Sector in Interesting Times: Case Studies in a Changing Sector* (Montreal: McGill-Queen's University Press, 2003). See also Miriam Catherine Smith, *A Civil Society?* and Miriam Catherine Smith, ed., *Group Politics and Social Movements in Canada* (Peterborough, ON: Broadview Press, 2008).

See the following by Paul A. Pross for an historical analysis of advocacy groups in Canadian policy dating from confederation to recent changes: *Group Politics and Public Policy*, 2nd ed. (Toronto: Oxford University Press, 1992); "Canada in the American Arcade: Is Pluralism a Distorting Mirror?" in *Policy Studies in Canada: The State of the Art*, ed. David Laycock (Toronto: University of Toronto Press, 1996), 33–48; "An Unruly Messenger: Interest Groups and Bureaucracy in Canadian Democracy" (paper presented at the annual meeting of the Institute of Public Administration of Canada, Charlottetown, PEI, August 2006). See Paul A. Pross and Kernaghan R. Webb, "Embedded Regulation: Advocacy and the Federal Regulation of Public Interest Groups," in Brock, ed., *Delicate Dances*, 63–121, on how seemingly unrelated regulations embedded in Canadian law undermine the democratic potential of community-based advocacy.

Chapter 1: Canada's Health Policy Landscape

1 Bob Russell, "From Workhouse to Workfare: The Welfare State and Shifting Policy Terrains," in *Restructuring and Resistance: Canadian Public Policy in the Age of Global Capitalism*, ed. Mike Burke, Colin Mooers, and John Shields (Halifax: Fernwood, 2000), 26–29, provides one critical account of Canada's move away from welfare state to the market values of neoliberalism. Jane Jenson and Susan D. Phillips, "Regime Shift: New Citizenship Practices in Canada," *International Journal of Canadian Studies* 14 (1996): 113–35, argue that Canada's postwar programs socially constructed the meaning of Canadian citizenship and that the transition to conservative governance regimes redefined citizenship. See the Canadian Museum of History's online exhibit "Making Medicare: The History of Health Care in Canada 1914–2007" for an account of the debates on health care, through nine decades, posted April 21, 2010, accessed October 11, 2016, http://www.historymuseum.ca/cmc/exhibitions/hist/medicare/medic00e.shtml.

2 Joel Lexchin, "New Directions in Canadian Drug Regulation: Whose Interests Are Being Served?" in *Power, Politics and Pharmaceuticals*, ed. Orla O'Donovan and Kathy Glavanis-Grantham (Cork, Ireland: Cork University Press, 2008), 153, summarizes the federal-provincial split in responsibilities in health care and drug regulation.

3 For the Senate report, see Canada, Parliament, Senate, Standing Committee on Social Affairs, Science and Technology Subcommittee on Veterans Affairs, *Time for Transformative Change: A Review of the 2004 Health Accord* (March 2012), 41st Parliament, 1st session (Ottawa: Public Works and Government Services Canada, 2012). As of February 14, 2017, the Standing Committee on Health was still hearing testimony from witnesses and receiving written briefs, which are available on its website, accessed February 14, 2017, http://www.parl.gc.ca/Committees/en/HESA/StudyActivity?studyActivityId=8837577.

4 Ronald W. Lang, *The Politics of Drugs: A Comparative Pressure-Group Study of the Canadian Pharmaceutical Manufacturers Association and the Association of the British Pharmaceutical Industry, 1930–1970* (London: Saxon House/Lexington Books, 1974), provides an analysis of the industry's history, structure, and lobbying efforts to strengthen the patent system that informs much of the discussion in this chapter.

5 In antiquity, recipes for pharmacy products from botanicals, minerals, and animal substances were compiled in pharmacopoeia, special books that public health authorities published to ensure that the apothecaries that prepared the medicines for physicians did so correctly and safely. See Teresa Huguet-Termes, "Islamic Pharmacology and Pharmacy in the Latin West: An Approach to Early Pharmacopoeias," *European Review* 16 (2008): 229–39.

6   See Henry Letheby, "Adulteration," *Encyclopaedia Britannica: A Dictionary of Arts, Sciences and General Literature*, 9th ed., vol. 1 (Chicago: R.S. Peale, 1888), 175, on the UK Adulteration of Food and Drink Act of 1860 and the events that led up to it. See Philip J. Hilts, *Protecting America's Health: The FDA, Business, and One Hundred Years of Regulation* (New York: Knopf, 2003), 27, and Paul Soucy, "The Proprietary or Patent Medicine Act of Canada," *Food, Drug, Cosmetic Law Journal* 8 (1953): 706–16, on regulations to control the patent medicine market in the United States and Canada respectively.

7   See Gary Gnirss, "A History of Food Law in Canada," *Food in Canada* 68, 4 (2008): 38.

8   See Hilts, *Protecting America's Health*, on the events leading up to the creation of the FDA, the agency's political significance, and industry opposition; ingredients whose disclosure remained mandatory included opium, morphine, and alcohol. See Patricia I. Carter, "Federal Regulation of Pharmaceuticals," *Loyola of Los Angeles International and Comparative Law Review* 21, 2 (1999) on industry victories. See Gnirss, "History of Food Law," on the replacement of Canada's Adulteration Act with the Food and Drugs Act of 1920.

9   On the rise of today's chemically based pharmaceutical industry and early discoveries, see Lang, *Politics of Drugs*; Jim Harding, "The Pharmaceutical Industry as a Public-Health Hazard and as an Institution of Social Control," in *Health and Canadian Society: Sociological Perspectives*, 2nd ed., ed. David Coburn, Carl D'Arcy, George Torrance, and Peter New (Richmond Hill, ON: Fitzhenry & Whiteside, 1992), 545–64; and Ilana Löwy, "Trustworthy Knowledge and Desperate Patients: Clinical Tests for New Drugs from Cancer to AIDS," in *Living and Working with the New Medical Technologies*, ed. Alberto Cambrosio (New York: Cambridge University Press, 2000), 49–81. See James T. Patterson, *The Dread Disease: Cancer and Modern American Culture* (Cambridge, MA: Harvard University Press, 1987), for a history of the postwar search for cancer drug treatments.

10   See Lang, *Politics of Drugs*, including Appendix C, on the dominance of particular countries in the control of the pharmaceutical market.

11   See Carter, "Federal Regulation of Pharmaceuticals," 218, and Fran Hawthorne, *Inside the FDA: The Business and Politics behind the Drugs We Take and the Food We Eat* (Hoboken, NJ: John Wiley & Sons, 2005), 42, on the sulfanilamide deaths and the Food, Drug, and Cosmetic Act of 1938. See Carter, "Federal Regulation of Pharmaceuticals," and Gary Gnirss, "A History of Food in Canada, Part V," *Food in Canada* 68, 8 (2008): 21, on the passing of Canada's 1954 Food and Drugs Act.

12   See Nicholas M. Regush, *Safety Last: The Failure of the Consumer Health Protection System in Canada* (Toronto: Key Porter Books, 1993), 9–10, and Jerry Avorn, "Teaching Clinicians about Drugs – 50 Years Later, Whose Job Is It?" *New England*

Journal of Medicine 364 (2011): 1185–87, on Chemie Grünenthal's failure to test for
birth defects.

13 Carter, "Federal Regulation of Pharmaceuticals," 220.

14 Ibid., 221.

15 See Hilts, *Protecting America's Health*, and Avorn, "Teaching Clinicians about Drugs,"
for discussions of the Kefauver hearings and the Kefauver-Harris Amendments. Carter,
"Federal Regulation of Pharmaceuticals," discusses the regulation of pharmaceuticals
in Canadian law. Regulation of pharmaceuticals in Canada is a "residual subject" –
that is, an area of concern not specifically named in the constitution as either provincial or federal. Löwy, "Trustworthy Knowledge and Desperate Patients," discusses
the common elements of drug laws in Western countries.

16 The reviews are still carried out in a similar fashion, though changes to the law's
content and the government regulatory structure have been introduced over the
years, as I discuss in the subsequent paragraph. See Marcia Angell, *The Truth about
the Drug Companies: How They Deceive Us and What to Do about It* (New York:
Random House, 2004), 27, on the testing of Phase 1 cancer and AIDS drugs.

17 On the passing of Vanessa's Law, see Laura Eggertson, "Ottawa Passes Drug Safety
Law," *Canadian Medical Association Journal* 186, 11 (2014): 818. Efforts to improve
drug safety tend to succeed following drug tragedies that harm children, as with
Vanessa's Law and laws passed after the Elixir of Sulfanilamide and thalidomide
tragedies.

18 Lang, *Politics of Drugs*, 16.

19 Ibid.

20 See Lang, *Politics of Drugs*, 28, n10, and 44, on the Green Book, based on an inquiry
undertaken by the Combines Division of the Restrictive Trade Practices Commission (1958 to 1961), and on the Royal Commission on Health Services (the Hall
Commission), a public inquiry that held hearings across the country and produced
two reports, in 1964. Both inquiries concluded that Canada's drug prices were the
highest in the world and that the US patent system was the heart of the problem. The
House of Commons Special Committee on Drug Costs and Prices (the Harley Committee) issued a report in 1967 on Canada's compulsory licensing law; see Jillian
Clare Cohen, "Canada and Brazil – Dealing with Tension between Ensuring Access
to Medicines and Complying with Pharmaceutical Patent Standards: Is the Story
the Same?" *Comparative Program on Health and Society*, Working Paper Series
(2003/2004): 7.

21 For discussions of the change in Canadian law to encourage compulsory licensing,
see Lexchin, "New Directions," Carter, "Federal Regulation of Pharmaceuticals," and
Cohen, "Canada and Brazil."

22 In 1999, PMAC changed its name to Canada's Research-Based Pharmaceutical Companies, or Rx&D; in a 2015 rebranding, the association became Innovative Medicines Canada; the Association of Canadian Drug Manufacturers (sometimes called the Canadian Drug Manufacturers' Association) now goes by the name Canadian Generic Pharmaceutical Association.

23 See Lang, *Politics of Drugs*, 53, on the antipathy between members of PMAC and the Association of Canadian Drug Manufacturers and on the market share of generic and brand-name companies. He provides the global market share of various countries in 1938 and 1963; in both years, Canada's market share was 1 percent.

24 Ibid., 44 and 33. Lang provides a detailed discussion of the two reports.

25 Michael Sheldon, the industry insider mentioned, is a former director of public relations for Smith, Kline and French, and was on loan to PMAC to prepare its case before the Special Parliamentary Committee on Drug Costs and Prices (ibid., 42).

26 Lang (ibid., 136) discusses the behind-the-scenes work of senior civil servants and their assessment of industry arrogance. See Joel Lexchin, "After Compulsory Licensing: Coming Issues in Canadian Pharmaceutical Policy and Politics," *Health Policy* 4, 40 (1997): 69–80, on the success of compulsory licensing. See Cohen, "Canada and Brazil," 7–8, on the 1986 US price comparison and the Eastman Commission's recommendation to keep compulsory licensing.

27 Forty-three of sixty-nine compulsory licences issued by 1971 were appealed in the courts; see Joel Lexchin, "Pharmaceuticals, Patents and Politics: Canada and Bill C-22," *International Journal of Health Services* 23, 1 (1993): 147–60. In a 1987 case, C.E. Jamieson & Co. Ltd. *v.* Canada 12 F.T.R. 167, the court decided that, under the Canadian constitution, the Food and Drugs Act spanned two subject areas: the regulation of public safety, and of trade and commerce; however, its dominant subject matter (its "pith and substance") is the regulation of public safety (Carter, "Federal Regulation of Pharmaceuticals," 222). Carter further notes that the US Food and Drug Administration's primary role has, similarly, been determined to be protecting consumers (p. 225).

28 See Carter, "Federal Regulation of Pharmaceuticals," 229.

29 See Regush, *Safety Last*, 12–13 for a discussion of Canada's review system on paper and in reality, and 56–57 on trade agreements and lower global drug safety standards. See William Wassenaar, "Canada: Evolution of Drug Regulation within the Health Protection Branch," *Food Drug Cosmetic Law Journal* 35 (1980): 451–61, on the establishment of the Health Protection Branch.

30 Avorn, "Teaching Clinicians about Drugs," 1187.

31 The literature on drug promotion techniques is now voluminous; see, for example, Barbara Mintzes, "'Ask Your Doctor': Women and Direct-to-Consumer Drug Advertising," in *The Push to Prescribe: Women and Canadian Drug Policy*, ed. Anne

Rochon Ford and Diane Saibil (Toronto: Women's Press, 2010), 17–46, on drug advertising; Jeremy A. Greene, "Attention to Details: Etiquette and the Pharmaceutical Salesman in Postwar America," *Social Studies of Science* 34 (2004): 271–92, on the history of detailing techniques; and Michael J. Oldani, "Thick Prescriptions: Toward an Interpretation of Pharmaceutical Sales Practices," *Medical Anthropology Quarterly* 18 (2004): 325–56, on detailing in the 1990s. See David Healy, *Pharmageddon* (Oakland, CA: University of California Press, 2012), for Healy's critique of the 1962 decision to rely on clinical trial evidence as the basis of drug approvals.

32 On DES and vaginal cancers, see Annekathryn Goodman, John Schorge, and Michael F. Greene, "The Long-Term Effects of In Utero Exposures – The DES Story," *New England Journal of Medicine* 364 (2011): 2083–84. On the Dalkon Shield, see Regush, *Safety Last*, 10–11, and Mary Florence Hawkins, *Unshielded: The Human Cost of the Dalkon Shield* (Toronto: University of Toronto Press, 1997).

33 See Nicholas M. Regush, *Condition Critical: Canada's Health Care System* (Toronto: Macmillan, 1987), for a description of strategies used to promote Depo-Provera; see Ruth Cooperstock and Henry L. Lennard, "Some Social Meanings of Tranquilizer Use," *Sociology of Health & Illness* 1 (1979): 331–47, on gender and the social construction of anxiety as a disease; see Mintzes, "'Ask Your Doctor,'" 31, for a 1975 ad for an antidepressant depicting a distressed-looking woman standing next to a vacuum cleaner.

34 See Steering Committee of Women and Health Protection, "Introduction," in Ford and Saibil, *The Push to Prescribe*, 1–13.

35 The federal government's contribution to health spending can be calculated in several ways, and not all analysts agree on the 15 percent figure; for a discussion, see Roy J. Romanow, *Building on Values: The Future of Health Care in Canada; Final Report* (Ottawa: Commission on the Future of Health Care in Canada, 2002), 35–40.

36 See Pat Armstrong and Hugh Armstrong, *Health Care* (Halifax: Fernwood, 2016), on the impact on federal funding cuts to the provinces in health care spending. See Josephine Rekart, *Public Funds, Private Provision: The Role of the Voluntary Sector* (Vancouver: UBC Press, 1993), for a case study in British Columbia of public sector downsizing and the province's subsequent reliance on civil society organizations for cheap substitute services.

37 On drug review times in Canada and the United States in the 1970s, from a 1980 US General Accounting Office report, see Carter, "Federal Regulation of Pharmaceuticals," 235, n165; on the slowing of review times in Canada and the pressure to speed them up, see Regush, *Safety Last*, 15–16. On the four government reports, see Regush, *Safety Last*, 17–18.

38 Clearly a drug lag skeptic, Hilts devotes an entire chapter of his book to the issue of "so-called drug lag" (*Protecting America's Health*, 191). He notes that structural factors

such as staff capacity and training affect the time it takes to conduct a proper review (p. 368). On drug lag as a social construct, see also Lexchin, "New Directions." On varied estimates of the percentage of drugs approved that are innovative versus "me too," see Regush, *Safety Last*, 15–16; for a more recent analysis, see Joel Lexchin, *Who's Calling the Tune: Harmonization of Drug Regulation in Canada* (Ottawa: Canadian Centre for Policy Alternatives, 2011), 10. On the argument that a careful review may ultimately save more lives, see Hilts, *Protecting America's Health*, 376; on the practice of prioritizing innovative drugs, see Regush, *Safety Last*.

39 See Regush, *Safety Last*, on Napke's and Henderson's efforts to improve PMS in Canada. Reports in the United States (for example, United States Congress, Office of Technology Assessment, *Post-marketing Surveillance of Prescription Drugs* [Office of Technology Assessment: Washington, DC, 1982]), and in Europe (e.g., Barbara Culliton and Wallace K. Waterfall, "Post-marketing Surveillance," *British Medical Journal* 280 [1980]: 1175–76) also flagged PMS as a key area of concern for drug safety.

40 Regush, *Safety Last*, 2–3.

41 The Même was manufactured in the United States and was distributed in both Canada and the United States. The product was heavily marketed in Quebec, where a critical mass of affected women began to organize, and where Regush made it a topic of ongoing journalistic investigation. Regush (ibid., 85–86) discusses complications from breast implants.

42 Ibid., 3. Catley-Carlson requested a meeting with Regush to discuss articles he had written about breast implant safety that had upset the minister of health.

43 See Lexchin, "New Directions," 155–56, on the TPD's move to user fees and the government memo defining the review unit's client as, "in many cases ... the person or company who pays for the service."

44 See Ann Silversides, "Lifting the Curtain on the Drug Approval Process," in Ford and Saibil, *The Push to Prescribe*, 127–28, for an account of the controversy over Relenza's NOC/c designation. See the PBS *Frontline* website for an interview with Michael Elashoff in which he describes the FDA's approval of Relenza, posted November 13, 2003, accessed February 24, 2016, http://www.pbs.org/wgbh/pages/frontline/shows/prescription/interviews/elashoff.html.

45 See Lexchin, "New Directions"; Mintzes, "'Ask Your Doctor'"; and Barbara Mintzes, Steve Morgan, and James M. Wright, "Twelve Years' Experience with Direct-to-Consumer Advertising in Canada: A Cautionary Tale," *PLoS One* 4 (2009): e5699, on the Canadian government's relaxation of the prohibition against DTCA. David M. Gardner, Barbara Mintzes, and Aleck Ostry, "Direct-to-Consumer Prescription Drug Advertising in Canada: Permission by Default?" *Canadian Medical Association Journal* 169 (2003): 425–27, note the government's failure to act on violations.

46 This discussion is restricted to drug treatments for breast cancer patients, but many
of the general trends apply to other cancers as well. These include an increased reliance on chemotherapy treatments, an expansion of the pharmaceutical menu,
and a rise in chemotherapy costs. On access to expensive cancer chemotherapy as
a relatively recent phenomenon, see Turner & Associates, *Cancer Drug Access for
Canadians: Report for the Canadian Cancer Society* (Toronto: Canadian Cancer
Society, 2009). See Patterson, *The Dread Disease*, 196–97, on the largely unsuccessful
postwar American program to test drugs for chemotherapy. See Barron H. Lerner,
*The Breast Cancer Wars: Hope, Fear, and the Pursuit of a Cure in Twentieth-Century
America* (New York: Oxford University Press, 2001), on how breast cancer came to
be understood as a systemic disease. The structural tendency for specialized medical
care to concentrate in major centres contributes added cost and inconvenience for
patients living in rural and remote areas; rural/urban resource inequalities also
contribute to regional variations in treatment.

47 In his historical analysis, Lerner *(Breast Cancer Wars)* notes that surgeons, who had
been the mainstays of breast cancer care, were especially reluctant to accept evidence
that cancer was systemic.

48 See Michael W. DeGregorio and Valerie J. Wiebe, *Tamoxifen and Breast Cancer*, 2nd
ed. (New Haven, CT: Yale University Press, 1999), 18–24, and Susan M. Love, *Dr.
Susan Love's Breast Book*, 1st ed., with contributions by Karen Lindsey (New York:
Addison-Wesley, 1990), 388–90, for two virtually identical lists of the "most commonly used" cytotoxic agents found to be effective in treating breast cancer.

49 On the reluctance of some specialists to use chemotherapy treatments without evidence of gain, see Patterson, *The Dread Disease*, 306–7.

50 See DeGregorio and Wiebe, *Tamoxifen and Breast Cancer*, 17 and 30, on tamoxifen's
mechanism of action.

51 S.M. Love, *Breast Book*, 390, identifies all hormonal drug treatments for breast cancer
as taken orally, once or twice day.

52 See Turner & Associates, *Cancer Drug Access*, on the variations in private medical
insurance plans' coverage for cancer treatments depending on province or territory
of residence and the terms of employee-sponsored or private drug plans.

53 See DeGregorio and Wiebe, *Tamoxifen and Breast Cancer*, 26–27, on high-dose
chemotherapy with bone marrow transplantation. This procedure is sometimes
referred to as high-dose chemotherapy with autologous bone-marrow transplant or,
colloquially, "high-dose chemo."

54 See Robert Bazell, *Her2: The Making of Herceptin, a Revolutionary Treatment for
Breast Cancer* (New York: Random House, 1998) on the development of Herceptin.
Vivien Walsh and Jordan Goodman, "Cancer Chemotherapy, Biodiversity, Public
and Private Property: The Case of the Anti-cancer Drug Taxol," *Social Science &*

Medicine 49, 9 (1999): 1215–25, tell the history of Taxol as a treatment for ovarian and breast cancer.

Chapter 2: Health Advocacy Organizations in Canada

1 Interview with author, October 2008.
2 See Paul A. Pross, *Group Politics and Public Policy*, 2nd ed. (Toronto: Oxford University Press, 1992), on the history of pressure groups in Canada.
3 Jane Jenson and Susan D. Phillips, "Regime Shift: New Citizenship Practices in Canada," *International Journal of Canadian Studies* 14 (1996): 113–35, frame Canada's civil society organizations as central to the country's postwar nation-building project; thus, when neoliberal regimes redefined the role of civil society, they also altered the meaning of citizenship. See Paul A. Pross and Kernaghan R. Webb, "Embedded Regulation: Advocacy and the Federal Regulation of Public Interest Groups," in *Delicate Dances: Public Policy and the Nonprofit Sector*, ed. Kathy L. Brock (Montreal: McGill-Queen's University Press, 2003), 63–121; Miriam Catherine Smith, *A Civil Society? Collective Actors in Canadian Political Life* (Peterborough, ON: Broadview Press, 2005); and Nick Acheson and Susan Hodgett, "Introduction: Narratives of Citizenship; Welfare State Reform and Civil Society in Canada," *British Journal of Canadian Studies* 25, 2 (2012): 151–59, for further analyses of this process.
4 See Patricia Kaufert, "Women, Resistance and the Breast Cancer Movement," in *Pragmatic Women and Body Politics*, ed. Margaret Lock and Patricia Kaufert (Cambridge: Cambridge University Press, 1998), 287–309, on the early breast cancer movement in North America.
5 See Marina Morrow, "'Our Bodies Our Selves' in Context: Reflections on the Women's Health Movement in Canada," in *Women's Health in Canada: Critical Perspectives on Theory and Policy*, ed. Colleen Varcoe (Toronto: University of Toronto Press, 2007), 33–63, for a comparison of health advocacy in Canada's first-, second-, and third-wave women's movements.
6 The VON website includes a brief history of the organization; see "About VON," VON Canada, accessed January 27, 2016, http://www.von.ca/en/history.
7 Terry Crowley, "Hunter, Adelaide Sophia (Hoodless)," *Dictionary of Canadian Biography*, vol. 13 (University of Toronto/Université Laval, 1994), accessed January 28, 2016, http://www.biographi.ca/en/bio/hunter_adelaide_sophia_13E.html.
8 Linda M. Ambrose and Margaret Kechnie, "Social Control or Social Feminism? Two Views of the Ontario Women's Institutes," *Agricultural History* 73 (1999): 234. In this article, Ambrose and Kechnie discuss the class tensions within the WI.
9 On the importance of consciousness-raising groups, see Morrow, "'Our Bodies Our Selves'"; on "undone science," see David J. Hess, "The Potentials and Limitations of Civil Society Research: Getting Undone Science Done," *Sociological Inquiry* 79, 3

(2009): 306–27, and Scott Frickel, Sahra Gibbon, Jeff Howard, Joanna Kempner, Gwen Ottinger, and David J. Hess, "Undone Science: Charting Social Movement and Civil Society Challenges," *Science, Technology, & Human Values* 35 (2009): 444–73; on feminist epistemologies and socially constructed ignorance, see Nancy Tuana, "Coming to Understand: Orgasm and the Epistemology of Ignorance," *Hypatia* 19, 1 (2004): 194–232.

10 In its origins, the *Birth Control Handbook* is more aptly described as a project of the 1960s New Left student movement than of the women's health movement; subsequent editions increasingly took on a feminist identity (millions of copies were distributed, in Canada and internationally, and by 1975, the *Handbook* was in its twelfth edition). See Christabelle Sethna, "The Evolution of the *Birth Control Handbook*: From Student Peer-Education Manual to Feminist Self-Empowerment Text, 1968–1975," *Canadian Bulletin of Medical History* 21, 2 (1999): 89–118.

11 Abortion and the dissemination of birth control information had been illegal in Canada since 1869, subject to a maximum penalty of life imprisonment. See Catherine Dunphy, *Morgentaler: A Difficult Hero* (Toronto: Random House, 1996), on Dr. Morgentaler's battle to have abortions legalized and the collective work of women's health activists. On the formation and activism of provincial abortion rights' groups, see Sari Tudiver, *The Strength of Links: Building the Canadian Women's Health Network* (Winnipeg: Winnipeg Consultation Organizing Committee, 1994).

12 See Morrow, "'Our Bodies Our Selves,'" on women's centres becoming sites for feminist analysis; see Kathleen McDonnell, ed., *Adverse Effects: Women and the Pharmaceutical Industry* (Penang, Malaysia: International Organization of Consumer Unions, Regional Office for Asia and the Pacific, 1986), on the prominence of pharmaceutical critique in the women's second-wave health movement. See Nicholas M. Regush, *Condition Critical: Canada's Health Care System* (Toronto: Macmillan, 1987), 237, on the founding of DES Action Canada. At the time, Health Canada was called the Ministry of National Health and Welfare.

13 The Epcot Center is a Disneyland-style centre highlighting different cultures.

14 For works by Canadian health professionals writing critically about pharmaceuticals in the 1980s, see Ruth Cooperstock, *Social Aspects of the Medical Use of Psychotropic Drugs* (Toronto: Alcoholism and Drug Addiction Research Foundation of Ontario, 1974); Ruth Cooperstock and Henry L. Lennard, "Some Social Meanings of Tranquilizer Use," *Sociology of Health & Illness* 1, 3 (1979): 331–47; Joel Lexchin, *The Real Pushers: A Critical Analysis of the Canadian Drug Industry* (Vancouver: New Star Books, 1984); and Jim Harding, "Mood Modifiers and Elderly Women in Canada: The Medicalization of Poverty," in McDonnell, *Adverse Effects,* 51–86.

15 See Tudiver, *Strength of Links*, and Connie Clement, *Remembering Ruth Cooperstock: The Past* (Toronto: Women and Health Protection, 2006), 3–6, on the play *Side Effects*.

Feminist health groups supported pharmaceutical birth control options but critiqued the safety standards and risk and benefit information as inadequate; moreover, they wanted improvements in women's access to education and employment, not drugs, as a long-term population control strategy. See the following chapters in McDonnell, *Adverse Effects*: Cary LaCheen, "Population Control and the Pharmaceutical Industry," 89–136; Vimal Balasubrahmanyan, "Finger in the Dyke: The Fight to Keep Injectables out of India," 137–58; and Lynn Duggan, "From Birth Control to Population Control: Depo-Provera in Southeast Asia," 159–65.

16 See Marc LaLonde, *A New Perspective on the Health of Canadians: A Working Document* (Ottawa: Government of Canada, 1974); Jake Epp, *Achieving Health for All: A Framework for Health Promotion* (Ottawa: Health and Welfare Canada, 1986); and World Health Organization (WHO), *The Ottawa Charter for Health Promotion* (Geneva: WHO, 1986).

17 Josephine Rekart, *Public Funds, Private Provision: The Role of the Voluntary Sector* (Vancouver: UBC Press, 1993), 16–30.

18 Alexandra Dobrowolsky, "Of 'Special Interest': Interest, Identity and Feminist Constitutional Activism in Canada," *Canadian Journal of Political Science* 31, 4 (1998): 724. Note that, from 1942 to 2003, the party was officially the Progressive Conservative Party of Canada (PCP) but (as in this excerpt) was often referred to simply as the Conservative Party. The PCP merged with the Canadian Alliance party in 2003, changed the name to the Conservative Party of Canada, and moved to the political right.

19 Anne Rochon Ford, "An Overview of Select Social and Economic Forces Influencing the Development of In Vitro Fertilization and Related Assisted Reproductive Techniques," in *New Reproductive Technologies and the Science, Industry, Education and Social Welfare Systems in Canada* (Ottawa: Royal Commission on New Reproductive Technologies, 1993): 85.

20 Neutropenia causes a deficiency in the white blood cells the body uses to fight off infections. The California-based biotechnology company Amgen makes Neupogen.

21 The Department of Consumer and Corporate Affairs was dismantled in 1993 and replaced by Industry Canada, which includes an Office of Consumer Affairs.

22 For examples of alternative treatments for cancer patients and related access campaigns, see Max Gerson, *A Cancer Therapy: Results of Fifty Cases & the Cure of Advanced Cancer by Diet Therapy*, 5th ed. (1958; repr., Bonita, CA: Gerson Institute, 1990); Ralph W. Moss, *Cancer Therapy: The Independent Consumer's Guide to Nontoxic Treatment & Prevention* (New York: Equinox Press, 1992); David J. Hess, *Evaluating Alternative Cancer Therapies: A Guide to the Science and Politics of an Emerging Medical Field* (New Brunswick, NJ: Rutgers University Press, 1999); and David J. Hess, "Beyond Scientific Controversies: Scientific Counterpublics, Countervailing

Industries, and Undone Science," in *The Public Shaping of Medical Research: Patient Associations, Health Movements, and Biomedicine*, ed. Peter Wheling, Willy Viehöver, and Sophia Koenen (London: Routledge, 2015), 151–71.

23 Ann Silversides, *AIDS Activist: Michael Lynch and the Politics of Community* (Toronto: Between the Lines, 2003), 198.

24 On meetings between Canadian AIDS and women's health activists, see ibid., 80, 132–33.

25 See Steven Epstein, *Impure Science: AIDS, Activism, and the Politics of Knowledge* (Berkeley: University of California Press, 1996), 223, and Philip J. Hilts, *Protecting America's Health: The FDA, Business, and One Hundred Years of Regulation* (New York: Knopf, 2003), 291–308, on AIDS activists' demands regarding drug regulation.

26 Hilts, *Protecting America's Health*, 296.

27 New York AIDS activists Mark Harrington and Jim Eigo, quoted in Hilts, ibid., 304 and 305.

28 See John Abraham and Courtney Davis, "Deficits, Expectations and Paradigms in British and American Drug Safety Assessments: Prising Open the Black Box of Regulatory Science," *Science, Technology, & Human Values* 32 (2007): 399–431, for their analysis of changes in drug regulation in the United States and the United Kingdom; for their discussion of AIDS activism and regulation, see pp. 424–25.

29 Lori Waserman, "Before Pink Ribbons: Understanding the Invisibility of Breast Cancer in the Canadian Women's Health Movement during the 1970s and 1980s" (MA thesis, Carleton University, 1997), 56.

30 See Jacques Derrida, "Plato's Pharmacy," in *Dissemination*, trans. Barbara Johnson (Chicago: University of Chicago Press, 1981), 61–172, and Michael Montagne, "The Pharmakon Phenomenon: Cultural Conceptions of Drugs and Drug Use," in *Contested Ground: Public Purpose and Private Interest in the Regulation of Prescription Drug*, ed. Peter Davis (New York: Oxford University Press, 1996), 11–25, on the pharmakon and the meaning of drugs.

31 Emily Martin, "The Pharmaceutical Person," *BioSocieties* 1 (2006): 275.

32 Barron H. Lerner, *The Breast Cancer Wars: Hope, Fear, and the Pursuit of a Cure in Twentieth-Century America* (New York: Oxford University Press, 2001), 253.

33 On the modest benefits of drugs to treat most cancers, see ibid., 254.

34 Gianni Bonadonna, Ercole Brusamolino, and Pinuccia Valagussa, et al., "Combination Chemotherapy as an Adjunct Treatment in Operable Breast Cancer," *New England Journal of Medicine* 294 (1976): 405–10.

35 Gabriel N. Hortobagyi and Aman U. Buzdar, "Current Status of Adjuvant Systemic Therapy for Primary Breast Cancer: Progress and Controversy," *CA: A Cancer Journal for Clinicians* 45 (1995): 199–226.

36 Adjuvant or "helping" chemotherapy is used in combination with surgery and/or radiation to reduce the burden of cancer cells in the body before there is detectable spread, to prevent or delay recurrence; see Susan M. Love, *Dr. Susan Love's Breast Book*, 1st ed., with contributions by Karen Lindsey (New York: Addison-Wesley, 1990), 433. Not all analysts agreed that surviving ten or twenty years post-diagnosis meant the woman was effectively cured. Christopher John Williams, ed., *Introducing New Treatments for Cancer: Practical, Ethical and Legal Problems* (Chichester, West Sussex: John Wiley & Sons, 1992), 248, describes chemotherapy regarding women diagnosed as stage 1 or stage 2 as "an investment with uncertain payoff [because] most patients with operable breast cancer relapse and die of the disease." Both authors concur, however, that for any given case, the evidence of life extension was slim and uncertain, whereas the evidence for reduced quality of life was significant and certain.

37 Lerner, *Breast Cancer Wars*, 252.

38 Williams, *Introducing New Treatments for Cancer*, 233.

39 S.M. Love, *Breast Book*, 324; Michael W. DeGregorio and Valerie J. Wiebe, *Tamoxifen and Breast Cancer*, 2nd ed. (New Haven, CT: Yale University Press, 1999), 47; V. Craig Jordan, "Tamoxifen: A Most Unlikely Pioneering Medicine," *Nature Reviews Drug Discovery* 2 (2003): 205.

40 S.M. Love, *Breast Book*, 324.

41 See Williams, *Introducing New Treatments for Cancer*, 232, and Ilana Löwy, "Trustworthy Knowledge and Desperate Patients: Clinical Tests for New Drugs from Cancer to AIDS," in *Living and Working with the New Medical Technologies*, ed. Alberto Cambrosio (New York: Cambridge University Press, 2000), 49–81, on surrogate endpoints as the basis for approving cancer drugs.

42 Löwy, "Trustworthy Knowledge and Desperate Patients," 60.

43 See Early Breast Cancer Trialists' Collaborative Group, "Effects of Adjuvant Tamoxifen and of Cytotoxic Therapy on Mortality in Early Breast Cancer: An Overview of 61 Randomized Trials among 28,896 Women," *New England Journal of Medicine* 319 (1988): 1681–92; and Early Breast Cancer Trialists' Cooperative Group, "Effects of Chemotherapy and Hormonal Therapy for Early Breast Cancer on Recurrence and 15-Year Survival: An Overview of the Randomized Trials," *Lancet* 365, 9472 (2005): 1687–717.

44 Williams, *Introducing New Treatments for Cancer*, 232.

45 Waserman, "Before Pink Ribbons."

46 Ibid., 14, 68.

47 Ibid., 69–70.

48 See Maren Klawiter, *The Biopolitics of Breast Cancer: Changing Politics of Disease and Activism* (Minneapolis: University of Minnesota Press, 2008), 166–67, for a similar

analysis of breast cancer's invisibility in the women's health movement in this era in the San Francisco area.

49 For other early political analyses, see Audre Lorde, *The Cancer Journals* (San Francisco: Spinsters Ink, 1980), and Deena Metzger, *Tree and the Woman Who Slept with Men to Take the War Out of Them* (Oakland, CA: Wingbow Press, 1983).

50 On Kushner's political analysis as a precursor of the breast cancer movement, see Sharon Batt, *Patient No More: The Politics of Breast Cancer* (Charlottetown: Gynergy, 1994); Marcy Jane Knopf-Newman, *Beyond Slash, Burn and Poison: Transforming Breast Cancer Stories into Action* (New Brunswick, NJ: Rutgers University Press, 2004); Lerner, *Breast Cancer Wars*; and Barron H. Lerner, "Patient, Public Activist: Rose Kushner's Attack on Chemotherapy," *Bulletin of the History of Medicine* 81, 1 (2007): 224–40.

51 Lerner, "Patient, Public Activist."

52 Ibid., 227.

53 Kushner, cited in Lerner, "Patient, Public Activist," 229.

54 Ibid., 238.

55 Ibid., 239.

56 On tamoxifen's known toxicities, the World Health Organization's International Agency for Research on Cancer and National Institutes of Health in the United States both list tamoxifen as a "known human carcinogen" because the drug causes endometrial cancer.

57 Lerner, "Patient, Public Activist," 240. The following two quotations are at p. 239.

58 See Shannon Brownlee, "Doctors Without Borders: Why You Can't Trust Medical Journals Anymore," *Washington Monthly*, April 2004, http://www.washington monthly.com/features/2004/0404.brownlee.html; Jerome P. Kassirer, *On the Take: How Medicine's Complicity with Big Business Can Endanger Your Health* (New York: Oxford University Press, 2005); and Howard Brody, *Hooked: Ethics, the Medical Profession, and the Pharmaceutical Industry* (Lanham, MD: Rowman and Littlefield, 2007), for assessments of professional ethical norms, contemporaneous with Lerner's article, that contrast the lax conflict-of-interest standards in medicine with those in journalism. Kassirer extends his comparison to the American judiciary, the legal profession, and government employees, noting that all have well-entrenched professional norms, including sanctions for serious violations.

Chapter 3: Beginnings of the Breast Cancer Movement

1 Sources for this vignette are Pat Kelly's testimony in Canada, House of Commons, Subcommittee on the Status of Women, *A Study of Breast Cancer*, Minutes of Proceedings and Evidence, 3rd sess., 34th Parl., October 22, 1991, 35–43; and Pat Kelly, interview with the author, September 2007. I recognize that the representatives from

the Canadian Cancer Society might well have a different telling of this meeting; however, the account captures a view of knowledge control on the part of professionalized cancer organizations at the time, which other activists I interviewed spoke of as well.

2 Sharon Batt, "Cancer Victims Can Learn from AIDS Sufferers," *Montreal Gazette*, July 4, 1989, and Carolyn Gibson Badger, interview with the author, April 2009.

3 Paula McPherson's testimony in Canada, *A Study of Breast Cancer*, February 25, 1992.

4 Ibid., 17–20.

5 In the 1970s, public interest research groups (PIRGs) were established on university campuses in the United States and Canada, with the goal of encouraging action for social change. Funds are made available to campus and community organizations whose work fits the PIRG mission.

6 Marcella Tardif's testimony in Canada, *A Study of Breast Cancer*, February 11, 1992, 34.

7 Sources: André Picard, "Montreal Woman's Ordeal Uncovers Inner Beauty," *Globe and Mail*, January 17, 1992, and ibid.

8 For theoretical discussions of lay scientific knowledge, see Massimiano Bucchi and Frederico Neresini, "Science and Public Participation," in *The Handbook of Science and Technology Studies*, 3rd ed., ed. Edward J. Hackett, Olga Amsterdamska, Michael Lynch, and Judy Wajcman (Cambridge, MA: MIT Press, 2008), 449–72; Michel Callon, "The Role of Lay People in the Production and Dissemination of Scientific Knowledge," *Science, Technology and Society* 4 (1999): 81–94; and Brian Wynne, "May the Sheep Safely Graze? A Reflexive View of the Expert-Lay Knowledge Divide," in *Risk, Environment and Modernity: Towards a New Ecology*, ed. Brian Wynne (Thousand Oaks, CA: Sage, 1996), 44–83.

9 The subcommittee was part of the Standing Committee on Health and Welfare, Social Affairs, Seniors and the Status of Women. Members were Barbara Greene, chair (Progressive Conservative), Edna Anderson (Progressive Conservative), Mary Clancy (Liberal), and Dawn Black (New Democratic Party).

10 Canada, *A Study of Breast Cancer*, February 25, 1992, 28.

11 Witnesses included twenty-nine researchers of varied specialties, nine patients and/or representatives of patient organizations (including one American), six representatives of traditional charities or foundations, two clinicians, and two representatives from the pharmaceutical industry.

12 The Canadian Cancer Society, the YWCA, and the newer, but rapidly growing, Canadian Breast Cancer Foundation all discussed their services to breast cancer patients. See Paul A. Pross, *Group Politics and Public Policy*, 2nd ed. (Toronto: Oxford University Press, 1992), 119, on policy communities.

13 From Sylvia Morrison's testimony in Canada, *A Study of Breast Cancer*, October 22, 1991, 45–49.

14 Ibid., 46. Which of the two drugs she is referring to is not clear from the testimony. The following three quotations are at pp. 47, 48, and 48.

15 Barbara Greene, Subcommittee on the Status of Women, *Breast Cancer: Unanswered Questions* (Ottawa: Parliament of Canada, 1992), 36.

16 For discussions of the treatment, its use in the United States, and its risks to patients, see Barron H. Lerner, *The Breast Cancer Wars: Hope, Fear, and the Pursuit of a Cure in Twentieth-Century America* (New York: Oxford University Press, 2001), 254–55, and David M. Eddy, "High-Dose Chemotherapy with Autologous Bone Marrow Transplantation for the Treatment of Metastatic Breast Cancer," *Journal of Clinical Oncology* 10 (1992): 665. On the fraud in HDC clinical trials, see Raymond B. Weiss, Robert M. Rifken, F. Marc Stewart, Richard L. Theriault, Lori A. Williams, Allen A. Herman, and Roy A. Beveridge, "High-Dose Chemotherapy for High-Risk Primary Breast Cancer: An On-Site Review of the Bezwoda Study," *Lancet* 355 (2000): 999–1003. *Dr. Susan Love's Breast Book*, which has appeared at five-year intervals since 1990, provides a telling record of the procedure's rise and fall. The 1990 edition makes no mention of high-dose chemotherapy; the 1995 edition devotes seven pages to describing the procedure, emphasizing its toxicity, including the high mortality rate, as well as the high cost, which tempted hospitals in the United States to see HDC as good business. Noting the lack of reliable effectiveness data, because studies to that point were historical comparisons, not non-randomized trials, she urges patients considering HDC to enter a clinical trial, so that future generations will know if it works. By 2000, she reports that four randomized clinical trials have shown HDC has no additional benefit over standard therapy but has more complications; she also cites the case of research fraud in South Africa and deplores the fact that, in nine years, twelve thousand American women underwent high-dose chemotherapy outside of clinical trials because physicians and hospitals were "selling dreams" (384). By 2005, she dismisses the procedure in a single paragraph as more toxic than standard chemotherapy regimens but with no greater benefits.

17 In 1999, PMAC changed its name to Rx&D and in 2015 the organization became Innovative Medicines Canada.

18 See Canada, *A Study of Breast Cancer*, May 11, 1992, 4–17, for Marks's and Postlewaite's testimony, and Appendix "Femm 14" 17A, 1–22, for the supplementary brief.

19 Ibid., Appendix "Femm 14," 17A, 2.

20 Ibid., 13.

21 These initiatives included funding to community-based health groups and setting up endowed chairs in women's health at universities.

22 P.L.C. Torremans, "Compulsory Licensing of Pharmaceutical Products in Canada," *International Review of Industrial Property and Copyright Law* 27 (1996): 316–30.

23 Patricia I. Carter, "Federal Regulation of Pharmaceuticals in the United States and Canada," *Loyola of Los Angeles International and Comparative Law Review* 21, 2 (1999), 215–58.

24 Eileen McMahon, "NAFTA and the Biotechnology Industry," *California Western Law Review* 33 (1996–97): 31–48.

25 See Jillian Clare Cohen, "Canada and Brazil – Dealing with Tension between Ensuring Access to Medicines and Complying with Pharmaceutical Patent Standards: Is the Story the Same?" *Comparative Program on Health and Society*, Working Paper Series (2003/2004), on Bill C-91 and the Patent Act Amendment Act in Canada's strategy to balance compliance with international patent standards against access to medicines. Pharmaceutical companies have challenged the Patented Medicine Prices Review Board's powers to control prices in court but without success; see Margaret Smith, *Patent Protection for Pharmaceutical Products in Canada: Chronology of Significant Events* (Ottawa: Library of Parliament, 2000), and Carter, "Federal Regulation of Pharmaceuticals," 246.

26 Cohen, "Canada and Brazil," 10.

27 Greene, *Breast Cancer*, xv.

28 Ibid., 41.

29 Ibid.

30 In a response to the subcommittee's report, the minister of health articulated a program that would reinforce the role of the Canadian Cancer Society and move the activists back to the margins; see Benoît Bouchard, *Government Response to the Fourth Report of the Standing Committee on Health and Welfare, Social Affairs, Seniors and the Status of Women on Breast Cancer* (Ottawa: Government of Canada, 1992), 29.

31 On Davis and the environmental causes of cancer, see D.L. Davis, D. Hoel, J. Fox, and A. Lopez, "International Trends in Cancer Mortality in France, West Germany, Italy, Japan, England and Wales, and the USA," *Lancet* 336 (1990): 474–81, and Karen Wright, "Going by the Numbers," *New York Times Magazine*, December 15, 1991. Over the next two decades, a loosely organized international network of breast cancer groups formed, now known as the environmental, or green, breast cancer movement; see Barbara Ley, *From Pink to Green: Disease Prevention and the Environmental Breast Cancer Movement* (New Brunswick, NJ: Rutgers University Press, 2009).

32 Health Canada hired Pat Kelly and me on contract for seven months, initially as cochairs and then as vice-chair and chair respectively. The two latter roles were virtually identical, except that I was responsible for the subcommittee's budget. The

other three subcommittees, dedicated to prevention and screening, treatment, and research, consisted predominantly of professionals, but each had several lay women as members.

33 Rod Mickleburgh, "Forum on Breast Cancer Hailed as Watershed Event in Canada: Patients Emerge as Full Partners in Setting Priorities," *Globe and Mail*, November 17, 1993.

34 World Health Organization (WHO), *Declaration of Alma-Ata, International Conference on Primary Health Care* (Alma-Ata, USSR: WHO, September 6–12, 1978), 1.

35 World Health Organization (WHO), *The Ottawa Charter for Health Promotion* (Geneva: WHO, 1986), 2; WHO, *The Sundsvall Statement, 3rd International Conference on Health Promotion* (Sundsvall, Sweden: WHO, June 9–15, 1991), 4.

36 Deena White, "Consumer and Community Participation: A Reassessment of Process, Impact, and Value," in *Handbook of Social Studies in Health and Medicine*, ed. Gary L. Albrecht, Ray Fitzpatrick, and Susan C. Scrimshaw (Thousand Oaks, CA: Sage, 2000), 468.

37 Ibid., 476.

38 Patricia Kaufert, "Women, Resistance and the Breast Cancer Movement," in *Pragmatic Women and Body Politics*, ed. Margaret Lock and Patricia Kaufert (Cambridge: Cambridge University Press, 1998), 287–309.

39 Pat Kelly, interview with the author, September 2007.

40 At this time, Bristol-Myers Squibb was in the process of applying to have the new ovarian cancer drug Taxol approved as a breast cancer treatment. The company also owned the rights to the Même implant, making it a player in the still-unsettled breast implant scandal.

41 The fund had a partnership structure, including established research agencies and cancer foundations that contributed additional monies (excluding, once again, the pharmaceutical industry).

42 Maren Klawiter, "Racing for the Cure, Walking Women, and Toxic Touring: Mapping Cultures of Action within the Bay Area Terrain of Breast Cancer," *Social Problems* 46 (1999): 104–26, introduced the term "cultures of action" to capture the diversity of groups within the breast cancer movement in the San Francisco area, and their fluidity. As in the United States, groups in Canada varied in the emphasis they put on such issues as support or advocacy, and (among the latter) cure or prevention.

43 The founders of this new breed of groups made efforts to ensure that "survivors" were included in their decision-making structures; thus, Willow set a 50 percent survivor minimum on its board; Breast Cancer Action Nova Scotia set an 80 percent minimum. The Canadian Breast Cancer Network's board consists entirely of survivors, with an additional requirement for regional representation.

44 In 1999, Rhône-Poulenc merged with Hoechst AG of Germany to form Aventis, which merged in 2004 with Sanofi-Synthelabo to create Sanofi-Aventis, based in Paris.

45 Alecia Swasy, *Soap Opera: The Inside Story of Procter and Gamble* (New York: Touchstone, 1993). Swasy, a journalist working for the *Wall Street Journal*, examines the company's environmental practices and the marketing campaigns of products marketed mainly to women.

46 By the fall of 1995, Pat had left Willow.

47 The quotation "view each case ..." is from the minutes of the Willow board meeting, November 28, 1995.

48 I was a member of the board at the time and represented the group at the meeting in San Antonio.

49 On pharma funding in the early American movement, see Barbara Brenner, "Sister Support: Women Create a Breast Cancer Movement," in *Breast Cancer: Society Shapes an Epidemic*, ed. Anne S. Kasper and Susan J. Ferguson (New York: St. Martin's Press, 2000), 325–53; Mary K. Anglin, "Working from the Inside Out: Implications of Breast Cancer Activism for Biomedical Policies and Practices," *Social Science & Medicine* 44 (1997): 1403–15; and Mary K. Anglin, "'You and *What* Army?' US Breast Cancer Treatment Activism and Big Pharma" (paper presented at the annual meeting of CASCA, Vancouver, May 2009).

50 Anglin, "Working from the Inside Out" and "'You and *What* Army?'"

51 Anglin, "Working from the Inside Out," 1411.

52 For Fugh-Berman's critique of the Prevention Trial, see Adriane Fugh-Berman, "Tamoxifen in Healthy Women: Preventive Health or Preventing Health?" *National Women's Health Network News*, September/October, 1991, 3, and Adriane Fugh-Berman and Samuel Epstein, "Tamoxifen: Disease Prevention or Disease Substitution?" *Lancet* 340 (1992): 1143–45. Other critics of the BCPT included Kara Smigel, "Breast Cancer Prevention Trial Under Scrutiny (Again)," *Journal of the National Cancer Institute* 84 (1992): 1692–94; Trudy L. Bush and Kathy J. Helzlsouer, "Tamoxifen for the Primary Prevention of Breast Cancer: A Review and Critique of the Concept and Trial," *Epidemiological Review* 15 (1993): 233–43; and Michael W. DeGregorio, Johanna U. Maenpaa, and Valerie J. Wiebe, "Tamoxifen for the Prevention of Breast Cancer: No," *Important Advances in Oncology*, February (1995): 175–85.

Researchers who supported the trial include Richard A. Love, "Issues in the Design of a Tamoxifen Health Trial," in *Introducing New Treatments for Cancer: Practical, Ethical and Legal Problems*, ed. Christopher John Williams (Chichester, West Sussex, England: John Wiley & Sons, 1992), 341–56, and Alison L. Jones and Trevor J. Powles,

"The Development of Cancer Chemoprevention Trials," in Williams, *Introducing New Treatments for Cancer*, 323–39.

See Jennifer R. Fosket, "Constructing 'High-Risk Women': The Development and Standardization of a Breast Cancer Risk Assessment Tool," *Science, Technology, & Human Values* 29 (2004): 291–313, and Ley, *From Pink to Green*, on the decade-long feminist opposition to the trial and its links to the green breast cancer movement. See Lerner, *Breast Cancer Wars*, on Bernard Fisher's decades-long breast cancer research program.

53 The quotation "You wouldn't normally ..." is from the transcript of the panel discussion "Breast Cancer Prevention: Best Guesses" (Montreal: Breast Cancer Action Montreal, 1992).

In a brief to the National Institutes for Health, the NWHN argued that the government agency should fund research into the preventable causes of age-related diseases from which women suffered, a program eventually launched as the Women's Health Initiative.

54 In 1991, tamoxifen was the world's bestselling anticancer drug. Nolvadex was still under patent in the United States, where the annual cost for a standard dose of twenty milligrams per day was US$750 a year (R.A. Love, "Tamoxifen Health Trial," 354). If taken for five years (the recommended duration for women with breast cancer), the cost to a healthy American woman would be US$3,750. The estimate that 29 million healthy women would meet the researchers' definition of "high risk" is from Leslie Ford, associate director, Division of Cancer Prevention of the National Cancer Institute, quoted in Susan Okie, "Tamoxifen Lowers Risk of Breast Cancer," *Washington Post*, April 7, 1998, Z07.

55 See Vivien Walsh and Jordan Goodman, "Cancer Chemotherapy, Biodiversity, Public and Private Property: The Case of the Anti-cancer Drug Taxol," *Social Science & Medicine* 49 (1999): 1215–25, and Vivien Walsh and Jordan Goodman, "From taxol to Taxol®: The Changing Identities and Ownership of an Anti-cancer Drug," *Medical Anthropology* 21, 3–4 (2002), 307–36, on Taxol's discovery and subsequent history.

56 Dr. Joe Pater's testimony in Canada, *A Study of Breast Cancer*, December 10, 1991, 10.

57 Newspaper columnist Christie Blatchford lent media support to the lobby; seventeen years later she cited the 1994 Ontario lobby as an example of successful drug access advocacy (Christie Blatchford, "Pitiable Tale of Mother Denied Coverage for Cancer Treatment Is Just a Rerun: In Ontario, Ministerial Dissing of Breast Cancer Victims Is Nothing New," *Globe and Mail*, March 17, 2011).

58 Justice Horace Krever headed the Royal Commission inquiry into the HIV and hepatitis C contamination of blood used for transfusions. Problems included failure

to properly screen blood donors, failure to properly test blood, and failure to warn the public about the risks of blood products.

59 Canada, *Commission of Inquiry on the Blood System in Canada: Final Report* (Canada: Minister of Public Works and Government Services, 1997), vol. 3, 1071. Comparing Canada's response with seven other high-income countries in which blood supplies were contaminated, Krever concluded that, as evidence about blood-borne transmission of HIV and methods of screening blood donations accrued, Canadian agencies responsible for blood safety lagged behind similar agencies elsewhere – particularly in the United States – in taking action (André Picard, *The Gift of Death: Confronting Canada's Tainted Blood Tragedy* [Toronto: HarperCollins, 1995], 64–65. Cost was the main reason the Canadian agencies delayed these procedures. For Justice Krever's discussion of international harmonization in Canada, see Recommendation 44 in Canada, *Commission of Inquiry on the Blood System,* vol. 3, 1071.

60 Canada, *Commission of Inquiry on the Blood System,* vol. 3, 1048.

61 Ibid., 1049. Blood products are a subset of biologic drugs and are regulated within the Biologics and Genetic Therapies Directorate of Health Canada's Health Products and Food Branch (HPFB). Pharmaceutical drugs derived from chemical manufacturing are regulated in an almost identical fashion by the parallel Therapeutic Products Directorate within the HPFB.

62 John H. Bryden, *Canada's Charities: A Need for Reform* (Ottawa: House of Commons, 1996).

63 Gordon Floyd, "The Voluntary Sector in Canada's New Social Contract: More Responsibility but No Voice?" *Philanthropist* 13, 2 (1996): 39–45.

64 Bryden, *Canada's Charities.*

65 See Peter R. Elson, "A Short History of Voluntary Sector-Government Relations in Canada," *Philanthropist* 21, 1 (2007): 36–73, for a history of government regulation used to shape of charitable organizations in Canada from pre-Confederation to 2007.

66 Pat Armstrong, Hugh Armstrong, Jacqueline Choiniere, Gina Feldberg, and Jerry P. White, eds., *Take Care: Warning Signals for Canada's Health Care System* (Toronto: Garamond Press, 1994), discuss the FTA, the NAFTA, and the discourse about health care.

67 On single-payer versus private health care delivery costs, see Morris L. Barer, Robert G. Evans, Clyde Hertzman, and Mira Johri, "Lies, Damned Lies, and Health Care Zombies: Discredited Ideas that Will Not Die," HPI Discussion Paper, vol. 10 (Houston: University of Texas, 1998), and Armstrong et al., *Take Care,* 31–51.

68 Carter, "Federal Regulation of Pharmaceuticals," 249–50, discusses the Regulatory Efficiency Act and the Reinventing Government Initiative undertaken in the United States the same year.

69 Todd Weiler, "The Straight Goods on Federal Regulatory Reform," *Government Information in Canada/Information Gouvernementale au Canada* 2, 2 (1995).

70 Canada's Regulatory Efficiency Act, if passed, would have allowed a corporation or industry group to gain an exemption from regulations based on a "compliance plan" that met the intention of the regulations while speeding approval or reducing investment uncertainty. At its discretion, the regulating agency could accept the plan in place of existing regulations, perhaps charging a cost recovery fee. For critiques of the act, see Brian Pannell, "Anti-regulation Bill Will Lull Public's Watchman to Sleep," *Toronto Star*, April 13, 1995, and Michael Valpy, "A Repugnant Assault on the Rule of Law," *Globe and Mail*, April 28, 1995. The US Food and Drug Administration Modernization Act was passed in 1997.

71 See Carter, "Federal Regulation of Pharmaceuticals," on the use of expert advisory committees.

72 See Nicholas M. Regush, *Safety Last: The Failure of the Consumer Health Protection System in Canada* (Toronto: Key Porter Books, 1993), on the training and supervision of outside reviewers.

73 Health Protection Branch, cited in Carter, "Federal Regulation of Pharmaceuticals," 251. The United States adopted user fees to expedite drug reviews and approvals in 1992 with the Prescription Drug User Fee Act (ibid., 251). The figure $40 million is from McMahon, "NAFTA and the Biotechnology Industry."

Chapter 4: Advocacy Redefined

1 On the government's renewal of the 1993 law, see Jillian Clare Cohen, "Canada and Brazil – Dealing with Tension between Ensuring Access to Medicines and Complying with Pharmaceutical Patent Standards: Is the Story the Same?" *Comparative Program on Health and Society*, Working Paper Series (2003/2004), and Patricia I. Carter, "Federal Regulation of Pharmaceuticals in the United States and Canada," *Loyola of Los Angeles International and Comparative Law Review* 21, 2 (1999).

2 Canada's Senate is the upper house of Parliament, its members appointed by the government of the day; once appointed, senators hold office until age seventy-five. On the two inquiries, see Roy J. Romanow, *Building on Values: The Future of Health Care in Canada; Final Report* (Ottawa: Commission on the Future of Health Care in Canada, 2002), and Michael Kirby and Marjory LeBreton, *The Health of Canadians: Study on the State of the Health Care System in Canada* (Ottawa: Senate of Canada: Standing Committee on Social Affairs, Science and Technology, 2002). In the latter six-volume report, see especially "Spending on Drugs in Canada," chap. 2, in vol. 2, *Current Trends and Future Challenges*, and "Expanding Coverage to Include Protection against Catastrophic Prescription Drug Costs," chap. 7, in vol. 6, *Final Report: Recommendations for Reform*.

3 On Canada's patchwork pharmaceutical policy, see Ingrid S. Sketris, Susan Bowles, and R. Manuel, "Canadian Public Policies and Practices Impacting Drug Prices, Utilization and Expenditures," *Journal of Pharmaceutical Finance, Economics and Policy* 12, 1 (2004): 23–54.

4 On the ICH, see John Abraham, "Pharmaceuticals, the State and the Global Harmonisation Process," *Australian Health Review* 28 (2004): 150–60; Joel Lexchin, "New Directions in Canadian Drug Regulation: Whose Interests Are Being Served?" in *Power, Politics and Pharmaceuticals*, ed. Orla O'Donovan and Kathy Glavanis-Grantham (Cork, Ireland: Cork University Press, 2008); and Joel Lexchin, *Who's Calling the Tune: Harmonization of Drug Regulation in Canada* (Ottawa: Canadian Centre for Policy Alternatives, 2011). On the reorganization of the ICH to become the International Council for Harmonisation, see the ICH website, accessed November 6, 2016, http://www.ich.org/about/organisational-changes.html.

5 Paul Martin, House of Commons *Debates*, February 21, 1994, p. 1713, and February 27, 1995, p. 1709, cited in Paul A. Pross, "An Unruly Messenger: Interest Groups and Bureaucracy in Canadian Democracy" (paper presented at the annual meeting of the Institute of Public Administration of Canada, Charlottetown, PEI, August 2006), 10.

6 Rachel Laforest, *Voluntary Sector Relations and the State: Building New Relations* (Vancouver: UBC Press, 2011).

7 See Paul A. Pross and Kernaghan R. Webb, "Embedded Regulation: Advocacy and the Federal Regulation of Public Interest Groups," in *Delicate Dances: Public Policy and the Nonprofit Sector*, ed. Kathy L. Brock (Montreal: McGill-Queen's University Press, 2003), 63–121, on the silencing effects of funding cuts, tightened rules on charitable status, and the use of project funding.

8 See Alexandra Dobrowolsky, "The Chrétien Legacy and Women: Changing Policy Priorities with Little Cause for Celebration," *Review of Constitutional Studies* 9 (2004): 171–98, on the Liberal government's adaptation of the SIS model.

9 Ibid. Dobrowolsky also provides a feminist analysis of Canada's SIS state.

10 See Kathy L. Brock, ed., *Delicate Dances: Public Policy and the Nonprofit Sector* (Montreal: McGill-Queen's University Press, 2003); Kathy L. Brock and Keith G. Banting, eds., *The Nonprofit Sector in Interesting Times: Case Studies in a Changing Sector* (Montreal: McGill-Queen's University Press, 2003); and Susan D. Phillips, "In Accordance: Canada's Voluntary Sector Accord from Idea to Implementation," in Brock, *Delicate Dances*, 17–51, on the Voluntary Sector Accord.

11 See Rachel Laforest, "Governance and the Voluntary Sector: Rethinking the Contours of Advocacy," *International Journal of Canadian Studies* 31 (2004): 185–203, on how funding programs retooled advocacy as nonconfrontational and professionalized. See Pross and Webb, "Embedded Regulation," on the seemingly unrelated federal regulations that constrained advocacy.

12 See Patricia Kelly, Charmaine Condy, and Sandra Harder, *Together to an End: The First Canada-US Breast Cancer Advocacy Conference, Final Report* (Burlington, ON: PISCES, 1997).

13 For a discussion of Open Space Technology, see Harrison Owen, ed., *Tales from Open Space* (Cabin John, MD: Abbott, 1995).

14 Kelly, Condy, and Harder, *Together to an End.*

15 The other twenty-one issues included genetic testing for cancer genes, the role of survivors on peer-review panels, correcting inaccurate information in media articles, breast cancer and chemical pesticides, diet, and First Nations issues.

16 Ibid., 56.

17 See Peter R. Elson, *High Ideals and Noble Intentions: Voluntary Sector-Government Relations in Canada* (Toronto: University of Toronto Press, 2011) on the changes to the tax law concerning registered charities.

18 Kelly Condy, and Harder, *Together to an End,* 57.

19 Ibid., 66.

20 Ibid.

21 Statements about Therapeutics Initiative's and Public Citizen's independence from corporations and government are available on their websites: "About Us," Therapeutics Initiative, accessed February 14, 2016, http://www.ti.ubc.ca/about-us/; "About Us," Public Citizen, accessed February 14, 2016, http://www.citizen.org/Page.aspx?pid=2306.

22 Following the publication of *Unsafe at Any Speed* (New York: Grossman, 1965), Nader founded the organization Public Citizen to investigate corporate and government corruption in environmental, health, and consumer product safety.

23 Kelly, Condy, and Harder, *Together to an End,* 69–70.

24 Ibid., 69, emphasis added.

25 Ibid., 70.

26 Rosanna Baraldi, "Drug Company Money: To Accept or Not to Accept? Is That the Question?" *DES Action Canada Newsletter* 51 (1997), accessed November 7, 2016, http://www.descanada.ca/anglais/anglais.html. The summary description of the panel is based on this article.

27 Baraldi, "Drug Company Money."

28 Anne Rochon Ford, *A Different Prescription: Considerations for Women's Health Groups Contemplating Funding from the Pharmaceutical Industry* (Toronto: Institute for Feminist Legal Studies at Osgoode Hall, York University, 1998).

29 John Martens, in an interview with Barbara Mintzes, cited in Barbara Mintzes, *Blurring the Boundaries: New Trends in Drug Promotion* (Amsterdam: HAI-Europe, 1998), 23.

30 Eric G. Rule and Hayley Chapman, "Alliances between Disease-Specific Non-profit Organisations and Private-Sector Pharmaceutical Companies" (paper presented by PricewaterhouseCoopers, Toronto, April 7, 1999).

31 Fred Mills, *Patient Groups and the Global Pharmaceutical Industry: The Growing Importance of Working Directly with the Consumer* (London: Urch, 2000).

32 Karen L. Miller, "Patient Advocacy: Leveraging the Newest Dimension of Health Care Public Relations" (paper presented to the Public Relations World Conference, Public Relations Society of America, Chicago, October 24, 2000).

33 Joanna Breitstein, "For Love of the Game," *Pharmaceutical Executive* 21, 6 (2001), 48–55 onward.

34 Rule and Chapman, "Alliances," 21.

35 Rule and Chapman, "Alliances"; Mills, *Patient Groups and the Global Pharmaceutical Industry;* and Breitstein, "For Love of the Game," reference the diversity of diseases that patient organizations represent; Mills documents the range of countries in which patient groups engage in political advocacy.

36 Breitstein, "For Love of the Game," 55.

37 Rule and Chapman, "Alliances," 9.

38 Miller, "Patient Advocacy," slide 38.

39 Rule and Chapman, "Alliances."

40 Liz Whamond and Durhane Wong-Reiger, "[PD08] NGO and Industry Partnerships: Lessons Learned" (paper presented at the eighth Cochrane Colloquium, Capetown, October 25–29, 2000).

41 Mills, *Patient Groups and the Global Pharmaceutical Industry*, 31.

42 Ibid., 31.

43 Ibid., 69.

44 Ibid., 70–71, quotation at p. 71.

Chapter 5: The Movement Fractures over Pharma Funding

1 Published accounts of amounts awarded from pharmaceutical companies to Canadian groups in this era include that of a $100,000 grant to a breast cancer group in 2000 (Donna Nebenzahl, "Do Drug Firms Call the Tune?" *Montreal Gazette*, April 1, 2003), 70 percent of a national colorectal cancer organization's $500,000 budget in 2000, and $1.8 million of a national arthritis group's $30 million budget in 2000 (André Picard, "Charities 'Thank God' for Drug Firms' Money," *Globe and Mail*, January 4, 2001).

2 AstraZeneca makes the breast cancer treatments Nolvadex D (tamoxifen citrate) and Arimidex.

3 Annmarie Mol, *The Logic of Care: Health and the Problem of Patient Choice* (London: Routledge, 2008).

4 Between 1990 and the present, Johnson & Johnson has reorganized its biotech subsidiary a number of times. The company established Ortho Biotech in 1990; it became Centocor Ortho Biotech in a 2008 merger, and in 2011, Janssen Biotech. For a detailed timeline, see the Janssen biotech website, accessed December 11, 2016, https://www.janssenbiotech.com/company/history.

5 The policy is online at http://bcam.qc.ca/policy (accessed December 11, 2016).

6 From the group's board minutes, December 2001.

7 From the group's board minutes, February 2002. For an account of Health Canada's gradual loosening of its DTCA prohibition and industry strategies to expand DTCA, see Joel Lexchin, *Private Profits vs. Public Policy: The Pharmaceutical Industry and the Canadian State* (Toronto: University of Toronto Press, 2016), 103–10.

8 The bulletin was published by one of five regional "information exchange" projects and was initially funded by the Canadian Breast Cancer Initiative; like the breast cancer groups themselves, these projects were advised to become self-sufficient.

9 On how civil society organizations in Quebec resisted neoliberal pressures to become contract service providers, see Deena White, "Interest Representation and Organisation in Civil Society: Ontario and Quebec Compared," *British Journal of Canadian Studies* 25 (2012): 199–229.

10 The quotation is from Patricia Kelly, Charmaine Condy, and Sandra Harder, *Together to an End: The First Canada-US Breast Cancer Advocacy Conference, Final Report* (Burlington, ON: PISCES, 1997), 70.

11 The federal government restricts the advocacy activities of registered charities through the Canada Revenue Agency, which defines what activities count as advocacy and how much of the organization's annual revenues can be spent on these activities. Peter Elson provides a detailed analysis of how these definitions, spelled out in policy circulars, changed under different governments from 1978 to 2003: Peter R. Elson, "Where Is the Voice of Canada's Voluntary Sector?" *Canadian Review of Social Policy* 60/61 (2007/2008): 1–20. Throughout the 1990s and up to 2003, all charities were governed by a "10 percent rule" that limited their advocacy to 10 percent of resources. Pat Kelly puts the CACC's annual budget in its early years at $190,000, all of which could be spent on advocacy; see Patricia Kelly, "Begging Your Pardon: Exploring the Impacts of Pharmaceutical Industry Funding of Non-profit Organizations," 2002, 4–5. Elson describes new guidelines, introduced in 2003, that relaxed the restrictions for smaller charities; those with an annual income less than $50,000 could spend up to 20 percent on political activities; those with revenues the previous year between $50,000 and $100,000 had a limit of 15 percent; and for those with a previous year income between $100,000 and $200,000, the limit was 12 percent. The 10 percent rule still applied to those with revenues over $200,000.

12 "New Chemotherapy Regimen out of Reach for Canadian Women," *Cancer Care in Canada*, Fall 2000, 22; see also "What's Keeping New Chemotherapy Regimen Out of Reach for Canadian Women with Breast Cancer?" *Cancer Advocacy Coalition*, September 2000, accessed December 12, 2016, http://www.canceradvocacy.ca/pages/breast-cancer.htm.

13 Ibid.

14 Adjuvant Therapy for Breast Cancer, *National Institutes of Health Consensus Development Conference Statement*, 17, 4 (November 2000): 1–23, accessed April 19, 2015, http://consensus.nih.gov/2000/2000AdjuvantTherapyBreastCancer114html.htm.

15 Barron H. Lerner, *The Breast Cancer Wars: Hope, Fear, and the Pursuit of a Cure in Twentieth-Century America* (New York: Oxford University Press, 2001), 254–55.

16 Murtuza M. Rampurwala, Gabrielle B. Rocque, and Mark E. Burkard, "Update on Adjuvant Chemotherapy for Early Breast Cancer," *Breast Cancer: Basic and Clinical Research* 8 (2014): 125–33.

17 Margaret A. Somerville, "Do We Have a Legal Right to the Best Cancer Treatments?" *Cancer Care in Canada*, Fall 2000, 6. The article summarized a few key points developed in a longer article, Margaret A. Somerville, "The Ethics and Law of Access to New Cancer Treatments," *Current Oncology* 6, 3 (1999), 161–74.

18 Canadian Medical Association, *CMA Code of Ethics*, updated 2004, reviewed March 2015, accessed February 14, 2015, http://policybase.cma.ca/dbtw-wpd/PolicyPDF/PD04-06.pdf.

19 "The Stein Case," *Cancer Care in Canada*, Fall 2000, 6.

20 Jennifer Shapiro, "Winning Strategies for Cancer Care: A Look at BC's Integrated Approach," *Cancer Care in Canada*, Fall 2000, 20–21.

21 Lisa Priest, *Operating in the Dark: The Accountability Crisis in Canada's Healthcare System* (Toronto: Doubleday, 1998), recommends greater public accountability as a way to reduce physician errors and improve hospital performance. Priest's newspaper articles calling for more rapid and widespread access to novel cancer drugs include "Pioneer Wouldn't Give Up on Breast Cancer Drug," *Globe and Mail*, October 21, 2005; "Fighting Cancer in a Bureaucratic Catch-22," *Globe and Mail*, December 18, 2009; "Dying Woman Wins Access to Cancer Drug Combination," *Globe and Mail*, January 29, 2011; "Health Minister Reaches Out to Cancer Patient Refused Herceptin," *Globe and Mail*, March 18, 2011; "Breast-Cancer Patient Gets Access to Costly Treatment," *Globe and Mail*, April 12, 2011; and "Dying Woman Takes Out Line of Credit to Pay for Herceptin," *Globe and Mail*, April 28, 2011.

22 See the website of the North American Association of Cancer Registries, NAACCR, accessed November 15, 2016, http://www.naaccr.org; limited NAACCR records from 2000 are available via the Internet Archive, https://web.archive.org/web/20000819085242/http://www.naaccr.org/Stats/index.html.

23 For the CACC's 2000 report card, see the organization's online archive, accessed November 15, 2016, http://www.canceradvocacy.ca/2000.htm. News coverage of the CACC's report card includes Helen Branswell, "Survival Rates Higher for US Cancer Patients, Group Says," *Kitchener-Waterloo Record*, September 26, 2000; Steve Buist, "Cancer Care Report Card Doesn't Tell the Whole Truth," *Hamilton Spectator*, September 26, 2000; Brad Evenson, "Toll from Cancer Higher Than in US: Report; Investigation Demanded; British Columbia and Alberta Defy the Trend," *National Post*, September 25, 2000; Krista Foss, "Cancer Report Card Gives B.C. High Marks: Death Rates Low in West, High in East; Is the Reason Good Care or Cleaner Lifestyle?" *Globe and Mail*, September 26, 2000; and Susan Murray, "Cancer Report Card Sparks Dispute," *Winnipeg Free Press*, September 26, 2000.

24 Foss, "Cancer Report Card Gives B.C. High Marks," cites the prevalence of Mormons in Utah as the reason for that state's low incidence and death rates. Many studies have documented the low cancer incidence among Utah's Mormon population; see, for example, Ray M. Merrill and Joseph L. Lyon, "Cancer Incidence among Mormons and Non-Mormons in Utah (United States) 1995–1999," *Preventive Medicine* 40, 5 (2005): 535–41.

25 See Buist, "Cancer Care Report Card," and Murray, "Report Card Sparks Dispute," for claims that cancer survival rates in Canada's are better than comparable US rates. The articles by Buist and Murray, as well as by Branswell, "Survival Rates Higher," all include critical assessments of the group's use of survival data.

26 For a summary of this session, titled "How Can We Reduce Breast Cancer Mortality in the Next Ten Years?" see Kelly, Condy, and Harder, *Together to an End*: 69–70.

27 See Lou Fintor, "Canada-US Mortality Comparison Highlights Analytical Pitfalls," *JNCI* 93, 2 (2001): 89–92, and Lou Fintor, "International Data Comparisons: Caveat Emptor," *JNCI* 93, 2 (2001): 90.

28 See Fintor, "Canada-US Mortality Comparisons"; the quotation from Pat Kelly is at p. 92.

29 Erica Johnson, "Drug Marketing: Promoting Drugs through Patient Advocacy Groups," CBC Television, *Marketplace*, televised November 14, 2000, accessed November 12, 2016, http://www.cbc.ca/consumers/market/files/health/drugmarketing, via the Internet Archive (https://www.archive.org).

30 The book Pat refers to is Robert Bazell, *Her2: The Making of Herceptin, a Revolutionary Treatment for Breast Cancer* (New York: Random House, 1998).

31 Personal communication, Pat Kelly, October 31, 2016.

32 Charlotte Gray, "There's a *New* Sheriff at Tunney's Pasture," *Canadian Medical Association Journal* 161, 4 (August 24, 1999): 426–27; quotation at ibid., p. 427.

33 Lexchin, *Private Profits*, 24–31, quotation at p. 30.

34 See Steven Epstein, *Impure Science: AIDS, Activism, and the Politics of Knowledge* (Berkeley: University of California Press, 1996), 327, on the shift in advocacy goals within the AIDS movement from rapid access to promoting "good science" that will eventually produce a cure or therapy.

35 Sham Mailankody and Vinay Prasad, "Overall Survival in Cancer Drug Trials as a New Surrogate Endpoint for Overall Survival in the Real World," *JAMA Oncology* (2016): doi: 10.1001/jamaoncol.2016.5296.

36 For an overview of cytotoxic chemotherapy's limited benefits for most solid cancers, including breast cancer, see Peter H. Wise, "Cancer Drugs, Survival and Ethics," *BMJ* 355 (2016), i5792. He concludes that cancer drugs for breast and other common cancers increase five-year survival by less than 2.5%, an overall benefit of around three months, with expensive new drugs rarely better than old ones; risk of side effects is high, including the risk of dying from treatment; and patients are poorly informed of these limitations. Graeme Morgan and colleagues, in a 2004 assessment of chemotherapy's contribution to five-year survival in adult cancers, conclude that breast cancer is "the best example of the 'overselling' of chemotherapy." They give the survival benefit after five years for breast cancer patients as a range, from 2.8% to 6.8%, depending on the woman's age and nodal status (Graeme Morgan, Robyn Ward, and Michael Barton, "The Contribution of Cytotoxic Chemotherapies to 5-Year Survival in Adult Malignancies," *Clinical Oncology* 16 [2004]: 549–60; quotation at p. 557). In clinical trials, premenopausal women who took tamoxifen for five years had a 6.8 percent reduction in death after ten years; for postmenopausal women, the figure was an 8.2 percent reduction in death after ten years, with the benefit varying depending on the type of breast cancer the woman had and her risk of mortality; see Early Breast Cancer Trialists' Cooperative Group, "Effects of Chemotherapy and Hormonal Therapy for Early Breast Cancer on Recurrence and 15-Year Survival: An Overview of the Randomized Trials," *Lancet*, 2005: 1687–717. In general, with tamoxifen, says Susan Love, the higher the risk, the higher the benefit; thus, women whose risk is low to begin with might expect only a 1 or 2 percent reduction in mortality risk, and might decide that the side effects are not worth the potential for gain; Susan Love, *Dr. Susan Love's Breast Book*, 5th ed. (Boston: Da Capo, 2010), 354.

37 Atul Gawande, *Being Mortal: Medicine and What Matters in the End* (Toronto: Doubleday Canada, 2014), 177–78. For the original study findings, see Jennifer S. Temel et al., "Early Palliative Care for Patients with Metastatic Non-Small-Cell Lung Cancer," *New England Journal of Medicine* 363 (2010): 733–42; median survival among patients receiving early palliative care integrated with standard care was 11.6 months, versus 8.9 months for those who received standard oncological care only.

38 Ibid., 171–72.

39 Alan S. Coates and John R. Simes, "Patient Assessment of Adjuvant Treatment on Operable Breast Cancer," in *Introducing New Treatments for Cancer: Practical, Ethical and Legal Problems,* ed. Christopher John Williams (Chichester, West Sussex: John Wiley & Sons, 1992), 447–58; Peter M. Ravdin, I.A. Siminoff, and J.A. Harvey, "Survey of Breast Cancer Patients Concerning Their Knowledge and Expectations of Adjuvant Therapy, *Journal of Clinical Oncology* 16, 2 (1998): 515–21; Vlatka M. Duric and Martin R. Stockler, "Patients Preferences for Adjuvant Chemotherapy in Breast Cancer," *Lancet Oncology* 2 (2001): 691–97; and Vlatka M. Duric et al., "Patients' Preferences for Adjuvant Chemotherapy in Early Breast Cancer: What Makes AC and CMF Worthwhile Now?" *Annals of Oncology* 16, 11 (2005): 1786–94.

40 Duric et al., "Patients' Preferences for Adjuvant Chemotherapy," 1791.

Chapter 6: Pharma Funding as the New Norm

1 Joanna Breitstein, "Partnerships and Perspectives," *Pharmaceutical Executive* 22, 1 (2002): 68.

2 Ibid.

3 See also Teri P. Cox, "Forging Alliances: Advocacy Partners," *Pharmaceutical Executive,* suppl. PR Power (September 2002): 8–13.

4 For this quotation and the two that follow, see Cohn & Wolfe, "Partnership Report" (Cohn & Wolfe: Toronto, 2003), 1.

5 All quotations are from Cohn & Wolfe, "Partnership Report": the shift from chequebook philanthropy, 11–12; reciprocal partnerships, 10; multilayered, multifaceted relationships, 15–17; the value of credibility for nonprofits, 37, 25; meaningful metrics, 19–20.

6 See, for example, Walter W. Powell and Kaisa Snellman, "The Knowledge Economy," *Annual Review of Sociology* 30 (2004), 199–220.

7 Daniel Vasella and Kathy Bloomgarden, "Courage under Fire," *Pharmaceutical Executive* 23, 4 (2003): 14. Vasella is the chairman and CEO of Novartis; Bloomgarden is CEO of the PR firm Ruder Finn.

8 Joanna Breitstein, "Patient Advocacy: For Love of the Game." *Pharmaceutical Executive* 22, 6 (2001), 48–55.

9 Best Practices, *Patient Advocacy & Professional Organizations: Building Effective Relationships* (Chapel Hill, NC: Best Practices, LLC, 2004). I cite the company's online promotional material rather than the booklet itself because the sixty-page guide boasts a price tag of US$4,950 and was beyond my research budget. All quotations pertaining to Best Practices, LLC are from the company's website, accessed November 20, 2016, http://www.best-in-class.com/bestp/domrep.nsf/products/patient

-advocacy-professional-organizations-building-effective-relationships!Open Document.

10 On the Vioxx scandal, see Jeanne Lenzer, "FDA Advisors Warn: COX 2 Inhibitors Increase Risk of Heart Attack and Stroke," *BMJ* 330 (2005): 440; Joseph S. Ross, David Madigan, Kevin P. Hill, David S. Egilman, Yongfei Wang, and Harlan M. Krumholz, "Pooled Analysis of Rofecoxib Placebo-Controlled Clinical Trial Data: Lessons for Post-market Pharmaceutical Safety Surveillance," *Archives of Internal Medicine* 169 (2009): 1976–85; and Steven Woloshin and Lisa M. Schwartz, "Bringing the FDA's Information to Market: Comment on 'Pooled Analysis of Rofecoxib Placebo-Controlled Clinical Trial Data,'" *Archives of Internal Medicine* 169 (2009): 1985–87.

11 See Patricia Kelly, "Begging Your Pardon: Exploring the Impacts of Pharmaceutical Industry Funding of Non-profit Organizations" (MA thesis, Royal Roads University, Colwood, British Columbia, 2002).

12 Deborah Tannen, *The Argument Culture: Moving from Debate to Dialogue* (New York: Random House, 1998).

13 This quotation is from Kelly, "Begging Your Pardon," 40; the preceding three are from ibid., p. 74.

14 Ibid., 6–7.

15 Ibid., 101.

16 Ibid., 94.

17 Ibid., 110.

18 Peter Dauvergne and Genevieve LeBaron, *P®otest Inc.: The Corporatization of Activism* (Cambridge, UK: Polity, 2014). A Gramscian analysis is based on the work of Italian political theorist Antonio Gramsci; see ibid., 21.

19 Kelly, "Begging Your Pardon," 100; the following quotation is at p. 110.

20 Ibid., 122.

21 CBCN, "2001 Guidelines for Corporate Partnerships," on file with author; see also http://cbcn.ca/en/our-approach. For the CCAN Code of Conduct Governing Corporate Funding, see http://www.canceradvocacy.ca/.

22 CCAN Code of Conduct, ibid., Section 2, Policies for CCAN Member Organization, 2.2, p. 4.

23 The guidelines for working with patient groups came out under the banner of Rx&D and appear to be in effect despite the organization's 2015 rebranding as Innovative Medicines Canada. *Rx&D Guidelines for Transparency in Stakeholder Funding* has seven principles and eight guidelines on stakeholder relations; see https://www.cag-acg.org/images/about/rxandd_2009.pdf (accessed November 20, 2016). An accompanying "interpretation document" provides the rationale for each of the guidelines and gives an example of how the guideline might be applied. Thus, the first guideline is that projects undertaken with stakeholders should not be used to promote specific

medicines; the rationale is that the company should help maintain the credibility of a partner organization and not be seen as circumventing direct-to-consumer advertising rules. The example provided posits a company that wants its new product placed on a provincial formulary; rather than a project that will secure reimbursement just for the company's product, the company should work with the stakeholder to design a project that will seek reimbursement for all appropriate medications in the class. A third document, *Rx&D Guidelines for Stakeholder Funding – Qs & As*, lists nine questions about the guidelines, such as whether "in-kind" contributions count as funding (they do). See http://sharingnetwork.canadapharma.org/CM Files/Commitment_to_Ethics/WithStakeholders/Transparency%20Guidelines/ Transparency_Guidelines-Qs_and_As.pdf.

24 *Rx&D Guidelines, Qs & As* (2009), see Q & A no. 5.

25 See *Rx&D Guidelines* (2009), preamble to the seven principles.

26 The explanation for the conditional wording in the section about relationships with patient groups is based on a March 13, 2013, telephone communication with Chrisoula Nikidis of Rx&D.

27 For an example of the logic model, see Quality Improvement and Innovation Partnership, *Logic Model Resource Guide* (Mississauga, ON: Ontario Ministry of Health and Long Term Care), January 2010, amended December 2010, http://www. hqontario.ca/portals/0/Documents/qi/qi-rg-logic-model-1012-en.pdf.

28 For an ethnographic case study of OCAPI, see Mavis Jones and Janice E. Graham, "Multiple Institutional Rationalities in the Regulation of Health Technologies: An Ethnographic Examination," *Science and Public Policy* 36, 6 (2009): 445–55.

29 See Strategy 4 of this document, *Serving Canadians – Now and into the Future: Strategic Plan 2004–07 for Health Canada's Health Products and Food Branch* (Ottawa: Health Canada, 2004): 15–17, available via the Internet Archive, https://web.archive. org/web/20050527191354/http://www.hc-sc.gc.ca/hpfb-dgpsa/strat_plan_e.pdf.

30 For an iteration of the information form dated April 27, 2010, see http://hc-sc.gc.ca/ ahc-asc/pubs/cons-pub/vsi_pvi_form2010-eng.php. The quotation "recognize the importance ..." is from a preamble (dated 2008) to the same form that stresses the importance of openness and transparency but nonetheless underlines that completing the form is wholly voluntary. An archived Health Canada web page for a consultation on dietary sodium reduction includes both the preamble and the *Voluntary Statement of Information Form for the Public Consultation on Dietary Sodium Reduction*, http://www.hc-sc.gc.ca/fn-an/consult/sodium/vsi-fdv-eng.php (both web pages accessed November 21, 2016).

31 Canada, *DRAFT HPFB Policy on Voluntary Statement of Information for Public Involvement* (Ottawa: Office of Consumer and Public Involvement, Health Products and Food Branch, August 20, 2004), 3, note 1 (author's files).

32 On the opposition of civil society groups to the free trade agreements, see Miriam Catherine Smith, *A Civil Society? Collective Actors in Canadian Political Life* (Peterborough, ON: Broadview Press, 2005), 76–78.

33 Tom Flanagan, *Harper's Team: Behind the Scenes in the Conservative Rise to Power* (Montreal: McGill-Queen's University Press, 2007), 264.

34 Flanagan, in an interview with Kathleen Petty on CBC Radio's *The House* (September 22, 2007).

35 On the Progressive Conservative Party's support of socially progressive causes, see Jared J. Wesley, "The Collective Center: Social Democracy and Red Tory Politics in Manitoba" (paper presented at the annual meeting of the Canadian Political Science Association, York University, Toronto, June 2, 2006).

36 Canada, House of Commons, Standing Committee on the Status of Women, *The Impacts of Funding and Program Changes at Status of Women Canada*, 1st Sess., 39th Parl., May 2007.

37 For the effect on the CAC of its loss of core government funding, see John Church and Wendy Armstrong, "Health Consumers in Canada: Swimming against a Neo-liberal Tide," in *Democratizing Health: Consumer Groups in the Health Policy Process*, ed. Hans Löfgren, Evelyne de Leeuw, and Michael Leahy (Northampton, MA: Edward Elgar, 2011), 193–207.

38 Janice E. Graham, "Smart Regulation: Will the Government's Strategy Work?" *Canadian Medical Association Journal* 173 (2005): 1469–70.

39 Treasury Board of Canada Secretariat, *Summary Report of the Public Workshops on the Draft Government Directive on Regulating* (Ottawa: Treasury Board of Canada Secretariat, 2007); emphasis in original.

40 Ibid. See also Gilles Bibeau, Janice E. Graham, and Usher Fleising, "Bioscience and Biotechnology under Ethnographic Surveillance: Where Do Canadian Medical Anthropologists Stand?" in *Medical Anthropology: Regional Perspectives and Shared Concerns*, ed. Francine Saillant and Serge Genest (London: Blackwell, 2006), 3–22, for scholarly perspectives on the proposals.

41 Health Canada, *Blueprint for Renewal II: Modernizing Canada's Drug Regulatory System for Health Products and Food* (Ottawa: Government of Canada, Health Products and Food Branch, Health Canada, 2007).

42 On the likely impact of progressive licensing on Canada's drug review times, transparency, and accountability, see James M. Wright, "Progressive Drug Licensing: An Opportunity to Achieve Transparency and Accountability?" *Canadian Medical Association Journal* 176 (2007): 1848–49; Neil Yeates, David K. Lee, and Maurica Maher, "Health Canada's Progressive Licensing Framework," *Canadian Medical Association Journal* 176 (2007): 1845–47; and Joel Lexchin, *Private Profits vs. Public*

Policy: The Pharmaceutical Industry and the Canadian State (Toronto: University of Toronto Press, 2016), 130–34.

43 Bonnie Brown, *Opening the Medicine Cabinet: First Report on Health Aspects of Prescription Drugs* (Ottawa: Standing Committee on Health, House of Commons, Government of Canada, 2004).

44 Robert G. Evans, "The Unsustainability Myth: Don't Believe Claims that Medicare Is Becoming Unaffordable," *The Monitor* (CCPA), July 1, 2010.

45 Pat Armstrong and Hugh Armstrong, *Health Care* (Halifax: Fernwood, 2016), 20.

46 "What Is the Health Accord?" *Canadian Health Coalition*, accessed April 25, 2015, http://healthcoalition.ca/what-is-the-health-accord/.

47 On concerns about the high cost of new cancer drugs to the system in Canada, see Wayne Kondro and Barbara Sibbald, "Patient Demand and Politics Push Herceptin Forward," *Canadian Medical Association Journal* 173 (2005): 347–48; Lauren Vogel, "Pan-Canadian Review of Cancer Drugs Will Not Be Binding on Provinces," *Canadian Medical Association Journal* 182, 9 (2010): 887–88; and Erin Walkinshaw, "National Assessment of Cancer Drugs Commences," *Canadian Medical Association Journal* 183 (2011): 109. On costs in the United States, see Debra Sherman, "Cancer Care Too Much for U.S Patients," *Globe and Mail*, June 6, 2011; Thomas J. Smith and Bruce E. Hillner, "Bending the Cost Curve in Cancer Care," *New England Journal of Medicine* 364 (2011): 2060–65; Andrew Pollack, "New Drugs Fight Prostate Cancer, but at High Cost," *New York Times*, June 27, 2011; "Extremely Expensive Cancer Drugs" (editorial), *New York Times*, July 6, 2011; and Donald W. Light and Hagop M. Kantarjian, "Market Spiral Pricing of Cancer Drugs," *Cancer* 119 (2013): 3900–02. For critical assessments on why the price tags on new drugs are so high and what can be done, see Henry Mintzberg, "Patent Nonsense: Evidence Tells of an Industry out of Social Control," *Canadian Medical Association Journal* 175, 4 (2006), 374–76, and Aaron S. Kesselheim, Jerry Avorn, and Ameet Sarpatwari, "The High Cost of Prescription Drugs in the United States: Origins and Prospects for Reform," *Journal of the American Medical Association* 316, 8 (2016): 858–71.

48 Examples of critical texts on conflicts of interest include Wendy Armstrong, "Public Engagement: Wherefore Art Thou? A View from the Trenches," Consumers' Association of Canada (Alberta) and PharmaWatch (paper presented at the UBC Centre for Health Services and Policy Research annual conference, Vancouver, February 22, 2007); Sharon Batt, "Who Pays the Piper? Industry Funding of Patients' Groups," in *The Push to Prescribe: Women and Canadian Drug Policy*, ed. Anne Rochon Ford and Diane Saibil (Toronto: Women's Press, 2010), 67–89; and Barbara Mintzes, "Should Patient Groups Accept Money from Drug Companies? No," *BMJ* 334 (2007): 935.

49   Maren Klawiter, *The Biopolitics of Breast Cancer: Changing Politics of Disease and Activism* (Minneapolis: University of Minnesota Press, 2008); Barbara Ley, *From Pink to Green: Disease Prevention and the Environmental Breast Cancer Movement* (New Brunswick, NJ: Rutgers University Press, 2009); and Margaret Woodell, "Codes, Identities and Pathologies in the Construction of Tamoxifen as a Chemoprophylactic for Breast Cancer Risk Reduction in Healthy Women at High Risk" (PhD diss., Rensselaer Polytechnic Institute, 2004), all include discussions of the Canada-US coalition.

50   Brown, *Opening the Medicine Cabinet.*

51   In addition to the loss of the popular website administrator, the rise of Facebook and a proliferation of online sites for cancer patients took a toll on the online community, which was no longer the only game in town.

52   See Cohn & Wolfe, "Partnership Report," 1–3, 9–20, on the shift in private sector funding strategies.

53   For discussions of neoliberalism and civil society and voluntary sector groups in Canada, see Miriam Smith, *A Civil Society?* and Rachel Laforest, "Rerouting Political Representation: Is Canada's Social Infrastructure in Crisis?" *British Journal of Canadian Studies* 25, 2 (2012): 181–97.

Chapter 7: Advocacy Groups and the Continuing Struggle over the Pharma-Funding Question

1   Kathleen Sharp, *Blood Feud: The Man Who Blew the Whistle on One of the Deadliest Prescription Drugs Ever* (New York: Dutton, 2011), documents the rivalry between the two companies. Eprex and Epogen are biosimilar products (both are epoetin alfa); although not identical, the differences in formulation have no clinical impact (Michael Lissy, Marité Ode, and Karsten Roth, "Comparison of the Pharmacokinetic and Pharmacodynamic Profiles of One US-Marketed and Two European-Marketed Epoetin Alfas: A Randomized Prospective Study," *Drugs in R&D* 11 [2011]: 61–75). The other ESAs on the market are Procrit, which Johnson & Johnson sold for the HIV market, and Aranesp, which Amgen sold for the dialysis market (Fadlo R. Khuri, "Weighing the Hazards of Erythropoiesis Stimulation in Patients with Cancer," *New England Journal of Medicine* 356 [2007]: 2445–48).

2   See Alex Berenson and Andrew Pollack, "Doctors Reap Millions for Anemia Drugs," *New York Times*, May 9, 2007, A1, and Otis Webb Brawley, *How We Do Harm: A Doctor Breaks Ranks about Being Sick in America*, with Paul Goldberg (New York: St. Martin's Press, 2012), 73, on the money at stake in EPO sales. See Sharp, *Blood Feud*, on the corporate feud between Amgen and Johnson & Johnson.

3   On cycling deaths linked to EPO, see Laurence M. Fisher, "Stamina-Building Drug Linked to Athletes' Deaths," *New York Times*, May 18, 1991. See Timothy D. Noakes,

"Tainted Glory – Doping and Athletic Performance," *New England Journal of Medicine* 351 (2004): 847–49, for a medical discussion of EPO as a performance-enhancing substance and its effects on health.

4 Brawley, *How We Do Harm*, 76–77.

5 Ibid.

6 Ibid.

7 Nicole Casadevall et al., "Pure Red-Cell Aplasia and Antierythropoietin Antibodies in Patients Treated with Recombinant Erythropoietin," *New England Journal of Medicine* 346 (2002): 469–75. For a news account of the study, see Andrew Pollack, "Rebellious Bodies Dim the Glow of 'Natural' Biotech Drugs," *New York Times*, July 30, 2002.

8 See Khuri, "Weighing the Hazards," on early concern about ESAs promoting tumour growth.

9 Michael Henke et al., "Erythropoietin to Treat Head and Neck Cancer Patients with Anaemia Undergoing Radiotherapy: Randomised, Double-Blind, Placebo-Controlled Trial," *Lancet* 362, 9392 (2007): 1255–60.

10 Brian Leyland-Jones et al., "Maintaining Normal Hemoglobin Levels with Epoetin Alfa in Mainly Nonanemic Patients with Metastatic Breast Cancer Receiving First-Line Chemotherapy: A Survival Study," *Journal of Clinical Oncology* 23 (2005): 5960–72.

11 Khuri, "Weighing the Hazards," discusses the risks of ESAs for patients with cancer, including the additional trials.

12 Ibid., 2445; see also Robert Steinbrook, "Erythropoietin, the FDA, and Oncology," *New England Journal of Medicine* 356, 24 (2007): 2448–51.

13 Brawley, *How We Do Harm*, 77–78, 72; examples of ads are also from there. See also Barbara Mintzes, Steve Morgan, and James M. Wright, "Twelve Years' Experience with Direct-to-Consumer Advertising in Canada: A Cautionary Tale," *PLoS One* 4 (2009): e5699. The ad campaign for Procrit was one of three advertising campaigns discussed on May 8, 2008, at a Congressional Hearing of the US House Committee on Energy and Commerce. The transcript of this hearing, titled "Direct-to-Consumer Advertising: Marketing, Education, or Deception?" is archived at http://web.archive.org/web/20150531014526/https://house.resource.org/110/org.c-span.205243-1.raw.txt (accessed November 23, 2016).

14 Brawley, *How We Do Harm*, 77.

15 Khuri, "Weighing the Hazards," 2448.

16 Berenson and Pollack, "Doctors Reap Millions," describe the rebate system to physicians.

17 Brawley, *How We Do Harm*, 96.

18 For press releases from the FDA and Health Canada (with Amgen and Janssen-Ortho), see Food and Drug Administration (FDA), "FDA Strengthens Boxed Warnings,

Approves Other Safety Labeling Changes for Erythropoiesis-Stimulating Agents (ESAs)," press release, Washington, DC (2007), and Health Canada, Amgen, and Janssen-Ortho, "Health Canada Endorsed Important Safety Information on Erythropoiesis-Stimulating Agents (ESAs): Aranesp (Darbepoetin Alfa) and Eprex (Epoetin Alfa); 'Dear Health Care Professional' Letter from Amgen and Janssen-Ortho: Health Canada/Amgen/Janssen-Ortho," 2007, accessed April 11, 2017, https://www.janssen.com/canada/sites/www_janssen_com_canada/files/product/pdf/en_eprex_ddl_04162007.pdf.

19 On the risks of blood transfusions in Canada under the current system, see Noni E. MacDonald, Sheila F. O'Brien, Gilles Delage and Canadian Pediatric Society, Infectious Diseases and Immunization Committee, "Transfusion and Risk of Infection in Canada: Update 2012," *Pediatric Child Health* 17, 10 (2012): e102–e111.

20 Brawley, *How We Do Harm*, 96–97.

21 For the 1988 overview, see Early Breast Cancer Trialists' Collaborative Group, "Effects of Adjuvant Tamoxifen and of Cytotoxic Therapy on Mortality in Early Breast Cancer: An Overview of 61 Randomized Trials among 28,896 Women," *New England Journal of Medicine* 319 (1988): 1681–92.

22 Joseph Ragaz and Andrew Coldman, "Survival Impact of Adjuvant Tamoxifen on Competing Causes of Mortality in Breast Cancer Survivors, with Analysis of Mortality from Contralateral Breast Cancer, Cardiovascular Events, Endometrial Cancer, and Thromboembolic Episodes," *Journal of Clinical Oncology* 16 (1998): 2018–24.

23 After fifteen years' follow-up, average improvement in survival is 6.8 percent for premenopausal women and 8.2 percent for postmenopausal women; see Early Breast Cancer Trialists' Collaborative Group, "Effects of Chemotherapy and Hormonal Therapy for Early Breast Cancer on Recurrence and 15-Year Survival: An Overview of the Randomised Trials," *Lancet* 365 (2005): 1687–717.

24 Christina Davies et al., "Long-Term Effects of Continuing Adjuvant Tamoxifen to 10 Years Versus Stopping at 5 Years After Diagnosis of Oestrogen Receptor–Positive Breast Cancer: ATLAS, a Randomised Trial," *Lancet* 381 (2013): 805–16.

25 For early clinical trial results for Arimidex, see Michael Baum, Aman U. Budzar, Jack Cuzick, John Forbes, Joan H. Houghton, Jan G. Klijn, Tarek Sahmoud, and ATAC Trialists' Group, "Anastrozole Alone or in Combination with Tamoxifen versus Tamoxifen Alone for Adjuvant Treatment of Postmenopausal Women with Early Breast Cancer: First Results of the ATAC Randomised Trial," *Lancet* 360 (2002): 1520; for Femara, see Paul E. Goss et al., "A Randomized Trial of Letrozole in Postmenopausal Women After Five Years of Tamoxifen Therapy for Early-Stage Breast Cancer," *New England Journal of Medicine* 349 (2003): 1793–1802, updated in Paul E. Goss, James N. Ingle, Silvana Martino, et al., "Randomized Trial of Letrozole Following Tamoxifen

as Extended Adjuvant Therapy in Receptor-Positive Breast Cancer: Updated Findings from NCIC CTG MA.17," *Journal of the National Cancer Institute* 97 (2005): 1262–71; for Aromasin, see R. Charles Coombes et al., "A Randomized Trial of Exemestane after Two to Three Years of Tamoxifen Therapy in Postmenopausal Women with Primary Breast Cancer," *New England Journal of Medicine* 350 (2004): 1081–92.

26 Stephen A. Cannistra, "The Ethics of Early Stopping Rules: Who Is Protecting Whom?" *Journal of Clinical Oncology* 22 (2004): 1543.

27 Paul S. Mueller, Victor M. Montori, Dirk Bassler, Barbara A. Koenig, and Gordon H. Guyatt, "Ethical Issues in Stopping Randomized Trials Early Because of Apparent Benefit," *Annals of Internal Medicine* 146 (2007): 880.

28 Martine J. Piccart-Gebhart, "New Stars in the Sky of Treatment for Early Breast Cancer," *New England Journal of Medicine* 350, 11 (2004): 1140–42.

29 Polly Niravath, Mothaffar F. Rimawai, and C. Kent Osborne, "Aromatase Inhibitor Adverse Effects: Are We Sweeping Them under the Rug?" *Journal of Clinical Oncology* 32 (2014): 3779.

30 Ongoing reviews of the data include John Berry, "Are All Aromatase Inhibitors the Same? A Review of Controlled Clinical Trials in Breast Cancer," *Clinical Therapeutics* 27 (2005): 1671–84; Hope S. Rugo, "The Breast Cancer Continuum in Hormone-Receptor-Positive Breast Cancer in Postmenopausal Women: Evolving Management Options Focusing on Aromatase Inhibitors," *Annals of Oncology* 19 (2008): 16–27; Adnan Aydiner and Faruk Tas, "Meta-Analysis of Trials Comparing Anastrozole and Tamoxifen for Adjuvant Treatment of Postmenopausal Women with Early Breast Cancer," *Trials* 9 (2008): 47; and Niravath, Rimawai, and Osborne, "Aromatase Inhibitor Adverse Effects." Hirohisa Imai, Katsumasa Kuroi, Shozo Ohsumi, Michikazu Ono, and Kojiro Shimozuma, "Economic Evaluation of the Prevention and Treatment of Breast Cancer – Present Status and Open Issues," *Breast Cancer* 14 (2007): 81–87, conclude the treatments are cost-effective, while Danny Hind, Sue Ward, Enrico De Nigris, Emma Simpson, Chris Carroll, and Lynda Wyld, "Hormonal Therapies for Early Breast Cancer: Systematic Review and Economic Evaluation," *Health Technology Assessment* 11, 26 (2007): 1–152, withhold judgment, since long- and medium-term survival are still in question.

31 See "Notice of Compliance with conditions (NOC/c)" database, Health Canada, accessed May 7, 2015, http://www.hc-sc.gc.ca/dhp-mps/prodpharma/notices -avis/conditions/index-eng.php#a; search alphabetically for Aromasin, Femara, and Arimidex.

32 Alan Cassels, "Ideas: Manufacturing Patients," radio broadcast, Toronto, CBC Radio, November 28, 2003, see p. 4 of official transcript.

33 Cannistra, "Ethics of Early Stopping Rules," 1542–45, 1543–44.

34 Ibid., 1544.

35   Ibid., 1544.

36   A US FDA report published in January 2017 provides twenty-two examples that illustrate Dr. Ling's point about misleading early clinical trial results. The report documents twenty-two drugs, medical devices, or vaccines that showed promise in early (Phase 2) clinical trials, and yet the larger Phase 3 trials did not confirm the findings of effectiveness, safety, or both. The treatments were designed for a wide variety of conditions, including one (Iniparib) for metastatic breast cancer. See *22 Case Studies Where Phase 2 and Phase 3 Trials Had Divergent Results* (Washington, DC: FDA, 2017), 1–43, accessed February 12, 2017, http://www.fda.gov/downloads/AboutFDA/ReportsManualsForms/Reports/UCM535780.pdf.

37   See Joel Lexchin, *Private Profits vs. Public Policy: The Pharmaceutical Industry and the Canadian State* (Toronto: University of Toronto Press, 2016), 90–95, on PAAB's history and role.

38   See ibid., 103–4, on the loosening of the DTCA prohibition.

39   In Ray Chepesiuk, "Supported by an Unrestricted Educational Grant," *Canadian Medical Association Journal* 169 (2003): 421–22, PAAB Commissioner Ray Chepesiuk discusses industry abuses of the UREG designation.

40   See Mintzes, Morgan, and Wright, "Direct-to-Consumer Advertising in Canada," on Health Canada's administrative shifts and the blurred distinction between information and advertising.

41   Canada Food and Drugs Act, R.S.C. 1985, c. F-27.

42   Personal communication, March 16, 2009.

43   On Health Canada's approval of Femara, see Joel Lexchin, "Notice of Compliance with Conditions: A Policy in Limbo," *Healthcare Policy* 2, 4 (2007): 114–22, Table 1 (Appendix), and Health Canada's letter stating conditions of the drug's approval, Canada, Drugs and Health Products, "Dear Health Care Professional: Femara," September 18, 2006, accessed December 1, 2017, http://www.hc-sc.gc.ca/dhp-mps/prodpharma/notices-avis/conditions/femara_dhcpl_lapds_100323-eng.php. On the strategy of whipsawing, see Steve Morgan, Paige A. Thompson, Jamie R. Daw, and Melissa K. Friesen, "Inter-jurisdictional Cooperation on Pharmaceutical Product Listing Agreements: Views from Canadian Provinces," *BMC Health Services Research* 13, 34 (January 31, 2013), doi: 10.1186/1472-6963-13-34.

44   Polly Niravath, "Aromatase Inhibitor-Induced Arthralgia: A Review," *Annals of Oncology* 24 (2013): 1443–49, reviews the literature on aromatase inhibitors, joint pain, and noncompliance.

45   Hanna clarified in a personal communication that, although she had had a recurrence, she was not treated with tamoxifen and would not be a candidate for an aromatase inhibitor. Had her cancer been ER+, however, she would have opted to continue post-tamoxifen treatment on the new drug.

46 Susan M. Love, *Dr. Susan Love's Breast Book*, 6th ed., with contributions by Karen Lindsey (Boston: Da Capo Press, 2015), 268.
47 Harold J. Burstein et al., "Adjuvant Endocrine Therapy for Women with Hormone Receptor–Positive Breast Cancer: American Society of Clinical Oncology Clinical Practice Guidelines Focused Update," *Journal of Clinical Oncology* 32 (2014): 2255–69, 2266.
48 Ibid., 2266. See also Love, *Dr. Susan Love's Breast Book*, 6th ed., 432–33, who concludes that the decision whether to take tamoxifen and an aromatase inhibitor in sequence, and if so on what schedule, will depend on various individual factors, such as the woman's age, bone health, history of blood clots, and sexual activity.
49 Ali Shajarizadeh and Aiden Hollis, "Delays in the Submission of New Drugs in Canada," *Canadian Medical Association Journal* 187 (2015): E47–E51.
50 Personal communication from Pat Kelly, October 31, 2016.
51 See Charles E. Geyer, John Forster, Deborah Lindquist, et al., "Lapatinib Plus Capecitabine for HER2-Positive Advanced Breast Cancer," *New England Journal of Medicine* 355 (2006): 2733–43, on the improvement in time-to-disease progression; GSK funded and conducted this study (ibid., 2736).
52 On the expected gain of 0.12 QALYs, see Quang A. Le and Joel W. Hay, "Cost-Effectiveness of Lapatinib in HER-2-Positive Advanced Breast Cancer," *Cancer* 115, 3 (2009): 489–98, 494.
53 For two cost-effectiveness analyses of lapatinib used in combination with capecitabine, see ibid., and National Institute for Health and Clinical Excellence, "Final Appraisal Determination: Lapatinib for the Treatment of Women with Previously Treated Advanced or Metastatic Breast Cancer" (London/Manchester, UK: NICE), May 10, 2010, 1–46, accessed December 2, 2016, https://www.nice.org.uk/guidance/GID-TAG387/documents/breast-cancer-advanced-or-metastatic-lapatinib-final-appraisal-determination3.
54 Lisa Priest, "Fighting Cancer in a Bureaucratic Catch-22," *Globe and Mail*, December 18, 2009.
55 The Fraser Institute advocates "a free and prosperous world where individuals benefit from greater choice, competitive markets, and personal responsibility," according to a statement of purpose that appears in many of its reports (e.g., Nigel S.B. Rawson, *Has pCODR Improved Access to Oncology Drugs? Timeliness and Provincial Acceptance of Pan-Canadian Oncology Drug Review Recommendations* [Vancouver: Fraser Institute, 2014], 29). The institute published updated versions of *Access Delayed, Access Denied* between 2005 and 2012, as well as reports that focus on wait times in Canada's health care system, delays in approvals of cancer drugs, and whether these drugs have been added to provincial drug formularies; see Nigel

S.B. Rawson, *Access to New Oncology Drugs in Canada, Compared to the United States and Europe* (Vancouver: Fraser Institute, 2012): 1–10; Nigel S.B. Rawson, *Potential Impact of Delayed Access to Five Oncology Drugs in Canada* (Vancouver: Fraser Institute, 2013, 1–19; Rawson, *Has pCODR Improved Access;* and Baccus Barua and Nadeem Esmail, *Federal Delays in Approving New Medicines* (Vancouver: Fraser Institute, 2013), 1–28. The institute accepts no government funding but does accept corporate donations, including funds from research-based pharmaceutical companies (Mark Rovere and Brett J. Skinner, *Access Delayed, Access Denied: Waiting for New Medicines in Canada* (Vancouver: Fraser Institute, 2012), 42.

56 Turner & Associates, *Cancer Drug Access for Canadians: Report for the Canadian Cancer Society* (Toronto: Canadian Cancer Society, 2009), i.

57 Ibid., 29.

58 Kelly Crowe, "Fraser Institute's Wait-Time Survey: Does It Still Count If Most Doctors Ignore It?" *CBC Health News Analysis*, Toronto: CBC, November 25, 2016, accessed December 4, 2016, http://www.cbc.ca/news/health/fraser-institute-wait-time-survey -critique-1.3867927.

59 Jean replaced a participant who withdrew because she herself had not had breast cancer and thought that survivors should develop the document. Lynn replaced a workshop participant who doubted that the proposed document would have teeth.

60 Ranjana Srivastava, "Dealing with Uncertainty in a Time of Plenty," *New England Journal of Medicine* 365, 24 (2011): 2252–53.

61 For a federal government report on patients' charters of rights in Canada, see Margaret Smith, *Patients' Bill of Rights – A Comparative Overview* (Ottawa: Library of Parliament, Government of Canada, 2002). For a discussion in the medical literature, see the following by Lauren Vogel: "Patient Charters: The Provincial Experience," *Canadian Medical Association Journal* 182 (2010): E639–40; "Patient Charters All Buzz and No Bite, Advocates Say," *Canadian Medical Association Journal* 182 (2010): 1406–8; and "Patient Charters: The International Experience," *Canadian Medical Association Journal* 182 (2010): E641–42.

62 On patients' rights documents having no teeth, see Vogel, "Patient Charters All Buzz and No Bite"; on structural and economic constraints limiting patients' rights, see Margaret Smith, *Patients' Bill of Rights*, 10; on Quebec's *Loi sur les services de santé et les services sociaux*, see Vogel, "Provincial Experience."

63 See Pat Armstrong and Hugh Armstrong, *Health Care* (Halifax: Fernwood, 2016), 50–64, on the omission of many pharmaceutical drugs from the Medical Care Act. On recent efforts to extend universal health care coverage to pharmaceuticals, see Steve Morgan, John Law, Jamie Daw, Liza Abraham, and Danielle Martin, "Estimated Cost of Universal Public Coverage of Prescription Drugs in Canada," *Canadian Medical Association Journal* 187, 7 (2015): 491–97; Marc-André Gagnon and

Guillaume Hébert, *The Economic Case for Universal Pharmacare: Costs and Benefits of Publicly Funded Drug Coverage for All Canadians* (Ottawa: Canadian Centre for Policy Alternatives, 2010); and "Campaign for a National Drug Plan," Canadian Health Coalition, accessed May 7, 2015, http://pharmacarenow.ca.

64 Mark Lawler et al., "A Catalyst for Change: The European Cancer Patient's Bill of Rights," *Oncologist* 19, 3 (2014): 1–8.

65 Ibid., 5, clause 2.6.

Conclusion: The Fight for Medicine's Soul

1 Orla O'Donovan, "Time to Weed out the Astroturf from the Grassroots? Exploring the Implications of Pharmaceutical Industry Funding of Patient Advocacy Organisations" (paper presented at Concepts of the Third Sector: The European Debate, ISTR/EMES Conference, Paris, April 27–29, 2005), 12.

2 The phrase "food, flattery and friendship" is from Dana Katz, Arthur Caplan, and Jon Merz, "All Gifts Large and Small: Toward an Understanding of Pharmaceutical Industry Gift-Giving," *American Journal of Bioethics* 3, 3 (2003): 41.

3 See Michael J. Oldani, "Thick Prescriptions: Toward an Interpretation of Pharmaceutical Sales Practices," *Medical Anthropology Quarterly* 18 (2004): 325–56, for a study of how the industry carefully paces gift-giving to physicians to build relationships over a period of years.

4 See Oldani, "Thick Prescriptions."

5 As an example, the Canadian Agency for Drugs and Technologies in Health (CADTH), a national organization for health technology assessment, now provides travel awards to a quota of patients who apply to attend its annual symposium as representatives of patient organizations; CADTH's 2017 annual symposium meets the criteria of an international charter called "Patients Included"; that is, a patient is part of the program planning committee, all sessions are open to patients, and patients are eligible to submit abstracts for inclusion in the program. CADTH also has a Patient Community Liaison Forum, whose members are drawn from five patient-group coalitions, and the agency has implemented formal procedures for obtaining patient-group input on the drugs and devices it evaluates. I attended the 2016 CADTH symposium as a patient representative and was struck that many, if not most, of the fifty-nine patient representatives in attendance were from groups that receive unconditional educational grants from the pharmaceutical industry. At several of the sessions I attended, panel members and delegates openly discussed the problems this presents. CADTH reviews drugs and devices, then advises provincial agencies whether to place these products on their formularies; in recent years, the agency has put in place processes to incorporate the views of patient organizations in its assessments. Several drug researchers expressed exasperation that patients'

submissions came across as cheerleading, that they lacked nuance and authenticity, they invariably recommended that the drug be funded, and they occasionally even used the same phrases as appeared in the materials submitted by the drug's manufacturer. Patients, in turn, were frustrated that their opinions did not seem to change CADTH's recommendations – evidence, in their view, that the agency was not listening to them.

6 On industry funding of CME in Canada, see Laura Eggertson, "Debate Sparked over Pharma-Funded CME," *Canadian Medical Association Journal* 188 (2016): E65; see also the August 2013 report of the Task Force of the College of Family Physicians of Canada (CFPC), "The CFPC's Relationship with the Health Care/Pharmaceutical Industry," accessed February 4, 2017, http://www.cfpc.ca/uploadedFiles/Resources/_PDFs/Industry_Task_Force_recommendations_ApprovedNov2013.pdf, and David Bruser, Jesse McLean, and Andrew Bailey, "Drug Companies Wine and Dine Family Physicians," *Toronto Star*, February 16, 2016, accessed February 4, 2017, https://www.thestar.com/.

7 See Pharmaphorum, *Patient Opinion Leaders: The New KOLs for Pharma?* (UK: Pharmafourm Premium Media, June 2014), 1–32, accessed December 8, 2016, http://pharmaphorum.com/images/pdf_docs/Patient_Opinion_Leaders_preview_doc.pdf.

8 See Suwit Wibulpolprasert, Sheena Moosa, K. Satyanarayana, Sarath Samarage, and Viroj Tangcharoensathien, "WHO's Web-Based Public Hearings: Hijacked by Pharma?" *Lancet* 370 (November 24, 2007): 1754. For one of the many critiques of Sprout's use of an advocacy campaign to gain approval of flibanserin, see Steve Woloshin and Lisa M. Schwartz, "US Food and Drug Administration Approval of Flibanserin: Even the Score Does Not Add Up," *JAMA Internal Medicine* 176, 4 (2016): 439–42.

9 The quotations in this paragraph are from "Patient Advocacy & Professional Organizations: Building Effective Relationships" (slide presentation), slide 9, Best Practices, LLC, accessed May 23, 2015, http://www.best-in-class.com/bestp/domrep.nsf/products/patient-advocacy-professional-organizations-building-effective-relationships!OpenDocument.

10 Jerome P. Kassirer, *On the Take: How Medicine's Complicity with Big Business Can Endanger Your Health* (New York: Oxford University Press, 2005), 7. Daniel Carlat, "Dr. Drug Rep," *New York Times Magazine*, November 25, 2007, provides a detailed account of being a KOL and eventually rejecting the role.

11 Eggertson, "Debate Sparked over Pharma-Funded CME."

12 Marcia Angell, *The Truth about the Drug Companies: How They Deceive Us and What to Do about It* (New York: Random House, 2004).

13 Ray Moynihan, "Doctors' Education: The Invisible Influence of Drug Company Sponsorship," *BMJ* 336, 7641 (2008): 416–17.

14 Kassirer, *On the Take*, 93; Arnold S. Relman, "Separating Continuing Medical Education from Pharmaceutical Marketing," *Journal of the American Medical Association* 285 (2001): 2009–12; and Marjorie M.A. Bowman and David D.L. Pearle, "Changes in Drug Prescribing Patterns Related to Commercial Company Funding of Continuing Medical Education," *Journal of Continuing Education in the Health Profession* 8 (1988): 13–20.

15 See Navindra Persaud, "Questionable Content of an Industry-Supported Medical-School Lecture Series: A Case Study," *Journal of Medical Ethics* 40 (2014): 414–18, on bias in industry-supported material used to teach medical students in Canada. On how medical schools and hospitals go along, and calls for an end to pharma-funded CME, see Angell, *Truth about the Drug Companies*; Kassirer, *On the Take*; and Eggertson, "Debate Sparked over Pharma-Funded CME." See Sheryl Spithoff, "Industry Involvement in Continuing Medical Education: Time to Say No," *Canadian Family Physician* 60 (2014): 695, on France's tax on industry.

16 On boundary objects, see Susan Leigh Star and James R. Greisemer, "Institutional Ecology, 'Translations' and Boundary Objects: Amateurs and Professionals in Berkeley's Museum of Vertebrate Zoology, 1907–39," *Social Studies of Science* 19 (1989): 387–420; and Adele Clarke and Susan Leigh Star, "The Social Worlds Framework: A Theory/Methods Package," in *The Handbook of Science and Technology Studies*, 3rd ed., ed. Edward J. Hackett, Olga Amsterdamska, Michael Lynch, and Judy Wajcman (Cambridge, MA: MIT Press, 2007), 113–37.

17 These include Angell, *Truth about the Drug Companies*; Jerry Avorn, *Powerful Medicines: The Benefits, Risks and Costs of Prescription Drugs* (New York: Vintage, 2004); Kassirer, *On the Take*; Howard Brody, *Hooked: Ethics, the Medical Profession, and the Pharmaceutical Industry* (Lanham, MD: Rowman and Littlefield, 2007); Carl Elliott, *White Coat, Black Hat: Adventures on the Dark Side of Medicine* (Boston: Beacon Press, 2010); David Healy, *Pharmageddon* (Oakland: University of California Press, 2012); Ben Goldacre, *Bad Pharma: How Drug Companies Mislead Doctors and Harm Patients* (New York: Faber and Faber, 2012); Peter C. Gøtzsche, *Deadly Medicines and Organized Crime: How Big Pharma Has Corrupted Healthcare* (London: Radcliffe, 2013); Grahm Dukes, John Braithwaite, and J.P. Moloney, *Pharmaceuticals, Corporate Crime and Public Health* (London: Edward Elgar, 2014); and Joel Lexchin, *Private Profits vs. Public Policy: The Pharmaceutical Industry and the Canadian State* (Toronto: University of Toronto Press, 2016). For university-based projects, see the special issue of the *Journal of Law, Medicine & Ethics* 41, 3 (Fall 2013), 544–746, devoted to "Institutional Corruption and the Pharmaceutical Industry," produced by fellows of the Edmond J. Safra Center for Ethics at Harvard University; the WHO Collaborating Centre for Governance, Accountability, and Transparency in the Pharmaceutical Sector, at the University of Toronto; PharmedOut at Georgetown

University Medical Center; and the Drug Institute Document Archive at the University of California, San Francisco.

18   Kevin Outterson, "Punishing Health Care Fraud – Is the GSK Settlement Sufficient?" *New England Journal of Medicine* 367 (2012): 1082–85 (see the interview accompanying the article online). In the article, Outterson evaluates whether the fines fit the crimes. For Public Citizen's 2012 report on the seventy-four US prosecutions in just over twenty months, see "Pharmaceutical Industry Criminal and Civil Penalties: An Update," http://citizen.org/hrg2073; for details on the 2012 Johnson & Johnson settlement, see https://www.justice.gov/opa/pr/johnson-johnson-pay -more-22-billion-resolve-criminal-and-civil-investigations; for the Novartis settlement, see https://www.justice.gov/usao-sdny/pr/manhattan-us-attorney-announces -370-million-civil-fraud-settlement-against-novartis (all three sites accessed February 16, 2017).

19   For the case studies of Braithwaite and colleagues, see John Braithwaite, *Corporate Crime in the Pharmaceutical Industry* (London: Routledge and Kegan Paul, 1984), and Graham Dukes, John Braithwaite, and J.P. Moloney, *Pharmaceuticals, Corporate Crime and Public Health* (Cheltenham, UK: Edgar Elgar, 2014); for a collection of sixteen articles by lab fellows at the Edmond J. Safra Center for Ethics, see the theme issue "Institutional Corruption and the Pharmaceutical Policy," *Journal of Law and Medical Ethics* 41, 3 (Fall 2013). For Goldacre's analysis, see Ben Goldacre, *Bad Pharma*, and for the quotation by Kohler and colleagues, see Jillian Clare Kohler, Monique F. Mrazek, and Loraine Hawkins, "Corruption and Pharmaceuticals: Strengthening Good Governance to Improve Access" in *The Many Faces of Corruption: Tracking Vulnerabilities at the Sector Level*, ed. J.E. Campos and S. Pradhan (Washington, DC: World Bank, 2007), 29–62, 31.

20   Brody, *Hooked*.

21   This and the following quotation at ibid., 39.

22   Edward Nik-Khah, "Neoliberal Pharmaceutical Science and the Chicago School of Economics," *Social Studies of Science* 44 (2014): 489–517.

23   The Chicago School was an offshoot of the international organization of social scientists known as the Mont Pelerin Society, which is dedicated to understanding personal and political freedom.

24   Nik-Khah, "Neoliberal Pharmaceutical Science," 492–93.

25   Ibid., 509, n15.

26   Ibid., esp. 494–96.

27   Ibid., 498–99.

28   "Drug lag" meme: ibid., 501. "$800 million pill" meme: ibid., 502.

29   Ed Silverman, "Developing a Drug Costs $2.6 Billion, but Not Everyone Believes This," *Wall Street Journal*, November 18, 2014. For a critical assessment of the $2.8

billion figure, see Jerry Avorn, "The $2.6 Billion Pill: Methodological and Policy Considerations," *New England Journal of Medicine* 372, 20 (May 14, 2015): 1877–79. Avorn notes that the data used to generate the $2.6 billion figure are not available for verification and that public funds are used for much of the early research on which successful drug development is based.

30 Nik-Khah, "Neoliberal Pharmaceutical Science," 506.

31 Ibid.

32 Ibid., 500.

33 Ibid.

34 Ibid., 506.

35 For the Karolinska report, see Nils Wilking and Bengt Jönsson, *A Pan-European Comparison Regarding Patient Access to Cancer Drugs* (Stockholm: Karolinska Institute and the Stockholm School of Economics, 2005).

36 For a detailed critique and debate of the Karolinska Report with a rebuttal from one of the authors, see Michel Coleman, "New Drugs and Survival: Does the Karolinska Report Make Sense?" *Cancer World* (2006): 26–35. For a newspaper account of this campaign, including concerns about the analysis, Roche's sponsorship, and the lack of transparency, see Sarah Boseley, "Concern over Cancer Group's Link to Drug Firm," *Guardian*, October 18, 2006, accessed December 2016, https://www.theguardian.com/society/2006/oct/18/cancercare.health; "Campaigning for Transparency" (editorial), *Lancet Oncology* 7 (2006): 961, called for transparency and stressed the need for a balance of opinions in such collaborative advocacy campaigns. The same journal subsequently published a defence of the Cancer United campaign, including a claim that the Karolinska Report was only one research source on which it was based (John Smyth and Ingrid Kossler, "The Cancer United Campaign – Validity, Transparency, and a Cause for Good," *Lancet Oncology* 8, 2 (February 2007): 93–94.

37 Angell, *Truth about the Drug Companies*, 151.

38 Otis Webb Brawley, *How We Do Harm: A Doctor Breaks Ranks about Being Sick in America*, with Paul Goldberg (New York: St. Martin's Press, 2012), 230.

39 Gøtzsche, *Deadly Medicines*, 282. The preceding three quotations are at p. 280.

40 Goldacre, *Bad Pharma*, 266.

41 Ibid., 270.

42 Ibid.

43 David J. Hess, "To Tell the Truth: On Scientific Counterpublics," *Public Understanding of Science* 20 (2011): 627–41.

44 See Canadian Institute for Health Information, *National Health Expenditure Trends, 1975–2016* (Ottawa: CIHI, 2016), 6, accessed January 30, 2017, https://www.cihi.ca/en/spending-and-health-workforce/spending/national-health-expenditure-trends/nhex2016-topic1.

45 Jens Geissler, "Health Policy in Germany: Consumer Groups in a Corporatist Polity," in *Democratizing Health: Consumer Groups and the Policy Process*, ed. Hans Löfgren, Evelyn de Leeuw, and Michael Leahy (Cheltenham, UK: Edward Elgar, 2011), 127–42.

46 See Martin Delaney, "AIDS Activism and the Pharmaceutical Industry," in *Ethics and the Pharmaceutical Industry*, ed. Michael A. Sontoro and Thomas M. Gorry (Cambridge, UK: Cambridge University Press, 2005), 316–17, on the US-based AIDS Treatment Activists Coalition and strategies for managing pharmaceutical industry relationships.

47 On health care zombies and the enabling role of the pharmaceutical industry in keeping them alive, see Morris L. Barer, Robert G. Evans, Clyde Hertzman, and Mira Johri, "Lies, Damned Lies, and Health Care Zombies: Discredited Ideas that Will Not Die," HPI Discussion Paper, vol. 10 (Houston: University of Texas, 1998), and Morris L. Barer, "Evidence, Interests and Knowledge Translation," *Healthcare Quarterly* 8, 1 (2005): 46–53.

48 Donald W. Light and Hagop Kantarjian, "Market Spiral Pricing of Cancer Drugs," *Cancer* 119, 22 (2013), 3900–02.

Index

ABCS (Alliance of Breast Cancer Survivors): advocacy for access to Taxol, 112; advocacy for prevention, 104, 111; affiliated members (Kelly, Ford, Spinks, Groves), 293; BCPT tamoxifen trial debates, 96, 111; financial difficulties and closure, 167–68; pharma funding debates, 96–97, 104–5, 116–17, 206(f)

Abraham, John, 73

Access Delayed, Access Denied (Fraser Institute), 245–46, 343*n*54

access to new drugs: about, 21, 246–47; AIDS advocacy for, 10–11, 71–74, 134; alignment with neoliberal deregulation, 10; analysis of history of discourse on rapid access, 283–88; audit activities by pharma-funded groups, 287–88; causes for delays, 240–41; CBCN's webcast to Atlantic Canada, 244–45; compassionate access programs, 242–43; CSDD framing of "drug lag," 285–87; discourse of hope, 181–82, 272; Harper's restructuring, 209; history of, 55; injustice charges, 250–51; international comparisons, 171–77, 240–41; international harmonization, 114–15, 124; Krever Inquiry's influence, 114–15; legitimate fiscal limits in health

system, 173, 242, 254, 256, 268, 289; media influence, 323*n*57; patient urgency, 180–81; pharma's promotion of, 130–33, 141–42, 178; pharma's redefinition of concepts ("wait time"), 240, 278; quality research vs rapid access, 72, 73, 74, 180–81; reports on disparities, 240–42, 245–47; risk/benefit balance, 115, 185(t); testimony at parliamentary hearings, 90–91; women's vs AIDS movement, 74. *See also* drug approval review system, review times; formularies, drug; prices of drugs

access to new drugs, conditional approval for. *See* NOC/c (notice of compliance with conditions)

accountability. *See* transparency

AC+T (Adriamycin and cyclophosphamide plus Taxol) chemotherapy, 171–72

actors (advocacy groups, private sector, government): about, 282–83; blurring of boundaries between actors, 57; boundary objects, 280; drugs as actors, 75, 216; embodied knowledge, 10–11; implicated in unethical industry practices, 282–83, 288–92; neoliberal partnerships, 16–17, 142; patient groups, 56–57; power relations, 282–83;

resistance to neoliberalism, 15–16; stakeholders, 16–17. *See also* power relations

Addyi (flibanserin), 276

adjuvant treatments (with surgery and/or radiation), 76, 316*n*36. *See also* anti-hormonal drugs; chemotherapy (cyto-toxic drugs)

Adriamycin, 127, 171–72

Adverse Effects (International Organiza-tion of Consumers Unions), 63

adverse-event reports. *See* post-marketing surveillance (PMS)

advertising. *See* marketing

advocacy: about, 271–72, 288–92; Atlantic Canada webcast on disparities and advocacy, 244–45; confrontational vs nonconfrontational, 57, 59–60, 94–95, 126; critical questions, 127; as evidence-based policy consultations, 126; federal regulations as constraints, 126; KOLs (key opinion leaders), 190–91, 273, 274–78; pharma's distortion of public policy, 276; POLs (patient opin-ion leaders), 275–78; professionaliza-tion of patient groups, 22–23, 126; proposals to separate patient groups from pharma funders, 186(t); reports on disparities in access, 240–42, 245–47; restructuring by ethics of pharma funding, 183; service vs advocacy normalization, 133, 200–8, 272; targets on pharma vs government, 129, 185(t), 289, 292. *See also* access to new drugs; environmental advocacy; patient groups; pharma industry

A.H. Robins, 47

AIDS drugs and patients: activism for "drugs into bodies," 10–11, 13–14, 71–74; AZT as early drug, 13–14, 181; dependence on drugs for survival, 133; embodied knowledge, 10–11; HIV-positive women, 133–35; medical

stigmatizing of patients, 12–13; placebo-controlled trials, 9–10; Procrit, 220, 338*n*1; shift of priority from access to safety, 73, 181

AIDS movement: about, 9–11, 71–74; advocacy for access to new drugs, 71–74, 134, 179, 298*n*16; advocacy for changes to unethical practices, 73–74; advocacy for clinical trial changes, 71, 74; compared with women's move-ment, 12–13, 74; confrontational tactics, 12, 57, 71–72, 74; critique of pharma, 11, 71; critique of regulatory agencies, 71; Epstein's ethnography, 7, 9–12, 19, 22, 73, 298*n*16, 332*n*34; gender differences in activist strategies, 86; influence on women's movement, 79; media coverage, 71; as model, 18, 72; patient advocacy, 4; pharma's awareness of power of activism, 189; shift from rapid access to "good science," 332*n*34; visibility of, 86; Voices of Positive Women, 133–35

Alberta: defeat of patients' rights bill, 253

Alternatives (Kushner), 80, 81

Alzheimer's support groups, 19

Ambrose, Linda, 58

Amgen, 69, 127, 217, 219, 314*n*20, 338*n*1

Amnesty International, 215

anemia drugs, 153–54, 156, 184, 217–19, 221, 267

Angell, Marcia, 288

Anglin, Mary K., 109

antibiotics, 37–38

anti-hormonal drugs: about, 54–55, 77–78; coverage of drugs taken at home, 54–55; generic drugs, 54–55; mechan-ism of action, 54, 77, 223; risk/benefit balance, 181–82; surrogate endpoint, 77–78, 222. *See also* aromatase inhibit-ors; tamoxifen

approval of new drugs. *See* access to new drugs; drug approval review system;

Harding, Jim, 63
Harley Report, 42, 43–44, 307*n*20
Harper, Stephen, 208–11
HDC. *See* chemotherapy (cytotoxic drugs), high-dose (HDC)
Health Action International. *See* HAI (Health Action International)
health advocacy groups, 56–57. *See also* patient groups
Health Canada: difficulties in relations with patient groups, 155–56, 163; OCAPI's mandate on transparency, 200–2; patient representatives, 275–78, 345*n*5; restructuring, 179–80; structure of relations with groups, 103(f). *See also* drug approval review system; Health Products and Food Branch (HPFB); Health Protection Branch (later Health Products and Food Branch); National Forum on Breast Cancer (1993); regulation/deregulation of drugs and devices; Therapeutic Products Directorate (TPD)
health care system: about, 26–27, 31–36; compared with US system, 173–77, 195; coverage of drugs taken at home, 54–55; debates on, 33–34, 35–36; federal transfer payments, 32, 35, 48, 119, 211; federal/provincial jurisdiction, 32–33, 39, 307*n*15; government-funded health insurance, 31–36; inability of employees to lobby government, 195; legitimate fiscal limits in health system, 173, 242, 254, 256, 268, 289; lobbying using international comparisons, 173; medical associations' role, 34; Medical Care Act (1966), 32–33, 34–35, 254, 344*n*62; and neoliberalism, 48–53, 65–70; off-loading social services to nonprofits, 17–18, 48, 117–18, 119, 126, 309*n*36; overview of history of, 26–27; privatization vs medical commons, 270–71; public administration of, 35, 119;

public support for, 33–34, 119; shift of welfare era to neoliberal era, 35–36, 48, 65–66; welfare-state era, 31–36. *See also* breast cancer treatment; hospitals; pharmacare, lack of national; physicians; provincial/territorial health care systems
"health care zombies," 291
Health Products and Food Branch (HPFB): Biologics and Genetic Therapies Directorate, 39–40; blood products, 324*n*61; BMC's advocacy for shorter drug review times, 179–80, 184; regulatory vs risk management model, 180; transparency and accountability, 200–1. *See also* clinical trials; drug approval review system
Health Protection Branch (later Health Products and Food Branch): about, 45–46; approval of new drugs, 45–46; review backlog (1980s), 48; "trust-industry philosophy," 51. *See also* clinical trials; drug approval review system
Healthsharing, 59
Healy, David, 46, 47
hearings, parliamentary. *See* parliamentary hearings on breast cancer (1991–92)
Hébert, Paul, 20–21
help-seeking ads ("Ask your doctor" ads), 184, 234–35, 238
Henderson, Ian, 50
Herceptin (trastuzumab): about, 55, 110; supplementation of with Tykerb, 242; drug lag, 179; Genentech, 109, 138; mechanism of action, 110; pharma funding debates, 138; price comparison, 118; recruitment for clinical trials, 106–7, 108; side effects and toxicity, 241
HER2-positive cancers, 241–42
Hess, David, 14, 290
high-dose chemotherapy. *See* chemotherapy (cytotoxic drugs), high-dose (HDC)
Hill+Knowlton Strategies, 188

Opening the Medicine Cabinet (report of parliamentary committee), 210–11, 212
Optimizing Access to Cancer Drugs for Canadians (Canadian Cancer Society), 245
Oregon plan, 99
organizations, patient. *See* patient groups
Ortho Biotech: CBCN partnership, 153–57, 184, 217–18, 220–21, 267–68, 277; Eprex marketing, 153–54, 184, 219, 267; reorganization, 329n4
OS (overall survival), 231
Outterson, Kevin, 281, 282, 288, 348n18
ovarian cancer: Taxol (paclitaxel), 112, 321n40
Oxfam, 5

PAAB (Pharmaceutical Advertising Advisory Board), 232–33, 235
palliative care: Cancer Strategy mandate, 204–5; quality of life, 182, 291, 332n37
parliamentary hearings on breast cancer (1991–92): about, 88–94; access to new drugs, 90–91; BCPT tamoxifen trial debates, 111; on breast cancer and implants, 88–92; government funding for new groups as response to, 101–3, 103(f); nonconfrontational activism, 94–95; report *(Breast Cancer)*, 94–95; testimony from pharma, 91–92; testimony from survivors and families, 89–91, 94; themes in testimony, 90, 94
partnerships: benefits for pharma, 141–42, 188–89; biocitizenship, 18–19; "empowered patient," 188; ethical guidelines, 142–43, 196–200, 334n23; failed partnerships, 142; public opinion on, 195; stakeholders, as term, 16–17. *See also* patient groups, partnerships (2000s); PHANGO (pharma-funded NGO); pharma funding, partnerships (2000s)

Patent Act Amendment Act, 93, 320n25
Patented Medicine Prices Review Board, 93, 94, 123, 320n25
patents and intellectual property: court approvals of patents for generic drugs, 93; extract from Pacific yew trees (Taxol), 111–12; impact on drug prices, 42; Kefauver hearings, 41–42; US patent system's role in prices, 307n20. *See also* compulsory licensing; NOC/c (notice of compliance with conditions)
Pater, Joe, 112
Patient Advocacy & Professional Organizations (Best Practices), 190–91
patient groups: about, 4–5, 18–20, 137, 271–72, 282–83, 288–92; actor in unethical industry practices, 282–83, 288–92; astroturf groups (covert pharma funding), 7, 23, 194–95, 196–97, 297n8; biosociality, 18–19; conflicts of interest, 186(t); credibility as priority, 189; critical questions, 24, 56–57; DES groups, 60–61, 209; dissensus conferences, 290; diversity and types of, 19, 23, 301n43; funding autonomy for, 290–91; goal of safe, effective, affordable drugs, 282; history of, 56–57, 123; lay knowledge, 85–86; myth-busting of health care zombies, 291, 350n47; neoliberal advocacy goals, 271; pharma funding debates, 7; pharma's support as marketing strategy, 136–37; power relations, 280, 283; professionalization of advocacy, 22–23; proposals to separate patient groups from pharma funders, 134–35, 143, 186(t), 290–92; public trust in, 21–22; recommended changes, 289–92; scholarship on, 20–22; service vs advocacy normalization, 133, 200–8, 272; war among patient groups, 3–4, 178, 205. *See also* PHANGO (pharma-funded NGO); *and specific groups*

funding, 144; pharma funding debates, 67, 96–97, 104–9; pharma's increased influence, 96–97, 104–9; pharma's lack of influence, 27, 89, 96, 123

pharma funding, contestation (late 1990s): about, 123, 183–85; case-by-case policies, 161; CBCN's partnership, 184; formalization of norms, 183, 187; funding of Together to an End conference, 126–28; guidelines for collaboration with patient groups, 129–30; overview of pharma funding debates, 185(t)–186(t); panel on ethical issues (1997), 133–36; prelaunch promotional campaigns, 136–37; proposals to separate patient groups from pharma funders, 134–35, 143, 186(t), 290–92; public relations, 140–41; written policies on, 137–40, 144, 146–47, 149–51. *See also* CBCN (Canadian Breast Cancer Network); Together to an End conference; Willow

pharma funding, partnerships (2000s): about, 140–42, 187, 189, 206(f); alignment of patient and pharma goals, 184, 194–95, 286–89; astroturf groups (covert pharma funding), 7, 23, 194–95, 196–97, 297n8; benefits for pharma, 141–42; CACC's partnerships, 177–78, 206(f); Cancer Strategy funding, 202–3; CBCN's partnership, 153–57, 206(f); formalization of norms, 183, 187; groups with multiple funding sources, 199; guidelines for partnerships, 142–43, 189, 196–200, 334n23; lack of alternatives to pharma funding, 214–15; logic model for proposed projects, 199–200; many small vs few large amounts, 188–89, 328n1; pharma research firms, 190–91; PR firms, 187–92, 259–60; public relations, 140–41; as sites of knowledge production, 189; transparency of agreements, 199–200; trust

relations with patients, 192; unrestricted educational grants, 153, 203; Vioxx scandal, 191–92; written agreements, 153–56, 177, 189, 199–200; written policies refusing pharma funding, 164–66. *See also* CACC (Cancer Advocacy Coalition of Canada)

pharma industry: about, 273–74; AIDS activism's critique of, 11, 73–74; alignment of patient and pharma goals, 184, 194–95, 286–89; Canadian market for US industry, 92; Canadian subsidiaries of US companies, 42–43; conflicts of interest, 186(t); corporate integrity agreements, 281; echo chamber strategy, 285, 287, 289; financial pressures in partnership period, 141; gifts to working group members, 248–49, 274; history of, 37–41; off-label promotion, 281; patient representatives, 275–78, 345n5; penalties for crimes, 41, 281–82, 348n18; power relations and actors in, 282–83; profit motive, 36, 216, 280–82; self-regulation issues, 196; stopping of clinical trials, 224–26, 231–32; unethical industry practices, 36, 282–83, 288–92; user fees for drug reviews, 51–52, 120, 179, 310n43. *See also* marketing; United States, pharmaceutical industry

pharma industry, associations. *See* PMAC (Pharmaceutical Manufacturers Association of Canada) (later Rx&D; now Innovative Medicines Canada)

pharma industry as actor. *See* actors (advocacy groups, private sector, government)

pharmacare, lack of national: about, 33, 270–71; advocacy for, 292; impact on breast cancer patients, 53, 54, 55; recommendations for, 33, 292; strategy in 2004 health accord, 211

DoC